THE BIBLE AND THE AMERICAN FUTURE

The BIBLE and the AMERICAN FUTURE

Edited by Robert Jewett
with Wayne L. Alloway Jr. & John G. Lacey

CASCADE Books • Eugene, Oregon

THE BIBLE AND THE AMERICAN FUTURE

Copyright © 2009 Wipf and Stock Publishers. All rights reserved. Except for brief quotations in critical publications or reviews, no part of this book may be reproduced in any manner without prior written permission from the publisher. Write: Permissions, Wipf and Stock Publishers, 199 W. 8th Ave., Suite 3, Eugene, OR 97401.

Cascade Books
An Imprint of Wipf and Stock Publishers
199 W. 8th Ave., Suite 3
Eugene, OR 97401

ISBN 13: 978-1-60608-993-4

Unless otherwise noted, Scripture quotations are from the New Revised Standard Version of the Bible, copyright © 1989 by the Division of Christian Education of the National Council of the Churches of Christ in the USA and used by permission.

Cataloging-in-Publication data:

The Bible and the American future / edited by Robert Jewett with Wayne L. Alloway Jr. and John G. Lacey.

x + 296 p. ; 23 cm. Includes bibliographical references and index.

ISBN 13: 978-1-60608-993-4

1. Bible—Hermeneutics. 2. Church and the world. 3. Christianity and politics—United States. 4. Christianity—21st century. 5. Christianity and culture. I. Jewett, Robert. II. Alloway, Wayne L. Jr. III. Lacey, John G. IV. Title.

BS476 B50 2009

Manufactured in the U.S.A.

Contents

List of Contributors vii

Foreword ix
WAYNE L. ALLOWAY JR.

1. Recovering from the Long Nightmare of Amnesia 1
   WALTER BRUEGGEMANN

2. America in God's World: Perspectives from Biblical Theology 22
   KENNETH L. VAUX

3. Between Armageddon and the World Court:
   Reflections on the American Prospect 48
   ROBERT JEWETT

4. Isaiah, National Security, and the Politics of Fear 72
   J. J. M. ROBERTS

5. Interpreting the Prophets and Issues of Social Justice 92
   TERENCE E. FRETHEIM

6. The Bible and American Environmental Practice:
   An Ancient Code Addresses a Current Crisis 108
   SANDRA RICHTER

7. The Genius of the Mad Prophet: Ezekiel and the New Moral Self 130
   JACQUELINE LAPSLEY

8. Building Hope upon the Ruins in Jeremiah 146
   KATHLEEN M. O'CONNOR

9. Jesus, the Poor, and Mammon: A Look at Values from Luke-Acts 162
   DARRELL L. BOCK

Contents

10. Jesus and the Renewal of Covenantal Economics 181
    RICHARD A. HORSLEY

11. Divine Violence in the Christian Bible 208
    JOHN DOMINIC CROSSAN

12. Cultured Pearls:
    Changing the Future of America as an Exercise in Culture-Making 237
    BEN WITHERINGTON III

    Afterword: With God on Our Side 267
    JOHN G. LACEY

    Bibliography 269
    Index of Ancient Documents 283

Contributors

Wayne L. Alloway Jr., Senior Pastor of St. Mark's United Methodist Church, Lincoln, Nebraska. Member of the Nebraska Annual Conference of the United Methodist Church.

Darrell L. Bock, Professor of New Testament at Dallas Theological Seminary, Dallas, Texas. Member of Trinity Fellowship Church.

Walter Brueggemann, Professor of Old Testament Emeritus at Columbia Theological Seminary, Decatur, Georgia. Member of the United Church of Christ.

John Dominic Crossan, Emeritus Professor of Religious Studies at DePaul University, Chicago, Illlinois. Member of the Roman Catholic Church.

Terence E. Fretheim, Professor of Old Testament at Luther Seminary, St. Paul, Minnesota. Member of The Evangelical Lutheran Church in America.

Richard A. Horsley, Professor of Religion Emeritus at the University of Massachusetts, Boston. Member of the United Methodist Church.

Robert Jewett, Guest Professor of New Testament at the University of Heidelberg, Germany, and Theologian in Residence, St. Mark's United Methodist Church, Lincoln, Nebraska. Member of the Nebraska Annual Conference of the United Methodist Church.

John G. Lacey, Executive Pastor of St. Mark's United Methodist Church, Lincoln, Nebraska. Member of the Nebraska Annual Conference of the United Methodist Church.

Contributors

- **Jacqueline Lapsley,** Associate Professor of Old Testament, Princeton Theological Seminary, Princeton, N.J. Member of the Presbyterian Church U.S.A.

- **Kathleen M. O'Connor,** Professor of Old Testament at Columbia Theological Seminary, Decatur, Georgia. Member of the Roman Catholic Church.

- **Sandra Richter,** Professor of Old Testament, Wesley Biblical Seminary, Jackson, Mississippi. Member of the Anglican Mission in America.

- **J. J. M. Roberts,** Professor Emeritus of Old Testament at Princeton Theological Seminary, Princeton, N.J. Member of the Church of Christ.

- **Kenneth L. Vaux,** Professor of Ethics at Garrett-Evangelical Theological Seminary, Evanston, Illinois. Member of the Presbyterian Church U.S.A.

- **Ben Witherington III,** Professor of New Testament at Asbury Theological Seminary, Wilmore, Kentucky. Member of the North Carolina Annual Conference of the United Methodist Church.

Foreword

WAYNE L. ALLOWAY JR.

In the winter of 2008 I received a letter from Robert Jewett, my former New Testament professor at Garrett-Evangelical Seminary. Bob was Guest Professor of New Testament at the University of Heidelberg in Germany at the time, and in his letter he proposed a partnership. He would serve as theologian-in-residence at the church I serve as senior pastor, St. Mark's United Methodist in Lincoln, Nebraska, and the church would provide a venue for him to teach Bible classes and organize theological symposia with national and international appeal.

When we had the chance to visit in person, it became clear that there was a certain synchronicity to our visions. St. Mark's was completing a new, 2,000-seat sanctuary and was looking for opportunities to utilize this new facility for unique, broad-based activities outside of the weekend worship services, and Bob was interested in organizing relevant theological conferences. It seemed providential—St. Mark's had resources and a shared vision of public responsibility and Bob had the expertise and contacts in the scholarly world. The deal was done.

After much discussion of potential topics for the first theological conference, Bob and I felt the time was ripe for serious, clear-thinking Christians of differing theological perspectives to meet and discuss what they believe the Bible has to say about the future of America. To that end, we created an opportunity for conservative, moderate, and liberal religious scholars to articulate and debate the various points of view that exist within the Church and academy on this subject by hosting a confer-

Foreword — Wayne L. Alloway Jr.

ence called "The Bible and the American Future." Our aim was to engage experts in the field of biblical and theological scholarship to talk about what the biblical prophets, Deuteronomy, Jesus, Paul, and other biblical writers had to say about a responsible public ethic and vision for the future, outside of the dispensationalist apocalypticism that has been so prevalent in American religious culture of recent years.

Further, we determined it was imperative to make the content of this conference accessible to the general public, the result of which is the extraordinary collection of essays you now see before you. We are pleased that such diverse scholars were willing to gather under the same roof to debate such a timely issue from such a broad spectrum of theological viewpoints. Perhaps this is the gift that St. Mark's brings to the table—a "neutral" venue for scholars from the left, right, and center to offer relevant, passionate, and timely discourse on a subject so important to our world.

This project would not have been possible without the tireless and expert help of Mary Schwaner, our staff art/design specialist and computer wizard; Nancy Hammel, our copyeditor and faithful member of St. Mark's; and Rev. John Lacey, my colleague and proofreader. I also offer my deepest gratitude to my dear friend and mentor Robert Jewett, whose vision, hard work, and cheerful countenance have made this conference and book such a great joy and success.

1

Recovery from the Long Nightmare of Amnesia

WALTER BRUEGGEMANN

It is undoubtedly the case that biblical memory, figure, and imagination have played a major role in shaping the political imagination and history of the West, not least the United States. Bruce Feiler, moreover, has told me, out of his current research, that Moses and the imagery of the Hebrew Bible/Old Testament have been much more decisive for U.S. political imagination than has been Jesus or other facets of the New Testament. In U.S. usage, the Hebrew Bible/Old Testament has invited focus variously on God's *providential governance* of history, the conviction of *a chosen people*, and the conquest of *the new land of promise* that has powered continued colonial expansionism.[1] Because that textual tradition has shaped the past, it is legitimate and important to reflect yet again on this textual tradition as it may fund, correct, discipline, and nurture political imagination in our current socio-economic crisis.

Thus I will probe major reference points in that memory to see the analogues of assurance and requirement that continue to reverberate in the political imagination of our society. I will do so in three obvious moves that will end in a focus on our contemporary context, because the text itself characteristically has propulsion toward the contemporary.

Moses and Joshua

It is important to linger at some length over the founding narratives of Moses and Joshua to which later communities of interpretation have always returned. We may line out that founding narrative in three dramatic acts that continue to be definitional.

First, there is no doubt that the Exodus memory—whatever may have been its historicity—is defining for the entire textual tradition that follows. The Exodus narrative attests to YHWH as the propelling agent for emancipation who exhibits both the capacity and the will to challenge Pharaoh's sovereignty and eventually to overthrow it. Indeed, the culminating Song of Moses in Exod 15:1–18, which anticipates the entire history of Israel, concludes in exultation over the sovereignty of YHWH, "The LORD will reign forever and ever" (Exod 15:18).

That conclusion by Moses, moreover, echoes the more primitive celebration of Miriam, "Sing to the LORD for he has triumphed gloriously; horse and rider he has thrown into the sea" (Exod 15:21).

Israel deduced from this narrative and its liturgic replication that the saving God of Israel is the Lord of the universe who is set against all exploitative order, and who wills and enacts emancipation from every oppressive system.[2] Ancient Israel found it easy to transpose its singing from one circumstance of exploitation to another, from one empire to another because, judged by the will of YHWH, they are all the same, all sure to be judged and overthrown. It is for good reason that Michael Walzer has proposed that the Exodus narrative is the founding document for all social revolutions in the modern world.[3] He attests that such a seedbed of social revolution of course summons to bold action; but at the same time cannot be understood apart for reference to that inscrutable will and force behind human agency.

Second in the founding memory, Israel arrived at Sinai. The meeting at Sinai is shrouded in mystery and there is no doubt that the textual tradition is stylized for liturgical re-enactment in some sort of covenant renewal replication. At Sinai God spoke; at Sinai God spoke ten times; at Sinai God spoke only ten times. And in those ten terse utterances the God of the Exodus laid down an alternative path of communal practice and political power.[4] According to some critical judgment, the decalog comes late, and according to some it is only a device to preserve patriarchal control for the benefit of the male elites.[5] But that, of course, is not how the text has functioned in the interpreting community.

We are given a clue to its function by the awareness that already in Exod 19:8, well before the ten utterances in chapter 20, Israel assented to the commandments because Israel knew well ahead of time that any requirements by the Lord of the Exodus would be preferable to the commands of Pharaoh. Pharaoh's commands are always oppressive requirements for endless productivity and the inescapable commoditization of the human enterprise. Israel readily assented to the alternative counter-commandments and pledged its oath of allegiance to this alternative sovereign (Exod 24:3, 7). In that moment of pledging, Israel becomes what it had not been:

> This very day the LORD our God is commanding you to observe these statutes and ordinances; so observe them diligently with all your heart and with all your soul. Today you have obtained the LORD's agreement: to be your God; and for you to walk in his commandments, and his ways, to keep his statutes, his commandments, and his ordinances, and to obey him. Today the LORD has obtained your agreement: to be his treasured people, as he promised you, and to keep his commandments; for him to set you high above all nations that he has made, in praise and in fame, and in honor; and for you to be a people holy to the LORD your God, as he promised. (Deut 26:16–19)

In that moment of mutual pledging, something happened in the public history of the world that is irreversible, namely, the acknowledgement that the Holy Creator of heaven and earth is committed to and implicated in the public process of political power. And that process can never again be regarded as an autonomous or indifferent one.

Israel is pledged to two awarenesses. On the one hand, the first three commandments establish the primacy of the holy God and thereby render all political reality penultimate and without claim to absoluteness or ultimacy. These commands preclude the reifying of any form of political-economic power as an ultimate; from that moment Israel has been aware of the seduction of idolatry, seduction that becomes most visible and repellant in the massive statue of Nebuchadnezzar in Daniel 3. From this moment of Sinai utterance, Israel knows that it must resist every such political exaggeration. On the other hand, the last six commandments are designed to protect, honor, and lend dignity to the political processes of the human community. In the rule of YHWH, human persons are granted primacy that cannot be overridden by any acquisitiveness.

The *ultimacy of YHWH's rule* and the *proximate ultimacy of human persons* come together, even though the community of this text has been slow to see that linkage in terms of every social differentiation of class, race, or gender (see 1 John 4:20). This interface of what is ultimate and what is proximately ultimate issues in the belated awareness that the *love of God* takes the form of the *love of neighbor*. This convergence is manifest in the fourth commandment on Sabbath whereby both *creator* and *creatures* are at rest. This vision of Sabbath rest on earth and in heaven is a complete contrast to the restless, seething productivity of Pharaoh's regime of commoditization. Israel departed Sinai now pledged to the ultimacy that keeps political economic power under surveillance, and to a proximate ultimacy that refuses indignity or brutality whereby power can override the vulnerable treasure of human well-being.

Israel departed Sinai under oath. The oath pertains to the commandments from the mountain. But the commandments have behind them the emancipatory wonder of the exodus, so that the first and decisive commandment of YHWH's rules is narratively situated: "The Lord your God who brought you out of the land of Egypt, out of the house of bondage . . . The commanding God of Sinai is none other than the liberating God of the exodus" (Exod 20:2). And for the rest of the textual tradition of interpretation, both Jewish and Christian, the twinned themes of *emancipation* and *obligation* are decisive and definitional.

Third in the founding narrative, the primal commitment to emancipation and obligation was not an easy vision to sustain in practice, as attested by the wilderness quarrels. The defining memory, moreover, came sideways in the work of Joshua and the seizure of the land of Canaan. They did, nevertheless, manage to incorporate land seizure that is portrayed in the book of Joshua as a part of the story of emancipation.[6] Thus the crossing of the Jordan River is remembered—and perhaps liturgically reiterated—as a replication of the crossing of the waters from Egypt: "You shall let your children know, 'Israel crossed over the Jordan here on dry ground.' For the Lord your God dried up the waters of the Jordan for us until you crossed over, *as* the Lord your God did to the Red Sea, which he dried up for us until we crossed over" (Josh 4:22–23).

The answer to the children's question is stylized and so taken as narrative. The statement turns on what Garrett Green terms the "copula of imagination," "as," "as the Lord God did to the Red Sea. Land seizure is now emancipation."[7]

The founding narrative did not linger, as has subsequent interpretation, over the brutality against the indigenous population. It managed to accept such brutality through the subterfuge—a recurring subterfuge—that the Sinai vision of human worth and dignity did not extend to the Canaanites, that is, did not extend to those unlike us outside our covenantal agreement. Of course! That is how the historical is always managed when self-interest overrides visionary passion. And so we are able to say that a core of violence—authorized by divine utterance—belongs to the taproot of the normative tradition.[8] The God who authorizes land conquest is involved in the practice of violence and is not easily extracted from it. Thus the founding memory concerns emancipation and obligation, but emancipation and obligation that are shot through with deep measures of "justified" violence.[9]

I take this along with these founding memories to suggest that this narrative account is deep in Western political thought and in U.S. history. I am, without any expertise, aware that the founding figures of the United States were not passionate about the Bible and functioned from a deist perspective without the particular passion that belongs to the biblical tradition. But of course there was, always and everywhere, alongside what Robert Bellah has called "the republican tradition" an evangelical passion as well that focused on the imagery of exceptionalism, that had no trouble transposing from ancient Israel providential chosenness that issued in manifest destiny. During the recent election, with deep hopes for Obama's theological sophistication, I was caught up short by the observation that no one, not even Obama, could be elected president without a conviction of U.S. exceptionalism. Of course! That affirmation of exceptionalism over the centuries has continued to feature emancipation ("leader of the free world") and obligation ("imperial burden") and violent expansionism ("the land of promise") as the engine for self-understanding and self-justification. These founding traditions have continued to be palpable and immediate in the rhetoric and imagination of our society.

Solomon

Such founding traditions of emancipation and obligation are difficult to sustain and are readily seen to be inadequate. At least that is how it turned out in ancient Israel. Thus my second point is to expose Israel's season of amnesia whereby it used its energy to elude the unsettling of an emancipatory God, and whereby it substituted more palatable mandates for the commands of Sinai. It turned out that the other peoples and other cultures were not as inimical to Israel as the rhetoric of the book of Joshua had proposed. It turned out that the other peoples had alternative features in their life from which Israel borrowed and which Israel wanted to imitate. And of course the urge to imitate and replicate caused a cooling of exceptionalism, for the exceptionalism of Sinai turned out to be excessively demanding. By the time of Samuel, Israel wanted to be "like the other nations," not so rigorously distinguished by obligation (1 Sam 8:5, 20). Very soon they wanted a standing army (for an occasional militia was not enough) and a durable bank, a place in which to store and invest surplus value.

We may, in paradigmatic fashion, trace Israel's accommodation and amnesia in two steps. First, David is portrayed as a master politician who could regularly have it both ways, being larger than life and too agile to be stalled anywhere. David could manage at the same time to be YHWH's anointed and yet be a Canaanite king of a city-state who violated covenant in his self-aggrandizement (see 2 Samuel 11–12). That royal agility is dramatized in the fact that he installed two "high priests" who shared leadership, power, and prestige (see 2 Sam 8:17). On the one hand there was Abiathar, who early sided with David amid the rough and tumble battle for control (1 Sam 22:20–23). On the other hand there was Zadok, who had no narrative introduction and simply appeared among David's bureaucrats (2 Sam 8:17). While Abiathar is clearly rooted in old tribal, covenantal traditions, scholars suggest that Zadok may have been from among the Canaanite priests in the old city kingdom of Jerusalem (Jebus). In any case, the important thing is that he came from nowhere. These priests together evidence David's immense juggling act of *ancient tradition* and *contemporary opportunism*.

But second, David's son Solomon advanced the case of amnesia that loosened Israel's connection to the old narrative of emancipation and obligation. I will identify three facets of Solomon's narrative that show the huge departure from the old tradition that he enacted.[10]

First, it is reported no less than four times that he married Pharaoh's daughter (1 Kgs 3:1; 7:8; 9:24; 11:1). He is the son-in-law of the pharaoh of Egypt who is remembered as the one from whom Israel had been delivered. There are all kinds of evidence that Solomon's regime borrowed a great deal from Pharaoh's governmental practices, the outcome of which is clearly the relaxation of the intensity of exodus and Sinai.

Second, Solomon could not tolerate the dual priest system of David. When father David died, there had been a vigorous contest for succession to the throne. Alongside Solomon, his brother, Adonijah, was a candidate for the throne. As in all such contests, the leadership chose up sides. It is reported that among Solomon's supporters was Zadok the high priest, the one who is a priest without covenantal rootage (1 Kgs 1:8). And Abiathar, along with Joab, supported Adonijah (1 Kgs 1:7). And of course they were the losers, as Solomon prevailed in the contest. We are told, moreover, that Solomon promptly executed Joab (1 Kgs 2:28–35) and Adonijah (1 Kgs 2:13–25). We might expect that he would also kill Abiathar, a leader of the opposition; but it is, however, unwise to kill a priest unless absolutely necessary. And so Solomon banished Abiathar to his home village of Anathoth: "Go to Anathoth, your estate; for you deserve death. But I will not at this time put you to death, because you carried the ark of the LORD GOD before my father David, and because you shared in all the hardships my father endured" (1 Kgs 2:26).

Solomon disposed of the priest who was rooted in the old covenantal tradition. Abiathar must have been a reminder of that deep rootage; and now Solomon could forget.

Third, with the attraction of Pharaoh and the dismissal of Abiathar, it does not surprise us that Solomon went in a very different direction. It may have been a direction in which father David would liked to have gone, but he was still restrained. Once Solomon embraced Pharaoh and scuttled Abiathar, he had no more restraint. The narrative of Solomon makes clear that such carefully arranged amnesia leads to unfettered accumulation. Solomon became the great acquirer. Now, like Midas, everything he touched turned to a commodity. He seemed to have an incessant urge to acquire, collect, and accumulate. In this he is reminiscent of Pharaoh who could never have enough bricks. Solomon, moreover, is an anticipation of the man who built bigger barns and who, by the end of his story, is called a "fool" (Luke 12:20). With his reputation for wisdom, Solomon is given to us as a foolish wise one, the one who is thought wise but who is seen, in the end, to have preferred his own self-destruction.

Thus Solomon accumulated goods commensurate with the limitless appetite of his entourage: "Solomon's provision for one day was thirty cors of choice flour, and sixty cors of meal, ten fat oxen, and twenty pasture-fed cattle, one hundred sheep, besides deer, gazelles, roebucks, and fatted fowl" (1 Kgs 4:22-23). Solomon accumulated proverbs, enough to exhibit his pre-eminence in learning: "He composed 3,000 proverbs and his songs numbered 1,005" (1 Kgs 4:32). Solomon accumulated enough gold to make his temple a stunning tourist attraction:

> The interior of the inner sanctuary was twenty cubits long, twenty cubits wide, and twenty cubits high; he overlaid it with pure gold. He also overlaid the altar with cedar. Solomon overlaid the inside of the house with pure gold, then he drew chains of gold across, in front of the inner sanctuary, and overlaid it with gold. Next he overlaid the whole house with gold, in order that the whole house might be perfect; even the whole altar that belonged to the inner sanctuary he overlaid with gold. (1 Kgs 6:20-22)

> So Solomon made all the vessels that were in the house of the LORD: the golden altar, the golden table for the bread of the presence, the lamp stands of pure gold, five on the south side and five on the north, in front of the inner sanctuary; the flowers, the lamps and the tongs, of gold; the cups, snuffers, basins, dishes for incense, and fire pans of pure gold; the sockets for the doors of the innermost part of the house, the most holy place, and for the doors of the nave of the temple, of gold. (1 Kgs 7:48-50)

Solomon accumulated fortresses and weaponry:

> Solomon conscripted to build the house of the LORD and his own house, the Millo and the wall of Jerusalem, Hazor, Megiddo, Gezer . . . Lower Bethhoron, Baalath, Tamar in the wilderness, within the land, as well as all of Solomon's storage cities, the cities for his chariots, and the cities for his cavalry, and whatever Solomon desired to build . . . (1 Kgs 9:15-19)

> Solomon gathered together chariots and horses; he had 1,400 chariots and horses, which he stationed in the chariot cities and with the king in Jerusalem." (1 Kgs 10:26)

Solomon made Jerusalem to be the depository of global wealth:

> Once every three years the fleet of ships of Tarshish used to come bringing gold, silver, ivory, apes, and peacocks. Thus King Solomon

excelled all the kings of the earth in riches and in wisdom ... Each of them brought a present, objects of silver and gold, garments, weaponry, spices, horses, and mules, so much year by year. (1 Kgs 10:22–25)

And as though to cap it all off, Solomon collected women, no doubt designed to create a web of political alliances: "Among his wives were 700 princesses and 300 concubines, and his wives turned his heart away" (1 Kgs 11:3).

It is clear that Solomon had dramatically and decisively shifted the foundations and assumptions of society. Whereas Sinai had imagined *a covenantal community of neighbors*, Solomon had transposed it into *an aggressive economy of commodities*. We cannot tell about this convergence of amnesia and commodity, whether amnesia permitted commoditization or whether the pursuit of commodity generated amnesia. No doubt they came together and relentlessly reinforced each other.

Solomon did all of this, moreover, under the banner of YHWH. Thus the centerpiece of his narrative is the temple dedicated to YHWH, the God of the regime (1 Kings 8). The temple is now the place where YHWH would dwell: "I have built you an exalted house, a place for you to dwell in forever" (1 Kgs 8:13). YHWH is there as patron and as guarantor. The temple is the place for reciting the narrative of legitimacy: He said, "Blessed be the Lord, the God of Israel, who with his hand has fulfilled what he promised with his mouth to my father David saying, 'Since the day that I brought my people Israel out of Egypt, I have not chosen a city from any of the tribes of Israel ... but I chose David to be over my people'" (1 Kgs 8:15–16).

The temple is a place for sure blessing: "Blessed be the Lord, who has given rest to his people Israel according to all that he promised: not one word has failed of all his good promises, which he spoke through his servant Moses. The Lord our God be with us, as he was with our ancestors" (1 Kgs 8:56–57).

All the words and phrases and gestures are right. Except that now we have a truncated, diminished YHWH who fits completely into the state apparatus of amnesia. YHWH has been toned down and lost edge, has no freedom, and no capacity for truth-telling confrontation.

We are now able to see, in the remarkable Solomonic achievement, that the remembered tradition of Exodus-Sinai could be readily and completely accommodated to an aggressive acquisitiveness that was committed to systemic coveting. How odd that the God whose tenth word was "Thou shalt not covet" now becomes the sponsor of a system that covets. The important point is that there was no noticed contradiction between the old covenant and the new passion for commodity. It all seemed to fit in an ideology of self-aggrandizement.

And so it always is with the generation that cannot remember. So it was in Germany with the rise of National Socialism. The church was to a great extent swept along in the new folk ideology of blood and soil. There were, to be sure, important exceptions of dissent. But the accommodators produced the hyphen in "Deutche-Kristi," German Christians. The famous phrase of Bonhoeffer, "cheap grace," is not a generic phrase among us; rather it points exactly to the crisis of accommodation in which the claim of the gospel is shabbily pre-empted for ideology, and all without notice.

When we consider covenant-become-acquisitiveness under Solomon and the German Christians under Hitler, then it is an easy move to see how the claim of the gospel has been taken up among us in the service of imperial commoditization. For the most part, gospel and American Dream feel like synonyms to us. The exceptionalism of the United States has been a sustained theme as the newly chosen that may be traced in a tale of expansionism through the Mexican War of James Polk to the Spanish-American War of Teddy Roosevelt and eventually to Iraq. Whatever else we may say, it is characteristically a quest for territory, for resources, for markets, for oil, all of which bear the mark of entitlement. The role of much of the church, moreover, has been to bless and not to notice, to benefit and to forget, so that the ultimacy of God and the proximate ultimacy of the neighbor are lost in an ocean of commodities, and we cannot imagine life without them. As Solomon had to expel Abiathar and as Hitler had to dispatch Bonhoeffer, so U.S. amnesia has had to forego Niebuhr and King, and pretend that we had not yet been told of our immense capacity for self-deception.

The regime of Solomon came to a sorry end. On the ground, it took 400 years to complete the demolition job at the hands of the Babylonians. But the theological truth of the matter was enacted much more promptly. The text places an extended prophetic speech of judgment in 1 Kings 11. The indictment against Solomon is that he turned away from the first commandment concerning the ultimacy of YHWH:

> Then the LORD was angry with Solomon, because his heart had turned away from the LORD, the God of Israel, who had appeared to him twice, and had commanded concerning this matter, that he should not follow other gods; but he did not observe what the LORD commanded. Therefore the LORD said to Solomon, "Since this has been on your mind and you have not kept my covenant and my statutes that I have commanded you, I will surely tear the kingdom from you and give it to your servant. (1 Kgs 11:9–11)

What is ordained against Solomon, says the tradition, is loss—loss of power, loss of territory, loss of prestige, forfeiture of mandate from YHWH. The process of loss is slow. But the tradition asserts that it grinds on because the key claims of Sinai are, in the end, not negotiable.

Hosea, Deuteronomy, and Jeremiah

According to the books of Kings, the story of royal Jerusalem, David's royal city, grinds on in its amnesia, missing all the signs and gestures of divine judgment. The amnesia would seem to have been complete . . . never was heard a discouraging word.

In retrospect, however, we are able to identify a succession of re-memberers who lived and worked below dynastic radar. They lived a long way from Moses, but there are hints that there was a Levitic priesthood that held on tenaciously to the tradition of Moses, priests who did not succumb to the regnant amnesia.[11] In the eighth century, it appears that movements surfaced with some vitality. It could be that the pivotal person in this reassertion was Hosea who had connections to that ancient tradition. Hosea, commonly located about 740 BCE, could remember enough to see that Israel had forgotten everything important about its life with YHWH:

> I will punish her for the festival days of the Baals,
>   when she offered incense to them
> and decked herself with her ring and jewelry,
>   and went after her lovers,
>   and *forgot* me, says the LORD. (Hos 2:13)

> My people are destroyed for lack of knowledge;
>   because you have rejected knowledge,
>   I reject you from being a priest to me.

> And since you have *forgotten* the law of your God,
> I also will forget your children. (Hos 4:6)
>
> Israel has *forgotten* his Maker, and built palaces;
> and Judah has multiplied fortresses;
> but I will a fire upon his cities,
> and it shall devour his strongholds. (Hos 8:14)
>
> When I fed them, they were satisfied;
> they were satisfied, and their heart was proud;
> therefore they *forgot* me. (Hos 13:6)

The sum of these indictments is that Israel has practiced indulgent self-sufficiency and can no longer remember the source of its life or the purpose for which it is accountable. The inevitable outcome of such amnesia, says the prophetic poetry, is being punished so that good land is reduced to a forest (Hos 2:13), being rejected and forgotten by God (Hos 4:6), having fire sent on its citadels (Hos 8:14), and having God come against it like a lion, a leopard, a bear who will tear and destroy (Hos 13:6–8). Thus amnesia consists in breaking Israel's connection to Gods' holy, protective, nurturing power, and being left exposed to the forces of death.

We do not know all of the factors that led to the generative theological recovery of the Sinai tradition in the eighth century, nor do we know of the historical connection between the memory of Moses and the poetic recovery that clustered around the work of Hosea. What we do know is that after Hosea, in the eighth century and on into the seventh century, this theological-political recovery took on generative force and authority, and culminated in the Deuteronomic movement that came to full voice in the late seventh century.

The pivot point of this recovery is the book of Deuteronomy, almost universally taken as the scroll found in the temple in Jerusalem in 621 BCE (2 Kings 22). There it is reported that the reading of the scroll evoked a powerful response from King Josiah who, on the basis of the scroll, instituted a great socio-economic-liturgical reform of the realm. We do not know what so startled the king, but we may imagine that it was the long list of covenantal curses in Deuteronomy 28 that culminates with the most unbearable of all threats, a return to the bondage of Egypt: "The LORD will bring you back in ships to Egypt, by a route that I promised you would never see again; and there you shall offer yourselves for sale to your enemies as male and female slaves, but there will be no buyer" (Deut 28:68).

The covenantal tradition, at its extreme edge, can entertain the possibility that with enough willful forgetting, the entire tradition of emancipation and obligation can be undone; the community can lose its identity and return to a despairing condition of slavery. It would be as though the entire *providential action* of YHWH were nullified, the *exceptionalism* of Israel were voided, and *the land of promise* were forfeited. Amnesia can lead to a loss and reversal of history!

The most timely tradition of the Bible for us in the United States just now, I propose, is the book of Deuteronomy that is offered as an antidote to amnesia that inevitably comes along with the mad commitment to accumulation. We may focus in particular on two facets of Deuteronomy about which it is said concerning King Josiah: "When the king heard the words of the book of the law, he tore his clothes" (2 Kgs 22:11).

First, the book of Deuteronomy voices a vigorous warning against amnesia:

> When the LORD our God has brought you into the land that he swore to your ancestors, to Abraham, to Isaac, and to Jacob, to give you—a land with fine, large cities that you did not build, houses filled with all sorts of goods that you did not fill, hewn cisterns that you did not hew, vineyards and olive groves that you did not plant—and when you have eaten your fill, take care that you do not *forget* the LORD, who brought you out of the land of Egypt, out of the house of slavery. The LORD your God you shall fear him, you shall serve, and by his name alone you shall swear. Do not follow other gods, any of the gods of the people who are all around you, because the LORD your God, who is present with you, is a jealous God. The anger of the LORD your God would be kindled against you and he would destroy you from the face of the earth. (Deut 6:10–15)

Prosperity will talk Israel out of its passion for God and cause Israel to abandon the non-negotiable first commandment. Affluence will cause Israel to lose its identity in relationship to YHWH:

> For the LORD your God is bringing you into a good land, a land with flowing streams, with springs and underground waters welling up in valleys and hills, a land of wheat and barley, of vines

and fig trees and pomegranates, a land of olive trees and honey, a land where you may eat bread without scarcity, where you will lack nothing, a land whose stones are iron and from whose hills you may mine copper. You shall eat your fill and bless the LORD your God for the good land that he has given you.

Take care that you do not *forget* the LORD your God, by failing to keep his commandments, his ordinances, and his statutes, which I am commanding you today. When you have eaten your fill and have built fine houses and live in them, and when your herds and flocks have multiplied, and your silver and gold is multiplied, and all that you have is multiplied, then do not exalt yourself, forgetting the LORD your God, who brought you out of the land of Egypt, out of the house of slavery, who led you through the great and terrible wilderness, an arid wasteland with poisonous snakes and scorpions. He made water flow for you from flint rock, and fed you in the wilderness with manna that your ancestors did not know, to humble you and to test you, and in the end to do you good. Do not say to yourself, "My power and the might of my own hand have gotten me this wealth." But remember the LORD your God, fore it is he who gives you power to get wealth, so that he may confirm his covenant that he swore to your ancestors as he is doing today. (Deut 8:7–18)

Forgetting is a recipe for perishing: "If you do *forget* the LORD your God and follow other gods to serve and worship them, I solemnly warn you today that you shall surely perish. Like the nations that the LORD is destroying before you, so shall you perish, because you would not obey the voice of the LORD your God" (Deut 8:19–20).

This document of recovery poses for jeopardized Israel a sharp either/or.

Second, we may become more specific about the remembering that will correct the jeopardy of amnesia. The remembering is not primarily cognitive. It is practical, concrete, and performative. In the commandments of Deuteronomy, the commandments linked to Sinai that go beyond Sinai, the economy is the venue for intentional, countercultural, neighborly activity. There are at least four commandments explicitly motivated by Exodus memory, each of which concerns redress of the economic depletion of the vulnerable. The allusion to Exodus is not incidental; rather the remembered oppressive situation in Egypt was exactly one in which the vulnerable were exploited and then rescued by YHWH. Now

Israel is to recall the exploitation of remembered Egypt and the wondrous emancipation from that exploitation to reorganize economic practices according to the neighborly covenant of Sinai:

- In Deut 15:15, the commandment for the year of release concerns the cancellation of debts on poor people, so that there will be no permanent underclass in Israel. Moses provides that the emancipated debt-slave will be given wherewithal to re-enter the economy: "And when you send a male slave out from you a free person, you shall not send him out empty-handed. Provide liberally out of your flock, your threshing floor, and your wine press, thus giving to him some of the bounty with which the LORD your God has blessed you. *Remember* that you were a slave in the land of Egypt; and the Lord your God redeemed you; for this reason I lay this commandment upon you" (Deut 15:13–15).

- In Deut 16:12, the Festival of Weeks is to be a liturgic recognition of the promise of dignity for the economically vulnerable: "Rejoice before the LORD your God—you and your sons and your daughters, and your male and female slaves, the Levites resident in your towns, as well as the strangers, the orphans, and the widows who are among you—at the place that the LORD your God will choose as a dwelling for his name. *Remember* that you were a slave in Egypt, and diligently observe these statutes" (Deut 16:11–12).

- In Deut 24:17, Moses warns against requiring collateral for a loan for the vulnerable, for such a requirement amounts to injustice: "You shall not deprive a resident alien or an orphan of justice; you shall not take a widow's garment in pledge. *Remember* that you were a slave in Egypt and the LORD your God redeemed you from there; therefore I command you to do this." (Deut 24:17–18) Now we might think this is a sub-prime loan. But such a loan is a risky one only if the lender proposes to foreclose on the loan; Moses clearly intends no foreclosure against the vulnerable.

- In Deut 24:22, Moses provides what Crüsemann calls the first economic safety net in history by forbidding stripping fields and vineyards of olives, grapes, or grain. The residue of these money crops is to be left for foraging by the poor, a strategy for sharing the wealth:

> When you reap your harvest in your fields and forget a sheaf in the field, you shall not go back to get it; it shall be left for the alien, the orphan, and the widow, so that the LORD your God may bless you in all your undertakings. When you beat your olive trees, do not strip what is left; it shall be for the alien, the orphan, and the widow. And when you gather the grapes of our vineyard, do not glean what is left; it shall be for the alien, the orphan, and the widow. *Remember* that you were a slave in the land of Egypt; therefore I am commanding you to do this. (Deut 24:19–22)

This commandment pertains to the most important money crops in Israel, so that to some extent the money crops are to be diverted to sustain the vulnerable.

If we take all four of these commandments together—the year of release, the Festival of Weeks, the limit on collateral, and the residue of crops for the poor, it is clear that Moses intends to redirect the economy toward the neighbor. Moses is aware, in Deut 15:7, that one may be tempted to be "hard-hearted" or "tight-fisted" toward the poor. Such a posture, however, is overcome by a vigorous act in the economy, by a passionate remembering of one's own status as an exploited worker, by remembering the God who revamped the economy, and by a recall of Sinai where solemn oaths for an alternative economy were enacted. Everything depends upon remembering; everything is at risk in forgetting. Moses recognizes that amnesia is a huge threat to a covenantal ethic, but believes that the amnesia-producing power of affluence can be resisted and overcome. Such resistance, however, requires regular assembling in the midst of surplus, regular reiteration of the requirements that remain contemporary, and regular re-engagement with the old oaths. Where that action is not sustained, amnesia will win by default.

Deuteronomy is the primary antidote to the strategy of accumulation so well exemplified by Solomon. Indeed, the single commandment concerning kingship in Israel reads, as is often noticed, exactly as though it were intended to be anti-Solomon, anti-accumulation. Moses reluctantly allows a monarch in Israel. But he strongly limits the power of a centralized economy: "Even so, he must not acquire many horses for himself, or return the people to Egypt in order to acquire more horses, since the LORD has said to you, 'You must never return that way again.' And he must not acquire many wives for himself, or else his heart will turn away; also silver and gold he must not acquire in great quantity for himself" (Deut 17:16–17). The king is not to be an accumulator of horses, wives, silver, or gold, the big three of arms, allies, or wealth. The prohibition included the curious phrase, "not return the people to Egypt in order to acquire more horses." That is, the king is not to barter away the covenantal freedom of the community for the sake of weapons, for such barter will always end in exploitation.

Alongside Deuteronomy at the end of the seventh century—and close to the destruction of Jerusalem—we may notice one other important voice of covenantal alternative that was rooted in Sinai and situated in the tradition of Deuteronomy, namely, the book of Jeremiah. Jeremiah, like Deuteronomy, is compellingly committed to an Exodus vision of social power: "For I solemnly warned your ancestors when I brought them up out of the land of Egypt, warning them persistently, even to this day, saying, 'Obey my voice'" (Jer 11:7).

> You brought your people Israel out of the land of Egypt with signs and wonders, with a strong hand and outstretched arm, and with great terror; and you gave them this land, which you swore to their ancestors to give them, a land flowing with milk and honey; and they entered and took possession of it. But they did not obey your voice or follow your law; of all you commanded to them, to do, they did nothing. Therefore you have made all these disasters come upon them. (Jer 32:21–23)

Jeremiah develops the tradition of covenant to show that the memory of emancipation and obligation has been completely disregarded in Jerusalem, and so the disaster is sure to come.

We may pay attention to a notation in Jeremiah that completes the loop of our reflection. The very first verse of the book of Jeremiah identifies the prophet: "The words of Jeremiah son of Hilkiah, of the priests who were in Anathoth in the land of Benjamin" (Jer 1:1). Jeremiah is rooted in the old village of Anathoth; when we hear "Anathoth," we remember immediately old Abiathar, a priest of David who was banished by Solomon back to his home village . . . Anathoth. Jeremiah is a descendant of Abiathar; banished Abiathar is his ancestor and progenitor. The crucial theme of *forgetting and remembering* is carried in the Old Testament in a long line from Abiathar in the time of David to Jeremiah in the time of Josiah. The Abiathar-Jeremiah tradition stands as contrary to the royally sponsored amnesia of the Davidic house and the Jerusalem temple. This tradition constitutes a subversion of reality that subverts the amnesia and summons Israel to remember.

Our Own History

So we come to a three-fold analog in our own contemporary history:

- There is an initial tradition of providence, exceptionalism, and land promise: *Moses, Joshua,* and our Founding Fathers;
- There is a counter-practice of amnesia wrought through excessive prosperity: *Solomon* . . . and the current imperial seduction that has issued in mindless consumerism;
- There is a summons to recover memory in the face of amnesia: *Hosea, Deuteronomy, and Jeremiah*; it remains for us to ponder what the analogous point is for us in the recovery from amnesia.

Well, obviously in this conference we take the Bible to be a crucial resource for recovery; here we imagine that the religious community, specifically the church, has a role to play in recovery from mindless, brutalizing amnesia that has powered our economy of self-destructiveness.[12]

Ours is a time for recovery of a defining memory that contradicts amnesia. It is a demanding piece of work with great ideological forces bound to resist. We can point, here and there, to voices of recall . . . Jim Wallace, Daniel Berrigan, Naim Ateek, Michael Lerner, Martin Luther King . . . and you can continue the list. It is all very uphill, but it is urgent. Here is a piece of encouragement. For perhaps the only time in ancient Israel in its 400-year run of Davidic kings, the subversive tradition of covenantal remembering did impact public policy in the reign of Josiah. In the astonishing figure of King Josiah, the teaching of Deuteronomy (and perhaps Jeremiah) reached the king. Jeremiah says of this king, in contrast to his own son Jehoiachim:

> Did not your father eat and drink
> and do justice and righteousness?
> Then it was well with him.
> He judged the cause of the poor and needy;
> then it was well.
> Is this not to know me?
> Says the LORD. (Jer 22:15–16)

"Your father," Josiah, did righteousness and justice. He intervened for the poor and the needy; and he prospered! In that process, moreover, he came to know YHWH, the God of exodus, the Lord of Sinai, the giver of life. Such a king! Such a possibility! The king was possible only because of the tough resilient testimony of the remembering tradition. It is Deuteronomy that created an environment that made an alternative policy possible.

So consider the sequence:

- Initial passion and obligation
- Amnesia and accumulation
- Remembering and reconstitution.

We are well along, in our society, in amnesia and accumulation, a practice that has brought us to our current crisis. And now we ponder recovery.

I finish with two observations. First, it is useful to think of the work of active recovery. Recovery from any addiction requires intentionality, and certainly Solomon was addicted. But recovery is also a process that requires, along with intentionality, a lot of patience for advance and relapse. Recovery is no quick thing. But it does happen! It would matter among us if the moral teachers of our society were to be understood as intentional agents of recovery from the disease and addiction of amnesia. Good teaching will matter in the face of seduction, the teaching of another way, a more excellent way. What a way to think about local churches as centers for recovery of our societal disease!

Second, I have taken as my assignment the exposition of the biblical tradition, even though our context is global and pluralistic. This is not to impose that theological tradition amid the pluralism of the global public.

It is rather to take the Bible as paradigmatic in a way that permits other traditions to have their say about the same ailment. Every culture and every religious tradition has tales to tell of oppression and emancipation, of autonomy and covenantal righteousness, of wounds and hopes. The Bible is an invitation to identify those same deep human transactions everywhere, and to imagine the resilient power of holiness that is at work in every narrative of wound and hope.

Our social scene is indeed a nightmare that alarms. It is a nightmare of being lost and displaced and not having a reliable identity with staying power. It is a nightmare that produces waves of anxiety and acres of malfunction. Nightmares may be evoked by a guilty conscience. Or perhaps by an over consumption of rich food. Perhaps both apply to us in this nightmare, guilt over the neighborhood and excessive consumption of rich food. When President Gerald Ford pardoned Richard Nixon he wisely declared that "the long nightmare is over." Well, the long nightmare of amnesia and accumulation is not over and not so finally and easily ended. But it can be addressed and come to an end. The address is to remember, in performative ways, to re-engage our humanness that is rooted in God's own holiness and it not reached by the ersatz offers of an imperial consumerism. It turned out . . . it always turns out . . . that Pharaoh's prosperity was a death trap. There is no future in an endless round of production and consumption. Sinai is a sabbath from the rat race of accumulation. The narrative of restful neighborliness looms at the horizon and waits our engagement.

Endnotes

1. See Gunn, "Colonialism and the Vagaries of Scripture," 127–43 for an example of such expansionist use of the tradition.

2. On the recognition that this emancipatory impulse of YHWH extends beyond Israel to other peoples, see Amos 9:7, and my comment on the verse, in "Exodus in the Plural (Amos 9:7)," in *Many Voices*, 15–34.

3. See Walzer, *Exodus and Revolution*.

4. See Harrelson, *The Ten Commandments and Human Rights*; and Harrelson, *The Ten Commandments for Today*.

5. See Clines, *Interested Parties*, 26–45.

6. I have proceeded on the assumption that it is Exodus-Sinai and not the Abraham narrative that is foundational for Israel. But when it comes to the legitimacy of the land of promise, the Abraham narrative is drawn into a connection with the Joshua traditions so that the promise to the ancestors is the basis for entry into the land. In the final form

of the text, the Abraham narrative thus plays a crucial role in the claim of the whole of the tradition.

7. Garrett Green, *Imagining God*, 73, 140, and passim.
8. See Brueggemann, *Divine Presence amid Violence*.
9. See Schwartz, *The Curse of Cain*. Schwarz has made a formidable argument that violence is intrinsic to monotheism and is therefore readily "justified" against any "other."
10. See Brueggemann, *Solomon: Israel*.
11. The history of the tradition is complex and obscure. The most helpful proposals are those of Cross, *Canaanite Myth and Hebrew Epic*, 195–215; and Wilson, *Prophecy and Society in Ancient Israel*, 135–252.
12. See Fishbane, *Sacred Attunement*. In his recent study, Fishbane has reflected on the disciplines of "mindfulness" in Judaism that provide an alternative to the "mindlessness" of contemporary society.

2

America in God's World: Perspectives from Biblical Theology

KENNETH L. VAUX

Pentecost was past. The embers of *Shavu'ot*, *Taurut*, and indeed the universal festival of grain and warmth, God, law and renewal, still glowed around the earth. Rabbis, priests, and *imams* of old had hallowed these days to celebrate the receiving of Torah, covenant (*berit*), and divine law for the world, to exult in the release of the oppressed and to bask in the gift of the grain harvest and sustenance of all life through God's opened hand. God's threefold benediction on the earth—security, economy, and ecology—was gratefully received. This was the compound, noble heritage of Sinai, liberation that brought Pentecost pilgrims and that missionary to the Gentiles—Saul, now *Paulos*—back to Jerusalem for *Shavu'ot*. So it was that the covenant of life—the bestowal of God to the world through the mediation of Abraham and Moses, then Jesus and soon after Paul, and eventually Muhammad—would be established in earth history.

It was at a commemoration of these salient days of Pentecost that, after a brief visit to King Abdullah in Riyadh in which the extraordinary moment of interfaith Scriptural Reasoning that accompanied the king's still-extant Middle East peace proposal was reaffirmed, President Barack Obama's Air Force One landed in Cairo.

I rose at 5 a.m. that morning so I would not miss these long-anticipated words. I had written in a recent homily, which had something to do with the theme of this conference, about the interfaith scriptural setting of recent Middle East peace initiatives. I also mentioned Ambassador

Tony Blair accompanying his peace-with-justice proposals for the region with an interfaith scriptural portfolio.

President Obama's speech strangely warmed the Wesley chamber of my heart, as it did Muslim hearts the world over, even as it inflamed the passions of some Israeli and Christian Zionists. Even though the president's purpose was to address the Muslim world, and although the sacred texts selected were those of Islam—that irascible second sibling in the Abrahamic family of faith—his speech did not disappoint. It far surpassed all expectations. Several passages spoke to my specific persuasion, and that of our assembling mandate at this symposium, on the bearing of scriptural study, biblical theology, and the drama of America's role today in the conflicts and prospects in God's world. By way of introduction, I mention a few:

> I have come here to seek a new beginning between the United States and Muslims around the world; one based upon mutual interest and mutual respect . . . I do so recognizing that change cannot happen overnight . . . But I am convinced that in order to move forward, we must say openly the things we hold in our hearts, and that too often are said only behind closed doors. There must be a sustained effort to listen to each other; to learn from each other; to respect one another; and to seek common ground. As the Holy Qur'an tells us: "Be conscious of God and speak always the truth." (Qur'an, Sura 12.108)
>
> Part of this conviction is rooted in my own experience. I am a Christian, but my father came from a Kenyan family that includes generations of Muslims. As a boy, I spent several years in Indonesia and heard the call of the *azaan* at the break of dawn and the fall of dusk.
>
> All of us have a responsibility to work for the day when the mothers of Israelis and Palestinians can see their children grow up without fear; when the Holy Land of three great faiths is the place of peace that God intended it to be; when Jerusalem is a secure and lasting home for Jews and Christians and Muslims, and a place for all of the children of Abraham to mingle peacefully together as in the story of Isra (Qur'an, Sura 17.1, 60), when Moses, Jesus, and Muhammad (peace be upon them) joined in prayer.
>
> The Holy Qur'an tells us, "O mankind! We have created you male and female; and we have made you into nations and tribes so that you may know one another." (Qur'an, Sura 49.13)[1]

Although not quoted by President Obama, the passage continues, "because Allah has full knowledge and is acquainted with all."

Then came a passage with echoes in ancient and Kabbalah Judaism. It resonates with that elusive literature in which Jewish Aramaic Christianity morphed into pre-Islamic Arabic poetry, then into Islam: "whoever kills an innocent, it is as if he has killed all mankind; and whoever saves a person, it is as if he has saved all mankind" (Qur'an, Sura 5.32). Who can tell whether that sublime mystical logic is biblical? Is it Aegean, Aryan, or Semitic? Is it a "one-in-the-many and many-in-one" metaphor from Greece or India? Paul in Corinthians affirms it—"one has died for all; therefore all have died" (2 Cor 5:14). I know that Oskar Schindler had it engraved on the ring forged from the hundreds of tooth crowns gathered from those he saved from the Polish crematoria in his factories.

One further passage from Obama's Cairo speech calls to mind the full-orbed message of what we will call the substance of biblical theology as it pertains to world affairs. Anticipating his impending visit to Buchenwald with Elie Wiesel—Wiesel's family had been killed there, and Obama's ancestors had been part of the liberation—President Obama continued:

> Around the world, the Jewish people were persecuted for centuries, and anti-Semitism in Europe culminated in an unprecedented Holocaust. Tomorrow, I will visit Buchenwald, which was part of a network of camps where Jews were enslaved, tortured, shot, and gassed to death by the Third Reich. Six million Jews were killed, more than the entire Jewish population of Israel today . . . (At the same time), it is also undeniable that the Palestinian people—Muslims and Christians—have suffered in pursuit of a homeland. For more than sixty years, they have endured the pain of dislocation. Many wait in refugee camps in the West Bank, Gaza, and neighboring lands for a life of peace and security that they have never been able to lead. America will not turn our backs on the legitimate Palestinian aspiration for dignity, opportunity, and a state of their own.[2]

Echoing the historic Scriptural Reasoning conference attended by King Abdullah and President Peres, President Obama invoked the Noachic law: "Too many tears have flowed. Too much blood has been shed."

There we have it, all the processional dimensions of biblical theology—1) the divine bestowal of God's way in this good earth; 2) the ubiquity of danger and temptation along with divinely proffered duty and hope within human crisis; 3) the recognition of human frailty amid the crescendo power of ominous evil; 4) covenant with its absolute proscription of murder and the command to heal and save; and 5) the transcending efficacy of associative love. All this is within the covenantal canopy of awareness of our radical contingency under the justice and mercy of a God whom we are given to know and love in the great blessing of *imago Dei*.

In this indwelling Spirit, the *Emmanuel* God tones and supplies every human intention and action. This natural and supernal endowment animates security, economy, and ecology—the template of divine/human/world interaction in the creation that is the substance of biblical theology. I've come to believe that these three dimensions constitute the kingdom of God come to this world. In annunciating the kingdom, Scripture elucidates this new and better world and indeed this blessed reign of God embedded in the divine-human, inter-human, and cosmic associations. The fulfillment of this substance indeed vindicates the authority of those Scriptures.

Soon Barack Hussein Obama was off again on Air Force One, now to Buchenwald and Normandy, then to a weekend in Paris with Michele and the girls, leaving Bo back on the lawn of the *Maison Blanc* to walk himself and do his duty on the lawn. What a crazy, wonderful, paradoxical world—in Galen's words, "*Inter faeces et urinam.*"

My thesis in this essay recapitulates that litany of convictions that are the essence of biblical realism. That realism, which I see as the genius of this symposium, is the best force available in these critical times to incline public policy away from the apocalyptic and the utopic—both enticements hinted at as eschatological options in Scripture, but both treacherous and misguided and both unworthy of our assent. I commend this company toward the more normative, though much less thrilling, biblical ethos of realistic and irenic justice and peace.

In kingdom foretaste, we live at once in a veil of tears and a cosmos of thwarted dreams, yet at the same time in a tantalizingly provocative and resplendent world. Paradoxically, we yearn for the end of the world and the Coming of Christ (*maranatha*) and for the kingdom to emerge here on the earth. At the same time, for some strange reason, we hold out for (and do our best to bring on) the human projects of permanent war or perpetual peace—Hobbes or Kant, Rambo or Francisco—in secular public policy. But in this Lincoln symposium, positioned somewhere between the symposia of Tim LaHaye and Hal Lindsey on the one hand and Erasmus and Plato on the other, I admonish that we best *wait* in nondemanding patience and *work* in strenuous public duty for Scripture's all-so-clear God-portrayal of the justice and benediction of creation and new creation. After some preliminaries, I will set out this realistic persuasion and illustrate it in the work of several luminaries of this assembled biblical "Dream Team"—our own Michael, LeBron, and Kobe, and don't forget the sweetness of Candace. We'll then let the church and the world assess the wisdom or folly (as the case may be) of the project.

Before reviewing several representative practical biblical theologies offered by our own circle of scholars, let us sketch a few touchstones of the biblical theology movement, recognizing that, although that movement is much maligned, the world today still seeks to find there insights pertinent for understanding and negotiating world crises.

My education as a theologian took place in the heyday of the biblical theology movement. The G. E. Wright and John Bright texts of the "God-who-acts" school were standard. Gerhard von Rad had just finished a stint at Edwardian, Witherspoonian, and Wilsonian Princeton, where I hung my hat for a few years. Here von Rad worked through his *Theology of the Old Testament* and his provocative, although somewhat embarrassing, statement in this post-*Shoah* era—that the view of God in Jewish Scripture was one saturated by the manic and Manichaen idea of holy war.

Part of the Barthian biblical awakening sought to excise Scripture from its cultural anti-Judaic bias and to stimulate its inherent cultural critique through the power of "living word." Von Rad articulated this biblical renewal movement, which supplied inspiration to war-and-peace concerns, economic matters, and ecological endeavors—all issues of social justice.

At the same time, the biblical theology movement had a dark side. It was triumphalist on gender and sex-preference matters, was excessively phobic in regards to socialism and Islam, and condoned Euro-Anglo-American supremacy in world affairs. The God-who-acts agenda was peppered with Manifest Destiny and dispensationalist disdain for the hurting and lost for whom Christ lived and died. This searching God of Scripture—the God of the weak, poor, and oppressed—was "not wanting any to perish" (2 Pet 3:9), certainly not at the hand of the Amalek-exterminating Jews, Christ-sword-from-the-throat-slashing Christians, or Janjaweed-marauding Muslim conquerors.

The cold-war historical context of this moment in the history of biblical interpretation moved popular convictions toward Marcionite and Manichaen directions—where ultimately John Kennedy's passions censuring Cuba (while endorsing the Peace Corps) would end in the Reagan era of global hegemony, unrestrained economic exploitation and greed, and unbridled ruination of the good earth. This house of cards would come crashing down in these post-September 11th years. Only in recent months do we see the dark side of American Puritan impulses, of value and disvalue and aggression both active and passive. Today, a world in turmoil seeks a new interfaith scripto-centric biblical theology. The verdict is still out as to whether such interfaith concord will be forthcoming, and whether the "peoples of the book" can arise in concert after millennia of genocidal and eco-cidal, even Deicidal, strife.

My own *Doktorvater*, Helmut Thielicke, was part of the historical anguish of the biblical theology movement and had been associated with the July 20th conspiracy to assassinate Hitler, a conspiracy that assured the death of another great pioneer of biblical theology, Dietrich Bonhoeffer. Here again, America and Europe intertwined as Bonhoeffer took sail and returned to the *dénouement* of the Third Reich from that other citadel of biblical theology, Union Seminary in New York.

Langdon Gilkey—who in the next decade would challenge the premises of the God-who-acts movement in favor of a God who confines action to Newton's secondary causes—was then studying at Union. A neo-orthodox renegade, Gilkey had critical reservations about God-who-acts theology that came not only from his penchant for the predictabilities of science, but also from his genuine biblical insight that in the regularities of the natural world—"for he makes his sun rise on the evil and on the good, and sends rain on the righteous and on the unrighteous" (Matt 5:45)—"God is working His purpose out as year succeeds to year . . ."[3]

The concern with the theological validity of nature's law takes us into the heart of the biblical theology template. Was natural theology a move toward Canaanite Baalism or Hitler's blood and soil? Von Rad rehearses the basic recital of biblical divine action that arises within the purview of a conjoined Wellhausian evolutionary developmentalism—a naturalistic scheme—and a Barthian transcendental kerygmatics—a supernaturalistic scheme. This is the classical synergy and dialectic of reason and revelation, critique and conformism, nature and history.

The sequence of great acts and deeds, a natural and historical template, might result in the following patterns as sacred history unfolds:

- *Israel*—liberation from Egyptian oppression, promised land, gift of Sinai Torah;
- *Jesus*—bondage to sin and death, efficacious crucifixion, resurrection and reconciliation;
- *Paul*—new creation, *en Christou*, enfolds the Gentile world into the Hebrew covenant;
- *Islam*—resistance to inculturations of Judaism and Christendom, *Taurut/Injil, salaam*;
- *Nazi time*—idolatrous Judaocidal state, creedal witness against authorities, new world; and
- *Today*—militaristic, economic, and ecological injustice, hope for global justice and peace.

Von Rad's later work—followed by the God-who-acts entourage and the rich array of biblical and theological scholars who have furthered the inquiry in the last half-century—has appropriated an anthropology, political theology, historiography, and ethics that are responsive to the crises and challenges of our contemporary world.[4] This symposium is a sample of that prophetic work.

Another new element in prophetic hermeneutics today is the understanding of scriptural texts in the world of religious discourse within which we labor in modern history (Abrahamic/interfaith studies). Here, texts are seen as historical and provincial as well as eschatological and universal. They thereby command attention and currency even in a secular, post-religious world. For the Abrahamic (monotheistic) traditions, this requires an admixture of worldly and spiritual insights on ultimate theological matters and on penultimate secular issues. Despite the enormous difficulty of interfaith exegesis, hermeneutics, and prophetic application, one advantage of this nascent practice of interfaith Scriptural Reasoning is its cross referential and corroborative possibility. As evidenced by the scholars of this symposium, this new intellectual disposition enlarges the context and the receptive range of our scholarship.

Historical crisis and "crisis theology," together with "interfaith theology," is the milieu of the continuing biblical theology movement. In my modest work in this field, I have come to believe with President Obama and the world interfaith trialogue movement, that the bedrock theological task of our time will be to explore and refine, where necessary, the conjunction of Christian and Muslim theologies of Hebrew scripture. These two offspring of Judaism, comprising sixty percent of the world's population, are at the epicenter of the global spiritual prospect and the world's secular problem. My Chicago colleague, Don Wagner, director of the Center for Middle Eastern Studies at North Park University, co-directs the evangelical-Muslim dialogue movement in the world with longtime colleague Mahmoud Ayoub, former professor at Temple University. That our symposium brings together evangelical and liberal voices from the Christian camp is a reason for great hope. F. E. Peters is insistent that, if for no other reason than the trauma that now tears at the whole world, our work must be done "in triplicate."[5]

At the dawn of this new millennium, Walter Brueggemann, along with James Barr, summarizes the current status of biblical theology. Brueggemann especially has struggled, both in his expositions of biblical theology itself and in his address of particular societal issues, to help us see the pertinence of scriptural renewal to public issues. The following principal points of his work serve to summarize the vitality and viability of biblical theology.

In his introduction to von Rad's first volume, *Old Testament Theology*, Brueggemann finds these summarial assertions: "That the God of Israel is rendered narratively and in utterance; That the God of Israel keeps opening futures and 'expels from the safety of old saving traditions'; That the dynamic of 'old and new' is defining for biblical faith."[6]

In his own *Theology of the Old Testament*, Brueggemann offers equally striking assertions by surveying Israel's core testimony and counter-testimony as well as its unsolicited and embodied testimony.[7] Studying these telephone-book-like tomes this summer actually brought me a happy surprise. Unable to read them on my Kindle, I took Brueggemann in hand along with von Rad and Barr—obviously, I have great arms like Michelle Obama. When I came up for air at summer's end, it was with the conviction that such work, at least in its next mutation, is exactly what the world needs now. Some suggestions of potential outlines for such endeavors are part of what I hope to contribute to this symposium.

I get at Brueggemann's analysis of the "way and word of Israel" and its reception in Christianity by reflecting on two days in June. These all-too-typical days reveal events and interpretations that allude in their meaning to that root of global monotheism, the blessing and bane of human existence—Hebrew scripture—as exegeted in the history of the three Abrahamic faith traditions: Judaism, Christianity, and Islam. Four experiences over forty-eight hours impinged on my study on June 9–10, 2009.

My friend and colleague was a retired professor at Northwestern. A secularized Jew from Canada, he lived an ironic, laconic existence especially since he contracted an excruciating, chronic, yet nonterminal, spine condition. He had the aggravating habit of always throwing the *schreckliche vielleicht* (the horrifying possibility question) right between the eyes of this so-called pastor-theologian: "Why shouldn't I commit suicide?" I did no better than that pitiful pastor in Bergman's *Winter Light*, who was not able to dissuade his anguished parishioner from the *coup de grâce*. Unable to accept Bernanos' country priest's *"tout est grace,"* I asked him to explore Yahweh—the "I am," the God of life, of Abraham, Isaac, and Israel. This offered slight challenge to this post-Holocaust sociologist. I offered witness to Jesus, with an embarrassing pause common to those who live the life of critical research, especially pastors and professors. Like most of us who gathered at his memorial, my thanksgiving and hope was muted by shame and frustration.

On the same day, another suicide occurred—this one in Peshawar near Islamabad, Pakistan. A truck with three drivers drove through the gates to a luxury, five-star hotel and detonated the 100-pound explosives. Killing and wounding a combined 100 people, word had it that Pakistani Taliban or even al-Qaeda was responsible. Various rationales were offered: protecting the homeland from foreign infidels; the America-encouraged push on the Swat valley to counter terrorism; resentment and retaliation for the Palestine horror; or some imprecise charge involving Jews, Christians, Muslims, and maybe even Hindus—standard fare in our post-September-11th world.

America in God's World

Two other footnotes on this typical day in the *Heilsgeschichte* of our time: Today, representatives of several of the big banks rescued with public funds from their misbehaviors have said they will begin to repay those funds—in order to evade regulations like executive-compensation limits and to avoid taking on toxic assets. Calling to mind the admonition of the prophet Amos, investment bankers of the day ask, "When will the Sabbath be over so we can get back to the business of setting exorbitant interest and continue rendering the poor destitute?" (paraphrase of Amos 8:5).

Finally, at midday, an old and sick 88-year-old man walked suicidally, like Dr. Tiller's assassin as a self-deceived martyr the preceding week, into the Holocaust Museum in Washington, DC. A Holocaust denier and hater of Jews and blacks—the product, it seems, of decades of bad preaching and teaching—he lowered his shotgun.

This pathetic world is so like that of the biblical epoch in Israel with the recitation of Torah and prophets. It is like the appearance of the Christian movement with its *euangelion* (gospel or good news) within the diabolical Roman and Holy Roman State. It recalls the travail of iconoclastic and invasive Islam in the waning centuries of the Christian Empire with its restatement of *Taurut* and *Injil*. And so *Nazizeit* and our own postmodern day, which has been called the end and refutation of biblical history. All moments of our times follow suit with their own unique idolatries and injustices and their own fragile kerygmatic witness.

Brueggemann understands the point/counterpoint, adherence/iconoclasm dialectic and dynamic of the Hebrew scriptural tradition. Pericopes often bear point/counterpoint dialectical paradox: "on the one hand/on the other hand." Like Tevye the dairyman fiddling on the roof of Chagall's world, Scripture taunts us with seemingly opposite views: "Take your son . . . and offer him" vs. "Do not lay your hand on the boy" (Gen 22:2, 12); and "Celebrate the drowning of the Egyptians" vs. "What are you doing, they are also my people?" (*Exodus Rabbah*).

With hermeneutical acuity, Brueggemann wisely sees that Hebrew Scripture offers premonition of a postmodern perception of reality. A new "sociopolitical interpretive situation" tempers what we can know and say while being true to sacred text. In this skeptical (and argumentative, Amartya-Sen) posture, both epistemology and assertion are of necessity *modest* because of the mystery and power of the One God, Yahweh, before and within whom all human intuition and articulation is of necessity finite and penultimate. This is the clear recognition of Tanakh, Mishnah, and Talmud, of Christian gospels and writings, and of Qur'an and *hadith*. Semitic, Abrahamic texts: This composite corpus firmly acknowledges both the human and divine side: "For my thoughts are not your thoughts, neither are your ways my ways . . ." (Isa 55:8).

This pause and reservation is totally opposite to the certainty and self-apotheosis of fundamentalist and orthodox presumptions and posturing found in each faith of Abraham. It is defensive and aggressive ploys in Jewish, Christian, and Muslim history that bring on such idolatrous and destructive maneuvers. History, including our own, is replete with the savagery of these presumptions and usurpations.

After reading James Barr's magnificent overview of the movement,[8] I need to clarify my own approach. Not being a technical biblical scholar in the modern sense, I operate on three assumptions. First, as a bred Calvinist and trained Lutheran, I know that theology begins and ends with Scripture. Second, I have been sculpted by interfaith studies and Scriptural Reasoning (tri-faith Abrahamic reading), and, since my doctoral studies on Holocaust and medical experimentation in Germany, I try to always carry in my tool-kit Hebrew text, Septuagint, Nestle, and Qur'an—along with a very modest linguistic facility at least—in order to honor the sacred texts and traditions of these fraternal partners. Finally, I am shaped by the Barth, Bonhoeffer, von Rad, and the vintage American God-who-acts movement of biblical renewal. I know from plain-sense experience that the wise and simple, young and old, rich and poor are our best Bible scholars, theologians, and ethicists—persons who can and do fathom and live out Scripture.

With this background and context before us, let me turn to my assignment, which is to offer several scenarios of prophetic Bible critique and hopeful construction. With the help of this company of the nation's best Bible scholars, I offer several selected reflections on the Bible, America, and the future.

I believe that Scripture points to three dimensions of corporate existence within which human weal and woe is mediated via divine provision and human justice or lack thereof. These three parameters are: security, economy, and ecology. How we choose and act in these three realms proffers or negates the divine gifts of peace, prosperity, and health.

America in God's World

Jewett on Security

First, from Bob Jewett, our convener and author of the landmark Hermeneia commentary on Romans, I take a couplet of overarching themes—shame and zealotry—to illustrate the transcendental of security. Several immediate events set the stage for this biblical consideration. The first is a CNN documentary called "American Radical: The Lone Wolf," which aired June 12, 2009.

This country is distinguished in the world not only by the thousands of children killed by guns (thirty-seven in Chicago alone this year), but also by a new semi-invisible class of "leaderless loners" or "lone-wolf subversives" who are lethally predisposed to tear down government entities and take down threatening others, such as Jews, blacks, Muslims, immigrants, abortion doctors, and homosexuals, to name a few. These purveyors of hate crimes are immersed in brooding resentment, willfully conducting their suicidal, self-conceived heroic acts out of a contorted world view—Manichaean, dualist, zealous, and apocalyptic—coercively ushering in a new order through violent destruction of the old. The names are familiar:

- *Ted Kaczynski* (the Unabomber), from his Montana cabin (the overland pass from Russia and all things red), mailed bomb letters to universities (including our own Northwestern) and various technology centers.
- *Timothy McVeigh* at Alfred P. Murrah Federal Building in Oklahoma City avenged the Justice Department's firebombing of the Branch Davidians at Waco, Texas.
- *James von Brunn* served six years in jail for hate crimes before entering the Holocaust Museum in Washington, DC, with his shotgun. His vendetta was against Jews, blacks, and the "Jews' black president"—Obama. Eighty-eight years old, he was quoted as wishing to go out "in a blaze of glory."
- *Scott Roeder* had long been stalking doctors and clinics that performed abortions. Like the self-appointed executioners of Thomas Becket, he chose the sanctuary of a Lutheran church in Wichita, Kansas, to kill Dr. George Tiller, purportedly saving innocent lives by offering his own in martyrdom.

- *Abdulhakim Mujahid Muhammad* entered the military recruiting station in Little Rock, Arkansas, and killed a soldier.

Two interesting repenters heighten the theological drama at hand and give our issue a twist toward the redemptive.

- *T.J. Leyden* was a leading skinhead, neo-Nazi racist confronted with the impact of his actions one night by his toddler son, who turned off the television and said, "Daddy, you know we don't watch shows with niggers." Leyden was so shocked to see that his three-year-old son was racist that he was forever changed: "and a little child shall lead them." (Isa 11:6) T.J. now works with the Simon Wiesenthal Center, offering a moving testimony of being liberated from what he came to see as a demonic bondage.
- *Frank Schaeffer*, son of famous Swiss preacher Francis Schaeffer, now believes that their anti-abortion rhetoric of decades-past led many into violent un-Christian murder of health professionals and patients.

Jewett believes that such a display of cases reveals an underlying fabric of misguided religious zeal derived from erroneous biblical interpretation. Where the grace of God is operative in the Spirit, there is no room for imperial, fanatical devotion (zealotry) or for the humiliation of others out of honor/shame designation and disregard. In *Mission and Menace*, Jewett develops an historical depiction of how this unfortunate pattern of belief and action became so pervasive.[9] In the masterwork on Romans, he then gives Scripture's remedy.

My own analysis of biblical theology and America's future is most deeply shaped by this theologian and historian—Bob Jewett, especially in *Mission and Menace*—and also by Kevin Phillips in *Bad Money: Reckless Finance, Failed Politics, and the Global Crisis of American Capitalism*.[10] These works both address the underlying religious atmosphere that provokes social and political disarray.

Both are analysts of the American religio-political ethos. It seems appropriate that this first symposium is at St. Marks, Lincoln, Nebraska, here in the great heartland of this nation—a region so magnificent and mischievous in world history, a region marked by its particular spiritual ardor and its exemplary serenity and solidarity. This is the perfect place

America in God's World

to pursue the theme of the Bible and the American future. Plus it is Bob's home on the range.

Both Jewett and Phillips find this nation's unique and constitutive ethos to be grounded in American Puritanism—Max Weber's and Alexis de Tocqueville's zone of fascination. Originating in East Anglia and the Rhineland-Palatinate, we find in this community a pioneering independence and interdependence—a worldview and way of life. Let us also recall that these immigrants we call Pilgrims and Puritans came to America to escape religious persecution. When Judeophobia and Islamophobia did not provide enough lethal glee and lust for destruction, old Europe took out after Catholics, evangelicals, and nonconformists. So our pioneer ancestors came here, deporting themselves pretty much at the same time as they were deporting African chattel slaves and depopulating the indigenous people in the New World.

Weltanschauung in this new land was a new proleptic horizon, one especially involving a pristine new frontier of unspoiled Eden—soon dispossessed of one native race and despoiled by the enslavement of another—a place to clear and build a secure homestead, all against the background of hardship, frugality, cattle-rustling, greed, and guns. Ecology, economy, and security—Adam and Eve, Cain and Abel, Jacob and Esau—the fabric and texture of life on the frontier depicts the well-being conveyed in scriptural justice, health, and peace. This new land also raises the specter of the persistent nemesis of the "lone wolf" and the seeming necessity of the "lone ranger" for every high noon.

In *Mission and Menace*, Jewett pours out a litany of contemporary zealotry played out against the psychosocial background of honor and shame—these dispositions derivative of the impulses of salvation and damnation.

Here is the architectural event-flow of the 400-year epoch of America that Jewett traces:

- the millennia city set upon a hill, flushed with Manifest Destiny;
- God's new Israel—exodus, promised land, and *ḥerem* of the Amalek (natives);
- the theocratic experiment—the resistance of a separationist church-state counter-experiment;

35

- the displacement of a permanent and persistently subversive counter-culture;
- enlightenment and awakening—the paradox of an emerging pious world empire;
- civil religion, where the Cheshire cat is gone but the ubiquitous sinister smile remains;
- zealous nationalism, Vietnam, civil rights, and the Green movement; and
- then, as Jewett's time line is fading—September 11th, terrorism, Iraq, Afghanistan, Israel/Palestine, *Nakba* 1 and 2, invasion and occupation, Christian right and cosmopolitan left, Obama—and here we are.

Jewett's new-world hope is forged in the formation of the American constitutional system (1787), which was a decisive choice for "prophetic realism" and against "zealous nationalism." This vision, he asserts, resonates with the Isaianic vision of the Bible: "of a future world court that would enable conflict resolution through impartial adjudication and make war unnecessary."

The vision would be further constituted by the international system that arose in the world after the global wars which ended in 1945 with the establishment of the United Nations, the World Court, and other such entities: "It was late in Isaiah's ministry, probably after the terrible Assyrian invasion of 701 BCE had buried his country's preference for imperial crusading, that the prophet developed the vision of global coexistence under law."[11]

Jewett then quotes the oracle of Isa 2:4, which is etched on a wall across from the United Nations building in New York. The modern European community—home base for institutions such as the World Bank, the World Court, the World Health Organization, the Hague, the War Crimes Tribunal, and many other transnational structures, many rejected by his beloved native America—is now his adopted homeland. All of this historical unfolding, fragile though it is, is for Jewett the continuing commitment of a struggling world to the New Testament's tantamount kingdom portrayal of a vision in which apocalyptic terror is repudiated by the life, death, resurrection, and ascension of the Lord of history.

The dramatic American narrative of the 400 years unfolds in the turbulent history precipitated by that biblical moment. Jewett indeed is holding the American drama over against the tracing paper of biblical *Heilsgeschichte,* where Romans becomes the interpretive paradigm in the declining American Empire as it was for Paul in the Roman Empire, Luther in the peaking Holy Roman and Ottoman Empires, Wesley in the struggling British Empire, and Barth in the dawning Empire of the Third Caesar-Reich.

Jewett traces this historical panorama of American history through the onionskin of his own two commentaries of Romans onto the brass-rubbing template of the great treatise itself. Using the metaphor of honor and shame and the dynamic process of zealotry, this protégée of Luther, Wesley, Barth, von Rad, Käsemann and company paints a picture of a *faux* righteousness based on the "pump-up" of honor or the "put-down" of shame. This denigration of human solidarity—added to an exhilaratingly derived zealotry, a human folly that contradicts the divine wisdom, equity, impartiality, forgiveness, and bestowal of dignity—is the breach of divine justice and peace, the righteousness of God on which depends the reconstitution of the world, creation, and new creation. Free gift and free task—*Gabe* and *Aufgabe*—this is the kingdom of God, the Trinitarian dispensation, on earth as in heaven.

The culmination of biblical theology we draw from Jewett's discussion of honor and shame is the life-or-death distinction of the Sinai and Shechem covenants, which I interpret in my own biblical theology as the distinction between might and power. When this, our nation, is commanded to "choose this day who we will serve," this is the choice we must make. I use these biblical words with definitions as taught by Walter Wink and Dan Migliore.[12]

Might is the artifice of strength growing out of the hasty and audacious religiosity we call zealotry; *power* is derived from the Spirit of God expressing itself in what Jewett calls "prophetic realism." This responsive, responsible, and righteous energy brings creative and constructive impulses into the common life: care; justice; mutual aid; help for the weak, sojourner, and stranger; solidarity and duty toward women and children.

Might is defensive and fearful; *power* rests in divine comfort and human community. *Might* seeks hegemony over others; *power* seeks reciprocal empowerment and cooperation. *Might* seeks national supremacy; *power* seeks universal sharing. *Might* seeks religious domination and uniformity; *power* seeks persuasion and pluriformity. *Might* finds divine mandate in war; *power* finds divine judgment and mercy toward all parties in conflict. *Might* usurps divine power for itself; *power* seeks to find it in all. *Might* seeks a reign of threat in which a global empire dominates the earth through the subjecting authority of security, economy, and ecology; *power* finds these gifts of *shalom* mediated in the Isaianic bestowal.

This topsy-turvy realm or state of affairs has appeared in our midst according to scriptural witness. In contradistinction to the shame/honor destruction of humanity, the wisdom of the cross, the holy agony, is a shame that transfigures all humanly instigated shame—becoming the honor and glory, the power and wisdom, the joy and delight of God. Hereby all humanity is crowned with glory and honor (Psalm 8; Romans 8; Revelation 6).

The signature passage for my thesis is Rom 1:14–17:

> I am debtor both to the Greeks, and to the Barbarians;
> both to the wise, and to the unwise.
> So, as much as in me is,
> I am ready to preach the gospel to you that are at Rome also.
> For I am not ashamed of the gospel of Christ:
> for it is the power of God unto salvation to every one that believeth;
> to the Jew first, and also to the Greek.
> For therein is the righteousness of God revealed from faith to faith:
> as it is written, The just shall live by faith.

Paul here claims that the messianic fulfillment, the Christ gospel, has taken nature (including humanity) into decisive, qualitative transformation and history into crossroads and a new departure. This "fullness of time" occurs in the space/time continuum within the worlds of Greece, Rome, and Israel and is variously labeled "the gospel of God," "the righteousness of God," or "the gospel of Christ." The power and glory of this shameless transfiguration of reality led me to offer at my Jewish friend's funeral service the words from *Les Miserables*, a tribute to this so tormented yet gracious man, "To love another person is to see the face of God."

Paul claims that this eruption/culmination that is this kingdom, gospel, or righteousness of God occurs within three historical transformations:

1. *A Roman Empire (Greek and Latin).* At once cosmopolitan and salutary—*Pax Romana/*"the fullness of time" (Gal 4:4) and yet diabolical—it was awash with idolatry and injustice, pretension and violence.

2. *A Jewish state.* Now Diaspora community (the Jacobean model of the Church/twelve tribes), it was destined as a force in the world for Torah and prophetic peace (Isaiah 40), but was involved in the enigma of the reception/rejection of the Messiah.

3. *The nascent Roman and Asia Minor house churches and their replication among Diaspora Jewish and righteous Gentile communities throughout the Hellenistic world and beyond.* Here was a new community of sacrificial liturgy and sacramental service that was to transform a tribal universe into communes of forgiveness, reconciliation, and mutual service—One sacred world for the One God (Shema/John 17)—companies of the basin and towel, proffering semiotic bread and baptismal wash, ministrations of death into life, violence into justice, self-absorption into local and global service, discord into peace.

As this great congregation on this great mid-continental plain lives out that same litany of word and work and invites our company of teaching-elders to support you and shed your vision into nation and world, we together find our security not in missile silos—targeted on Russia, China, and Iran—but on this missive of justice and peace.

Economy is the second command/gift/grace to which we now turn our attention. From the bedrock consideration of the "economy of God" to the profuse concern about money, manna, and mammon, Scripture is pervaded by an attention to wealth and impoverishment—as a decisive dimension of common life in the faith community and world society.

Horsley on Economy

In his new study, Richard Horsley considers the way in which the conviction of "covenant" might pertain to contemporary American economics.[13] As I have argued in *America in God's World,* America is now awash in a bewildering shipwreck involving not only profound economic crisis, but also an accompanying underlying spiritual-ethical malaise that seems to have contributed to the America-epicentered tsunami that has sent tidal waves of anguish sweeping around the world.[14] Russia's version of Rush Limbaugh spews rhetoric about America owing the world more than $53 trillion.

The typhoon's etiology seems to be multifactoral. We speak of inevitabilities, stupidities, and injustices: corrections (cycles), bubbles, and greed are operative. There are, in the first case, natural and necessary global economic patterns. Much economic philosophy scans history and finds recurring rhythms and patterns much like the seasons of nature—spring and summer, autumn and winter.

Inflations and deflations, progressions and depressions also seem to be brought on by human miscalculations and failures of prediction and prevention. A high-tech banking or housing bubble can be seen coming, and appropriate regulating and protecting measures can be enacted to sustain equilibrium.

But finally, the deliberate exploiting and expropriating impulses—human selfishness, injustice and greed, impulses that often deface human life—catch fire in dark rooms of deceit and destruction, and human community is seared and burned by the malevolence one to another. Bernie Madoff defaces himself and family, breaks love with his own faith community at Yeshiva and the Elie Wiesel Foundation, and fractures trust with vast numbers of unknown faces on myriad stock-account reports.

Horsley identifies this worldly maelstrom and its causal spiritual malaise as breach of "covenant." In his introduction to *Covenant Economics,* he follows the American saga and its belief in biblical provocation and undergirding much along the lines of Jewett. Biblical exodus is rehearsed in the deliverance from persecutorial Europe. New land is received, and—here our stolid New Englander demurs—*ḥerem* is executed as the indigenous people (Canaanites and Amalikites or Algonquins and Cherokees, I suggest) are exterminated or concentrated. The land is consecrated and constituted, even in the Federalist rhetoric of the Deists. Horsley goes on to argue that America must repent, return, and again claim the duties incurred with the biblical covenant—especially in the realm of economics.

Economic rights, Horsley correctly asserts and we often forget, are part and parcel of the covenant to which we profess we are bound. Throughout his fine corpus of work, he shows that if we follow biblical covenant, we see rights as both formal and substantive.

Today, we argue intensely and insipidly "which is the best—the most godly nation in the world?" As I write on Independence Day, the rhetoric is profuse and problematic. After a frightful abrogation of all democratic principles on free-speech protesters by the gangs of thugs called *Basij*, the barring of all free press and the killing of innocents symbolized by the young woman named Neda Soltan, Ahmadinejad's Iran is proclaimed by the "supreme leader" as the "only religious-democracy in the world." In an interesting dissent, the Assembly of Qum Seminary Scholars and Researchers sees fraud. Meanwhile, still flush with our own "chosenness," we Americans pursue our invasions and occupations in Iraq and Afghanistan and by proxy in Palestine and Gaza.

Amid these unseemly assertions, we might well examine Horsley's claim that in biblical purview substantive rights—food and shelter, work and health care, retirement and provision for women, children, the poor and refugees, all economic rights—are as important as formal rights such as speech, assembly, worship, travel, and others.

As a sometimes unsolicited adviser to President Obama, along with Cornel West and Michael Dyson, I offered critique of a phrase he used in the early days of his campaign. At the stirring Kate Smith conclusion of every speech—"God bless you, and may God bless the United States of America . . ."—he often would add, "America is the last, best hope of Earth . . ."

I am thankful that he dropped this felicitous Puritan pretense so patently unbecoming in this world of myriad great and honorable nations: France and Russia, China and India, Iran, Iraq and Israel, Uganda and Uruguay, Honduras and Haiti, Singapore, Japan and Australia, among 130 others. All nations under heaven are established under the One God who "made of one blood all nations of men . . . and hath determined the times before appointed, and the bounds of their habitation" in space and time (Acts 17:26).

Covenant economics—drawn from the paradigm of Torah and Decalogue Horsley summarizes—"include the right to the integrity of people's life, the right to integrity of marriage and the family, the rights of the elderly (do I hear an "Amen"?) and the right to the basis of livelihood for individuals, families, and households (the right to jobs and income) . . . for adequate livelihood, adequate education, decent health care, transportation, day care for children, adequate care for the elderly, clean air and water, safety of life and limb . . ."[15] Perhaps we recognize again the triadic template, the *shalom* of security, economy, and ecology, the provision of God for all that ought not to be curtailed or stifled by human injustice or hoarding.

In America today, all these rights are falling under the budgetary axe of nation and states in favor of the more-sacred cows of military and homeland security budgets, bank-buster corporate salaries, exorbitant legal-fees, and out-of-control medical and insurance costs—among other demonic powers.

Not only does Horsley see the analogies and continuities of biblical imperatives for today's world, he sees clearly the threats. Idolatrous projection and powers of the world conspire to rob humanity of its rightful inheritance. Humanly imposed impediments thwart the flow of Godly provisions for the human family. Sensitive to the biblical antagonists to the way of God found in the worldly powers of the enveloping cultures—Egypt, Babylon, Assyria, then Greece and Rome—Horsley finds contemporary analogy in the alien powers of nation-states, governments, self-serving professions, and huge unresponsive corporations. In this age of AIG, General Motors, and Exxon, who can miss his point?

In the past thirty months, America has learned that only the biblical prognostics of prophecy and the biblical imperatives of Torah—scriptural *prohibitiva* and *imperativa*—can rescue us now and save us from humanly contrived destruction. We are taking the world fast to a hellish inferno of unsafe securities, impoverishing economics, and "wasteland" ecologies. The ubiquity and malignancy of economic phenomenon is particularly pronounced. Persons of modest means are castigated for taking their families into the calamity of bankruptcy and foreclosure by taking on unmanageable sub-prime mortgages. Respected three-piece-suited Presbyterian bankers are condemned for selling the instruments of high-risk that decimated the savings and pensions of most of their clients. All of these fast-buck con-men should have consulted their heritage of faith for truth and justice before they concocted the facile impossibilities of Ponzi and sub-Ponzi schemes. Now as they head for prison, their pastors and rabbis—those who parroted the mega-church prosperity gospel, the Wall-Street line—should be forced to go up the river with them.

But economics is also a realm of profound liberation and enrichment. The time for theological renaissance grounded in biblical wisdom has come. As I attempted to show in *America in God's World*, under the frenzy of the idolatrous and unjust public actions of our congregants are the shaky-sands of fallacious theology purveyed by the malpreaching of a thousand false prophets and—dare I say?—we, their teachers. Beyond the perquisite cleansing, biblical theology in refreshed modalities can still serve us well. For now, Horsley's admonitions need be taken to heart to rescue church and world while there is yet time.

The most compelling and, I find, relevant part of Horsley's proposal is his discussion of economics and the poor and needy: land foreclosure and Jubilee, debt-slavery and redemption, and the issue of charging loan-interest to the poor, sabbatical rotation—all arcane and outmoded virtues are dusted off and commended. No interest for the poor is an issue most faithfully applied today in Islamic banking and most grotesquely violated in Jewish and Christian banking. The *mullah*-scholars of Qum contrasted with Lehman Brothers are no contest in this summer of our economic discontent.

In summary, the realm of economy reveals, on close view, its profound reach. In this difficult year of economic downturn, America's gross product will diminish five percent while China's will increase by the same. Even now, America's generated wealth will likely amount to almost more than that of all the other nations of the world combined. Even California's shaky ship-of-state is still the globe's sixth-largest economy.

The economy is the composite wealth of the people, government, corporations, and institutions of the society. It is *ecos* (the whole house substance) of this particular nation. In terms of meaning, this invokes the biblical, covenantal mandate that "to whom much is given, much will be required" (Luke 12:48). In the great undergirding justice governing all of life, we come with nothing and leave with nothing. It doesn't matter whether we are Michael Smith or Michael Jackson. After economic debts are settled and legal fees collected, we all end at zero sum. Here

God is all in all. Now economy verges philosophically and theologically into ecology. We stand responsible before God to this nation, one habitation in this vast ecosphere that Scripture addresses as *oikumene*—the one world-house of the One God who brought it in, upholds it and will take it away—a God who was and is and will be. So the final word is accountability for who we are and for what we have been given in God's world house—ecology.

Richter and Ecology

Obama's environment program was not supported by a single opposition representative. Could so many get something as obvious as the onrushing ecological calamity so utterly wrong? In our own circle, it is the women exegetes and philosophers who seem to have a gift of sensitivity when it comes to the environment and eco-theology. My home university, Northwestern, was home for many years to two of our country's most eminent eco-theologians—Mary Daly and Rosemary Radford Ruether.[16] Our Candace Parker on this Dream Team is Sandra Richter. To close this paper, I address her contentions in *The Epic of Eden*.[17]

Richter is a pastor-scholar, an expert in what may be called the Christian Old Testament, one identified as part of the evangelical movement within contemporary Christianity. Her doctoral work set the direction for her salient and provocative career with a study on the issue of whether the divine Name of Yahweh actually conveyed divine "presence" at shrines and sanctuary, or whether this was simply a nominal and representational designation.

This recent work, setting forth a cognate direction of research that includes the Lincoln essay, is a persuasive biblical-theological argument for Christians to take seriously the Hebrew Bible, rather than seeing it as a prelude only to the Christian Scripture and tradition. The root of her contentions are: 1) the Bible in both Old and New Testaments is an inspired text about God and the project of human redemption; and 2) creation, mediated via Scripture, is both the setting and the doctrine for the exposition of this truth. I find here a groundbreaking contribution to a biblical theology of creation and ecology for America in God's world.

The "evangelical Bible" (the Greek and Hebrew texts deemed closest to the "autographs," along with the highly esteemed King James and

Scofield Bibles, all admittedly at some variance with Roman Catholic, Eastern Orthodox, and certainly Hebrew *Tanakh* and Islamic *Taurut* and *Injil* scriptures) begins with Eden and ends with the New Jerusalem. Scripture, thus conceived, sees these alpha and omega realms as concrete places (realities) in the unfolding redemption of God, both now firmly "in place."[18] Richter's goal is to "deal a mortal blow"[19] to the syndrome of "closet Christianity" that barricades itself off from the Old Testament. In this move, she firmly asserts that the narrative of the Hebrew people and the redemptive plan of the God of Israel is part and parcel of Christian faith and not just a prelude to the "real way."

Richter, we may assume, endorses the project of Christians reaching out to understand biblical and contemporary Israel in order to better understand her own story drawn from Hebrew Scripture. It will be interesting to explore with her what she thinks of comparative Scripture study by Christians with contemporary Jews and Muslims. Resonating with John Calvin's conviction that the two essential subjects of the minister's study are the history of Israel and the history of the Church, she claims that God's redemptive history can only be discerned by fathoming the content and "merchandise" of that biblical narrative. This is the "truth of redemption."[20]

This immersion and engagement with Israel that Christian tradition has always understood as the substance of its own faith culminates in our knowledge of and relationship with God through Christ. The grounding of universal faith begins with God's redemptive dealing with the people of Israel.

The Bible is therefore about real time and space, contends Richter. The covenant—all about gardens, trees and rivers, sun and moon, and all the creatures on earth—holds the experiences of all called to its liberating and binding life-agreement into a coherent pattern of meaning. Here, for Richter, is found the pattern and paradigm of stewardship on the earth.

The covenant that became explicit at Sinai was implicit at Eden and complicit in the New Jerusalem. The beginnings and endings, alpha and omega, of the covenant are not datable or scientifically verifiable, but here and now, they are binding and obligatory on the people of God. We are also responsible to pursue political, security, economic, ecological policies—local, national, and international—to implement these commands. An archeologist, Richter believes that these redemptive realities are profoundly true, guaranteed in the promises of God and dependent on the reciprocal obedience of humans to the covenantal commands. The latest souvenir of redemption is as near as the latest *tel*.

As far as the kingdom-composite of redemption is concerned, just as *shalom* is the primal security imperative and Jubilee is the primal economic imperative, Sabbath is the primal ecological imperative. Sabbath is the proleptic new and proximate now, heaven and earth. In Sabbath, God hallows the creation through redemptive love expressed as divine provident sustenance and hard, yet rewarding, human work and rest.

The creation and fall texts in Genesis 1–3 view creation in her promise and prospect and in her trauma and tribulation. Humanity (Adam and Eve)—once the safe guardians of Eden, then the banished despoilers of the garden—are now caught up in the cosmic redemptive drama marked by the oscillation between obedient observance and the calamitous crisis of disobedience, the redemptive agony of new birth (Romans 8). The "being-redeemed" creation of "holy agony" is covenantal. This rapture—not the one where we are "taken away" or "blown away"—is the very substance of times, places, and peoples; of visions, commands, and prophesies; and of rivers, trees, and gardens known in the paradisal imagery of the Scriptures of Christians, Jews, and especially Muslims. My son, a professor at Cambridge, sits today at his computer at King's College under a magnificent amber and gold Qum carpet depicting the door to paradise and the tree of life.

Richter's mandates are anchored in these biblical codes that pertain to the world around us that is our home. This good earth/fallen cosmos is tuned by those codes so that nature herself "groans in travail" to human justice or injustice, responsible stewardship, or opportunistic exploitation and abuse.

This biblical-theological essay has been an offering of the diverse teaching team of the Lincoln conference. We have distilled here a composite vision of God's way for America in this crucial moment in world history. Elucidated in a triadic template of biblical and gospel values—security, economy, and ecology—we offer to church and broader religious community, as well as nation and world, what we trust is being proffered to the world by the One who speaks "I will be whom I will be" (Exod 3:14) and "Come, follow me" (Luke 18:22).

Endnotes

1. Obama, "New Beginning" speech, Cairo.
2. Ibid.
3. Ainger, "God is Working His Purpose Out."
4. See von Rad, *Old Testament Theology*, vol. 2.
5. See Peters, *The Children of Abraham*.
6. Von Rad, *Old Testament Theology*, vol. 1, 27.
7. Brueggemann, *Theology of the Old Testament*, 9–10.
8. See Barr, *The Concept of Biblical Theology*.
9. See Jewett, *Mission and Menace*.
10. See Phillips, *Bad Money*.
11. Jewett, *Mission and Menace*, 294.
12. See Wink, *The Powers That Be*; and Migliore, *The Power of God*.
13. See Horsley, *Covenant Economics*.
14. See Vaux, *America in God's World*.
15. Horsley, *Covenant Economics*, 166.
16. See Ruether, *Gaia and God*.
17. See Richter, *The Epic of Eden*.
18. Ibid., 15.
19. Ibid., 19.
20. Ibid., 23.

3

Between Armageddon and the World Court: Reflections on the American Prospect

ROBERT JEWETT

Two Visions of the Future

From the beginning of the American colonies, two biblical visions of the future have vied for dominance, the millennial dominion of the saints in the new Jerusalem after the battle of Armageddon, and the establishment of arbitration between states that allows them to beat their swords into plowshares. The former comes from Revelation 20 and the latter from the oracle in Isaiah 2 and Micah 4. Elements of both visions appear in various combinations as the defining content of Matthew's image of the city set upon a hill (Matt 5:14) that is so frequently employed for America. These two visions of the American future come from the same Bible, but have encouraged policies and attitudes that are diametrically opposed. The vision of Revelation encourages military conflicts with crusading expectations of peaceful achievement, while the oracle in Isaiah and Micah encourages the development and maintenance of constitutional systems of conflict management that eliminate the need for war. Revelation assumes the need to annihilate all adversaries so that only the peaceful saints remain in an untroubled paradise. With Satan bound for a thousand years, the saints are expected to rule the world without complicated governmental systems because conflicts allegedly cannot arise among the righteous. In contrast, Isaiah and Micah are realistic in expecting the continuance of conflicts between groups and nations, which need to be adjudicated in an impartial court, making peaceful coexistence possible.

In the decades after the Second World War, the development of international institutions followed the logic of Isaiah and Micah, while the Cold War teetered on the edge of a battle of Armageddon until the turning point of 1989–90. But a decade earlier, the election of Ronald Reagan expressed disillusionment with institutional restraints in governance, economy and international relations, along with a militant preparation for Armageddon. This vision dominated American politics for decades, justifying military conflicts and sowing the seeds of the global economic collapse of September 2008. A resurgence of hope in constitutional forms of conflict management and peaceful coexistence occurred in the last election, but the implications for a biblical assessment of the American prospect are not yet clear.

My thesis is that the experiences of these recent decades reveal the need for Americans to become self-critical about their choice of future visions. While the vision of an untroubled paradise produced by Armageddon should be abandoned, the vision of Isaiah and Micah needs to be cleansed of its theocratic and imperialistic elements. This process of reinterpretation began in early American history and now provides the basis for a viable hope of peaceful coexistence under the rule of law for the entire world.

The Dominant Vision of Apocalyptic Warfare

The first generation of immigrants in New England derived from the book of Revelation their dualistic world view and their belief that violence would inaugurate God's kingdom.[1] They thought of themselves as standing in the succession of Christian warriors and martyrs from the Bible down to sixteenth-century England.[2] Preachers such as John Davenport, John Cotton, Increase and Cotton Mather, and Thomas Hooker worked on the task of building a holy and invincible commonwealth. Between 1629 and 1640, when their cause declined in England, more than 20,000 Puritans immigrated to America with this in mind. It was the call to battle that quickened their spirits, and they were fully convinced that such warfare had to be waged in the civil realm against the forms of corruption they felt were afflicting England. Their hope was that with the successful completion of such a war, the millennial kingdom promised in Revelation 20 would surely arrive.

Michael Walzer has pointed out the decisive role of such ideas among Puritan radicals who believed that "the saints did know the purposes of God": Beginning at some point before 1640, a group of writers ... began the work of integrating the spiritual warfare of the preachers with the apocalyptic history of Daniel and Revelation. The religious wars on the continent and then the struggle against the English king were seen by these men as parts of the ancient warfare of Satan and the elect, which had begun with Jews and Philistines and would continue until Armageddon.[3]

The Puritan thinkers shifted the thousand-year kingdom of Revelation 20 from the past to the immediate future and used martial categories to reinterpret the role of the saints. When the revolution came in England, preachers rose to proclaim the final battle with Satan. Stephen Marshall exhorted the troops in Parliament in 1644: "Go now and fight the battles of the Lord ... Do now see that the question in England is whether Christ or Anti-Christ shall be lord or king." Henry Wilkenson wrote that Parliament's "business lies professedly against the apocalyptical beast and all his complices."[4] The battle was directed not only against the Cavaliers but also against moral corruption everywhere. The purge of heretics, worldlings, and the licentious was viewed as part of the same battle by which "the whore of Babylon shall be destroyed with fire and sword."[5] This terminology derives almost exclusively from the book of Revelation.

With the revolution's overthrow in 1660 England, Puritans saw the American colonies as the new bearers of Protestant destiny. Ernest Tuveson has noted the impact of Jonathan Edwards' idea that with the conversion of the New World, the last corner of the globe, "divine providence is preparing the way for the future glorious times of the church, where Satan's kingdom shall be overthrown throughout the whole habitable globe."[6] Frederic Baumgartner went farther to show that "for the Puritans, the French and Indian War in North America also served as a millennial event ... The French and their native allies served antichrist by waging war on the people of God, and their early victories were signs that the great tribulation was beginning. The British victory in turn confirmed the deeply held belief among the English colonists that they were a chosen people building the New Kingdom in America."[7]

Between Armageddon and the World Court

By the eve of the American Revolution this vision of participating in a millennial age was clearly developed.[8] Timothy Dwight's poem, "America"[9] (1771) described the hopeless state of the world before the discovery of the new promised land and sets forth the promise of the millennial peace that would soon be administered by the saints in America. Dwight was a Congregational minister and poet (1752–1817) who became president of Yale University;[10] America is extolled as the emerging millennial empire:

> Hail Land of light and joy! Thy power shall grow
> Far as the seas, which round thy regions flow;
> Through earth's wide realms thy glory shall extend,
> And savage nations at thy scepter bend . . .
> Then, then an heavenly kingdom shall descend,
> And Light and Glory through the world extend.
> And every region smile in endless peace;
> Till the last trump the slumbering dead inspire,
> Shake the wide heavens, and set the world on fire.

The idea of the heavenly kingdom descending to earth at the conclusion of the battle of Armageddon, of course, comes from the book of Revelation. The kingdom's glory and power will extend as "far as the seas" and "savage nations" will submit to the rule of the saints. Such peace, of course, could only come through violence that "sets the world afire." Dwight pictures the American troops as joining with the heavenly host in the manner of the ancient Israelite ideology.[11]

In the period before and during the Civil War, the apocalyptic language employed by both sides produced an expectation of violent upheaval. Harriet Beecher Stowe spoke of an imminent "last convulsion" that would remove the blight of slavery from the chosen people.[12] Hundreds of abolitionist preachers took up this line,[13] until, with the opening of hostilities in 1861, Hollis Read wrote *The Coming Crisis of the World: or, The Great Battle and the Golden Age*, depicting the apocalyptic strife that would usher in the millennium. It was to be the battle of the North, "carrying the standard of Christ, against the South, ranged under that of the Beast," just as in the book of Revelation.[14]

The most powerful embodiment of this zealous ideology was "Battle Hymn of the Republic," written in 1862. Its terminology and imagery, as Tuveson shows, is derived almost exclusively from the apocalyptic portions of the Bible.[15] In the marching of the Union soldiers was "the glory of the coming of the Lord." With God marching on the side of the Northern armies, victory was viewed as inevitable. It would be strenuous and bloody, and many would die in the certainty that they would receive his "grace" for their faithfulness in battle. But they could fight to the last man with the certain knowledge that they were following the victorious signal:

> He has sounded forth the trumpet that shall never call retreat;
> He is sifting out the hearts of men before His judgment-seat:
> O, be swift, my soul, to answer Him! Be jubilant, my feet!
> Our God is marching on.

Who is this martial God who leads the Northern troops into battle? Who is the "Lord" who crushes the grapes of his wrathful wine by the feet of his troops? It is none other than the loving Christ seen through the lens of the book of Revelation. The contradictory redemptive images of the peaceful suffering servant and the marching Lord of battle are joined in the final stanza. The redemptive task of the Northern soldiers is neatly shifted from annihilating the enemy to altruistically setting people free. The unselfish mission of the suffering, dying servant is incorporated into that of the warrior. The soldier dies, not killing others, but suffering for others. With this, the stage is set for the 140 years of altruistic, martial zeal in America:

> In the beauty of the lilies Christ was born across the sea,
> With a glory in His bosom that transfigures you and me:
> As he died to make men holy, let us die to make men free,
> While God is marching on.

This ideology steeled the North for the long, bloody, and frustrating war. In time, such wars to "make men free" would not be able to halt their course until the entire world was involved. As the following citation from Rev. George S. Phillips reveals, global millennial prospects were in view even during the most discouraging hours of the war: "Our mission . . . should only be accomplished when the last despot should be dethroned, the last chain of oppression broken, the dignity and equality of redeemed humanity everywhere acknowledged, republican government everywhere established, and the American flag . . . should wave over every land and encircle the world with its majestic folds. Then, and not till then, should the nation have accomplished the purpose for which it was established by the God of heaven."[16]

These ideas led directly to the Spanish-American War. A Cuban independence movement had struggled against Spanish colonial authorities from 1895 to 1898 in a bloody campaign with atrocities that were widely reported in the American press.[17] Public opinion in the United States favored the insurgents, and people were outraged by the reports of genocide occurring only ninety miles away. After the mysterious sinking of the battleship *Maine* in the harbor of Havana, an enormous groundswell of crusading spirit swept the country headlong toward a war to free Cuba. Selfless idealism echoing "The Battle Hymn of the Republic" was articulated by Henry Watterson's editorial in 1898:

> It is a war into which this nation will go with a fervor, with a power, with a unanimity that would make it invincible if it were repelling not only the encroachments of Spain but the assaults of every monarch in Europe . . . It is not a war of conquest. It is not a war of envy or enmity. It is not a war of pillage or gain . . . We find in it the law supreme . . . the law of man, the law of God. We find in it our own inspiration, our own destiny. . . [which] says that liberty and law shall no longer be trampled upon . . . by despotism and autocracy upon our threshold. That is the right of our might; that is the sign in which we conquer.[18]

After negotiations failed to halt the Spanish occupation and the genocide seemed otherwise unstoppable, President William McKinley reluctantly asked Congress for a declaration of war. The Spanish troops and fleet were quickly dispatched, but Cuba was not immediately handed over to the insurgents, in part because they were mostly Afro-Cubans whom the American commander characterized as "degenerates, absolutely devoid of honor or gratitude. They are no more capable of self government than the savages of Africa. "[19] Liberal Protestants and especially missionaries supported the war and subsequent colonialism with theological arguments. A pamphlet of 1898 stated, "One thing, as Christian men, I hold we cannot do. We cannot, as Christian men, tolerate the statement that the unendurable woes of Cuba are no business of these United States . . . The cause of freedom in Cuba is the cause of God and Man."[23]

One missionary declared, "I believe in imperialism because I believe in foreign missions... The imperialism of the Gospel is the emancipation of humanity."[20] President McKinley was a committed Methodist who agreed with these sentiments. He was hailed as *"a providential man. Like the prophets of old, he is on an errand. He is the prophet of our times,"* in the sermon of Bishop C. H. Fowler.[21] His postmaster general, Charles Emory Smith, stated that "the hand of Providence has been in this work as distinctly as the hand of Providence was in the war of the Revolution, or in that great war of 1861."[22] Expressing the ideology of the "Battle Hymn of the Republic," the aims in Cuba and the Philippines were altruistic and thus victory was allegedly inevitable. Henry Van Dyke's sermon on Thanksgiving Day 1898 expressed this thought very succinctly: "Not for gain, not for territory, but for freedom and human brotherhood! That avowal alone made the war possible and successful."[23]

America's entrance into the European conflict in 1917 not only turned the "Great War" into a world war but also changed it from a misguided conflict over the control of Europe and its colonies into a global crusade to establish democracy. The nation had entered the war after much hesitation, because of Germany's violation of neutrality on the high seas. But the justification President Woodrow Wilson developed had little to do with self-defense. He demanded that the country enter a crusade for millennial goals: "The world must be made safe for democracy. Its peace must be planted upon the tested foundation of political liberty. We have no selfish ends to serve. We desire no conquest, no dominion... We are but one of the champions of the right of mankind. We shall be satisfied when those rights have been made as secure as the faith and the freedom of nations can make them."[24]

That military action could guarantee the triumph of liberty and change the global condition to make democracy "safe" was a belief shaped by the theology of Revelation 20 as adapted by the "Battle Hymn of the Republic." Henry van Dyke,[25] a Presbyterian clergyman and hymn writer who was serving temporarily as a Navy chaplain, wrote an additional stanza for the hymn that was widely used in training camps:

> We have heard the cry of anguish, from the victims of the Hun,
> And we know our country's peril if the war-lord's will is done.
> We will fight for worldwide freedom till the victory is won,
>   For God is marching on.[26]

A powerful surge of enthusiasm swept over the country in the wake of President Wilson's call to a millennial battle for freedom. Theodore Roosevelt told the Harvard Club, "If ever there was a holy war, it is this war."[27] Randolph H. McKim proclaimed from his Washington pulpit: "It is God who has summoned us to this war. It is his war we are fighting . . . This conflict is indeed a crusade. The greatest in history—the holiest. It is in the profoundest and truest sense a Holy War . . . Yes, it is Christ, the King of Righteousness, who calls us to grapple in deadly strife with this unholy and blasphemous power."[28]

In the past decade, this same ideology led President George W. Bush to justify the "war against terrorism" as a millennial strategy to "rid the world of evil."[29] He explained the war in Iraq in terms that can be traced back to the interpretation of Revelation 20 by early Puritans and whose secular formulation was developed by Woodrow Wilson: "The establishment of a free Iraq in the heart of the troubled Middle East will be a watershed event in the global democratic revolution . . . The advance of freedom is the calling of our time. It is the calling of our country. From the Fourteen Points to the speech at Westminster, America has put our power at the service of principle. We believe that liberty is the design of nature . . . It is the right and capacity of all mankind."[30]

This vision assumes that war in the hands of the chosen nation is redemptive, capable of changing the conditions of human existence so that freedom is guaranteed. It assumes the innocence of America and the essential evil of its adversaries. In the words of Timothy Dwight, its power is destined to spread "Far as the seas . . . And savage nations at thy scepter bend." This is the vision that has brought us to the impasse of 2009.

The Vision of Constitutional Coexistence

A more realistic vision derived in part from Isaiah and Micah emerged in the last decades of the eighteenth century. This vision presupposes that although conflicts will inevitably arise between states and nations, they can be resolved by fair and impartial adjudication so that wars are no longer necessary. While the placement of this court on Mount Zion originally involved a decisive element of imperial precedence,[31] its adaptation in America started a process by which it came to embody the hope of constitutional democracy.

> All the nations shall flow to it,
>> and many peoples shall come, and say:
> "Come, let us go up to the mountain of Yahweh,
>> to the house of the God of Jacob;
> that he may teach us his ways
>> and that we may walk in his paths. "
> For out of Zion shall go forth the law,
>> and the word of Yahweh from Jerusalem.
> He shall judge between the nations,
>> and shall decide for many peoples;
> and they shall beat their swords into plowshares,
>> and their spears into pruning hooks;
> nation shall not lift up sword against nation,
>> neither shall they learn war any more. (Isa 2:3–4; Mic 4:1–3)

This vision raised the hope among Puritans that a future theocratic imperial realm would guarantee world peace. That government derives its authority from God and acts in God's behalf was the universal assumption until the rise of the United States. The early colonies shared this premise, creating theocratic realms in New England and established churches in most of the other colonies. The British crown that provided the warrant for these colonial systems was thought to be divinely established, with authority to determine the religious beliefs of citizens.

The theocratic premise was challenged for the first time in North America by Roger Williams, who had arrived with the first Massachusetts settlers in 1631 as a clergyman trained in Cambridge.[32] He had a friendly attitude toward Native Americans and acknowledged their ownership of the land, which undermined the alleged right of colonists to take it without payment. He campaigned against the enforcement of religious conformity by civil authorities and argued for a separation of religion and government.[33] Forced to flee from Massachusetts in 1636, Williams established a church and later a colony in the primitive area of Providence, Rhode Island. In 1644 he wrote *The Bloody Tenet of Persecution for Cause of Conscience*, which for the first time advocated religious freedom on principle.[34] This idea was not derived from any of the Old Testament prophets but from the Pauline letters, the only biblical writings that use the word "conscience." Williams argued that "although it be groundless, false, and deluded, 'conscience' is not by any arguments or torments easily removed . . . I speak of conscience, a persuasion fixed in the heart and mind of man, which enforceth him to judge—as Paul said of himself a persecutor—and to do with respect to God."[35] Moreover, Williams argued that any form of "religion cannot be true which needs such instruments of violence to uphold it."[36] In 1651 he wrote the letter to Massachusetts governor John Endicott, protesting the persecution of Baptists on the grounds that "conscience is found in all mankind," and reflects a "persuasion fixed in the mind and heart of man," as St. Paul taught.[37] The tiny colony of Rhode Island, of which he was governor from 1654 to 1657, became the haven for persecuted Quakers and Baptists fleeing from other colonies.

These themes were taken up by other independent colonists. An outstanding example was Ann Hutchinson, who emigrated in 1634 to Boston and came under the influence of the Puritan preacher John Cotton. A bold, intelligent, and charismatic leader who could interpret the Scriptures for herself,[38] she began to have religious meetings in her home where the absolute dependence of believers on God and the need to accept divine grace were advocated. On the basis of 1 Cor 15:44–45, she taught that believers could become totally new creations in Christ, a radical doctrine whose popularity threatened to destabilize the situation of the churches in New England.[39] Her challenge of the complacent religiosity of others aroused serious opposition. Four years later she was charged with antinomianism and insubordination "not fitting for your sex," in the words of Gov. John Winthrop.[40] She replied that what she did was a "matter of conscience," to which Winthrop responds that she should "keep her conscience to herself," i.e., keep silent about it, or "it must be kept for you." That is, the theocratic government alone has the right to determine whether conscience is correct or not and should be followed or not. Here the conscience of the individual believer was pitted against the consensus of the religious community, reflected in its government. She was condemned, banned from the colony, and fled to Rhode Island where Roger Williams was providing a refuge for the freedom of conscience.

In the course of the Great Awakening, a new religious majority emerged that was inclined to follow Williams's line. One of the results of the rise of independent churches was to challenge the tax system supporting the established clergy in various colonies, viewed now as a violation of conscience. By the end of the Great Awakening, Baptist congregations temporarily gained the right to be exempt from such taxes in Massachusetts. There were similar struggles in the other colonies against the Anglican tax system. Since the time of Roger Williams, the Baptists had argued for freedom of religion and the noninterference of the state in religious affairs. Isaac Backus,[41] a Baptist itinerant preacher in Connecticut and Massachusetts, wrote a book titled *A Fish Caught in His Own Net* (1768), arguing that Congregationalists had violated their own principles in giving clergy associations the right to determine eligibility for ministry, and using public power to enforce such decisions to disallow Baptist clergy. He argued for the complete freedom of conscience and the complete separation of church and state because religion should rely on "persuasion alone" rather than on coercion.[42] This line of argument was taken up in Backus's appeal to the Massachusetts legislature in 1774, protesting the tax on Baptist congregations to support Congregational churches.[43] Backus argued that Baptists would refuse to pay such taxes because that would be "implicitly allowing to men that authority which we believe in our consciences belongs only to God. Here, therefore, we demand charter rights, liberty of conscience."[44] Backus and his Baptist colleagues are not demanding tolerance in the usual enlightenment sense but intrinsic rights of religious freedom, based on their reading of the Pauline letters. This reveals the link between the cause of political liberty and the Great Awakening that gave such growth to the Baptists and other independent churches.[45]

Leaders like Backus ended up supporting the revolution against England on religious grounds, in defense of their view of religious freedom that they felt the Anglicans and other establishment figures as well as the British government were threatening.[46] In the decades leading up to the Revolution, there were conflicts over religious establishment in almost all of the colonies. These conflicts contributed to the ultimate triumph of religious freedom. The Anglican efforts to install their establishment in New England and elsewhere were strongly opposed by dissenting churches, so that the battle for freedom of religion came to be blended with the struggle against "taxation without representation." This helps to account for the fact that two very different traditions came to the same opinion about religious freedom: the evangelicals shaped by the Great Awakening and the Deists. The evangelicals wanted above all else to prevent harassment by established churches that could use the power of the state to enforce religious conformity.[47] The Deists advocated religious liberty as related to intellectual freedom. The most important arena for the legal struggle for religious liberty was Virginia, where the Anglican establishment was opposed by dissenting churches and deist political leaders. On the eve of the Revolution, Thomas Jefferson estimated that two-thirds of Virginians were associated with dissenting churches,[48] whose members supported religious liberty. After his graduation from Princeton in 1771, having studied an additional year with John Witherspoon who was advocating independence from Great Britain and a constitutional establishment, James Madison returned to Virginia and became enraged at the prosecution of Baptist clergy for preaching without an Anglican-approved license.[49] He wrote, "That diabolical, Hell-conceived principle of persecution rages among some, and to their eternal infamy, the clergy can furnish their quota of imps for such business. This vexes me the most of anything whatever."[50] Among the rights that should be protected in a just republic, Madison believed that "none was literally more sacred than the liberty of conscience."[51] In 1779, Jefferson submitted a bill to the Virginia Assembly stating that since "Almighty God hath created the mind free" and "chose not to propagate" the truth "by coercions," it is "sinful and tyrannical" to force people to support of churches in which one is not a member.[52] After years of debate, this bill abolishing an established religion and providing a separation between church and state was finally passed under the leadership of James Madison in 1786. In Lambert's words, "And with its passage, the law signaled one of the most revolutionary moments in the entire American revolution."[53] Madison argued that freedom of religion was "an unalienable right"[54] and that there is an "equal right of every citizen to the free exercise of his Religion according to the dictates of conscience."[55] This line of argument was strongly supported, with the very same arguments and terminology, by the dissenting Baptists and Presbyterians who had developed this line of thinking from the time of Roger Williams. One result of this coalition between Evangelicals and Deists was that the Constitution itself does not refer to God, and thus became the first political system in the western world that did not involve a church establishment.[56] Thus the issue of freedom of conscience that Roger Williams had advocated in the seventeenth century came to be embodied in the Constitution.[57] Although its passage was viewed as a fulfillment of the ancient vision of Micah and Isaiah, as we shall see, the theocratic element was removed.

A decisive feature of the prophetic vision was that only a great king could usher in the new age by means of imperial power, thus producing justice. This was altered in the colonial environment by convictions that were shaped by the Pauline letters. In a country where Calvinism turned out to be the most significant political force, the Puritan settlers in New England were Calvinist extremists who promoted their version of the egalitarian impulse.[58] A group of forty-one Puritans emigrated to Massachusetts in 1620, and on the ship Mayflower, they drafted and signed an agreement concerning self-government under God with the sixty-one other passengers, the famous "Mayflower Compact." Based on the Old Testament concept of covenants between God and Israel, they agreed "solemnly and mutually in the Presence of God and one of another, [to] covenant and combine ourselves together into a civil Body Politick." Here we find the Calvinist mixture of religion and politics, in that a covenant between a church and its Lord, often referred to as a "compact" in older English, was extended into the political sphere and signed by the religious and secular colonists who had traveled on the Mayflower.[59] In place of a royal system organized from the top, this covenantal system rested on the voluntary agreement of those at the bottom. Legitimacy now derived from the consent of the governed, who were conceived as equals.

The Pilgrims also tried to implement the egalitarian principle of *koinonia*, "holding things in common" that they found in the Pauline letters and the book of Acts.[60] In 1630 John Winthrop's sermon aboard the ship under way to Massachusetts made plain that all of the partners in the new commonwealth were "fellow members of Christ" who had agreed to establish "a due form of Government both civil and ecclesiastical."[61] In contrast to the Plymouth Colony, the form of *koinonia* in Massachusetts Bay Colony was to create a commonwealth by giving private property to citizens. They established independent congregations that had the power to appoint their own clergy. In the conviction derived from the New Testament that Christ, rather than the Pope or bishops, was the head of the church, and that all church members should have a voice in theological questions, they developed a radically democratic church system. They came to be called "Congregationalists," following the idea that each local congregation should organize its own affairs in response to the covenant between that congregation and God. They projected the same covenantal thinking into the political sphere. The New England Puritans established a parliamentary form of government that was separate from the churches, yet was dominated by their influence. Historian Ralph Barton Perry argues that these early Congregationalists, along with the even more radical Calvinists, the Baptists and Quakers, "were saturated with democratic feeling" that they derived from the New Testament.[62] James Hastings Nichols showed that the Puritan groups advocated a democratic social order because in their small congregations they "had practical and indeed daily experience of a fellowship united in a common purpose beyond themselves, to which purpose each and every member was found to have something to contribute."[63] The later political philosophy of John Locke, which exerted the greatest influence at the time of the American Revolution in advocating these ideas, "was a true son of the Puritan Independents," in Perry's words.[64] A congregational church order was established by which members elected their leaders and their ministers in a covenantal manner. This led to the development of the "New England town meeting," in which each citizen was entitled to speak about public issues.

This idea that each citizen was equal to any king was decisive in the period of the American Revolution. The widely distributed oration by the Baptist preacher in Boston, John Allen, proclaimed that "Liberty... is the native right of the Americans" because "they were never in bondage to any man."[65] He went on to argue that no institution of royal government had a right to tax the Americans without their consent, and that the Americans should stand "upon their own strength" in resisting such efforts. The Congregational minister Samuel Sherwood placed the revolution for the sake of liberty in the millennial context of defending a democratic church order: "Liberty has been planted here; and the more it is attacked, the more it grows and flourishes. The time is coming and hastening on, when Babylon the great shall fall to rise no more; when all wicked tyrants and oppressors shall be destroyed forever . . . These commotions and convulsions in the British Empire may be leading to the fulfillment of such prophecies as relate to his [i.e., Satan's] downfall and overthrow, and to the future glory and prosperity of Christ's church."[66]

Part of this fervor derived from the religious resentments felt by the free church Protestants. The Congregationalists remembered former leaders burned at the stake by Catholic and Anglican authorities and resented Anglican efforts to re-establish their dominance in colonies that had enjoyed a form of democratic self-government for more than a century. The Baptists opposed all efforts to impose governmental control over churches.[67] The Scottish Presbyterians harbored centuries of resentment against English domination and the Scotch-Irish had experienced forcible relocation to Northern Ireland followed by legislation that discriminated against their rights to Presbyterian activities; they emigrated to the colonies with these resentments still fresh and unforgotten.[68] These segments of colonial population resonated positively to the Declaration of Independence, which depicted King George as thoroughly wicked and therefore illegitimate.

That a king can be sinful was related to the widespread sense that all humans are fallible and inclined toward evil. James Madison always maintained that "if men were angels, there would be no need for government." Timothy Dwight believed that humans always "remain the children of Adam and Eve, prone to error and weakness, capable of working harm and, in the right circumstances, gigantic evil."[69] No human, therefore, should ever be trusted with absolute power. In *The Ideological Origins of the American Revolution*, Bernard Bailyn has shown how these traditions joined in the Revolutionary period "into a comprehensive theory of politics."[70] This provided a definition of political liberties that were thought to be endangered by the misuse of royal authority. It encouraged the creation of a Constitution based on the principle of separation of powers; it preferred resolution of conflicts by lawful procedure, and the idea of federal union between existing states.[71] As law professor Marci A. Hamilton has shown, these ideas were advocated in the Constitutional Convention by students of John Witherspoon, the Presbyterian theologian who served as president of Princeton University.[72] Several members of the convention were his friends and former students, including James Madison,[73] and they advocated his ideas that "all rulers, including the people if they were rulers, would be tempted to abuse their powers," that liberty could only be achieved by separating powers, and that these must be balanced in an interdependent manner.[74] The biblical text lying behind this conviction was Romans 1–3 that demonstrates universal participation in wickedness. The Enlightenment version of this doctrine was that power always corrupts and absolute power corrupts absolutely.

These ideas were embodied in the Virginia Plan that Madison and his colleagues presented to the Constitutional Convention, which provided the framework for subsequent deliberation. The Constitution that emerged from this deliberation shares a crucial premise with the vision of Isaiah and Micah, that conflict between groups is inevitable and should be managed by lawful arbitration.

In an important regard, however, this constitutional development departs from the prophets who expected that the impartial court would be established on Zion by divine fiat. In the words of Isa 1:26, "I will restore your judges as at the first, and your counselors as at the beginning. Afterward you shall be called the city of righteousness, the faithful city." The covenantal thinking that came to be widely accepted in the American colonies assumed that human cooperation and consent should replace the system of allegedly divine authority imposed from above. The idea of the "consent of the governed," that we have traced from the Mayflower Compact onward provides a decisive place for human cooperation with what was perceived to be the divine will as conveyed in the Bible. The resultant preamble was a path-breaking replacement of the royal principle: "We the people . . . do ordain and establish this constitution. " As James Wilson said, the Constitution "is laid before the citizens of the United States, unfettered by restraint . . . By their *fiat*, it will become of value and authority."[75] The biblical allusion to Gen 1:3, *fiat lux* ("let there be light"), was extended by James Madison, that the Constitution would remain "a dead letter, until life and vitality were breathed into it by the voice of the People," alluding to Gen 2:7, "And the LORD God formed man of the dust of the ground, and breathed into his nostrils the breath of life, and man became a living soul."[76] Almost two centuries of covenantal thinking lie behind this language, giving humans the responsibility to create "compacts" to establish governmental systems based on the consent of the governed. The language of "ordain and establish" also had religious resonance in a society in which church members rather than royally authenticated bishops claimed the right to establish churches and ordain pastors. As Alexander Hamilton explained, this language was a "recognition of popular rights."[77] Since these rights were perceived to be supported by the same Bible as the visions of world peace through conflict adjudication, there was a widespread sense of providential guidance in the triumph over imperial England and the establishment of the republican Constitution.

Joel Barlow's 1787 epic poem, *The Vision of Columbus*, celebrated "the United States as the most advanced embodiment of an enlightened Republican culture," conceived on the model of Isaiah and Micah.[78] In the final section of the poem, an angel reveals the rise of "a world civilization, a league of states resembling the United Nations with the individual member states all modeled after the newly established American republic."[79] Here the prophetic vision of the impartial world court on "the mountain of the Lord" that would allow nations to "beat their swords into plowshares" is fulfilled by the Republican triumph:

> From all the bounds of space (their labours done),
> Shall wing their triumphs to the eternal throne;
> Each, from his far dim sky, illumines the road,
> And sails and centres tow'ard the mount of God . . .
> So, from all climes of earth, where nations rise,
> Or lands or oceans bound the incumbent skies,
> Wing'd with unwonted speed, the gathering throng
> In ships and chariots, shape their course along . . .
> There, hail the splendid seat by Heaven assign'd,
> To hear and give the counsels of mankind . . .
> To give each realm its limit and its laws;
> Bid the last breath of dire contention cease,
> And bind all regions in the leagues of peace . . .[80]

Barlow intended to show that with the constitutional settlement, not only "good government" but also the "hopes of permanent peace must be founded,"[81] not just for the United States of America but for "all regions" of the earth. These themes reappear in the remarkable celebrations of the ratification of the Constitution. The most elaborate of these was the Grand Federal Procession that occurred in Philadelphia on July 4, 1788.[82] The biblical theme of Micah/Isaiah's peaceable kingdom was represented by the master blacksmith hammering plowshares and pruning hooks out of old swords.[83] The vision of peaceful coexistence between adversaries was conveyed as clergymen of different denominations, including a Jewish rabbi, appeared in the parade, "all walking arm in arm."[84]

American religious and political leaders labored hard in the earlier part of the twentieth century to enshrine these principles in the Covenant of the League of Nations, whose charter the country unwisely decided to reject. Although mostly forgotten today, generations of theologians and religious leaders also supported institutional embodiments of the law of nations, including many writers in publications such as *The Christian Century* since its establishment in 1900. They were convinced that the impartial administration of international law could resolve conflicts and ultimately rid the world of the scourge of war. After the most destructive war in history, religious leaders supported the establishment of the United Nations as a partial fulfillment of the vision of Isaiah and Micah. The final lines of their oracle are chiseled in the United Nations building in New York—the origin of a modern hope for world peace through international law.

Conclusion: The Choice between Two Visions

The two master visions of the future contained in the Bible provoke legitimate human choice. While some forms of American religion remain reluctant to reject one vision over the other, they all are loyal to the same Bible in which Jesus said, "You have heard that it was said to the men of old, ... but I say to you" (Matt 5:21–22). Both Jesus and Paul made choices in favor of an imperfect international system of justice that partially embodied the vision of Micah and Isaiah. They tolerated Roman rule while criticizing its imperial pretensions and its violation of the principle of due process of law. But they rejected the popular alternative of Jewish zealotism that expected divine intervention in establishing a theocratic empire to replace Rome. In decisive ways, the healthy side of the biblical heritage follows this vision rather than that in Revelation 20.[85]

Since 1967, and especially after 1980, the American rejection of the vision of Isaiah and Micah has led to the impasse we currently face. Since the capture of Jerusalem and the West Bank of the Jordan in 1967, the United States acquiesced in the unlawful seizure of Arab lands on the West Bank of Palestine. We have provided the means for the occupation of the West Bank, in explicit violation of the United Nations Charter, which has evoked the rise of Islamic terrorism. An overwhelming majority of Americans supported the Iraq war in 2003 as an appropriate response to such terrorism, in violation of the U.N. Charter that forbids preventive wars. In other arenas the same choice has been visible. For example, despite our formal commitment to the International Court in

1946, the Reagan administration withdrew from compulsory jurisdiction in 1985 while the Nicaragua harbor mining incident was under review. In the following year, the court declared the United States had violated international law in a variety of ways in connection with Nicaragua, the "first time in the history of the Court that the United States was found in violation of international law in a matter involving the use of force against another nation."[86]

This disregard for international institutions was sustained by a widespread expectation of a final battle as predicted in the book of Revelation. A schedule for the end-time events was developed by a number of popular writers, including Hal Lindsey who wrote books like *The Late Great Planet Earth* and *The Terminal Generation*.[87] Their premise was that the re-establishment of Israel in 1948 marked the beginning of the final generation of world history. Assuming that a generation in the biblical sense is no more than forty years, this meant that the final battle would occur no later than 1988. In Lindsey's version of this scheme, the Rapture was expected to occur before the tribulation, which would begin seven years before 1988, at the latest.[88] While repeatedly intoning Jesus' saying about no one knowing the day or the hour, Lindsey and others persistently and forcefully made the claim that the generation that began in 1948 would indeed be the final generation in world history and that preparations for the final battle should begin.[89]

That the Rapture should have occurred no later than 1980–81 is connected with some important political developments. In 1978, just before the latest date on which the Rapture was supposed to have inaugurated the end-time scenario, one of the most remarkable political movements in American history suddenly emerged. Under the leadership of Jerry Falwell and other Rapture advocates, the Moral Majority movement attracted the political involvement of tens of thousands of pastors and churches that had never been involved in the political process before.[90] In the conviction that the final crisis of world history was at hand,[91] the Moral Majority movement promoted candidates and policies suited for the battle of Armageddon, including a stronger nuclear force and enlarged military budget, a resistance to any compromise with the Soviet Union, an unquestioning support of Israel, a rejection of Palestinian claims for autonomy, a renunciation of the United Nations and international law, a dismantling of the complicated controls over the economic system, and an uncompromising position on moral issues such as abortion. They saw these policies as preparation for righteous victory in the forthcoming apocalyptic conflagration. Despite the alliance with nonapocalyptic groups, the impetus and all of the state and national leaders of the Moral Majority movement reflected the conviction that the Rapture was virtually within sight.

The impact of the Moral Majority movement on American political life has been enormous, far larger than the rather short-lived organization itself would indicate. It contributed decisively to the election of Ronald Reagan in 1980 and brought into office the entire generation of leadership within the Republican party, including Newt Gingrich, Dick Armey, Tom Delay, and others.[92] Within a short time it largely transformed the conservative Republican party, which had hitherto been committed to federalism, capitalism, and the international rule of law, into a millennial party resistant to federal authority, hostile to the traditional American politics of compromise, rejecting governmental controls over the banking and business systems, and profoundly suspicious of international law and peacekeeping. The choices made in 1980 and thereafter also brought an extraordinarily combative tone to American politics, matching the vocabulary of an apocalyptic holy war.[93] They provided the atmosphere in which the misguided war in Iraq was rationalized and prosecuted in 2003. The vision of the book of Revelation also encouraged the repeal of effective controls over the national and global financial systems, thus contributing to the collapse in September 2008.

The election of 2008 represents a turn away from the Armageddon option and toward the American consitutional and democratic heritage with its prophetic foundation. There is now a need for the religious community to reflect on these underlying issues and to clarify the choices it wishes to make. It should be clear to all that the choices we make have global consequences. My conviction is that the current impasse was caused in large part by allegiance to the millennial vision of Revelation, and that we should now choose a clarified, constitutional form of the vision of Micah and Isaiah.

Endnotes

1. The historical details in this essay are adapted from my study, *Mission and Menace*.
2. Hudson, *Nationalism*, 7.
3. Walzer, *Revolution of the Saints*, 291.
4. Ibid., 295.
5. Ibid., 296.
6. Edwards, *Work of Redemption*, cited by Tuveson, *Redeemer Nation*, 100.
7. Baumgartner, *Longing for the End*, 131.
8. See Ahlstrom, *Religious History*, chapter 52.
9. Cited from Tuveson, *Redeemer Nation*, 105-6; text in McTaggart and Bottorff, *Timothy Dwight*, 1-12.
10. See Dowling, "Dwight, Timothy," 192-94.
11. McTaggart and Bottorff, *Timothy Dwight*, 10.
12. Tuveson, *Redeemer Nation*, 191.
13. See McKivigan, *War Against Proslavery Religion*, 183-201; Dorrien, *American Liberal Theology*, 199-204.
14. Tuveson, *Redeemer Nation*, 192ff; see also Moorhead, *American Apocalypse*, ix-x, 42-59; Shattuck, *Shield and a Hiding Place*, 15-19.
15. Tuveson, *Redeemer Nation*, 197ff.
16. Cited from Hudson, *Nationalism*, 74; see also Butler et al., *Religion in American Life*, 257 and James Moorhouse's description in *American Apocalypse*, 216, of the essay by George Prentiss of Union Seminary in New York that depicts "God the destroyer. Never content with the world as it was, he subverted, one by one, the barriers to the millennium."
17. See Tone, *Cuba*, 1-152; Kagan, *Dangerous Nation*, 379-400; McCartney, *Power and Progress*, 87-95.
18. Louisville *Courier-Journal*, April 20, 1898; cited also in Watterson, *Annals of America*, 12.194.
19. Cited by Tone, *War*, 283.
20. William Radcliffe, "Presbyterian Imperialism, " *Assembly Herald* (1899) 6, cited by McCartney, *Power and Progress*, 73.
21. Cited by McCartney, *Power and Progress*, 162; italics in original.
22. Cited by ibid., 161.
23. Cited by Hudson, *Nationalism*, 121. According to Buggeln, *American National Biography*, 22.208-09, Van Dyke was a Presbyterian minister, poet, professor of literature, who later served as a diplomat during the Wilson administration.
24. Wilson, *Annals of America*, 14.81.
25. See Buggeln, *American National Biography*, 22.209; Henry Van Dyke's view of the war is in *Fighting for Peace*, 65-145.
26. Cited by Abrams, *Preachers Present Arms*, 117.
27. Roosevelt, *Foes*, 33.
28. Cited by Abrams, *Preachers Present Arms*, 55.
29. Bush, "National Day of Prayer and Remembrance."
30. Cited by McCartney, *Power and Progress*, 1.
31. See Roberts, "War in the Zion tradition," 119-28.

32. See Gaustad, *Roger Williams*; Moore, "Roger Williams," 100–115.
33. See Hall, *Separating Church and State*, 29.
34. See ibid., 86–91.
35. Cited by Ziff, *Puritanism*, 106.
36. Cited by Hall, *Separating Church and State*, 87.
37. Cited by Gaustad and Noll, *Documentary History*, 1.77.
38. Noll observes in "Bible in American Culture," 1078, that Hutchinson "was able to quote lengthy portions of Scripture at her trial."
39. See Wills, *Under God*, 344.
40. Cited in Gaustad and Noll, *Documentary History*, 1.96–98; according to Cohen, "Winthrop," 663, Winthrop referred to Hutchinson as a "hydatidiform mole" that had experienced a "monstrous birth." His dislike of Hutchinson is described in Bremer, *John Winthrop*, 299–300.
41. See Dunn, *American National Biography*, 1.836–38; McLoughlin, *Isaac Backus*, 110–92.
42. See Lambert, *Founding Fathers*, 201; see also McLoughlin, *Isaac Backus*, 127.
43. See Gaustad and Noll, *Documentary History*, 1.225–27.
44. Ibid., 1.227.
45. See Miller, "Religious Liberty in Colonial America," 149–50.
46. See McLoughlin, *Isaac Backus*, 136–37.
47. Miller, "Religious Liberty in Colonial America," 550.
48. Lambert, *Founding Fathers*, 226.
49. For a listing of Madison's activities in support of religious freedom, see Wills, *Under God*, 374.
50. Letter cited by Banning, *Sacred Fire of Liberty*, 81. See also Rakove, *James Madison*, 6 and McCoy, *Last of the Fathers*, 228, 239.
51. Banning, *Sacred Fire of Liberty*, 84; see also 102.
52. Gaustad and Noll, *Documentary History*, 1.229–32; see also Wills, *Under God*, 363–72.
53. Lambert, *Founding Fathers*, 235.
54. Gaustad and Noll, *Documentary History*, 1.233.
55. Ibid., 1.237.
56. In Article 6 of the constitution and in the first amendment of 1791 no religious qualifications for office holders are allowed and congress is prohibited from passing a law "to establish a religion or prohibits the free exercise thereof." See "The Constitution of the United States, " in Morris, *Basic Documents*, 49–70.
57. See Moore, "Religious Liberty," 57–76.
58. See Butler et al, *Religion in American Life*, 56.
59. See Philbrick, *Mayflower*, 40–43.
60. See Ziff, *Puritanism*, 37–39.
61. Gaustad and Noll, *Documentary History*, 1.67–68; Allitt, *Major Problems*, 61–62. For an assessment of John Winthrop's sermon, see Bremer, *John Winthrop*, 173–83.
62. Perry, *Puritanism and Democracy*, 195.
63. James Hastings Nichols showed that the Puritan groups advocated a democratic social order because in their small congregations they "had practical and indeed daily experience of a fellowship united in a common purpose beyond themselves, to which purpose each and every member was found to have something to contribute."

64. Perry, *Puritanism and Democracy*, 32.
65. Gaustad and Noll, *Documentary History*, 1.221–22.
66. Ibid., 1.228.
67. Clark, *Language of Liberty*, 372–81.
68. Albanese, *Sons of the Fathers*, 42.
69. Dowling, *American National Biography*, 7.193.
70. Bailyn, *Ideological Origins*, 54.

71. For a comprehensive account of the realistic, constitutional principles actually adopted after the American Revolution, in contrast to later "constitutional myths" about continued state sovereignty, co-equal branches of government, and intentional inefficiency, see Wills, *Necessary Evil*, 57–122. See also Koch, *Jefferson and Madison*, 33–61, and especially 219: Jefferson believed that the greatest of all political calamities would be in his words, "submission to a government of unlimited powers."

72. Hamilton, "Witherspoon," 54–66.

73. Leibiger, *Founding Friendship*, 6 observes: "While at Princeton, Madison imbibed Whiggish principles and a commitment to personal liberty, especially freedom of speech and conscience."

74. Hamilton, "Witherspoon," 57–58; see also Fechner, *John Witherspoon*, 239–54, 276–85.

75. Cited by Amar, *America's Constitution*, 7.
76. See Amar, *America's Constitution*, 506.
77. Cited by Amar, *America's Constitution*, 11.
78. Schloss, "Joel Barlow's *Vision of Columbus*," 139.
79. Ibid., 143.
80. Bottorff and Ford, *Works of Joel Barlow*, 2.256–57.
81. Schloss, "Joel Barlow's *Vision of Columbus*," 143.
82. See Schloss, "Nation as Spectacle," 44–62.
83. Ibid., 57.
84. Ibid., 48.

85. The advocacy of coexistence of enemies by Jesus and Paul and the books of Jonah and Ruth carry forward Isaiah's vision that "The wolf shall dwell with the lamb, and the leopard shall lie down with the kid, and the calf and the lion and the fatling together ... They shall not hurt or destroy in all my holy mountain" (Isa 11:6, 9). It is also significant that the identical wording of the Isaianic vision appears in Mic 4:1–3, thus placing this vision in the opening of both the major and the minor prophets. Kessler lifts up the element of conflict resolution in *Micha*, 185–86. In "Micah," 1160, Holman observes that Micah implies that "for the establishment of international peace human effort and dedication are indispensible, but ultimately it remains a gift from God."

86. Moynihan, *Law of Nations*, 147.

87. Lindsey, *Terminal Generation*; see the restatement of these views in *The Rapture* and *Planet Earth*.

88. Boyer, "Fundamentalist Apocalyptic," 167; see "Lindsey's Prophetic Timetable," in O'Leary, *Arguing the Apocalypse*, 147–54.

89. See for example, Jeffrey, *War in the Middle East*, 11, he calculates the battle will occur within a generation of from "forty to seventh years" starting with 1948; a new dating scheme is presented in his *Armageddon: Appointment with Destiny*. Hicks appears to fit this time frame in *Another Look at the Rapture*, 15–22. In *Beginning of the End*, 194.

LaHaye claimed it was "probable" that the generation beginning in 1948 will see the end times, but in *No Fear of the Storm*, he seemed less sure. For a survey of this date setting, see Boyer, *When Time Shall Be No More*, 187–90.

90. See Georgianna, *Moral Majority and Fundamentalism*, 26–29; Wilcox, *God's Warriors*, 95–96, 120–21. See also Liebman and Wuthnow, *New Christian Right*.

91. See Jorstad, *New Christian Right*, 17–19; Hill and Owen, *New Religious Political Right*, 43. See also Snowball, *Moral Majority*, 40–53.

92. See Domke, *God Willing?* 9–10; Roebuck, "Fundamentalism and Pentecostalism," 97.

93. See the chapter on "The War Metaphor," in Snowball, *Moral Majority*, 123–49; also O'Leary, *Arguing the Apocalypse*, 172–93.

4

Isaiah, National Security, and the Politics of Fear

J. J. M. ROBERTS

The underlying premise for this conference on the Bible and the American Future is that there are two contrasting visions for the American and global future based on two competing visions within the biblical tradition. One is an apocalyptic vision of cataclysmic wars in which the future is secured by our military victory over evil enemies. The second is a less understood biblical vision of peaceful cooperation with other nations that offers the foundations for a more responsible public ethic and a more realistic vision for the future. Moreover, the apocalyptic vision was the one informing the policies of the Bush administration, and the vision of peaceful cooperation is the one informing the policies of the Obama administration. Now as a lifelong Republican and perhaps the only Republican speaking at this conference, I have serious difficulties with this premise. Quite apart from my political prejudices, which are easily criticized and would probably be dismissed out of hand, I have more serious difficulties with the easy separation of these two biblical traditions in this analysis. In my reading of the biblical text, the apocalyptic and cooperative visions within the biblical text are woven together in such a complex and intricately interconnected fashion that I do not believe they can be medically separated and played off against one another in this fashion without killing both visions.

I will try to illustrate this point by particular attention to the prophetic visions of the eighth-century prophet, Isaiah of Jerusalem, and the refraction of his message within the pages of the New Testament. In the process I will also attempt to show how complex and difficult it is to

Isaiah, National Security, and the Politics of Fear

find clear political directions for the present from the Bible, a difficulty that I think is vastly underestimated by conservative evangelicals and "mainstream" liberal theologians alike. Let me begin with the "politics of fear." In what passes for political discourse in our era—a discourse marked by extreme, misleading, inflammatory remarks on both sides of the polarized debate—a great deal has been made of the "politics of fear." The Democratic left has charged the Republican right with unfairly playing to the general public's irrational fears of the developing policies of the Obama administration. Whether those fears are actually irrational is quite another matter, and after eight straight years of the left's demonization of Bush and his administration, it is hard to imagine why the left expected any better treatment of the Obama administration by the right, but our task is not to adjudicate the current debate, but to ask what the Bible might contribute to it.

As it happens, Isaiah of Jerusalem speaks directly to the topic of "the politics of fear" in an oracle that dates from the time of the Syro-Ephraimitic War of 735–732 BCE.[1] Because of the fear of Assyrian expansion, most of the small states along the Mediterranean coast, including Tyre, Philistia, and north Israel had rebelled against their Assyrian suzerain and joined a defensive coalition led by the Arameans of Damascus. Judah on their southern border was still an independent state, free from the Assyrian yoke, having paid no tribute to Assyria after the disaster at Kullani in 738, when all the other western states rushed with tribute to submit.[2] But with the Kullani disaster still fresh in their minds, the Judean court, first under Jotham, and then under his successor Ahaz, refused to join the defensive alliance, preferring to remain neutral and stay out of the conflict. This refusal of Judah to join the alliance created what the allies regarded as a frightening and intolerable strategic situation on their southern border. The allies needed Judah's military and financial resources for their imminent war with Assyria, and Israel and the Arameans could not afford to have a potentially hostile state on their southern borders when Assyria moved against their northern front. With very limited time to deal with the situation, the allies decided to make a lightning-fast surprise attack on Jerusalem, cut it off from the rest of Judah, breach its walls, and replace Ahaz, whom they regarded as a traitor, with a ruler more amenable to their coalition, thus securing their southern front. There is some confusion about the person they planned to put on Ahaz's throne, because the text has been intentionally garbled, but possibly it was a non-Davidide from the Tyrian royal house, the son of Ittobaal.[3] Given the political and military situation, everyone on both sides of the issue was operating out of a very rational and profound fear. When members of Ahaz's court heard that the Aramean army had already joined up with the Israelite army in Samaria, they were terrified and trembled like trees in a windstorm (Isa 7:2), and when this combined army bypassed Judah's northern border fortifications at Mizpeh and suddenly passed by unprepared Judean villages to appear on Mt. Scopus just north of Jerusalem, there was sheer panic (Isa 10:27b–32).[4] Both sides accused the other of treason, and Isaiah, apparently fearing that Ahaz was about to do something precipitous, finds himself repeatedly sent by God to Ahaz with reassurances of divine support and deliverance,[5] based on the ancient Zion Tradition. This theological tradition, which was formed during the period of the Davidic-Solomonic empire, held that:

1. Yahweh, the God of Israel, was the imperial God of the whole world;
2. Yahweh had chosen David and his dynasty, granting him an eternal covenant that a Davidide would always sit on the throne in Jerusalem as God's human representative; and
3. Yahweh had chosen Jerusalem as his earthly dwelling place.[6]

Despite Isaiah's reassurances, however, Ahaz refused to trust in the promises of the Judean royal theology, and decided instead to reject Judah's previously neutral stance, appeal to Assyria for help, and accept Assyrian vassalage.

The oracle in Isa 8:11–15 is a response to this situation:

> For thus said Yahweh to me as his hand seized me, and he turned me aside from going in the way of this people, saying:
> "Do not call everything treason that this people calls treason,
> and do not fear what it fears,
> and do not be terrified by what terrifies it.
> But Yahweh of Hosts, sanctify him;
> let him be your fear,
> let him be your terror.
> He will become either a sanctuary,

or a stone of collision,
and a ledge of stumbling,
to both houses of Israel;
a snare and a trap to the inhabitants[7] of Jerusalem.
And many will stumble over them,
and fall and be broken,
and be snared and caught."

Since all of the imperatives in vss. 12–13 are in the plural, the admonition is addressed to Isaiah and his followers, not to the prophet alone. It encourages Isaiah and his followers to take a different path than the rest of his society. By sanctifying Yahweh of the heavenly hosts, the militant God of Israel, and making him one's primary object of fear and terror, all the lesser fears and terrors of the larger society, no matter how rational, would be put in perspective. Thus by making God one's primary fear, Isaiah implies that one could defang those lesser fears, enabling one to continue to obey God even in the face of genuine and frightening threats. The admonition is backed up by a promise and a corresponding threat. To those who sanctify God and make him their primary fear, God will become a *miqdaš*, "a sanctuary, or temple," where one can find refuge from life-threatening dangers. To those who put other fears first, this sanctuary will become only a trap. Isaiah makes an unusual word play here. Both stone (*'eben*) and ledge or rock (*ṣur*) are normally used in Israel's cultic vocabulary to refer to God as a place of refuge,[8] but here Isaiah reverses that expected meaning by the modifiers he juxtaposes to those cultic terms. God will become the stone, not of help, but the stone one stubs one's toe on, and the rocky ledge, not of refuge, but the ledge one trips over. Isaiah is trying to convince his audience that the threat from God for human disobedience is more destructive and terrifying than any credible threat from the armies of Aram and Israel or even the imperial armies of Assyria.

In the larger context of Isaiah's message, this centering on the fear of God as one's primary motivation for action, undergirds Isaiah's remarkably consistent political message throughout his very long prophetic ministry of at least thirty-eight, and perhaps as long as fifty years. From the Syro-Ephraimitic War in 735–732 BCE, through the Samaria revolt of 725–722, the Hamath-Gaza-Samaria revolt of 720, the Ashdod affair of 715–711, and Hezekiah's revolt against Sennacherib in 705–701, Isaiah urged Judah to avoid involvement in defensive alliances with foreign nations and trust instead in the promises of God to the Davidic dynasty and Zion/Jerusalem, God's chosen city. Such promises, of course, presupposed that the Davidic king and his court would respond positively to these promises and attempt to fulfill the royal ideal associated with these promises. As Isa 7:9 puts it, "If you (plural) do not firmly believe, you (plural) will not be firmly established." I have worked out the details of this general viewpoint in a paper to be published in the *Stone-Campbell Journal* 13/1 (2009), so I will not repeat them here, though we will come back to the royal ideal. Instead, I want to address the difficulty of using Isaiah's comments on fear and his consistent opposition to Judah's temptation to enter into foreign military alliances as providing any support for isolating a biblical vision of international cooperation independent of the supposedly rival apocalyptic vision.

In all of Isaiah's oracles of promise and warning that can be reasonably dated to any of the historical crises mentioned above, Isaiah's promises are mixed with a military, even apocalyptic element. In the Syro-Ephraimitic crisis of 735–732, Isaiah reassured Ahaz and his court that within five to six years their two main enemies would be destroyed—Ephraim would be shattered from being a people, and Damascus would be removed from being a city.[9] When that did not convince the Judean court, Isaiah promised that by the time his pregnant wife weaned her expected child, that is, in three to four years, the land of the two kings the Judean court so feared would be abandoned. Finally, he promised that before his next child could say, "Momma" or "Papa," that is, in one to two years, both Damascus and Samaria would be plundered by the king of Assyria. Isaiah 17 describes this imminent and thorough destruction of Damascus and Ephraim in very apocalyptic terms, comparing them to the chaotic sea monster of myth before they are chased away in a mere moment by the rebuke of God (Isa 17:12–14). A number of other oracles that appear to have been re-edited to refer to a later setting may also date in their original form to this crisis, and they share the same features. Isa 10:33–34 has Yahweh chopping down the forest of the Aramean-Israelite coalition, Isa 10:16–19 has Yahweh sending a wasting sickness into his—presumably Israel's—warriors (cf. Isa 17:4) and decimating his forest, in Isa 10:20–23 only a remnant of Jacob will return from God's judgment. Isaiah 2, which I also date to this period, has a very apocalyptic portrayal of God's judgment on Israel and its Aramean and Philistine allies, where they are warned to "enter into the rock, and hide in the dust from the terror of Yahweh and from the glory of his majesty."[10] Finally in Isa 28:1–6, an oracle that could date as late as the revolt of Samaria in 725–722, Isaiah portrays God as destroying in a devastating flood the drunken remnant of Ephraim.

The oracles in Isaiah 19 may possibly date to the Hamath-Gaza-Samaria revolt of 720 and its aftermath,[11] and in the initial oracles Yahweh rides on a swift cloud to terrify the gods of Egypt, throw Egypt into civil war, deliver them into the hands of a fierce ruler, devastate the economy of the Nile, and turn the wisest of the Egyptian counselors into fools (Isa 19:1–15). It is only in the series of short and very unusual oracles in Isa 19:18–25, which offer a remarkable portrayal of international cooperation between Israel, Egypt, and Assyria as equal partners, that one finds material that could be construed as offering a vision of peaceful cooperation independent of any apocalyptic element. Even here, however, Yahweh's healing of Egypt is subsequent to his smiting of them (Isa 19:20–22). Moreover, most scholars date all this material much later than Isaiah of Jerusalem, though I would at least consider the possibility of a date immediately after the 720 revolt, or sometime between 720–715, when there was a brief détente and trade accord between Assyria and Egypt.

All of the oracles dating to the Ashdod affair in 715–711 envision God's military destruction of the Philistine ringleaders of the revolt and their Egyptian and Nubian supporters. In Isaiah 20 the Philistine rebels, besieged in their cities, will be utterly dismayed when they see the members of the Egyptian and Nubian relief force on which they had relied for help led away captive to Assyria, naked and barefoot. In Isaiah 18 Yahweh will calmly watch from Jerusalem while the Nubian host is cut down and left as food for birds and beasts like shoots pruned from a grapevine. In Isa 14:28–32 Yahweh warns the Philistines who are rejoicing over the death of Ahaz, that Hezekiah, his new Davidic king, far from joining their revolt, will be an even worse enemy than Ahaz, and that Yahweh and his king as well as the Assyrians, the smoke from the north, will participate in the extermination of the Philistine remnant.

Then, in the oracles dating to the time of Hezekiah's revolt, an element reappears that was last found in the oracles from the time of the Syro-Ephraimitic War. Because Ahaz had refused Isaiah's repeated reassurances from God during that crisis, Isaiah had consigned Judah to a limited measure of the same judgment that had overtaken Damascus and Ephraim—the flood of Assyria would sweep into Judah and reach up to its neck (Isa 8:5–8). In Isaiah 28 the prophet actually reworks an earlier oracle against Israel as the introduction to an oracle of judgment against the rulers of Jerusalem. The same sweeping flood that earlier devastated Samaria will once again overwhelm Judah, spreading sheer terror among its leaders, because they sought refuge in an alliance with Egypt rather than trusting in Yahweh. Judah's Egyptian allies will not save them, and Judah will be devastated because they trusted in Egypt rather than in God (Isa 30:17; 31:1–3). In none of these texts is there any non-apocalyptic vision of peaceful cooperation between nations.

One should note, however, that Isaiah's word of judgment on Jerusalem is not his last word, the influence of the Zion Tradition's promises to David and to Zion had too great a hold on Isaiah's theological imagination to permit that. God's judgment on his city was simply a means to an end. His judgment was simply to refine Zion, so that it would once more be called a city of righteousness (Isa 1:21–28). The Assyrians were his agents for this refining process, but when God had finished his work on Mount Zion and Jerusalem, he would punish the Assyrians in turn (Isa 10:5–15). In this strange work of Yahweh (Isa 28:21), God himself would besiege and distress Jerusalem until it was like a dead person whose ghostly voice a soothsayer called up from the underworld, but then, at the last moment, God would miraculously intervene in a frightening theophany, and the multitude of foes fighting against Jerusalem would vanish in a moment, like a dream when the dreamer awakes (Isa 29:1–8). God would come down like a lion to fight against Mount Zion, but Yahweh the destroying lion would miraculously turn into a flock of protective birds, and he would protect, deliver, spare, and rescue Jerusalem (Isa 31:4–5), and the Assyrian enemy would be destroyed, not by human hands, but by Yahweh (Isa 31:8–9; also see Isa 14:24–27). In a raging tempest Yahweh would come against Assyria, and its king would perish in a firepit of human sacrifice (Isa 30:27–33). When Yahweh had burned up his foreign enemies who destroyed his people, and had terrified the sinners among his own people in Zion by this pyrotechnic display, the inhabitants of this purified and redeemed Jerusalem would look with wonder on their wide land and peaceful Jerusalem, marveling at the sudden disappearance of the hated enemy, and rejoicing in Yahweh their true king (Isa 33:1–24).[12] This note of future hope is also found in the idealized portrait of the future Jerusalem in Isa 2:1–4 and Mic 4:2–6, as well as in Isaiah's portrayals of the ideal future king in Isa 8:23–9:6; 11:1–10; and 32:1–8, passages to which we may have occasion to return.

To return to Isa 8:11–15 and the prophet's message about making God one's primary object of fear, a little reflection on this passage will also indicate the difficulty of applying it in any direct way to the modern political scene. Isaiah's argument in this passage and in his policy of quiescent, noninvolvement in international treaty alliances growing out of this principle of primary fear, depended on ancient and widely accepted religious promises by God to the Davidic dynasty, to Jerusalem, its capital city, and to Israel, God's chosen people. Whatever his most partisan supporters may think, our president, whether a Bush or even an Obama, is not a son of David or an heir to the Davidic throne, much less the Messiah. Washington, DC, is not Zion nor the new Jerusalem. Nor is the United States the new Israel. In short, there are no specific ancient and widely accepted religious promises by God to our president, our capital, or our nation upon which one can rationally espouse Isaiah's foreign policy views as in any way directly relevant, much less prescriptive, for the foreign policy of the United States. In fact, when Isaiah's message about fear is refracted through the New Testament, it is not applied to a nation at all, but to the church.

With some slight changes, the author of 1 Peter quotes Isa 8:12–15 in the context of preparing Christians to stand up to persecution: "But even if you should suffer for doing what is right, you are blessed. Do not fear what they fear, and do not be terrified, but in your hearts sanctify Christ as LORD, being ready always to give your defense to anyone who asks you a reason for the hope that is in you; yet do it with gentleness and reverence, having a good conscience so that, when you are maligned, those who abuse your good conduct in Christ may be put to shame" (1 Pet 3:14–16). Isaiah's original admonition to national leaders is here transformed into an admonition to members of a minority religious community without any political power and under serious threat of persecution. The date and authorship of 1 Peter is disputed, but if the book is early, it could reflect the beginning of the Roman persecution of Christians under Nero in the 60s CE that the Roman historians Suetonius and Tacitus mention, and which Tacitus describes in gruesome detail.[13] If the book is later, it could reflect the ongoing state persecution of Christians under Trajan described in a letter to that emperor by Pliny the Younger.[14] In either context the early Christians had ample reason to be afraid of their enemies, but according to 1 Peter's adaptation of the Isaiah passage, it was the greater fear of God that allowed them to endure such sufferings despite their very rational and legitimate fears of their persecutors. As Jesus himself said, "Do not fear those who kill the body, and after that can do nothing more. But I will warn you whom to fear: fear him who, after he has killed, has authority to cast into hell. Yes, I tell you, fear him!" (Luke 12:4–5).

Even this New Testament appropriation of Isaiah's message, however, is hardly applicable to modern Christians in the United States without considerable rethinking and reinterpretation. Christians in the United States are not part of a minority religious community without political power and under serious threat of persecution by the dominant society. Christians in the United States have as much, if not more, access to political power, even oppressive political power, than members of any other group in United States society. Most of our politicians and elected officials, in fact, are at least nominally identified as Christians.

This is a far cry from the situation in 1 Peter, where the minority community is urged to keep its head down, to avoid calling attention to itself by behavior or teaching that could be construed as disruptive to the ordered hierarchical society envisioned in the Roman Empire as the ideal. This hierarchical Roman ideal, reflected in the typically Hellenistic household code of ethics adopted and promoted in 1 Pet 2:13—3:7, is no longer the ethical ideal of modern United States culture. Contemporary Western Christians no longer have to tolerate slavery to avoid the persecution of a dominant society for which slavery was seen as part of the natural order of things. Few modern Christians would even dream of defending slavery, much less encouraging slaves to willingly submit to it. But in precisely the same way, Western Christians no longer have to regard Paul's insight in Gal 3:28 that "in Christ there is neither Jew nor Greek, slave nor free, male nor female, for you are all one in Christ Jesus" as an unrealizable ideal in a hostile environment. If Peter's Christian community was in danger of bringing persecution down on itself as a disrupter of family and society by *granting* its women full rights with its men, the modern Christian community in the United States is far more likely to draw the larger society's opprobrium upon itself by *denying* its women those full rights. The social context of the modern Western church is totally different from that of the New Testament church, and the logic of the scriptural argument cuts in a different direction with that different context.

Given the changed cultural context for the modern believer in the United States from that of any of the original recipients of the Scriptures either in the Old Testament or in the New Testament, how is the modern believer to find direction for political ideals in the Bible? Obviously Scripture will not be able to answer our precise questions in a direct and simplistic fashion. It will require a bit more work on our part than that.

Nonetheless, there are certain general principles in Scripture that can provide some guidance in our struggle to address responsibly the political issues of our day. One such principle is the admonition given by Isaiah and repeated by 1 Peter that insists that God should be the believer's primary object of fear. This notion of making God one's primary source of fear is very biblical. The "fear of God" in the biblical idiom is the equivalent of "piety" or a "religious lifestyle." As Ecclesiastes puts it, "Fear God and keep his commandments, this is the whole duty of man" (Eccl 12:13). If one fears God more than anything else, one can obey God even when such obedience puts one in deadly peril. It is an antidote to fear as an excuse for disobedience, as an excuse for wholesale abandonment of proper procedure, and as an excuse for the adoption of immoral, illegal, and unjust means to a supposedly noble end.

This seemed self-evident to me until early this summer when in response to a church presentation on "fearing God," a woman in the congregation objected that the "fear of God" was an unworthy motivation for a truly moral person. In the following discussion I learned that a lot of people, including many Christians, have a very negative response to the idea of "fearing" God. In our permissive era, it has become popular even in the church to contrast the supposedly Old Testament idea of "fearing" God, with the supposedly superior New Testament idea of "loving" God, despite the fact that the Old Testament says a lot about "loving" God (Deut 6:5), and the New Testament says a lot about "fearing" God (Luke 23:40; Acts 13:16, 26; 1 Pet 2:17; Rev 14:7). It is true that 1 John 4:18 says, "There is no fear in love, but perfect love casts out fear; for fear has to do with punishment, and whoever fears has not reached perfection in love." But none of us in this life have reached perfection. As the same writer says, "If we say that we have no sin, we deceive ourselves, and the truth is not in us" (1 John 1:8), and "If we say that we have not sinned, we make him a liar, and his word is not in us" (1 John 1:10). As long as we are in this life, imperfect sinners, it serves us well to both love and fear God.

I think it is a very serious mistake to try to be more moral than Jesus, to be more perfect than our Lord, and yet you see religious people doing it all the time. I'll just love God and not fear him is an example of that, but there are many others. Jesus turned water into wine for a wedding banquet, and Jesus so frequently attended such banquets that his enemies branded him a wino and a glutton, but despite the model of our Lord, many Christians insist that a true Christian must not drink alcoholic beverages even in moderation. There are other Christians today who argue that true Christians ought to be vegetarians, despite Jesus' teaching that it is not what goes into a person's stomach that defiles a person, but what comes out of the heart, thus declaring all foods clean (Mark 7:18–19). Both the insistence on total abstinence from alcohol and meat were views held by some in the early church, but the New Testament regarded those who attempted to impose these and similar restrictions on all believers as heretics, not as heroes of the faith (Col 2:16–23; 1 Tim 4:1–5). It is enough for disciples to be like their Lord; there is no merit in trying to surpass him in piety. If Jesus said to fear God, we would do well just to obey him.

In addition to the fear of God, another general principle repeatedly enunciated by Isaiah is the concern for justice within society. In Isaiah's time a monarchical system of government was the only form of government that Judah and Israel had known for more than 200 years, and this concern for justice was embodied in a long-standing royal ideal of the king as the upholder of God's impartial justice and the provider of peace and well-being for his people.[15] This royal ideal is well expressed in such Psalms as Ps 72 and Ps 101. Psalm 101 is particularly striking, because in it the king appears to swear an oath promising that he will not put up with corrupt officials in his royal administration, that he will drive such corrupt officials from his presence, that he will cut off and destroy all such evildoers from the city of the Lord, the imperial capital. As an heir of this tradition, Isaiah embraced it with enthusiasm. One can see this particularly in the prophet's portrayal of the ideal king in Isa 9:6; 11:1–5; and 32:1–2. Isaiah 9:6 depicts this ideal king as reigning on the throne of

David and his kingdom during a period of endless peace, during which the king will establish and uphold his throne and kingdom "with justice and with righteousness from this time onward and forevermore." Isaiah 11:1–5 characterizes the rule of this king as carried out "with the spirit of Yahweh, the spirit of wisdom and understanding, the spirit of counsel and might, the spirit of knowledge and the fear of Yahweh":

> His delight shall be in the fear of Yahweh.
> He will not judge by what his eyes see,
> or decide by what his ears hear;
> but with righteousness he shall judge the poor,
> and decide with equity for the meek of the earth;
> he shall strike the earth with the rod of his mouth,
> and with the breath of his lips he shall kill the wicked.
> Righteousness shall be the belt around his waist,
> and faithfulness the belt around his loins.

The language suggests that this king, motivated by the fear of God, will not be swayed by surface appearances and popular opinion, but will cut to the heart of the matter, rendering righteous judgment for the oppressed, and punishing the evildoer. The third passage, Isa 32:1–2, envisions not only the ideal king, but ideal royal officials as well. The king will reign in righteousness and princes will rule with justice. Each, king and royal officials as well, will be like God in being for the oppressed "a hiding place from the wind, a covert from the tempest, like streams of water in a dry place, like the shade of a great rock in a weary land." One should note that in the larger context of the first two of these passages about the ideal king, the era of peace follows the destruction of Israel's enemies. In Isa 9:3 Yahweh has broken the yoke and rod of the Assyrian oppressor, and in Isa 11:4 the ideal king will smite the earth and kill the wicked. There is no vision here of peaceful international cooperation without the interconnected vision of military defeat of the enemy.

To return to the royal ideal, while Isaiah embraced it, he did not see it realized in the royal administrations of his time, and so the ideal became a weapon in his hand for critiquing contemporary kings and particularly their royal officials. He characterized the Jerusalem of his time, not as the idealized city of God filled with righteousness, but as a corrupt whore, full of murderers and corrupt royal officials, all of whom ran after bribes and perverted the justice due to orphans and widows (Isa 1:21–23). Despite their religious pretensions, the politically powerful unjustly oppressed the orphans and widows (Isa 1:10–17). The leaders had despoiled and crushed the poor, grinding them into the dust (Isa 3:13–15). Apparently much of this oppression was done legally, by passing oppressive decrees and laws that targeted smaller landowners, so that they had no recourse even in the courts (Isa 10:1–2). From Isa 5:8 and Mic 2:1–2 it is clear that part of the social problem in Isaiah's time was that the wealthy and powerful were buying up or otherwise appropriating all the arable land in the country. The devastation of Israel as a result of the Syro-Ephraimitic War had led to an enormous flight of refugees from the north to Judah. The population of Judah doubled in the eighth century. Since the majority of these refugees were now landless and in desperate need of work, there was a surplus of cheap farm labor, and the rich expanded their agricultural holdings at the expense of the poor to take advantage of this vast pool of cheap labor, and the more small landowners they dispossessed, the larger this labor pool grew.

In evaluating this situation, one should note that Judah in the eighth century was not a rustic backwater composed primarily of subsistence farmers and a modestly better off political class.[16] It was actually a very wealthy state. Judah sat astride the two-way southern trade routes from Arabia and farther east and south that continued on past Judah to the Mediterranean and farther west. With his political and military control of this area, the Judean king and his administration was in position to demand a twenty to twenty-five percent transit tax on all goods passing through his territory in either direction as well as demanding samples of particularly desired goods and other payments for ease of passage. The Toronto archaeologist John Holladay, based on the Assyrian tribute figures for the period, calculated the Judean kingdom's income from this transit tax during the reigns of Ahaz and Hezekiah as running somewhere in the neighborhood of 5 million dollars per year.[17] In the approximately thirty years between Ahaz's payment of tribute to Tiglath-Pileser III in 733–732 BCE, and Hezekiah's payment of tribute to Sennacherib in 701, the Judean treasury had to accumulate a surplus of almost $50 million in gold and silver bullion over and above its expenses in paying its military and royal officials to maintain this transit tax system and other government services.[18] That means that Judean society was marked by a sharp contrast between grinding poverty and ostentatious wealth, well reflected in Isaiah's parody of Judah's wealthy women in Isa 3:16—4:1 and 32:9–14. In short, given its much smaller size and population, the contrast between rich and poor in Isaiah's Judah, was not all that different from the disparities in wealth in the modern United States.

It is in this context that Isaiah argues that the secret to finding rest and repose, Isaianic shorthand for peace, prosperity, and well-being, is to give rest to the weary, to give repose to the needy (Isa 28:12).[18] For Isaiah governmental policies that favored the wealthy political class at the expense of the poor and impoverished were an abomination, and this was particularly true of a foreign policy with military options that imposed an undue burden on the poor. Isaiah characterized such policies as a rejection of Yahweh's promises and a reliance instead on "oppression and deceit" (Isa 30:12–17). For Isaiah, dependent as he was on the Zion Tradition's promises to David and Zion, the king and royal official's first order of business was to see that true justice was done at home, and then trusting in God's promises, without undue anxiety or haste, to deal with international issues.

Just as with Isaiah's emphasis on the "fear of God," Isaiah's emphasis on impartial justice and the relief of the poor and oppressed, are picked up and reiterated in the New Testament, though again, not primarily as admonitions to high government officials, but to ordinary believers. Jesus directed his ministry primarily to the poor and religiously outcast, and he emphasized "justice and mercy and faith" over the punctilious observance of ritual law (Matt 23:23). He relieved those who were suffering, even if it meant healing on the Sabbath and thus offending the religious authorities, and he insisted that if the religious leaders of his day had truly understood the prophet Hosea's words, "I desire mercy and not sacrifice," they would not have condemned the guiltless (Matt 12:1–14). His early followers continued this concern for the poor in their collections and almsgiving on their behalf, and in their insistence despite temptations to the contrary that there was no place in Christianity for partiality and preferential treatment of the rich and powerful (see 1 Tim 5:21; 6:17–19; and James 2:1–7).

But how do these general principles translate into useful categories for the contemporary political debate, particularly with regard to national security, economic reform, the health care debate, and the use of fear to achieve political ends? The first thing to note is a negative. Isaiah does not provide a blueprint to address any of these issues. Isaiah lived under a religious monarchy, one might even say a theocracy, and even in his most utopian portrayals of the future, he never envisioned anything but an idealized form of that same government structure. We live in a secular republic, a constitutional democracy in which every citizen has a more direct influence on the direction our government takes by the way the citizen exercises his or her right to vote. Our rights as citizens, even if we are in a political minority, are enshrined in a bill of rights and a constitution that are intended to protect us from the potentially abusive powers of our ruling class. And to further strengthen this protection, our government is set up with checks and balances by an ideally independent administration, legislature, and judiciary, so that any potential abuse of governmental power by any one of our three parts of government may be blocked by the intervention of the other two.

Isaiah's views on Judah's national security and foreign policy is dependent on Judah's very particular historical contexts during Isaiah's ministry and on very particular religious traditions concerning David and Jerusalem, historical contexts that we do not share at all, and religious traditions that we share only in very attenuated and highly transformed versions. In Christianity, as an heir of later Jewish developments in the approximately 600 years following the collapse of the Davidic monarchy and the destruction of Jerusalem in 597–586 BCE, the promises to David have been reapplied to Jesus of Nazareth as the Christ or Messiah, but Christianity also explicitly affirms, following Jesus, that his kingdom is not of this world. The promises to Jerusalem have been transformed from promises of divine protection and world leadership of the actual city in Israel to promises of divine protection to Jesus' followers, his church, the new Jerusalem, or even to their future glorified home in heaven following the last judgment. Given this radically different context, both politically and religiously, it would be highly irresponsible for a contemporary religious leader to claim that the United States should avoid defensive military alliances with foreign nations because Isaiah was opposed to eighth-century Judah entering such alliances. One should note that Micah, an eighth-century contemporary of Isaiah, appears to have envisioned with favor the future re-establishment of a south Syrian defensive league to block further Assyrian incursions into Israel during the future reign of the ideal David: "If the Assyrians come into our land and tread upon our soil, we will raise against them seven shepherds and eight installed as rulers. They shall rule the land of Assyria with the sword, and the land of Nimrod with the drawn sword; they shall rescue us from the Assyrians if they come into our land or tread within our border" (Mic 5:5-6).[19]

Isaiah and Micah both envisioned an idealized future for Jerusalem when all nations would come up to Jerusalem and its Davidic ruler (see Isa 11:10) to have their disputes arbitrated by God (Isa 2:2-4; Mic 4:1-5), and as a result of this arbitration there would no longer be a need for war or armaments to settle international disputes.[20] One might be tempted to claim that these two passages provide the alternate view of peaceful international cooperation independent of any apocalyptic vision of the defeat of one's enemies. Some very prominent Old Testament scholars have, in fact, taken these texts' declarative statements that in that ideal future nations would beat their swords into plowshares, their spears into pruning hooks, and cease to engage in warfare, not as declarative statements, but as imperatives to modern states to adopt a policy of disarmament. Yet both these interpretations ignore the profoundly imperialistic background of these visions. The reason the nations submit to this arbitration in this ideal future is because God will have made the imperial power of Jerusalem evident to the whole world. The implication is that God's imperial administration in Jerusalem is capable of enforcing its arbitration decisions on its vassal states. The Jerusalemite Peace portrayed here is no less imperialistic or lacking in the implicit threat of force than the Pax Romana of the Roman Empire. In the larger context in Isaiah, this vision of a future of worldwide peace centered in Jerusalem functions as the introduction to an appeal to the house of Jacob, the northern kingdom of Israel, to drop out of the Syro-Ephraimite alliance against their kinsmen and fellow religionists in Judah. Moreover, that further address goes on to threaten Israel with apocalyptic destruction from God. The larger context in Micah is not as clear, but the text goes on to promise the restoration of the former dominion and sovereignty to Jerusalem (Mic 4:8), and Mic 4:11-13 calls upon Zion to gore, trample, and beat in pieces all the nations that assemble against her. The only way to save either of these visions from entanglement with apocalyptic militarism is to isolate them as floating pericope, remove them from their present eighth-century context, thus denying their authorship by either Micah or Isaiah, and plop them down in an exilic or post-exilic setting without any real historical context at all. Such late dating for theological reasons is just as open to the charge of apologetic exegesis as any early dating by the most rigid fundamentalist. But even a late dating cannot strip the imagery of either passage of their clear imperialistic background, and there remains no justification for turning a declarative statement about the future into an imperative for today.

The establishment of the League of Nations after World War I, and the establishment of the United Nations after World War II, were noble attempts to bring an end to war through arbitration and sanctions against offending nations, but the League of Nations was a dismal failure, and the U.N., despite mixed success in particular areas, has given little reason for any nation to disarm and rely on it for its security against hostile neighbors. Moreover, apart from the aspect of arbitration, neither organization was or is remotely similar to the imperial Jerusalem envisioned by Isaiah and Micah.

One will have noted that I have spent disproportionally more time on Old Testament texts than on the New. In part that is because I am professionally an Old Testament scholar, but it is also because the Old Testament contains more material directly addressed to high government officials dealing with issues of national government and international politics. The New Testament is far more oriented toward life in a minority religious community where there is little opportunity to exercise significant influence on national or international political affairs. The ethical admonitions within the New Testament are more interpersonal ethics for life within such a community, with relatively little direct reflection on what good political government would look like, or the particular virtues that should characterize a good ruler. Yet even in the New Testament there is an apocalyptic framework that provides the ultimate incentive for a life of obedience. To return to the passage in 1 Peter, the reason why Christians can endure persecution following the model of their master is that there is a final judgment, when God will judge the living and the dead, punishing the wicked and rewarding those who have been faithful (1 Pet 4:1—5:11). This apocalyptic element is already found in the teachings of Jesus as portrayed in the Gospels (Matthew 24–25; Mark 13), it is an essential part of Paul's gospel (Rom 2:6-11; 2 Thess 1:5-10), it is elaborately spelled out in the book of Revelation, and is presupposed in all the other New

Testament writings even where it is not directly addressed. Thus I find it hard to justify the notion of a biblical vision of peaceful cooperation independent of and disentangled from an apocalyptic background of final judgment.

It should be clear from my preceding comments about the vast historical and cultural distance, and, with regard to the Old Testament, even the religious distance that separates us from the world of the Bible, that I am very suspicious of any claim, whether from the right, the left, or the middle of the road, that the Bible supports a particular political agenda, that a true Christian must vote in favor or against a particular legislative proposal, or even support a particular political party. Scripture does provide us with some underlying principles to guide our political reflections—the demand to make God our primary fear, the insistent call for social justice and righteousness, the absolute rejection of partiality in judicial process, particularly directed against the preferential treatment of the rich, and the imperative to protect and relieve the poor, oppressed, and powerless. These general principles do provide us some guidance in critiquing particular government policies in which these principles are egregiously violated. One could make the claim, for instance, that given our principles of government, any government action that infringed the constitutional rights of our citizens, particularly if it was rammed through the legislature and the courts by an administration in the name of national security and in response to overwhelming fear of our enemies, would come close to the kind of disobedient fear that Isaiah was addressing. Such actions would be a clear perversion of justice, a denial of our own principles of government, and could easily lend themselves to the economic exploitation of those whose rights were abrogated.[21] Nonetheless these general principles, as useful as they are to critique abuse, do not spell out in a positive way how such demands are to be concretely realized in our culture and under our form of government. They do not make clear what particular economic and diplomatic policy choices have the best chance of providing us lasting security and economic well-being in this dangerous world. They do not tell us whether a government-run health-care program will be more just, more affordable, and more sustainable in the long-run than health-care offered by private providers. These are issues for serious debate, but apart from insisting on these general principles from Scripture and no doubt others that I have overlooked, biblical scholars, theologians, and preachers have little to contribute to this debate as biblical scholars, theologians, and preachers, other than to critique the misuse of religion in the debate. The real heart of the debate requires, first and foremost, the expertise of diplomats, statesmen, constitutional lawyers, economists, and healthcare specialists, while always taking into account the cares and concerns of ordinary citizens, rich and poor alike.

Endnotes

1. The historical context of the beginning of the Syro-Ephraimitic War is spelled out in Isa 7:1–9 and its parallels in 2 Kgs 15:37–38 and 2 Kgs 16:5–9. For a detailed textual reconstruction and exegetical analysis of the Isaiah passage see my article, Roberts, "The Context, Text, and Logic of Isaiah 7.7–9," 161–70.

2. For the identification of Kullani and the background to this event, see my article, Roberts, "Amos 6.1–7," 155–66, and the literature cited there.

3. MT has son of Tab'al, "Good for Nothing," not NRSV's son of Tabeel, "God is good," but this can hardly be the original reading. Such disparaging alteration of proper names often happens in the OT in proper names that contain the divine name Baal—e.g., note Ishbosheth, "Man of shame," (MT of 2 Sam 2:8ff.) for the original Ishbaal, "Man of Baal," (LXX of same passages)—which is why the identification with the contemporary Phoenician name Itto-Baal is attractive.

4. For this interpretation of Isa 10:27b–32, see my article, Roberts, "Isaiah and His Children," 193–203, esp. 201, and the earlier literature cited there. MT's garbled ʿl mpny-šmn, "a yoke before fatness," in 10:27b, should probably be emended to ʿl(h) mpny-šmrn, "he went up from before Samaria," rather than following NRSV's peculiar emendation of the final word to Rimmon.

5. For Isaiah's repeated attempts to reassure Ahaz, see my article, Roberts, "Isaiah and His Children."

6. For a fuller discussion of the date, content, and importance of this Zion Tradition, see my discussion in Roberts, "Solomon's Jerusalem and the Zion Tradition," 163–70, and the earlier literature cited there.

7. Since the participle is a singular, one could also translate this word as the "ruler" of Jerusalem and see it as a specific reference to Ahaz. A similar usage of the term meaning "ruler" is found in Amos 6:5, 8.

8. See the discussion in my forthcoming paper, Roberts, "Security and Justice in Isaiah."

9. Roberts, "The Context, Text, and Logic of Isaiah 7.7–9," 161–70.

10. For a full discussion of this passage, see Roberts, "Isaiah 2 and the Prophet's Message to the North," 290–308.

11. For the possible dates of all the Egyptian and Nubian oracles, see my discussion in Roberts, "Isaiah's Egyptian and Nubian Oracles," 201–9.

12. For a full treatment of this passage see Roberts, "Isaiah 33: An Isaianic Elaboration of the Zion Tradition," 15–25.

13. One may find a convenient English translation of Tacitus and Suetonius' remarks in Barrett, *The New Testament Background*, 15–17.

14. A convenient English translation of Pliny's letter to Trajan and Trajan's fascinating reply may be found in the excellent Ferguson, *Backgrounds of Early Christianity*, 594–95, 605.

15. For the details on this royal ideal and its abiding theological significance, see my study in Roberts, "The Enthronement of Yhwh and David," 675–86.

16. Holladay, "Hezekiah's Tribute, Long-Distance Trade, and the Wealth of Nations," 309–31.

17. Ibid., 327.

18. For this reading see my short note, Roberts, "A Note on Isaiah 28:12," 49–51.

19. The eighth-century date and authenticity of this passage is debated, but for the defense of its early date and authenticity and this interpretation of the passage, see Hillers, *Micah*, 69.

20. See my discussion of this issue in Roberts, "The End of War in the Zion Tradition," 119–28.

21. An example far enough in the past to escape the hysterics of the contemporary debate comes easily to mind. After the Japanese attack on Pearl Harbor in World War II, there was a very real fear of a Japanese invasion of the West Coast. There was a very large Japanese immigrant population on the West Coast, and since Japanese agents in Hawaii were strongly and correctly suspected of playing a role in providing intelligence to Japan's military for the attack on Pearl Harbor, there was a legitimate, if exaggerated concern, that the Japanese immigrant population on the West Coast would provide a cover for similar hostile espionage. The general society of the period was also marked by far more virulent racism than in our time, and the treachery of the surprise attack on Pearl Harbor while negotiations were going on with Japan's representatives in Washington, DC, exacerbated the hatred of the Japanese, a hatred that was soon heightened by wartime propaganda that intentionally demonized our enemy to prepare our soldiers and sailors to kill them without hesitation or moral compunction. Given this context, it is not particularly surprising that our government took pre-emptive action against this whole immigrant community despite the fact that the vast majority of them had committed no act of treason or any other crime against the state, their sole demonstrable fault being their Japanese ancestry. Nonetheless, the state soon forcibly resettled these Japanese immigrants, U.S. citizens or not, into guarded internment camps away from the cities along the Pacific coast. In the process, much of the property and possessions of these unfortunates were expropriated by others, an economic injustice that has still not been adequately compensated to this day. Eventually, the vast majority of these immigrants proved their loyalty to their adopted country, and many of their young men were finally allowed to join the U.S. military and fought courageously for the U.S., primarily against Germany in special Japanese-American detachments. With the advantage of hindsight, most critics today would regard the government treatment of these Japanese-American citizens as a horrendous travesty of justice, an inexcusable abridgment of their constitutional rights, and as economic oppression of the most egregious sort. It was not the United States' finest hour.

5

Interpreting the Prophets and Issues of Social Justice

TERENCE E. FRETHEIM

In this conference devoted to the Bible and the American future, the topic I would like to explore is the interpretation of Israel's prophets and issues of social justice. The implications of this conversation have no little import for how we think about the Bible and our future as an American people.[1] My plan is to interweave concerns about social ministry today with the ministry of the prophets. Because most of the prophets were laypersons and not "clergy," it is necessary to think about ministry in a broad way.

Let me cite two texts which will serve as a way into these issues.

> Thus says the LORD: Act with justice and righteousness, and deliver from the hand of the oppressor anyone who has been robbed. And do no wrong or violence to the alien, the orphan, and the widow, or shed innocent blood in this place. For if you will indeed obey this word, then through the gates of this house shall enter kings who sit on the throne of David, riding in chariots and on horses, they, and their servants, and their people. But if you will not heed these words, I swear by myself, says the LORD, that this house shall become a desolation. (Jer 22:3–5; note especially the "if, if not.")

> Listen, you heads of Jacob and rulers of the house of Israel. Should you not know justice? You who hate the good and love the evil, who tear the skin off my people, and the flesh off their bones; who eat the flesh of my people, flay their skin off them, break their

bones in pieces, and chop them up like meat in a kettle, like flesh in a caldron. (Mic 3:1–3)

Being a prophet was not an ongoing office in ancient Israel, as if prophets hung out their shingle and awaited calls to problematic situations. Prophets were not even found in every generation of Israel's life. Prophets often appear when things seem to be going reasonably well in Israel, but those times often prove to be but a prelude to moments of sheer hell.

People often ask: Who are the prophets today? I think a more appropriate question is this: How might we in our ministries see faithfully to one or another aspect of the prophetic task? This might be a clear word of the Gospel, such as: "Comfort, comfort you my people, says your God, . . . for the LORD has forgiven you double for all your sins" (Isa 40:1). Or, it might be an especially sharp word of critique and judgment, as in the text from Micah quoted above. Or, some combination thereof.

We may be living through a time of identity crisis for prophets, or in other terms, a leadership crisis in the church. Ministry these days is often defined in therapeutic terms. One seeks conflict resolution, not stirring things up. We are living in a non-risk generation, intensified by certain economic factors. Who is going to risk one's job or salary or the money flowing into our congregation by upsetting someone's applecart? We'll be prophetic in this sense when in a close circle of friends, or when we can remain anonymous.

Two understandings of the Old Testament prophets have been common over the years and how we sort these out has implications for our topic.

Prophets and the Future

The prophet is one who predicts the future. This definition is problematic; the word "prediction" suggests that the prophets were concerned about precision regarding future times and places. It would be much truer to their message to speak of the prophet as one who *announces* a word. Their language about the future is seldom very specific; rather than a timetable, they almost always speak more generally of "in that day" or "the days are surely coming."

Two basic principles need to guide our thinking about the prophets and their word about the future.

1. There is *seldom a literal correspondence* between a prophecy and a fulfillment. An illustration may be suggested that will help illumine this point. In the late nineteenth century a father made a promise to his young son that, if he maintained certain patterns of behavior, the father would give him a horse and buggy on his twenty-first birthday. The years went by.... The son made good on his end of the bargain; the time for fulfillment of the promise was at hand. But, in the meantime Henry Ford had been at work and Model Ts were on the streets. The last thing that the son wanted was a horse and buggy. The father could have said: "I made you a promise, I am going to fulfill it precisely in the terms I made it." But the son would have wanted his father to change the form of the promise and give him a Model T. Indeed, to be true to the promise, the form of the fulfillment would have to be changed.

Similarly, the prophet's message was adapted for the audience to which it was directed. By the time we get to Jesus, however, many of his contemporaries were looking for a literal fulfillment of some of these prophecies, in terms of, say, God coming in on a white horse and delivering them from the Romans. The disciples got past the literal form of God's promises and saw that Jesus was indeed the one God promised, but in a form and content much more marvelous than the prophets ever imagined. It might be suggested that today some folks among us are busily looking for a horse and buggy; they may miss the car.

2. There is often, not always, *a contingent element* with respect to prophetic words of indictment and judgment. Recall the "if" and "if not" in Jer 22:3–5. That is, the way in which people responded to the prophet could affect the shape of the fulfillment of a specific prophetic word, though all such contingencies are understood from within God's larger saving will for Israel and the world. An illustration may be offered: In some ways, God is like parents who play chess with young children, knowing that they could win the game if they chose, but at the same time, because they value the relationship, they choose to play in a way that does not overpower the child. And, given this kind of relationship, as the children improve in their chess-playing, the parents will have to cope with the increasingly sophisticated moves the children make. So, the way in

which the game will progress and finally be won, and the amount of time it will take, will be shaped in light of the moves the child makes.

Similarly, the moves that the people of God make in their lives matter to God because of the relationship God has established with them—in real relationships both parties to the relationship count. And so God takes into account what people say and do in moving into the future. Think of God as a quilt-maker. God is one who takes the threads and the patches of our words and deeds and weaves them into the quilt of God's new heaven and new earth. What we do and say makes a difference regarding the shape the future will take.

I am amazed at how often the language of fatalism creeps into our thinking about the future. Take justice issues or environmental issues: It is commonly thought that it doesn't make any difference what we do regarding these matters; the future is in God's hands. God has got the future all mapped out, and what human beings do is finally irrelevant. I submit that to leave the future simply in God's hands is to denigrate human responsibility. To do such a thing would be similar to the devil's temptation of Jesus: Jump off the top of the temple and God will send his angels to save you from the rocks below. Jesus replied: that would tempt God (Matt 4:1–11). We can certainly leave the future *ultimately* in God's hands, but God's relationship with us is such that we are given a great deal to say about the shape of our own future, *and*, to our point, the shape of the future of those less fortunate than we are. The future is partly settled and partly unsettled. Partly settled, yes: there will be a new heaven and a new earth. But the future is also unsettled—our words and deeds with respect to the less fortunate in our midst will make a difference with respect to the shape of their future and ours.

From another perspective, there are those who think that the earth is in its last minutes of existence. God is about to wrap up the history of the world in our lifetime, and a few people have been clued in regarding its final stages. And so, given this short time frame, you don't need to take any special care for the less fortunate; heaven will be theirs soon, anyway. Or about the environment—it's all going to be destroyed soon anyway, so don't waste your time. We will continue to be subjected to speculation about the end of the world as we have for centuries. One possible effect has been and will be that people will get so caught up in thinking about the next world that responsibility for this world is diminished. As one individual told me: ever since I discovered all this about the end of the world, I quit making my weekly visits to the senior citizen's home and spend that time reading my Bible and praying. Let's put the point squarely in terms of our topic: How we think and speak and act about the future can have a massive effect on how we think about those less fortunate than ourselves and on our practice of justice more generally.

Prophets and Social Reform

A second understanding of prophet: The prophets are social reformers, instruments of social and religious reform (the word "prophetic" often has this sense). The prophets are very well informed about such issues, and they seek to discern how God is at work in the social, economic, and political spheres of their own times. The prophets absolutely refuse to separate faith and politics or social issues, not least because they know very well that how people do their politics can deeply affect, positively or negatively, how the less fortunate are treated. This perspective can be very helpful, but we do need to remember that the prophets have no new social programs to offer, nor do they make any suggestions for change in the structures of society. Moreover, they do not have a fixed system of socio-political thought that they apply in some unwavering way. For the prophets, the will of God must be discerned ever anew in changing times and places.

An error of judgment that modern Christians too often make is that the prophets (or their modern successors) should not speak to socio-political-economic matters. It is interesting that this encouragement to churchly silence is deep in the "tradition"; indeed, Mic 2:6, in its indictment, reports hearing this complaint from the people: "one should not preach of such things." But the prophets believed that issues of social justice were not simply matters of private morality and they voiced these concerns in the public square to their 'congregations.' Social justice is a matter in which the *community of faith* must become involved or it would face a disastrous future. To be true to the tradition, the prophets *must* preach it!

It is important to say that the prophets are not satisfied simply to engage in social and political analysis; they place societal abuses in relationship to issues of faithfulness to God. In a nutshell: injustice reveals infidelity. The people's mistreatment of the poor was a sign that their relationship to God was not what it ought to be. If we're not taking good care of those less fortunate in our midst, our relationship with God is not healthy, however good we might feel about that relationship or however well our congregation seems to be doing.

So, when it comes to stating how change is to be introduced, the most basic call from the prophets is for repentance. At the same time, they also call for action on the far side of repentance, for it is remarkable how even those who regularly repent can continue abusive patterns of behavior toward others. Isaiah 1:16–17 puts these ideas together very well: "Wash yourselves, make yourselves clean; remove the evil of your doings from before my eyes; cease to do evil, learn to do good; seek justice, rescue the oppressed, defend the orphan, plead for the widow." Repent and act on behalf of the poor and needy. Both spheres of action are important.

Now, a key question arises. What are the sources of this prophetic concern for issues of social justice?

The prophetic word about social justice is often associated with liberal causes, almost as if the prophets were free-floating radicals from the 1960s. But it must be emphasized that the prophets were fundamentally conservative in their approach to these issues. The prophets discerned that social justice was a deeply traditional value that had often been neglected or misinterpreted. It is not that the prophets had nothing new to say, but their radicality consisted more in their rhetorical strategy, their forceful and intense way of speaking the old word of God into a new time and place, of getting under our skin and in our face with respect to long-standing communal commitments.

If we were to seek to articulate this point in today's terms, we could say something like this: The concern for matters of social justice is deeply rooted in the tradition (more than 600 biblical texts could be cited!). Anyone who is committed to the Bible will be truly concerned about social justice and, in every age, will seek to address these issues anew with *communities* of faith in very public ways. To be concerned about social justice in this way is then, basically, a conservative agenda. It could be said that anyone who does not attend carefully and explicitly and publicly to issues of social justice in our life together betrays the cause of conservatism. Anyone who is concerned about the tradition will be concerned to address these concerns ever anew into the life of the people of God.

Sources of Prophetic Concern for Social Justice

Within that inherited tradition, what more particularly are the sources of this prophetic concern for social justice? We might speak of that concern as rooted in both gospel and law. First of all, *the gospel*.

The Gospel

Justice in the Old Testament has primary reference to what God has done and continues to do. Most basically, justice has reference to God's deliverance of Israel when they were enslaved in Egypt. The Israelites were the helpless victims of exploitation and abuse at the hands of the most powerful nation of that age. God did not command Moses: Go and tell them that their sins are forgiven. God said: Get them out of there! God liberated them from Egyptian cruelty and it is this gospel action of God that is to ground and shape Israel's own action on behalf of those comparably abused and marginalized. Notice how Deut 10:17–19 moves from God's action to Israel's action: "For the LORD your God is God of gods and Lord of lords . . . who executes justice for the orphan and the widow, and who loves the strangers, providing them with food and clothing. You shall also love the stranger, for you were strangers in the land of Egypt." It is often noted that this kind of formulation can be encapsulated in the phrase "imitation of God."

The book of Exodus in turn roots this divine deliverance even more deeply in the tradition, namely, "the covenant with Abraham, Isaac, and Jacob" (Exod 2:24). "Covenant" in this context is to be equated with promise, an obligation that God takes upon the divine self. The Israelites "groaned under their slavery, and cried out. Out of slavery their cry for help rose up to God" (Exod 2:23; cf. Judg 2:18). And God "heard" and "remembered his covenant" and "looked upon" them and "knew" what they were going through (Exod 2:24–25). The "covenant" or promise that God "remembers" is worded in this way in Exod 6:6: "I am the LORD, and I will free you from the burdens of the Egyptians and deliver you from slavery to them. I will redeem you." Importantly, what God will do on behalf of an abused and oppressed people is made a matter of divine promise. God liberated the Israelites from socio-political bondage because God had *promised* to do so. (See the divine promises to do so throughout Genesis, e.g., 15:12–16; 28:15; 17:6–8; 46:3–4; see also Deut 7:8.)

This *explicit link between divine promise and social justice* should not be lost on modern readers. That which grounded the prophets' concern for the less fortunate among them was not general good sense, or wise social planning, or family values, important as such matters may be. Caring for needy ones is a *religious* matter grounded in a *theological* claim about God, namely, that God keeps promises. God's deliverance of Israel from abuse in Egypt is believed to be the fulfillment of such a promise.

That this divine action is called "salvation" in Exod 15:2 should expand our understanding of what salvation is all about; salvation in the Old Testament is always understood in a full-bodied sense, and in a given context that may include a socio-political dimension.[2] What might it mean theologically that the language of salvation is associated with the *divine practice of social justice*? Might the *ongoing* practice of social justice be salvific in some basic sense? God's concern about matters of social justice was believed to be so pervasive that it was built into the very heart of the covenantal promises. And God will be faithful to such promises. In some basic sense, helping the poor is a saving act. This activity is a means whereby God's work of *salvation* is extended to the larger community. And so, for Israel not to extend that saving activity of God to those who were poor and disadvantaged among them was to violate their own history.

So, helping the less fortunate can never be simply a social or political activity; it is also a religious activity in which God has chosen to become involved. What this kind of reflection may help us see is that justice is *not* an end in itself. *Justice is in the service of salvation*, in the service of salvation in a full-bodied sense for everyone in the community.

The Law

The prophets also drew upon *the law*. For Israel, the law is understood to be a gracious gift of God, for the law's most basic concern is the life, health, and flourishing of individuals and communities. A key text, often neglected, that gathers some of these themes is Deut 15:7–11:

> If there is among you anyone in need, a member of your community in any of your towns within the land that the LORD your

God is giving you, do not be hard-hearted or tight-fisted toward your needy neighbor. You should rather open your hand, willingly lending enough to meet the need, whatever it may be. Be careful that you do not entertain a mean thought, thinking, "The seventh year, the year of remission is near [see vv. 1–6]," and therefore view your needy neighbor with hostility and give nothing; your neighbor might cry to the Lord against you, and you would incur guilt. Give liberally and be ungrudging when you do so, for on this account the Lord your God will bless you in all your work, and in all that you undertake. Since there will never cease to be some in need on the earth, I therefore command you, "Open your hand to the poor and needy neighbor in your land."[3]

Pentateuchal law is filled with such social justice concerns and, as far as I can discern, only three law texts are present in the Revised Common Lectionary (the Ten Commandments and the two love commandments). This absence of social justice texts in the law to which congregations are regularly exposed is a public witness against the church for its inattention to such matters. In any case, these laws are picked up by the prophets and used to indict people for neglecting their vocational responsibilities toward the less fortunate.

Let the concern of Isa 3:14–15 with respect to the point of Deut 24:19–22 regarding the leaving of some of the crop behind for the poor to gather illustrate the issue: "The Lord enters into judgment with the elders and princes of his people. It is you who have devoured the vineyard; the spoil of the poor is in your houses. What do you mean by crushing my people, by grinding the face of the poor? says the Lord GOD of hosts." Note the detail of Isa 3:18–24, a list of the contents of the closet of an affluent individual. This list needs to be more inclusive in today's terms, but the concern might be gathered in terms of a question such as this: how many pairs of shoes do you have? I will give you a moment to count.

What are the primary factors that led to the formulation of all these laws that are concerned about matters of social justice? Two key factors ground these legal and prophetic concerns.

1. The *creational concerns* of God for life, health, and the well-being, not only of individuals, but of the entire community. Deuteronomy 5:33 is a good example of such concerns: "Do as the Lord your God has commanded you . . . so that you may live, that it may go well with you, and that you may live long on the land." And so it is that matters of food

Interpreting the Prophets and Issues of Social Justice

and clothing, shelter and health, and other such daily needs, preoccupy Israel's laws. Recall that before sin entered the world, there were laws, and these laws were understood in vocational terms—be fruitful, multiply, fill the earth, have dominion, subdue the earth. These commands were designed to shape the vocation of human beings in the world. The laws of Moses are a further particularization of these creational laws for the sake of Israel's vocation. The laws regarding the less fortunate have the fundamental purpose of defining a vocation, a particularizing of what love of neighbor entails.

2. The very *nature of God*. God was compassionate, just, gracious (see Exod 22:27). God was one who did not remain aloof from the sufferings of people, but who entered into the plight of their lives. As God had acted, so were the people to act. Because such divine action on behalf of the less fortunate was so comprehensive, no law could finally encompass what it meant to be a neighbor, so God's people were always to be ready to go beyond the law, seeking to discern ever new situations in which care for the less fortunate might be exercised.

Again, for Israel, caring for these needy ones is a *religious* matter; or in other terms, social legislation has to do with Israel's relationship with God. The authority behind Israel's social legislation is the authority of God who gave the laws. We who live in more modern cultures can so easily escape from the force of such social legislation because—we often think—it is generated by legislators, the judiciary, and social agencies of various kinds, and God is not explicitly identified with their authors. Somehow we need to help people make the connection between our social policies and practices and the work of God, who works through agents to develop them. We need to help shape such policies and practices so that they conform to *God's* concern for the needy. And we are called to be watchdogs over that legislative/judicial process because the human agents in and through which God has chosen to work can make mistakes, some of them huge. We need to recover the sense of a community that seeks the public good of all.

Exodus 22:21–27 sets the agenda for the people of God in an especially sharp way. Severe judgment is set out for the people of God, should they move from being victims to becoming the victimizers. Note that these words are directed to the people of God who have just experienced the divine salvation at the Red Sea. Oppression of the poor is believed to be so heinous a crime that it carries the death penalty; it is a capital offense. Note also the intensely personal response of God; no cut-and-dried legal provision here. God lifts up the high importance of how the people of God treat the poor and disadvantaged. The language is not set in terms of what the courts will do, but what God will do. Courts will, of course, be agents of God, but the intensely personal way in which God becomes engaged in the formulation should set us back on our heels: If you abuse the widow and the orphan, God says, "I will kill you."

Why don't we pay more attention to texts such as these? Because they are uncomfortable? Because our priorities lie elsewhere? Because we have decided that other texts are more important than these? Because we back away from the note about God killing? Notably, this sharp response of God is directed not to matters of idolatry or worship or the spiritual life, but rather it focuses on the social and economic sphere, particularly the lending of money. Perhaps that is why a text such as this is so neglected.

In sum, the law is understood to be a gracious gift of God, whose basic concern was the life, health, and flourishing of individuals and communities. And we, like the prophets, are called to tend carefully to that law.

This quotation from Abraham Heschel's book, *The Prophets*, helps capture this strong sense of urgency with respect to such matters: "Our sense of injustice is a poor analogy to God's sense of injustice. The exploitation of the poor is to us a misdemeanor; to God, it is a disaster. Our reaction is disapproval; God's reaction is something no language can convey. Is it a sign of cruelty that God's anger is aroused when the *rights* of the poor are violated, when widows and orphans are abused?"[4]

Of what rights does Heschel speak? Rights that are related to fundamental everyday needs, such as the right to food, clothing, housing, fair wages, bribery-free trials, proper weights and measures, and care in matters of health. And to hit a little closer to home, perhaps: the right to be protected from the insatiable appetites of the affluent, who gobble everything in sight for themselves and store it in their pantries and bank accounts. The prophets become a voice—indeed the voice of God—for those whose rights are being neglected or violated. When justice is done, those rights are upheld in the community or they are restored.

While justice is the responsibility of every citizen, the prophets call leaders especially to account with respect to their pursuit of justice.

Interpreting the Prophets and Issues of Social Justice

Ezekiel 34:1–4 captures the point well: "Ah, you shepherds of Israel who have been feeding yourselves! Should not shepherds feed the sheep? You eat the fat, you clothe yourselves with the wool, you slaughter the fatlings; but you do not feed the sheep. You have not strengthened the weak, you have not healed the sick, you have not bound up the injured, you have not brought back the strayed, you have not sought the lost, but with force and harshness you have ruled them."

In the same train of thought, the prophets tend not to speak in generalities, such as "you have sinned" or "you have not loved your neighbor." They do not lay out a specific social or political agenda, but they do not hesitate to name the social sins. Perhaps they do so because to remain at the level of generality would allow for the possibility of escape from the charges being brought. If the prophetic word were only "You have sinned," then four factors could kick in: (1) We could all too easily pick and choose our sins, and you can be sure we would conveniently forget a few of them. (2) We need to hear these particulars, because we may not even realize some of our sins or the evils of our institutions. (3) The naming of the sin enables us to see more clearly what the particular will of God actually is for daily life. (4) In being so particular about things, the needs of real people can often be identified, and not just some general social concern.

Uncomfortable Dimensions

Moving toward a conclusion, I draw out three uncomfortable—indeed offensive—dimensions of these texts.

God Takes Sides

We often don't realize as clearly as we should that, in freeing the Israelites from Egyptian abuse, God took sides. God took the side of the exploited Israelites and acted sharply against the Egyptian oppressors. Now that is certainly an offensive word to many people. But there it is, at the heart of the Old Testament message: God takes sides.

Let me say several things that may help clarify that point. Certainly God loves all people and is concerned for the life and health of every person. That is clear. But, at the same time, it is important to say that God is more concerned about some people than others. Why? Because they need more help; they need more attention if they are to be brought up to the level of well-being that God wants for all people. In this sense, they do get from God a kind of preferential treatment. Think for a minute, if you as a parent were to rush your sick or injured child to the emergency room at the hospital, wouldn't you be rightfully ticked if the nurses and doctors paid just as much attention to you as they did to your child?

The strong and the affluent do not need the same level of help as do many of our brothers and sisters all over the world—and in our own backyard. I am bothered that we so often begrudge God's generosity at this point. We who have reaped the bounty of God's goodness in so many ways complain that God chooses to tend in a special way to those who are less fortunate than we are. Remember the question that ends Jesus' parable of the laborers in the vineyard (Matt 20:1–16) when those who had worked all day started complaining about receiving the same salary as those who were hired late in the day? "Am I not allowed to do what I choose with what belongs to me? Or, are you envious because I am generous?"

The Critique of Affluence

While wealth as such is apparently not condemned, the wealthy often are, because wealth is so easily, indeed is almost always gained on the back of the underprivileged and misused once it has been procured. Listen to Mic 6:12 without qualification: "Your wealthy are full of violence." Wealth is so dangerous for one's religious health, and we are seldom, if ever, as generous as we think we are. Martin Luther has some striking things to say about wealth in view of his time and place (and note the contemporary parallels!): "Foreign trade brings from Calcutta and India and such places wares like costly silks, articles of gold, and spices—which minister only to ostentation but serve no useful purpose, and which drain away the money from land and people; this would not be permitted if we had proper government and princes." Or, "It is not fitting that one man should live in idleness on another's labor, or be rich and live comfortably at the cost of another's discomfort, according to the present perverted custom."[5]

At the same time, the prophets saw no special virtue in the poor as such or in being poor. Amos seems to have been a successful animal dealer; Isaiah belonged to the upper class. But there was a kind and degree of wealth that the prophets held to be incompatible with justice. Let me paraphrase the language of James Mays.[6] If the acquisition of wealth and possessions costs the economic freedom and welfare of others, the prophets called it violence and oppression. If it fostered conspicuous consumption at the level of luxury that was enjoyed in heedless or minimal concern for the needs of others, it was wrong. If it set the values of profit above that of personal relationships, it was iniquitous. If wealth became the dominant motivation of those responsible for social well being, it was sin.

Social Justice and Worship

Finally, and most uncomfortably for me, *social justice is closely related to the practice of worship*. Another offensive dimension of this prophetic link is presented: Unless you practice justice on behalf of the less fortunate, your worship is, well, wasted. Hear several verses from Amos 5:21–24, with God as speaker: "I hate, I despise your festivals, and I take no delight in your solemn assemblies." For God to hate something is for God to focus the divine energies against something. Another possible translation of "despise" could be: "I consider them trash." And the more literal sense of "take no delight" is "I will not smell," or in our idiom, "I will hold my nose at all your worship services."

God continues in Amos 5:22: "Even though you offer me your burnt offerings and grain offerings and the offerings of your fatted animals, I will not look upon them." You could read this in terms of what you put in the collection plate, but it is probably more drastic than that, given the use of sacrifices as a means in and through which God bestowed forgiveness on the worshipers. The contemporary force of this text would be something like this:"Even though you properly celebrate the Lord's Supper, I will no longer consider it a means of grace for you. " And when the text says that God will no longer look upon these sacrifices, it means that God will not only hold his nose, God will close his eyes. God continues: "Take away from me the noise of your songs; I will not listen to the melody of your harps" (Amos 5:23). Read: "Your singing of hymns, the finest of your pipe organ music, and even the best choirs singing Bach—I will not listen to them." So God has placed his hands over the divine ears, too (see also Isa 1:11–15; 58:1–9; Mic 6:6–8; Jer 6:20; Hos 6:6).

The prophets manage to indict every form of worship imaginable. They condemn not only sacrifices, but hymns, musical accompaniment, and even prayers. It is important to note that Israel's worship in these texts is not being condemned because it is idolatrous (at other times and places, certainly), nor was it rejected because the people were being insincere. The problem was a disjunction between their worship and their treatment of the less fortunate. If there is no social justice, there is no acceptable worship to God. God will not tolerate comfortable worship and social and political isolation. God will not tolerate a full church and a vacuum of justice. If you don't take care of the less fortunate, God does not want your praises and prayers. There is no form of worship, however devout or solemn or rightly observed or full of praise and prayer, that is invulnerable to the judgment of God.

Worship will be evaluated at least as much by what happens outside the sanctuary as by what happens within. If worship fosters a disunity of faith and responsibilities toward the neighbor or considers that relationship immaterial, it deserves the prophetic critique. Whatever strategy we do pursue, we will be judged by this criterion: How well are the less fortunate members of your society being cared for? And what about the children?

Conclusion

The prophets understood that the future of Israel's society was deeply dependent upon how the people, both individually and corporately, tended to the care for the less fortunate. Israel's lack of such a concern was among the major factors that led to its destruction. And God was believed to be involved in that judgment.[7] Israel's only hope, finally, was a hope in God for the other side of disaster, that God would pick those who survived up off the rocks below the falls and send them on their way down the river once again.

A prophetic question for today is this: Where are we in the river of life? Are we being sucked into the pull of the falls and an inevitable and terrifying trip over the brink? What might the global economic crisis have to say about ways we treat our neighbors, not least the less fortunate?

Interpreting the Prophets and Issues of Social Justice

What of the increasing gap between the more fortunate and less fortunate among us, or our deep mistreatment and neglect of the needy, including millions of children living in poverty and without adequate health care. While no date soon is likely to trigger the end of the world, we may not have much longer before we experience the end of our world. Is it already too late? We must work as if it were not too late. And so the word of the prophets is: Repent, and let that repentance give a certain shape to life, that is, a concerted individual and corporate effort on behalf of the less fortunate among us. Who will speak a prophetic word for God today regarding the deep and pervading crises regarding the needy in our own culture? Who will listen?

Endnotes

1. This essay is cast in more popular terms in view of the audience to which it was originally directed. For more scholarly references and earlier considerations, see the Bibliography and Fretheim, "The Prophets and Social Justice," 159–68.

2. For an earlier reflection on salvation in the Old Testament with related references, see Fretheim, "Salvation in the Bible vs. Salvation in the Church," 363–72.

3. For several other key texts, see Exod 22:21–27; Lev 19:9–10, 18, 34 [note the identification of the 'neighbor'!]; Deut 10:17–19; 16:18–20; 24:19–22; 25:13–16.

4. Heschel, *The Prophets*, 285.

5. Martin Luther, "On Trade and Usury," *Luther's Works*, vol. 45, 245–46, 261; see also his explanation of the seventh commandment in the Large Catechism.

6. Mays, "Justice in the Prophets," 154.

7. For detail on this point, see Fretheim, *God and World in the Old Testament*, 157–65.

6

The Bible and American Environmental Practice: An Ancient Code Addresses a Current Crisis[1]

SANDRA RICHTER

Introduction

Although environmental ethics and creation care have received increased attention from the academic community of faith in recent years,[2] most lay people are still asking the question: "Is Environmentalism a Christian value... does the Bible actually speak to this topic?" This essay attempts to address these questions with an all-too-brief survey of the larger biblical theological perspective of humanity as God's steward of creation, and a focused investigation of the book of Deuteronomy. Through Deuteronomy's ancient code of faith and praxis, we modern heirs of Scripture catch a glimpse of God's expectations of the redeemed community as regards his good gifts of land, life, and living things.

In the Beginning

In Genesis 1 God reveals his plan for his creation. The interdependence of the cosmos is laid out within the literary framework of a perfect "week." On the seventh day, God is enthroned above his creation, and he rests. This communicates not only his complete satisfaction with what has gone before, but also that the perfect balance of God's ideal plan is dependent on the sovereignty of the Creator. Of great significance is the penultimate climax of the piece. On the *sixth* day, a steward is enthroned, under the Creator but over the creation: "Then God said, 'Let us make ʾādām in our image, according to our likeness; and let them rule . . .'" (Gen 1:26). Whereas the outworking of God's ideal design is dependent on the sovereignty of the Creator, so too, it is the privilege and responsibility of the Creator's stewards to facilitate this ideal plan by means of living their lives as a reflection of God's image. This was God's perfect plan.

The role of the human stewards within the created order is specified in Genesis 2: "Then Yahweh Elohim took the human and put him into the garden of Eden to tend it (*lĕʿobdāh*) and guard it (*lĕšomrāh*) (Gen 2:15). Thus, the larger message of these accounts is clear: the garden *belongs* to Yahweh, but ʾādām has been given the privilege to rule and the responsibility to care for this garden under the sovereignty of their divine lord. And so God's ideal is set in motion—a world in which ʾādām would succeed in constructing the human civilization by directing and harnessing the abundant resources of the garden under the wise direction of the Creator. Here there would always be enough, progress would not necessitate pollution, expansion would not demand extinction. The privilege of the strong would not require the deprivation of the weak. And humanity would succeed in these goals because of the guiding wisdom of God.

But as we all know, humanity rejected this perfect plan and chose autonomy instead. And because of the authority of their God-given position within the created order, humanity's choice cast the entire cosmos into disarray. As Romans 8 details, because of ʾādām, even "the creation was subjected to futility" and enslaved "to corruption" (Rom 8:20–21). The Christian community readily recognizes the results of ʾādām's choice in the arena of human relationships: poverty, greed, violence, etc. Moreover, we recognize and embrace the role of the redeemed community to stand in opposition to these societal norms. But what of the impact of humanity's rebellion on the garden? And how might the reality of redemption in our lives redirect our attitude toward the same?

Israel stands as the first model of God's relationship with a redeemed and landed citizenry in a fallen world. The document that articulates the national constitution of that citizenry is the book of Deuteronomy.[3] In this book, whose legal traditions reach back into the shadows of Israel's earliest settlement, there is a continuing chorus: if the people will remember the law of God, and obey it, they will live and prosper; but if they forget, and disobey, they will not prosper. To obey is life; to disobey death. "So choose life in order that you may live, you and your descendants!" (Deut 30:19). The incarnation of this blessing of life for Israel is the land—the land "flowing with milk and honey" (Deut 4:40; 6:3; 11:9; 26:9, 15; 27:3; 31:20).[4]

The Land and Its Produce

Throughout the book of Deuteronomy Israel is reminded that the land of Canaan is a gift. It is the land which Yahweh "swore to Abraham, Isaac, and Jacob, to them and to their descendants after them" (Deut 1:8). In the language of ancient international diplomacy, the land of Canaan is a land grant. But land grants could be recalled.[5] Thus, although the offspring of Abraham are invited to abide upon the land with joy and productivity, Deuteronomy is eminently clear that the land will never be truly theirs. Rather, as the curse sections of Deuteronomy 28 and the transitional materials of chapters 29–34 detail, Yahweh retains the right to reclaim his land; to uproot his people "from their land in anger and fury and in great wrath, and to cast them into another land as it is this day" (Deut 29:28). As it was in the garden, so it is in the land of Israel—God owns the land, and it is humanity's privilege to live upon it. Thus, both the land and its produce, and even its animal inhabitants do not actually belong to Israel, but to their suzerain lord, Yahweh.

This reality is most evident in the laws of the tithe, the first fruits, and the firstborn. In Israel's world, a populace was expected to pay a percentage of their produce to the central government and a vassal kingdom was expected to pay an annual percentage of the gross national product to its overlord. In Israel's pastoral and agricultural world this meant a percentage of their crops and flocks belonged to higher authorities. Thus, in Israel's theocratic government, Yahweh commands:

> You shall surely tithe all the produce of your seed, that which comes forth from the field year by year. And you shall eat in the presence of Yahweh your God, in the place where he chooses to place his name[6]—the tithe of your grain, your new wine, your oil, and the firstborn of your herd and flock[7]—in order that you may learn to fear Yahweh your God all your life. (Deut 14:22–23)

> You shall set aside each of the firstborn males that are born of your herd and your flock for Yahweh your God.[8] You shall not work with the firstborn of your herd, nor shear the firstborn of your flock. Rather, you and your household shall eat it year by year in the presence of Yahweh your God in the place that Yahweh chooses. (Deut 15:19–20)[9]

> This will be the priests' due from the people: when anyone sacrifices an ox or a sheep, they must give the priest the shoulder, the two cheeks, and the stomach. You shall also give him the first fruits of your grain, your new wine, and your oil, and the first fleece when you shear your sheep. (Deut 18:3–5)[10]

Patrick Miller observes that the cultures of Syria-Palestine commonly used the tithe as a "regular tax." But unlike surrounding practices, Miller points out that Deuteronomic law interprets the tithe as "a celebratory gift to God, implicitly serving as an expression of thanksgiving that was to be enjoyed and shared by the members of the family as an act of devotion at the central sanctuary if possible."[11] I concur that Deuteronomic law sees the practice of the tithe as celebratory, but I also concur that here we find the divinely-authorized taxation system. The ultimate mark that the people of Israel are only tenants on Yahweh's land is that the produce of that land belongs to their overlord. This is demonstrated by the fact that Israel is commanded to make regular offerings of the land's produce to the divine king throughout the year. In fact, the old legal core of Deuteronomy is introduced and concluded by imperatives regarding Israel's tenant status. Deut 12:10–12 opens the law code with the following:

> When you cross the Jordan and live in the land which Yahweh your God is giving you to inherit, . . . then you will bring to the place in which Yahweh your God will choose to place his name,[12] all that I am commanding you: your burnt offerings, and your sacrifices, your tithes and the contribution of your hand, and the choicest votive offerings that you vow to Yahweh. And you shall rejoice in the presence of Yahweh your God.

The great creedal pronouncement of Deuteronomy 26 closes the law code with a reminder of the same:

> When you have entered the land which Yahweh your God is giving you as an inheritance, . . . you shall take from the first of all the produce of the ground which you shall bring in from your

land that Yahweh your God is giving you, and you shall put it in a basket and go to the place where Yahweh your God chooses to place his name.[13] And you will go to the priest who is in office at that time, and say to him, "I declare this day to Yahweh your God that I have entered the land which Yahweh swore to our fathers to give us." Then the priest shall take the basket from your hand and set it down before the altar of Yahweh your God. And you shall testify before Yahweh your God, . . . (Yahweh) brought us to this place, and gave us this land, a land flowing with milk and honey. Therefore, I have now brought the first of the produce of the land which you have given me, oh Yahweh."

Deuteronomy makes it crystal clear that this good land and its produce belong to Yahweh and the tribes of Israel are only his tenants, appointed to their *naḥalâ* according to his good pleasure.[14]

The Produce and the Poor

Operating under the assumption that the produce of the land ultimately belongs to Yahweh, Deuteronomic law dictates that the Israelites not exhaust the produce of the land in their quest for personal or national economic security. Thus, although the cereal crops of wheat and barley were the mainstays of the community throughout Israel's tenure upon the land—essential for the survival of man and beast, and holding pride of place in Deuteronomy's description of the "good land" promised in Deut 8:7–10,[15] Yahweh commands that Israel refrain from fully harvesting these dietary anchors. Rather, he commands that they reserve a portion of the cereal harvest for the marginalized among them: "When you reap your harvest in your field and have forgotten a sheaf[16] in the field, do not go back to get it; let it be for the immigrant, for the orphan, and for the widow, in order that Yahweh your God may bless you in all the work of your hands" (Deut 24:19; cf. Lev 19:9–10; 23:22). The olive was of comparable importance to ancient Israel's economy. Its oil was not only critical to domestic survival, but it had long served Canaan as a significant export, a "cash crop" of sorts (cf. 1 Sam 8:14; 1 Kgs 5:11[25]; Hos 12:12; 1 Chr 27:28). As Lawrence Stager summarizes: "The production of olive oil was a major industry, accounting for much of the economic prosperity of the region. Surplus oil was exported to Egypt, Phoenicia, and perhaps even to Greece."[17] Yet Deuteronomy 24 commands: "When you beat your olive tree, do not go over the boughs again; let it (the unharvested portion) be for the immigrant, the orphan, and the widow" (Deut 24:20).

Likewise, the vineyards of ancient Canaan were very significant to the domestic and commercial venues of Israel's economy. Indeed, Canaan was famous for its wine, and viticulture thrived in this region as far back as the Early Bronze Age.[18] In fact, Thutmose III's famous Karnak Botanical Garden depicts grapevines imported from Canaan to Egypt.[19] Yet Deuteronomy commands that the gleanings of the vineyard be left for the poor. Leviticus particularizes this command stating that the smaller clusters (Hebrew *peret*) be left as well:[20] "When you gather the grapes of your vineyard, do not glean afterwards; let it (the unharvested portion) be for the immigrant, the orphan, and the widow. And remember that you were a slave in the land of Egypt; therefore I am commanding you to do this thing" (Deut 24:20-22; cf. Lev 19:9-10; 23:22). Thus, despite the critical role that grain, olives, and grapes played in the economy of Iron Age Israel, and despite the subsistence struggles of the typical "small holder" family farm,[21] God's command was that the produce of the land be shared. In Israel, the drive for economic security and surplus must always be tempered by God's command for charity, and not even economic viability served as an acceptable rationale for greed.

The Land and Agriculture

In concert with Israel's understanding that it was Yahweh who actually owned the land of Canaan, a number of laws address the longevity of the land's fertility. The core of these laws is the Sabbath rest—a command to humanity to regularly cease production so that the land might be allowed an opportunity to replenish itself.[22] Thus, in Exod 23:10-12 we read: "You shall sow your land for six years and gather in its yield, but the seventh year you shall let it rest and lie fallow, so that the needy of your people may eat; and whatever they leave the wild animal may eat. You are to do the same with your vineyard and your olive grove. Six days you shall do your work, but on the seventh you shall rest; in order that your ox and your ass may rest, and the son of your female servant and the immigrant may be refreshed." Leviticus 25:4-7 reiterates and particularizes this law:

> But during the seventh year the land shall have a sabbath rest, a sabbath belonging to Yahweh; you shall not sow your field nor

> prune your vineyard. Your harvest's after growth you shall not reap and the grapes of your untrimmed vines you shall not gather . . . Rather the sabbath (growth) of the land shall be your food: belonging to you, your male servant, your female servant, your hired man, your temporary resident, and the immigrants among you. Even your domesticated beast and the wild animal that is in your land shall have all its crops to eat. (Lev 25:4–7)

The sort of fallowing described here not only aided in the recovery of fertility, it "broke the natural cycle of noxious plant pests and diseases."[23] Moreover, fields were rotated such that livestock (accompanied by their restorative nitrogen and phosphorous-rich manure) were regularly grazed upon the fallow fields.[24] Crop rotation would be the third weapon in the arsenal of the ancient farmer as regards sustainable soil fertility. As any organic farmer would tell us, and the history of urbanization in Mesopotamia dramatically illustrates,[25] the continuous cultivation of a single crop in the same field depletes the soil of nutrients and encourages the proliferation of pests and diseases specific to that particular crop.[26] In contrast, crop rotation, fallowing, and the grazing of livestock enhances the microbiology of the soil, and the rotation of certain crops—such as legumes—actually restores soil nitrogen content.[27] Moreover, as these laws reiterate the consequence of the gleaning laws (that Yahweh intended for a portion of his harvest to remain in the field for the voiceless among his creatures), this system also guaranteed something agriculturalists speak of as "crop residue." Crop residue is that which remains in the field after the harvest is complete and thereby provides essential humus to the soil.[28]

Thus, we see that Israel's Sabbath law served to protect the long-term fecundity of the land. Then as now, such farming practices limited short-term yield.[29] But they helped to ensure long-term productivity. And as current agricultural science is demonstrating, failure to provide for long-term soil fertility by allowing the soil to rejuvenate itself (e.g., relying wholly on nonorganic, chemical fertilizers)[30] leads to decreased fertility, and eventually sterility. It also leads to a devastating effect for those living in poverty.[31] Perhaps most significant is that in Israel's fallow law we find a critical ideological principle: In Israel, it was not acceptable to take from the land everything that a populace *could*. Rather, God's people were commanded to operate with the long-term well-being of the land as their ultimate goal. They were instructed to leave enough so that the land might be able to replenish itself for future harvests and future generations—even though such methods would cut into short-term yield. Why? In Leviticus, "because I am Yahweh says your God" (Lev 25:17), and "the land is mine" (Lev 25:23; cf. Lev 26:34–35, 43). In Deuteronomy, so that "you shall prolong your days in the land" (Deut 4:40). In other words, because this is Yahweh's land and Yahweh's produce and Yahweh intends that his land be fruitful for the next generation of tenants.[32] In sum, the *politeia* of ancient Israel taught that economic growth was not a viable excuse for the abuse of the land, and true economic well-being would come only from careful stewardship of the same.

The Land and Warfare

Even in the midst of the crisis of warfare, we find that God's people are commanded to treat creation with care: "When you besiege a city for many days, to make war against it in order to capture it, you shall not destroy its trees by swinging an axe against them. Indeed you may eat from them, but you shall not cut (them) down. For is the tree of the field a man that it should be besieged by you? Only a tree that you know does not produce food may you destroy and cut down, and you may build your siegeworks against the city with which you are at war until it falls" (Deut 20:19).

Ancient Israel was blessed with an array of "food-bearing trees." Borowski lists the fig, olive, date, sycamore (that would be the fig-bearing *Ficus sycamorus*, not the enormous nonfruit-bearing sycamore of North America), apricot, carob, almond, pistachio, and walnut as indigenous to Canaan, as well as several that cannot be identified with certainty by means of their biblical appellatives.[33] All of these trees faced similar developmental realities—if maintained they would produce for generations, but full maturity preceded production (cf. Deut 20:6). Regarding the all-important olive tree, Stager reports that it takes five or six years for the trees to *begin* to flower, and as many as twenty years to reach full maturity. Even then, they bear fruit only every other year. "It is commonly said that one plants an olive yard not for one's self but for one's grandchildren."[34] Similarly, Steven Cole reports that the female date palm—a treasured source of preservable, calorie-rich fruit—"may take as long as twenty years before they produce their first fruit."[35] The crops born of these trees were a mainstay of the Iron II Israelite economy and diet.[36] And, of course, the great dream of the Israelite was a level of national security and prosperity in which every citizen might "live in safety, every man under his vine and his fig tree, from Dan even to Beersheba" (1 Kgs 4:25).

In light of the long-term value of food-bearing trees, it is no surprise that a standard aspect of the Assyrian war machine involved the decimation of a besieged enemy's vineyards and orchards. The goal was to cripple that city for decades beyond the actual assault, be that assault successful or not. As Jeremy Smoak and Jacob Wright ably illustrate, this strategy (and the threat of this strategy) were regularly communicated by the Assyrians through text and image.[37] Hence, Sargon II boasts regarding his assault on the store-city of Ursal: "I entered triumphantly . . . Into his pleasant gardens, the adornments of his city which were overflowing with fruit and wine . . . came tumbling down . . . His great trees, the adornment of his palace, I cut down like millet . . . The trunks of all those trees which I had cut down I gathered together, heaped them in a pile and burned them with fire."[38] In the Suhu annals of Shalmaneser III, the king declares, "We will go and attack the houses of the land of Suhu; we will seize his cities . . . we will cut down their fruit trees."[39] Cole offers an encyclopedic collection of these texts and images, showing that this particular military strategy was a staple of Assyrian war craft.[40] Michael Hasel demonstrates that this siege tactic was not new with the Assyrians, but may be tracked into the second millennia among the Babylonians, Assyrians, Hittites, and, especially, the Egyptians. His thesis, in fact, is that whereas the Assyrians used this tactic to cripple a community's agricultural support system *after* a siege, the only group to use this strategy during or *before* the successful capture of a city (for the express purpose of building seigeworks as is the stated purpose in Deut 20:19) is the New Kingdom Egyptians. Most specifically, Thutmose III at Megiddo.[41] In sum, it is apparent that the systematic annihilation of orchards was a staple of ANE warfare well before the time of Israel's settlement in the land. What then might be the rationale for Deuteronomy's law? To quote Hasel, Israel is forbidden from such retaliatory tactics because "it would not be in Israel's interest to destroy the very resources that would later sustain them."[42] Hence, it would seem that in Israelite law, even national security did not justify the abuse of the land or the magnificent flora residing upon it. Rather, in Israel the fact that it took a generation for an olive orchard to come to full fruition deserved deference, and human enterprise was not a worthy excuse for wiping out the future productivity of the land. I wonder what those stripping Canada of its boreal forests for catalog paper production (at a current rate of five acres a minute[43]), those creating lunar landscapes in eastern Kentucky by means of "mountain top removal" coal mining,[44] or those devouring 1.5 acres of rainforest a second (along with the 50,000 species a year that inhabit that acreage)[45] might say about God's law to Israel? I wonder what God might have to say to those of us who are growing rich from these endeavors?

The Creatures of the Land

And what do the Scriptures have to say regarding the creatures that inhabit the land with God's people? Throughout the Bible, we read that even in a fallen world, God rejoices in the beauty and balance of his creation. Moreover, God has designed the created order *so that* his wild creatures will have the food, water, and habitat they need to survive and prosper. It is Yahweh who "sent out the wild donkey free" and "gave to him the wilderness for a home" (Job 39:5–6). It is by his command that the eagle nests in the high country (Job 39:26–27). In the flood narrative, although God judges the world because of its corruption, he rescues animal-kind along with humankind, and his re-creational covenant is with "every living creature . . . the birds, the domestic animals, and every wild creature of the earth" (Gen 9:10–11). In the elegant verse of Ps 104 we hear the poetic celebration of the beauty and dignity of the wild animal and its habitat: "He is the one who sends forth the springs into the wadis; between the mountains they flow; giving drink to each of his wild creatures" (Ps 104:10–11).

In the Whirlwind Speeches of the book of Job, the Creator queries: Do *you* know the time the mountain goats give birth? Have *you* watched the calving of the deer? As any environmentalist would say that the single greatest cause of the extinction of animal species is the reckless destruction of their habitat—and in America we are presently devouring nearly 2 million acres a year for the noble quest of urban sprawl (and experiencing a related species extinction rate of as much as 1,000 times the historical loss ratio),[46] the fact that the wild animals' habitat was designed and given to them by God should give us pause.[47]

Returning to the book of Deuteronomy, what was God's specific command to Israel regarding the care of the wild creature? In the early stages of Israel's urbanization, we can safely assume that the impact of human development did not present a serious threat to the Levantine ecosystem. Yet in the *politeia* of Israel, Yahweh promulgates law that requires the long-term protection of the creatures who share the promised land with his people. Regarding wild animals, Deut 22:6–7 offers us a *pars pro toto*: "If you happen upon a bird's nest in front of you in the road, or in a tree, or upon the ground, with young ones or eggs, and the mother sitting upon the young or on the eggs, do not take the mother (who is sitting) upon the young. Rather, you will surely shoo the mother away, and the young you may take for yourself, in order that it may be well with you and that you may prolong your days."

Several have seen in this law the utilization of *analogia*: a vehicle of Wisdom literature that formulates a more abstract point by way of a practical example."[48] And many have specifically identified an analogy to Deut 20:19–20—the sparing of the fruit trees during siege warfare. The common idea between these texts? As McConville summarizes: "preserving the means of life."[49] Thus, to take both tree and fruit, mother and offspring, would result in the extermination of a particular species in a particular place. In fact, as the phrase "mother with her children" often appears in warfare contexts as an expression for wanton killing, Tigay and Christensen hypothesize that the language of this Deuteronomic law communicates the same—"total, cruel extermination" that would "mark one as ruthless."[50] Moreover, it is quite possible that seizing the mother bird *with* her young was an aspect of the iconography of royal prowess in Assyria. In one of the more obscure stone wall reliefs of Aššur-bani-pal, in which the king's return from the hunt is celebrated, this practice is depicted alongside the notorious royal slaughter of wild lions.[51]

But in Deuteronomy Israel is commanded to be different. In contrast to the practice of their neighbors, Israel is instructed in the wisdom of preserving the creatures with whom they shared the promised land. Indeed, Deuteronomy states that if Israel killed off the wild creatures without a thought as to the creatures' ability to replenish their populations, it would *not* "be well" with Israel in the land. I believe the same would apply to us.

As regards the treatment of the domestic animal, the Sabbath ordinance again applies.

> But the seventh day is a sabbath belonging to Yahweh your God; you shall not do any work, not you or your son or your daughter or your male servant or your female servant or your ox or your donkey or any of your domesticated beasts. . . . And remember that you were a slave in the land of Egypt, and that Yahweh your God brought you out of there with a mighty hand and with an outstretched arm, Therefore, Yahweh your God has commanded you to keep the day of the sabbath. (Deut 5:14–15)

Thus, according to the mandate of the covenant, and because of God's gift of redemption to his people, the Israelites were to honor *him* by allowing their livestock to rest.

As is true today, farm animals were maintained in Israel exclusively to facilitate the well-being of humanity. In Israel's case, to serve the people of Israel with their wool, milk, meat, and labor (and after the onset of Iron II, their eggs).[52] Yet these creatures were allotted a place in the Sabbath ordinance of God. Consider as well Deut 25:4 which commands that the Israelite not muzzle his ox while he drags the threshing sledge for his master. In the smallholder farms of the Central Hill Country, the cereal crop was absolutely crucial to the survival of the community.[53] And the Iron Age farmer relied heavily upon the labor of his beast for the long and arduous task of extracting the precious grain from the stalks in which it grew. Once cleaned and stored, this grain would serve as the primary food supply for man and beast. Moreover, in this subsistence economy, every kilo counted.

Baruch Rosen has done an arresting calculation of exactly how many calories were necessary to sustain the average Iron I Israelite village of one hundred souls. Operating off of data culled from the known sites, Rosen estimates that the typical village would experience an annual shortfall of 15,000,000 calories a year.[54] If his model is correct, anticipating that the average family included five people, this would mean an annual shortfall of sixty days of food per family. Rosen anticipates that the manner by which most villages accommodated for this shortfall was attempting to raise and store more grain and slaughtering additional animals from the flock. The point here is that the three to four kilos (5–7 lbs.) of grain that an ox might consume over the course of a day of threshing made a difference.[55] Yet God commands Israel to allow the beast who served them the opportunity to enjoy its life and work and to benefit from the fruit of its labors . . . even when that benefit and joy cut into the farmer's profits, or his essential food supply.

How might this ordinance speak to current practice on America's factory farms? Factory farming is the practice of raising livestock in confinement at high-stocking density, where the farm operates essentially as a factory whose end-product is protein units. Confined animals burn fewer calories, their excrement is mass-managed (or mismanaged as many argue),[56] and their fertility and gestation fully controlled. As regards America's most lucrative agricultural product, pigs, confinement has been distilled into an exact science: twenty 230-lb. animals per 7.5 foot-square pen,[57] housed upon metal-grated flooring, in climate controlled conditions, never actually exposed to the light of day. These animals are sustained in such crowded and filthy conditions that movement is difficult, natural behaviors impossible, and antibiotics are essential to the control of infection. Sows, typically a 500-lb. animal, are separately housed. They live out their lives in 7-foot-by-22-inch metal gestation crates from which they are never released, even in the process of giving birth. They are artificially inseminated to deliver an average of eight litters, litters inflated beyond their natural carrying capacity by fertility drugs. A staple of their diet is the rendered remains of their deceased pen-mates.[58] Surely if God is offended by boiling a kid in its mother's milk (Deut 14:21), we should be concerned that dead sows are routinely ground up and fed to their offspring.[59] But as the "New Agriculture" reports, all of these innovations make these production units (i.e., billions of animate creatures) easier to manage, maintain, medicate, and slaughter. And the rapidly escalating market for meat for human consumption, in the third world in particular, is voiced as the rationale for mass-confinement animal husbandry.[60] As Matthew Scully painfully illustrates in his 2002 exposé of the industry, *Dominion: The Power of Man, the Suffering of Animals, and the Call to Mercy*, the factory farm has not only taken the "live" out of livestock, but it has taken the "farmer" out of farming. And even the most casual perusal of the state of the American farm confirms this very fact. We have seen a revolution in our country in the past several decades regarding the production and consumption of meat; we eat more meat, more cheaply, than any other generation in history.[61] As a result, in our country, the abuses to which domesticated animals are routinely subjected are nearly too horrific to report. I find it difficult to believe that this is what Yahweh intended for the creatures he entrusted to ʾādām.

Consider as well the complex Levitical legal structures that accompany the slaughtering of animals. Israel was certainly allowed to slaughter and eat the animals they raised, but any domestic animal had to be taken before the priest first. According to Leviticus 17, this practice served in part to ensure that the animal's *nepeš* (life) had been considered.[62] In Israel, the life of the animal was not to be taken without thought or without mercy. Regarding the method of slaughter detailed in the Talmud, Milgrom states: "All of these [details] clearly demonstrate the perfection of a slaughtering technique whose purpose is to render the animal immediately unconscious with a minimum of suffering." Moreover, as regards the secular slaughterer, "by virtue of his training and piety, his soul shall never be torpefied by his incessant butchery but kept ever sensitive to the magnitude of the divine concession in allowing him to bring death to living things."[63] In Deuteronomy, even the wild gazelle must be slaughtered with due care (12:15, 22; 14:5; 15:22).[64]

Reflect upon these Israelite laws in comparison with the assembly line approach we employ in the raising, slaughtering, and mass-marketing of animal flesh in America. Few of us realize that animals used in agriculture have almost no legal protection. More than 95 percent of them—birds—aren't even included in the regulations implementing the federal Humane Methods of Slaughter Act, the law that requires an animal to be rendered insensible to pain before they are killed.[65] As regards the cattle industry, Scully reports that whereas in 1990 the typical American slaughter plant operated at fifty kills per hour, newer plants now run at 300 to 400 per hour. How does one go about slaughtering 400 800-lb. bovines in an hour? As Martin Fuentes, an IBP worker, told the *Washington Post*, "The line is never stopped simply because an animal is alive."[66] Ramon Moren—whose job is to cut off the hooves of strung-up cattle passing by at 309 an hour—reports that although the cattle are supposed to be dead when they reach him, often are not: "They blink. They make noises. The head moves, the eyes are open and still looking around. They die piece by piece."[67] In contrast, at every juncture, Israel was constrained to consider the *life* of the animal that served them and whom they consumed, by covenant law . . . even though such considerations were costly as regards time and resources.

Conclusions

In sum, the *politeia* of ancient Israel communicates that neither economic expansion, national security, nor even personal economic viability were legitimate justification for the abuse of the land, the abuse of the poor, or the abuse of the domestic or wild creature. Rather, all of these laws of land, tree, and creature communicate a similar theme: Israel was a tenant upon God's good land; a steward. The land, its produce, and its inhabitants belong to God, not humanity. And all members of Israel's society stood responsible before God regarding their care of his resources.

This brief survey also demonstrates that Israel's attitude toward the enduring fertility of their land, its wild residents, and the well-being of their livestock stood in some contrast to the practices of their time. Egypt and Mesopotamia were well known for their environmental terrorism in warfare. Assyrian iconography celebrates the wanton slaughter of the wild creature, and it is broadly believed that a contributing factor to the collapse of the Mesopotamian civilization was the agricultural sterility that resulted in part from the failure to fallow. According to my training, I should seek an explanation for Israel's distinctive mindset in the sociological realties of the evolution of their culture. Is Deuteronomy's concern for the long-term environmental impact of their civilization on the land the result of their uniquely challenging geographical setting, the psychological impact of their dependence on dry-farming as opposed to irrigation-based agriculture? Is it the outgrowth of their egalitarian societal structure, or a reaction against the practices of "the other"? Or might Israel's distinctive perspective be, perhaps, a reflection of the character of their God? A reflection that critiqued and censured their culture and their economy as much as it does ours?

Just like us, Israel struggled with the competing demands of a diverse society, insufficient yields, property loss, land tenure, poverty, and taxes. But underlying their response to these issues, at least in Deuteronomy, was one central tenet: this land, these creatures are not ours; they are on loan to us. We must manage them well so that each is preserved. And we must take God at his word that in response to our obedience, he himself will bring about the increase (Deut 30:9). Short-term, desperation management which exhausts current resources in answer to the cry of the urgent is not acceptable.

The Bible and American Environmental Practice

At the dawn of creation, ʾādām was appointed as the steward of the riches of creation. In our rebellion we rejected this calling. Yet throughout the great Story the message is reiterated—the land, its produce, and its creatures belong to God, not to us, and his expectation is that his people will behave accordingly. In the book of Deuteronomy we are offered a concrete illustration of the role of the redeemed community as regards creation care in the midst of this fallen order. Here the people of God are called to fulfill their role as steward by re-orienting their values to those of their heavenly sovereign, "to realize that everything about us, even the food we eat, should be governed by order, a respect for life, and a concern to represent Yahweh well before a watching world."[68] I believe the calling of this present community of faith is the same: to demonstrate with our *lives* "what the will of God is, that which is good and acceptable and perfect" (Rom 12:2). What is the will of God regarding creation? "Then Yahweh Elohim took the human and put him into the garden of Eden to tend it (*lěʿobdāh*) and protect it (*lěšomrāh*)" (Gen 2:15).

Endnotes

1. A version of this essay first appeared in Sandra Richter, "Environmental Law in Deuteronomy: One lens on a Biblical Theology of Creation Care," *Bulletin of Biblical Research* 2009, forthcoming. My thanks are due to a number of experts and practitioners who helped me navigate data outside the field of biblical studies: Dr. Ben Brammell of the Department of Biology at the University of Kentucky; Frank Allen Cross Jr., a second-generation row crop and small grain farmer in Madera County, California; Scot Hoeksema, a biochemical engineer and botanist, currently residing in Lexington, Kentucky; Ryan Strebeck of the Strebeck Family Ranch, a third-generation cattle rancher of the Curry and Roosevelt Counties in New Mexico and Elk City, Kansas; and Ann Bell Stone of Elmwood Stock Farm, a diversified agriculture farm in Georgetown, Kentucky.

2. The bibliography on this topic has become immense, but a few good points of entry include: Isaak, *The Old Testament in the Life of God's People*; the second volume of Abingdon Press's Studies in Christian Ethics and Economic Life; Derr, *Environmental Ethics and Christian Humanism*; *Ecotheology: The Journal of Religion, Nature and the Environment*; the Evangelical Environmental Network; Gottlieb, *A Greener Faith*; Moo, "Nature in the New Creation," 449–88; Davis, *Scripture, Culture, and Agriculture*. See as well calls from those who would not necessarily include themselves within the Christian community but recognize the Church as an important catalyst for change: Scully, *Dominion*; Wennberg, *God, Humans and Animals*, 289–95; Wilson, *The Creation*.

3. See McBride, "Polity of the Covenant People," 62–77.

4. See Forti, "Bee's Honey," 327–41. It had long been assumed that this "honey" is the sweet syrup ground from the pulp of grapes, dates, figs, and carobs. Tova Forti's compelling argument that Deuteronomy actually speaks of wild bee honey, has been

strengthened by the recent discovery of an industrial-sized apiary at Tel Rehov in an Iron Age IIA context (Mazar and Panitz-Cohen, "Honey and Bee-Keeping in the Bible and the Ancient Near East") 327–41.

5. See Weinfeld, "בְּרִית. berîth," *TDOT* 2:267; Beckman, *Hittite Diplomatic Texts*; Hess, "The Book of Joshua as a Land Grant," 493–506.

6. "To place one's name" is an ancient idiom which communicated that someone had inscribed their name and/or text on a monument, building, or votive offering and that item therefore belonged to the one named (Richter, *The Deuteronomistic History and the Name Theology*, 342–45).

7. Patrick D. Miller points out that "[t]he presentation of the firstborn may have served originally the same purposes as the first fruits of the harvest, that is, a dedication to the deity of the first of the flocks and herds as an acknowledgment of the rule and provision of the deity . . . " This system of offering and sacrifice served to acknowledge Israel's position as a tenant and subordinate in God's government, and as a means to address the needs of the landless among them (Deut 14:28–29; 26:12–15)" (Miller, *The Religion of Ancient Israel*, 120–21).

8. What makes the firstborn special? Ryan Strebeck of the Strebeck Family Ranch, a third-generation cattle rancher of the Curry and Roosevelt Counties in New Mexico and Elk City, Kans., states that for cattle, there are no obvious qualities that a firstborn calf might have that subsequent calves would not possess. "A significant observation here could have to do with the fragile nature of one's first birthing experience. Cows . . . often experience more trauma surrounding the first calving season. Miscarrying, or 'sloughing' a calf is more common for a heifer than a five-calf cow. Mindful of this, we could probably say that a firstborn calf is more prized because of the high risk of losing that first calf" (personal communication 8 Sept. 2008). Ann Bell Stone of Elmwood Stock Farm, a sixth-generation central Kentucky small family farmer, adds regarding their Suffolk/Dorset cross sheep herd, that the first birth is usually no different than later births, but it is the indicator of what sort of producer and mother a ewe will be (interview with author, 11 Sept. 2008).

9. The law of Exod 22:28 has changed here. Rather than the firstborn being sacrificed on the eighth day, now the sacrifice of the firstlings will occur once yearly in the context of a great feast at "the place" (McConville, *Deuteronomy*, 266; cf. Miller, *Religion of Ancient Israel*, 120). In addition, the firstborn is not to be worked or shorn, conditions that would have been impossible under the Exodus law. As the goal was for the ewes to birth twice per year, and always in the spring, and as traditionally the best meat is a weaned male, 2-5 months old, it is probable that the sacrifice at "the place" involved these male firstlings of the flock in the fall. The fact that the firstborn was reserved for special slaughter at the central cult site might explain the inordinately small number of immature caprovine and bovine bones recovered at 'Izbet Ṣarṭah (see Laniak, *Shepherds after My Own Heart*, 42–57; cf. Dahl and Hjort, *Having Herds*; cf. Hesse, "Animal Husbandry and Human Diet in the Ancient Near East," 203–22; Rosen, "Subsistence Economy in Iron Age I," 177–78; 347–51; and "Subsistence Economy of Stratum II," 156–85).

10. Each animal's function within Israelite society can be identified in these laws: ovines for wool, bovines for labor, and each for meat. The faunal assemblage throughout the Israelite period demonstrates that ovines greatly outnumbered bovines serving as the primary source of milk and meat, with bovines associated chiefly with the cultivation of cereals (Rosen, "Subsistence Economy," 339–49; cf. Prov 14:4; cf. Rosen, "Subsistence

Economy of Stratum II," 180).

11. Miller, *Religion of Ancient Israel*, 119.

12. See n. 6 above.

13. Ibid.

14. See the distribution of the *naḥălâ* in Joshua 13-24; the inalienable land law of Lev 25:13-17; 23, and Borowski on private land tenure in *Agriculture in Iron Age Israel*, 23-26.

15. Barley and wheat were well-suited to Levantine conditions, and their abundance in Canaan is frequently mentioned in Egyptian literature (*ANET*, 239; cf. Borowski, *Agriculture*, 3-5). Storage silos and carbonized seeds have been found "in almost every Iron Age I site" as have the tools and installations necessary to the sowing, reaping, threshing, winnowing and storing of these grains (Rosen, "Subsistence Economy in Iron Age I," 343; cf. Jane Renfrew, "Vegetables in the Ancient Near Eastern Diet," in *CANE* 1:195). The grain harvests were also central to the Israelite cultic calendar (Borowski, *Agriculture*, 33; cf. 47-69).

16. Borowski, *Agriculture*, 60.

17. King and Stager, *Life in Biblical Israel*, 96. Excavations at Philistine Ekron have produced more than 100 olive presses, and archaeologists speculate that Ekron produced "a thousand tons of oil annually, mostly for export" (ibid.; cf. Stager, "The Finest Olive Oil in Samaria" *JSS* 28 [1983] 241-25; "Shemer's Estate" *BASOR* 277/278 [1990] 93-107; Borowski, *Agriculture*, 117-26). Note that the full utilization of the olive required the long-term investment of a "deeply rooted sedentary society (as opposed to a settling society)," and is therefore more characteristic of Israel's Iron II era than Iron I (Rosen, "Subsistence Economy," 346-47).

18. See King and Stager, *Life in Biblical Israel*, 98.

19. Borowski, *Agriculture*, 102-14; cf. Paul and Dever, *Biblical Archaeology*, fig. 77.

20. See Borowski, *Agriculture*, 110.

21. Throughout its national period, the bulk of the Israelite populace lived on small family farms in which the main economy was a mixture of pastoralism and diversified agriculture. The goal of this economy was ensuring the survival of the family. Carol Meyers speaks of the Israelite farmers as "small holders: 'rural cultivators practicing intensive, permanent, diversified agriculture on relatively small farms'" (Meyers, "The Family in Early Israel," 3). Because of the typical Israelite family's sustenance approach to farming, agricultural production ran year round. The planting of grains occurred in the fall, legumes in the winter, and the care and pruning of vineyards and orchards throughout the year. The barley harvest began with the spring equinox, wheat in late April. Grapes and other fruits were harvested during the summer months, with the olive crop gathered from late August to late October. For further reading, see Borowski, *Daily Life in Biblical Times*, 13-42; King and Stager, "A Day in Micah's Household," in *Life in Biblical Israel*, 12-19; and Hopkins, "Life on the Land," 178-91.

22. McConville names Deut 5:12 a "conscious re-presentation" of Exod 20:8. He demonstrates that Deuteronomy knows the full version of the sabbatical ordinance that gives rest to the land as well as its creatures (McConville, *Deuteronomy*, 121-22, 128).

23. Hopkins, "The Subsistence Struggles of Early Israel," 185. Most organic farmers still practice fallowing for the same reasons. As Ann Bell Stone of Elmwood Stock Farm in Georgetown, Ky., points out, however, you must have the luxury of having enough fields to practice fallowing. Elmwood Stock Farm rotates their 350 acres of organically

grown grains, vegetables, and livestock on a seven-year cycle.

24. See Rosen, "Subsistence Economy in Iron Age I," 344–45; and Borowski, *Agriculture*, 145–48.

25. Jacobsen and Adams, "Salt and Silt in Ancient Mesopotamian Agriculture," 1251–58. Powell, "Salt, Seed, and Yields in Sumerian Agriculture," 7–38. Yoffee theorizes that the ever-present threat of salination of the Mesopotamian soils due to extensive irrigation was exacerbated by Hammurabi's centralization of the realm. "There may well have been a decision to abandon or shorten the period of fallow on lands the Crown controlled, thereby providing short-term fiscal relief, since the lands would initially provide more grain, but ultimately there would result a loss in productivity" (Yoffee, "The Collapse of Ancient Mesopotamian States and Civilization," 53).

26. Borowski, *Agriculture*, 148.

27. Ladizinski, "Origin and Domestication of the South West Asian Grain Legumes," 95, 150–51). Note that unlike Israelite law, federal law in the United States has actually discouraged crop rotation and fallow cycles. See Professor Patricia Muir of the Department of Botany and Plant Pathology at Oregon State University, http://oregonstate.edu/~muirp/orgmater.htm.

28. Organic material, i.e., humus, in soil is necessary for water-holding capacity, aeration, maintenance of beneficial soil organisms, and the input of natural fertilizers. Conversion to cropland is "almost universally associated with a rapid decrease in soil organic matter and soil nitrogen content" (Muir, "Consequences for Organic Matter in Soils." A dramatic example of this is in the Midwestern U.S., whose prairie soils have lost 1/3–1/2 of their organic material since they began being cultivated (ibid.).

29. Hopkins, "Life on the Land," 185.

30. See Muir, "Consequences for Organic Matter in Soils."

31. Scott Sabin, executive director of *Floresta* (an organization that addresses deforestation and poverty) has spent his life attempting to explicate the relationship between short-sighted environmental abuse and refugee populations (Sabin, "Environmental Emigration," 37–38). Cf. Sukhdev, "The International Economics of Ecosystems and Biodiversity."

32. Note that the law codes of both Egypt and Mesopotamia place great stress on the duty of the tenant to keep the soil in good working order (Eyre, "The Agricultural Cycle, Farming and Water Management in the Ancient Near East," 185).

33. Borowski, *Agriculture*, 114–16.

34. King and Stager, *Life in Biblical Israel*, 96.

35. Cole, "The Destruction of Orchards in Assyrian Warfare," 30; Wright, "Warfare and Wanton Destruction," 434.

36. Borowski, *Agriculture*, 133.

37. Smoak, "Building Houses," 9–35, and Wright, "Warfare and Wanton Destruction"; cf. Maeir, Ackermann, and Bruins, "The Ecological Consequences of a Siege."

38. Smoak, "Building Houses," 22; cf. *ARAB* 2:87, text 161.

39. Ibid., 21; cf. *RIMB* 2: 295.

40. Cole, "The Destruction of Orchards in Assyrian Warfare," 29–40.

41. Hasel, *Military Practice and Polemic*, 102–13. See Jacob Wright's review in *JBL* 125 (2006) 577.

42. Hasel, ibid., 35.

43. Hull, "The Final Frontier," 46.

44. Mountaintop removal (MTR) is a relatively new form of coal mining that requires the targeted site to be clear cut and then leveled by the use of explosives to reach the minerals desired. Demolition may extend as far as 1,000 feet below the surface. The "overburden" (the vegetation, topsoil, rock, etc.) is typically dumped into surrounding valleys. Due to the need to dump the "overburden," 6,700 "valley fills" were approved in central Appalachia between 1985 and 2001 and "[t]he U.S. EPA estimates that over 700 miles of healthy streams have been completely buried by mountaintop removal and thousands more have been damaged" (Reece, "Moving Mountains"). The environmental results of this method are literally devastating—water tables under the mountain are eliminated, surrounding ground water is frequently poisoned by the coal slurry byproduct, and the potential for the re-growth of forests or any type of plant life larger than grasses is rendered improbable (ibid.). The rationale for MTR is profit—the utilization of explosives and large machinery significantly reduces the coal companies' need for workers. See the Website "Appalachian Voices" for a grassroots perspective on the profound impact that this mining method is having upon the lives, income, property, and health of the poor in Appalachia (http://www.appvoices.org/index.php?/site/mtr_overview/.htm).

45. For an introduction to this enormous problem see http://www.rain-tree.com/facts.htm; and Laura Tangley, "Saving the Forest for the Trees."

46. One estimate for general land consumption is 365 acres per hour ("Smart Growth/Sprawl," http://www.nrdc.org/cities/smartGrowth/default.asp.htm. The American Farmland Trust estimates that more than one million of those acres are agricultural land, with a consumption rate of two acres a minute (http://www.farmland.org/programs/protection/default.asp; "America's Agricultural Land is at Risk," http://www.farmland.org/programs/protection/default.asp.htm. See Felicity Barringer, "Endangered Species Act Faces Broad New Challenges," *The New York Times* (June 26, 2005) and Daniel Glick "Putting the 'Public' Back in Public Lands," 26. Whereas the historically expected rate of species extinction should be about one species in a million annually "[s]tudies of various organisms (birds, mussels, fish, and plants) show that these groups are now disappearing more than 100 times faster, and in some cases up to 1,000 times faster, than the background rate. Even worse, the number of species currently threatened with extinction far exceeds those recently lost, bringing future extinction estimates to potentially 10,000 times the 'normal' rate" (Kyle S. Van Houtan, "Extinction and Its Causes," 15).

47. One of the most devastating results of urban sprawl in the United States has been the destruction of wetlands. The U.S. Fish and Wildlife Service reports that roughly 58,500 acres of wetlands are being destroyed annually ("Clean Water and Wetlands," *Sierra Club* n.p. Online: < http://www.sierraclub.org/wetlands/htm>. Cf. *Audubon Magazine*'s special May 2006 issue, "America's River," which provides an exposé of the broad impact of the long-term abuse of the mighty Mississippi.

48. Nelson, *Deuteronomy*, 268.

49. Ibid., *Deuteronomy*, 337.

50. Christensen, *Deuteronomy 21:10–34:12*, 500; Jeffrey Tigay, *JPS Torah Commentary: Deuteronomy*, 201. Cf. Sasson, op. cit. "Should Cheeseburgers Be Kosher."

51. Here among the Lion Hunt Reliefs, from the northern palace at Ḳuyûnjik, men are pictured carrying back dead lions, a hare, a bird and bird's nests (British Museum exhibit G10; big number 124889). These reliefs are well known for their graphic celebration of the slaughter of wild creatures as an illustration of royal prowess (Gadd, *The Assyrian Sculptures*, 72–73; cf. Jacob Wright "Warfare and Wanton Destruction," 454, figure 4).

52. See n. 10; Laniak, *Shepherds after My own Heart*, 42–57; and the Department of Animal Science at Oklahoma State University Website http://www.ansi.okstate.edu/breeds/sheep/awassi/index.htm and http://www.ansi.okstate.edu/breeds/goats/ anatolian black/index.htm for images and current animal husbandry practices involving these animals.

53. See endnotes 15, 21.

54. "Subsistence Economy," 348–49; cf. "Subsistence Economy of Stratum II," *'Izbet Ṣarṭah: An Early Iron Age Site near Rosh Ha'ayin*, 156–85.

55. This statistic emerges from a conservative estimate of the ancient working bovine at 600–700 lbs. (275–320 kg). Such an animal should be able to comfortably consume as many as four kilos of wheat during a day of labor (personal communication Ryan Strebeck of the Strebeck Family Ranch of the Curry and Roosevelt Counties in New Mexico and Elk City, Kans., 29 October 2008). This intake is reasoned off of the daily dry ration of a mature Angus steer in a feedlot—a ration based on a percentage of body weight, which in the arid conditions of southwest United States averages 800 lbs. In comparison, the weight of Boran cattle in East Africa under less-than-favorable conditions is 350–400 lbs. (160–180 kg), while its well-fed counterpart would average 990 lbs. (450 kg; Dahl and Hjort, *Having Herds*, 163–67). Nimrod Marom of the Laboratory of Archaezoology at the University of Haifa states that ancient bovine weight is difficult to determine, but estimates 400 kg +/- 50 kg (personal communication Nimrod Marom 28 October 2008). Marom's estimate would increase caloric intake and therefore increase the sacrifice of the Israelite farmer when choosing not to muzzle his ox (cf. Rosen's estimate of 5 kg per day, "Subsistence Economy of Stratum II" in *'Izbet Ṣarṭah: An Early Iron Age Site near Rosh Ha'ayin*, 156–85).

56. "Waste lagoon" management has received a lot of attention in the press over the past decade. For a summary see Scully, *Dominion*, 249. For definitions see the North Carolina Cooperative Extension Service Website: http://www.bae.ncsu.edu/programs/extension/publicat/wqwm/ebae103_83.html and the EPA's final rule on Concentrated Animal Feeding Operations http://cfpub.epa.gov/npdes/afo/cafofinalrule.cfm?program_id=7.

57. Most conventional hogs in this country are Duroc breed, going to slaughter at 220–40 pounds (personal communication 28 October 2008 Ann Bell Stone; cf. Scully, *Dominion*, 252).

58. See Scully, *Dominion*, 247–86. "Due to animal welfare concerns, the entire European Union has already banned both veal crates and gestation crates, effective 2007 and 2013, respectively. Yet, in the United States, the use of these abusive crates remains customary practice" ("Think Outside the Crate," http://www.hsus.org/farm/camp/totc/. For images see factoryfarm.com photo gallery at http://www.farmsanctuary.org/issues/factoryfarming/photos/pork.html.)

59. Jack Sasson has recently argued that Deut 14:21 involves cooking a kid in its mother's *fat*: "If so, we would be dealing not with an arcane or enigmatic dietary injunction, but with a wise counsel, an aphorism, instructing a farming community not to squander the bounties that God has given Israel" by slaughtering the mother and its young on the same occasion and thereby leading to a serious reduction in stock (Sasson, "Should Cheeseburgers Be Kosher?").

60. The enormous energy consumption required for mass-confinement animal husbandry is an interesting part of this equation. In his recent "An Open Letter to the Next Farmer in Chief," Michael Pollan states that the industry currently consumes 19% of the

annual national consumption of fuel. And whereas in 1940 each calorie of fossil fuel produced 2.3 calories of food, currently the ratio is ten calories of fossil fuel to every one calorie of food (http://www.nytimes.com/2008/10/12/magazine/12policy-t.htm).

61. Schlosser, "Cheap Food Nation," 36–39, online: http://www.sierraclub.org/sierra/200611/cheapfood.asp.

62. See Milgrom, *Leviticus*, 184–92.

63. Milgrom, *Leviticus*, 105–6.

64. Cf. Miller, *Religion of Ancient Israel*, 126.

65. See the Humane Society's "The Dirty Six: The Worst Practices in the Agribusiness," http://www.hsus.org/farm/resources/pubs/the_dirty_six.html. For images see the "Farm Sanctuary" factory farming Website photo gallery at http://www.farmsanctuary.org/issues/factoryfarming/photos/egg.html. For pending legislation designed to further protect livestock in America see "Proposed Legislation and Public Policy Federal Legislation" (http://www.trendtrack.com/texis/test/viewrpt? event= 47a0aa2797).

66. Interview with reporter Joby Warrick in 2001; cf. Scully, *Dominion* 284.

67. Ibid.

68. Block, "Recovering a Deuteronomic Theology of Animals," 305.

7

The Genius of the Mad Prophet: Ezekiel and the New Moral Self

JACQUELINE LAPSLEY

You may or you may not be aware that dozens of technical manuals have been written and published about *Star Wars*. These technical manuals are, like all technical manuals, not for the faint of heart: they describe in stupefying detail the vast array of vessels, weaponry, and associated matériel from George Lucas's intergalactic space epic. They tell of the inner workings of Superlaser Tributary Beam Shafts and the power-to-mass ratio of the Corvellian Corvette. Perhaps you, like me, are among the millions of parents of young Star Wars fans who have purchased or borrowed these books, and read them aloud to a five-year-old or an eight-year-old, a child whose rapt attention to every crumb of minutia resembles that of a devout monk poring over the Scriptures.

The reference to Scripture is not idle. As a pedagogical tactic with students, I have on several occasions compared reading these technical manuals to reading parts of Scripture, notably Leviticus, but also Ezekiel. The similarity lies in this: these texts give you—at one and the same time—both too much information, and not enough. In the case of *Star Wars*, you get too much information about each little component of the ships and not enough about the bigger picture, about the world in which they operate. Almost everything you need to know about how these ships participate in the larger story of *Star Wars* is left in the deep background, undisclosed in the books themselves. In the case of Leviticus, you have heaps of detailed information about specific rituals, and you intuit that

The Genius of the Mad Prophet

there must be a larger frame of reference that makes sense of what you are reading, but you can't quite get hold of that bigger picture—too much is left undisclosed. In the case of Ezekiel, you at least have a loose narrative framework—it tells a story, more or less—but it is a strange and mysterious story, the meaning of the details are difficult to grasp, and the relationship of one event to another is elusive. Already in the first few chapters in Ezekiel, for example, God has commissioned Ezekiel to be a prophet to Israel by causing him to lose the power of speech, and commanded him to eat bread cooked over excrement while lying on his side for a year. How are these events the word of God to us and for us?

Of the so-called three major prophets (with Isaiah and Jeremiah), Ezekiel is by far the most difficult to understand. In fact, by most ways of accounting, Ezekiel does not really qualify as a "major" prophet. Consider the evidence: Jeremiah is known in the Christian tradition for his moving laments ("confessions"), for the way he stands both over *against* the people, bearing the Lord's message of judgment, and yet also *with* them, embodying their suffering in his own person; Isaiah, of course, is the fifth gospel, its significance and place in the Christian tradition is unquestioned. But Ezekiel? There is the dry bones passage in chapter 37, thank goodness, and the promise of an everlasting covenant of peace in the same chapter. Many have heard the folk spiritual "Ezekiel Saw the Wheel," loosely based on the vision in chapter 1. But most people, even many theologically trained people, cannot come up with much more than that if asked. Even those who work closely with the prophet are uneasy: the biblical scholar Michael Fishbane, for example, who appreciates Ezekiel in many ways and has written professionally on the prophet, is still moved to declare that almost half the book is "shrill and hysterical."[1]

It is true that the New Testament does make a few allusions to Ezekiel. John 10 alludes to Ezekiel's image of the good shepherd (chapter 34) and applies it to Jesus. Images from the proto-apocalyptic material in chapters 38 and 39, and the temple vision in chapters 40 through 48 get picked up in the book of Revelation (Rev 20:8; 22:1–2, respectively). And several of the epistles allude to particular verses from Ezekiel[2] but the total is paltry when compared to Isaiah, or even Jeremiah.[3] It seems that the New Testament writers were also flummoxed by the strangeness of Ezekiel. This trend continues in the modern era. Texts from Ezekiel rarely appear in the Revised Common Lectionary, for example. The dry bones appear in the Great Vigil of Easter (they also make two other appearances in the RCL), but otherwise only five passages make the three-year cycle of offerings, and four of those five are listed as the alternate reading to another, apparently, preferred text.[4] Those who follow the RCL religiously consume a maximum diet of fewer than 100 verses of Ezekiel in three years, and probably a good deal fewer, given the alternate readings.

So why should we bother with Ezekiel? He offers little by way of messianic hope, or pithy, comforting, quotable thoughts on God's love and promises of redemption. In the current idiom, he's a bit of a "whack job." Yet I believe the book of Ezekiel constitutes one of the Old Testament's most profound theological reflections on human nature and the depth of God's will and passion to save humanity, and indeed, all creation from that which afflicts us. Despite that the book is bursting with bizarre symbolism and sexually explicit language, and seethes with divine fury,[5] it also offers intensely powerful expressions of God's desire to restore humanity and creation to wholeness. The book resists being diced into quotable bits, however; it demands, rather, to be read as a whole, for the integrity of its unpalatable but profound claim that though humanity's relationship with God seems inexorably broken, and indeed, that human moral agency itself is in fact broken beyond any human-initiated repair, God nevertheless reaches into that seemingly irreparable brokenness and makes humanity whole again.

In Ezekiel's view, Israel's long history has shown how human effort to maintain covenant relationship with God has failed, and indeed, it has shown how the endless human striving to contain and control God has failed. The book reveals the Lord as one who cannot and will not be contained or domesticated. In his understanding of the human condition and of the divine—human relationship as being irremediably broken unless healed by divine unilateral action, Ezekiel foreshadows the writings of Paul in the New Testament.

How does all of Ezekiel's theological profundity relate to the political order, the topic of this conference? At least in this way: the effort to domesticate God, to tie the deity to one's own aims and desires, which is a catastrophic consequence of the total failure of human beings as moral agents, results in a chaotically disordered political and social life, a disorder that Ezekiel describes in florid and sometimes sordid detail. The failure of human beings to know themselves and to know God results

The Genius of the Mad Prophet

in idolatry, injustice, and violence. Ezekiel reveals a God who is furious that humanity suffers, politically and economically, because people, and especially people with power, try to make God into an object to suit their purposes.

The rest of this paper will first examine Ezekiel's account of the people's failure to know God and themselves, that is, their failure as moral agents. Second, we will consider the devastating political and economic consequences of the distorted moral identity of Israel's leaders' for the people of God. The last part of the paper will take up the way Ezekiel envisions a solution to the problem he has so graphically exposed. Some concluding reflections will consider how Ezekiel offers us a constructive word in the twentieth-first century.

Failure to Know God and Self

More than any other prophet, or indeed any biblical writer, Ezekiel is explicitly concerned that Israel know God. But what constitutes knowledge of God? Most divine actions in Ezekiel are followed by the recognition formula ("that they/you may know YHWH"), revealing that knowledge of God is the ultimate purpose of all divine action, whether of punishment or of deliverance. The recognition formula offers some clues as to what constitutes the knowledge that Ezekiel has in mind. Though the seventy-two occurrences are parceled out to a diverse audience (Israel, the nations, even the land), they always follow a divine action, as mentioned, though they do not constitute an implicit call to human action in and of themselves, as Zimmerli suggests.[6] The evidence of the text suggests that the knowledge of Yahweh involves the whole self; it is at heart an orientation to existence that shapes human identity. This kind of knowledge is prior to and prerequisite for, in Ezekiel's way of thinking, any potential right action.

Ezekiel depicts the people—whether those who have remained in the land after the first deportation of 597, or those who, with Ezekiel and many other elites, were uprooted to a ghettoized life on the outskirts of Babylon—he depicts all of them as tirelessly attempting to control either their own fate, or to justify their despair by blame-shifting. Those who are trying to control their own fate either engage in rituals that they hope will induce YHWH to save them, or in rituals that seek the favor of other deities, who might be induced to save them. Those who seek to justify their despair fatalistically point to a seemingly inexorable law: we are doomed to live out the consequences of our parents' and grandparents' failings. So, on the one side, the people scurry frantically around, busying themselves with trying to fend off disaster without any realization that their complete disconnection from God—the same God who formed them as a people and has delivered them over and over again—their disconnection from this God, is the root of their problems. On the other side are those who refuse to take responsibility for the current situation and retreat into fatalism.

In Ezekiel 8, we encounter the first type. The prophet is given a tour of the temple and is asked to witness a series of idolatrous worship practices in the temple. Each one is worse than the last. In one case the elders of Israel are cowering in a dark room, trying to manipulate images in a desperate attempt to improve their fate: "Mortal, have you seen what the elders of the house of Israel are doing in the dark, each in his room of images? For they say, 'The LORD does not see us, the LORD has forsaken the land'" (Ezek 8:12). Margaret Odell rightly sees these actions as efforts by the people to prevent the impending Babylonian onslaught.[7] The scene highlights the desperation of the worshipers to "fix" their situation through their own efforts; they are trying to cope with reality by applying ritualistic bandages to their situation.

It is the people's lack of both self-knowledge and knowledge of God that Ezekiel skewers in this scene and in the other judgment passages in the book. These debilitating deficiencies in knowledge cause them to flail about in their anxiety and fear. They engage in their manipulative rituals and think that some god—YHWH perhaps, but any god will do—that some god somewhere will deliver them, but these efforts themselves serve as impediments to a right relationship with the living God of Israel; their frenzied activity becomes a kind of deafening static that prevents them from perceiving the truth of their situation.

The fatalistic view is well exemplified in chapter 18, where a popular proverb is cited: "The parents have eaten sour grapes, and the children's teeth are set on edge" (Ezek 18:2). The gist of this saying is that the present generation is merely experiencing the consequences of the sins of earlier generations. Reading from this script constitutes a refusal to take any responsibility for the unfolding catastrophe. Where have we heard this before? Even from the very first chapters of Genesis, the Bible gets the human condition right: when in doubt, we blame-shift. The rest of chapter 18 is a cogent refutation of the logic of this conviction. All are accountable before God; responsibility for the current situation cannot be evaded. Ezekiel punctures every pose, whether of self-sufficiency or of fatalism, that Israel strikes in response to the disaster of the Babylonian onslaught.

The people's failure to know *themselves* is revealed especially whenever Ezekiel refers to the benefits of the experience of shame, yes, the *benefits*, of feeling ashamed. For Ezekiel, shame is a profound gift, and an essential element of self-knowledge. The language of shame appears not in passages of judgment, curiously, but in passages describing God's deliverance of the people from their present travails. That is because, for Ezekiel, feeling ashamed is not a punishment for sin, but part of the first movement of being delivered from crippling ignorance. The sequence of events is of critical importance. Remembering our sins—what we have done that flies counter to God's will for us and for the world—remembering our sins is a crucial part of self-knowledge; and for Ezekiel, remembering the past is always accompanied by an appropriate sense of shame, spurred by the recollection of our past actions.

The end of chapter 16 offers a good example. The bulk of this chapter is a blistering discourse of judgment against Israel, using highly sexualized, and some argue, even pornographic, language.[8] But at the end of this discourse, the Lord promises that Jerusalem's fortunes will be restored "*in order that* [they] may bear [their] disgrace and be ashamed of all that [they] have done" (Ezek 16:53–54). Deliverance will come so that the people will feel ashamed. This is a peculiar turn of events for a culture like our own that understands the dreadful psychological consequences of toxic forms of shame. Shame that saves is a strange idea indeed. But some forms of shame lead to self-knowledge—the kind of shame that washes over when one realizes how one's actions are perceived and experienced by others. It is the sudden jolt that takes one out of oneself and one's own perceptions; an appropriate, non-toxic feeling of shame allows us to see ourselves from another's perspective, from outside our own narrow subjectivity.

A few lines after the gift of shame is promised, a future everlasting covenant is announced: "I will establish with you an everlasting covenant, *then* you will remember your ways and be ashamed . . ." (Ezek 16:60–61).[9]

The knowledge of God entailed by the covenant will initiate the people's experience of shame which in turn leads to self-knowledge. In the end, knowledge of God and human self-knowledge are not truly separate; they are inextricably intertwined. It is not surprising, then, that memory of the painful past corrects an amnesia of both divine and human identity. The connection is further illustrated at the very end of chapter 16: "I will establish my covenant with you, *then* you will know that I am Yahweh, *in order that* you may remember and be ashamed and not open again your mouth on account of your shame, when I forgive you all that you have done" (Ezek 16:62–63). Memory and shame: taking responsibility for past actions, and acknowledging our failures—Ezekiel affirms repeatedly that this kind of self-knowledge is necessary if a future of hope is to open before us.[10]

The Consequences of the Failure to Know God and Self

The consequences of failing to remember who we are and what we have done, of failing to know God and self, are everywhere in evidence in Ezekiel's view. The prophet repeatedly describes and decries idolatry, in which God's covenant people worship that which is not God. Idolatry is both primary cause and most significant symptom of the disordered self. But I wish to examine in this section not idolatry, but two other, lesser known, consequences of the people's self-delusion. Ezekiel is not usually associated with a message of social justice, but he should be. He returns again and again to the injustice and violence committed against the powerless; together with idolatry, these are the most pernicious consequences of failing to know God and self.

Ezekiel's indictment of the way violence and oppression are wielded against the powerless is quite pronounced (*ḥamas*, "violence," is fiercely judged in Ezek 7:11, 23; 8:17; 12:19; 22:26; 28:16; 45:9, and that's just one of Ezekiel's ways of referring to the evils of violence). In chapter 22 Ezekiel makes it especially explicit that literal violence (Ezek 22:3, 6, 9, 12, 25, 27), the abuse and oppression of the weak (Ezek 22:7, 10, 11, 29), and unjust economic practices that exploit the poor (Ezek 22:7, 12, 13, 25, 27, 29), are all violations of what lies at the heart of covenant faithfulness and will not be tolerated—they are as serious as the idolatry and cultic violations with which Ezekiel is customarily more closely associated. Indeed, for Ezekiel the "sin" of the ancient city of Sodom was not homosexual acts, but the people's enjoyment of their prosperity while neglecting the poor (Ezek 16:49)!

Where he is usually focused on violence done to people, in one memorable line Ezekiel accuses the priests of having done violence to the law (Ezek 22:26), which, as P. J. Harland explains, is not simply a set of rules to be followed, but incarnates God's will for the people, and thus violence against the law is violence against God.[11] Yet this too also comes around to violence done to people, for it is Ezekiel's way of saying that the priests, charged with helping the people to understand and uphold the law, have, by their failure to do so, become the catalyst for a cascade of violence throughout the land. As Harland summarizes: "When God's law is rejected, human life becomes subject to arbitrary exploitation."[12]

An early edition of the *Theological Dictionary of the Old Testament* defines ḥamas ("violence") as the "cold-blooded and unscrupulous infringement of the personal rights of others, motivated by greed and hate and often making use of physical violence and brutality."[13] This definition is useful except in its emphasis on "rights." In the Old Testament violence is not about the infringement of the "rights" of the victim—the idea of individual "rights" is a peculiarly modern one—rather, it is about the failure of the perpetrator to act responsibly toward others, to exercise ethical responsibility toward members of the community and in the interests of the common good.

Ezekiel also picks up on an economic theme that appears in other prophetic literature as well as in wisdom literature: chasing after unjust gain (*beṣaʿ*) is always at the expense of the less wealthy and powerful. In an extended discourse on unjust social and economic practices in chapter 22, Ezekiel judges those who seek *beṣaʿ*: "In you [the city of Jerusalem], they take bribes to shed blood . . . and you make dishonest gain (*beṣaʿ*) from your neighbors by extortion; and you have forgotten me, says the LORD GOD. See, I strike my hands together at the dishonest gain (*beṣaʿ*) you have made, and at the blood that has been shed within you" (Ezek 22:12–13). Later in the passage the city's leaders are again targeted: "Its officials within it are like wolves tearing the prey, shedding blood, destroying lives to get dishonest gain" (Ezek 22:27). The meaning of *beṣaʿ* is uniformly negative here, as it refers to the practice of defrauding other members of the community for financial gain, usually by means of violence, although not always. It always connotes the acquisition of wealth through immoral means, destroying lives for profit.[14]

The lure of *beṣaʿ* is not confined to the community in Jerusalem, but afflicts the exiled community in Babylon as well. In chapter 33 Ezekiel offers a revealing vignette of life among the exiles in Babylon, of the challenges facing the prophet as he seeks to convey the divine word to a people finally unable to hear it. They *seem* willing to attend to what God might be saying through the prophet ("Come and hear what the word is that comes from YHWH," they say in Ezek 33:30), but the words do not sink in ("they hear your words, but they will not do them" Ezek 33:31). The people do not act upon the prophetic words because "lust is in their mouths and their heart goes after unjust gain [*beṣaʿ*]" (v. 31b, a more literal translation than NRSV: "for flattery is on their lips, but their heart is set on their gain"). The "lust" and the "unjust gain" both denote conditions where something normal has been carried to an abnormal excess (uncontrolled desire, perhaps here akin to gluttony; profit inappropriately gained at the expense of others).[14] The problem of self-serving behaviors among those in power is not confined to the past, to pre-fall Jerusalem, but continues in Ezekiel's present, even as it does today. Ezekiel wrestles with the fundamental question of the human condition, and serves as a forerunner of later articulations by Augustine and others of the intractable nature of human sinfulness.

In chapter 34 Ezekiel continues the theme of failed leadership, but this time by offering a distinctive take on the classic Israelite metaphor of the people of Israel as sheep, with shepherds representing Israelite kings (e.g., 2 Sam 5:2; Jer 3:15; 10:21; 12:10), as well as other leaders (e.g., 2 Sam 7:7; Isa 44:28; Jer 17:16). Here in Ezekiel, it seems that the shepherds refer to Israelite kings, but also more broadly to other members of the ruling elite (those who wield political, religious, and economic power). The indictment, laid out in Ezek 34:1–8, is not simply that the powerful have been tending to their own needs instead of the needs of the people, but that they have been using the sheep for their own unjust gain—the failure is not one of neglect, but of abuse: "You eat the fat, you clothe yourselves with the wool, you slaughter the fatlings; but you do not feed the sheep" (Ezek 34:3). This is a similar accusation to those we have already seen not only in chapters 22 and 33, but elsewhere in the book as well, that is, that the political, economic, and religious establishment use their power for their own gain, at the expense of those whose interests these elites are supposed to serve (Ezek 22:12, 13, 27; 33:31, just discussed).

In sum, Ezekiel, like every Israelite prophet, has a powerful vision of the common good, embodied in God's gift of the law to the people. For it is the law, lived out in the context of the ongoing, life-giving relationship with the God who delivered them from Egypt, that makes the common good sustainable. In Ezekiel's worldview, no one is exempt from responsibility for the disasters that have befallen the nation, that have resulted from the abandoning of the law and of its Giver, but Israel's leaders are judged particularly harshly. They were supposed to uphold the laws that prevented the powerful from exploiting the weak, but the temptation to use their power to gain more power for themselves was too much for them, as it has been for so many throughout history.

How to Solve the Problem?

And so for Ezekiel the core problem lies deep within the human condition; indeed, Ezekiel comes to the conclusion that human beings, on their own, are inherently incapable of doing the right thing. When human beings *are* described as capable of choosing and acting for the good, it is because they have received the knowledge of God, and genuine knowledge of themselves, as a gift. Most of us in the West today think the way much of the Bible thinks: to be a virtuous person is to *act* rightly, obeying laws and doing commandments. But in much of Ezekiel, action recedes as the primary element in moral agency; rather, the moral agency given by God is constituted by *knowledge* (knowledge of God and knowledge of self) as its primary element, with moral action flowing out of that knowledge as an important, but derivative consequence.

Ezekiel wrestles with the relationship between action and knowledge in the moral life, resulting in considerable tension within the book. One result of this tension is that by the end of the book (esp. in chapters 36–48), people *do* less and *watch and listen* more. Watching and listening enables new insights into self and God, and fewer blundering errors brought about by greed and self-interest. As the book progresses, Ezekiel is fitfully but firmly articulating a movement toward a new way of thinking about the way human beings are constituted. Only with a more seriously reflective emphasis on self-understanding in the context of a complex world can the common good be the goal of life together.

Once God has acted to bestow knowledge on the people, with the result that they gain knowledge of God and of themselves, the text is largely silent on the role of human action in the future; people are not described as *doing* much of anything in the second half of the book, that is, once God has decisively acted to deliver the people. Action does not recede entirely from moral agency, however. It appears, for example, in the "new heart, new spirit" language of chapters 11 and 36. After the new heart of flesh and the new spirit are installed, God proclaims, "I will make it so that you follow my statutes and keep my ordinances and do them" (Ezek 36:26–27; cf. 11:19–20). The new self, empowered by the divinely given heart and spirit, will act rightly, but that action is secondary, a consequence of the newly constituted self (see also Ezek 37:24, after the dry bones have been revivified).

Similarly, when Ezekiel is to describe the temple to the people, a sense of shame must precede right action. "You, mortal, describe the temple to the house of Israel, that they may be ashamed of their iniquities and so that they may measure the proportion. If they are ashamed of all they have done, make known to them the plan of the temple, its arrangement, its exits, and its entrances, and its whole form—all its ordinances, and all its entire plan and all its laws; and write it before their eyes so that they may follow its entire plan and all its ordinances, and do them" (Ezek 43:10–11). The sequence of events proceeds from divine revelation ("describe the temple") to human self-knowledge (shame), to more specific divine revelation, and finally to appropriate, correct behaviors. Here again right identity precedes right action; moral action will emerge as an apparently natural consequence of an accurate sense of self.

Only the beginnings of a shift in the way the human moral agent is constructed are detectable in Ezekiel, but this shift gained a certain momentum, and a more forceful articulation, in the centuries that followed the Exile. By the time apocalyptic arrived on the scene, God-given knowledge takes on paramount importance in the construction of the human self; human action is derivative. This shift is especially clear in the sectarian documents from Qumran, where *identity* is paramount and right action flows out of knowledge of that identity.[16] The dominant view of moral agency (with action as primary) certainly continued to exist in postexilic Judaism, but not without having to wrestle with the challenge that Ezekiel articulated, a challenge that, as the efficacy of human moral action became a seemingly less reliable framework for understanding the world, took on increasingly persuasive power. This trajectory continues in the Apostle Paul, who even more forcefully emphasizes that only God's gift of a new identity makes genuine agency possible in the world.

Implications for Political Life

I want to end by drawing out more explicitly a few of the implications Ezekiel offers us for our reflections on political life in the twenty-first century. Ezekiel underscores the catastrophic consequences of the absence of the knowledge of God and human self-knowledge on the life of the community, and both of these are relevant for politics in our time, though much of Ezekiel's wisdom for us concerns human nature.

But before enumerating the implications of Ezekiel for us, the customary caveat when working with biblical texts bears repeating: Ezekiel's ethics is what Michael Walzer terms "thick" moral argument, that is, it is deeply particularist and contextual. Ezekiel's understanding of humanity is embedded in the particularity of the changing conditions of the Babylonian crisis, and thus a thin, universal morality cannot be extracted from Ezekiel or any biblical text without extreme violence to the text and to our own contemporary situation. Yet the "thickness" of Ezekiel's argument is instructive in and of itself, for where moral argument is thick, it has "the radical potential of an internal critique." As Waltzer observes, "social criticism in maximalist [that is, thick] terms can call into question, can even overturn, the moral maximum itself, by exposing its internal tensions and contradictions."[17]

Ezekiel, like many biblical writers, is engaged in a form of intelligent social criticism, that is, he does not adhere slavishly to inherited traditions, but struggles with those traditions, resulting in dynamic and constructive internal critique. And so we arrive at the first implication of Ezekiel's book for us: *the emphasis on identity over action*. By the end of Ezekiel's book *actions* are no longer primary in the moral life; they have been displaced by *identity*, by knowing who we are in relation to God and the world. Confident in their identity, the people's actions flow naturally out of that identity.

In American political life today it would be worth wrestling more explicitly with our two apparently polarized cultural and political traditions of self-reliance on the one hand, and commitment to the common good on the other. Many public policy decisions are made with hardly any reflection on the underlying commitments that fund those decisions—what kind of vision sustains the political actions we take? Are our actions congruent with our self-understanding? The United States has been formed by powerful narratives that emphasize self-reliance and individual rights, but the biblical narrative points overwhelmingly to the responsibility of citizens to foster the common good of all. How might we come to a better balance of our formative narratives?

A second implication concerns *genuine knowledge of God*. Ezekiel excoriates those who attempt to control and domesticate God for their own purposes. Most graphically in chapter 8, but also elsewhere in the book, the prophet reveals the pathetic self-destructive flailings of those who would harness the will of God for their own purposes, political or otherwise. It is entirely appropriate and desirable for those engaged in debates about public policy to disclose the motivations behind their positions (e.g., "I support this environmental initiative because, as a Christian, I believe that God wills for all creation, and humanity as a part of that good creation, to flourish . . ."). But it is an act of idolatry to claim special access to the divine will beyond what is revealed in Scripture by way of informed corporate interpretation in the context of real community needs. And it is counter to the overall trajectory of the Scriptures to strive for a seamless unity of the political and the religious: the United States has never been a "Christian country," and to strive for such an entity runs counter to the biblical witness, and particularly to that of the New Testament.

A third area in which Ezekiel may guide us derives from the other major alternative response to crisis that Israel evinced (other than fatalistic despair): *blame-shifting*. Just as Israel looked to previous generations in an effort to deflect blame for the present situation, so few in political life today are anxious to accept responsibility for the current difficulties we face. As long as acknowledging mistakes is seen as a weakness instead of a strength, we will not be able to improve our political life and so the welfare of all. Responsibility for this mind-set does not lie with leaders alone, although that is where Ezekiel puts his emphasis. In American politics we the people refuse to allow our leaders to make honest mistakes. Here I am not referring to the repeated and predictable script of personal sexual misconduct, but to the fact that sometimes well-intentioned policies have unforeseen consequences and require modification. Failure should be allowed to have some instructive value and not simply presage defeat at the polls.

Just as Ezekiel criticizes those who blame previous generations for present crises, he also upholds the need for the people to hold themselves accountable for the failures of the past that have led to the crises of the present. The primary path to self-understanding lies in experiences of shame, the acute self-awareness born of seeing one's actions as others see them (recall Nathan's cry to David over the Bathsheba affair: "You are the man!" [2 Sam 12:7]). Our tendency today is to view shame as having only negative effects (and to be sure, the deleterious effects of toxic shame are real), but Ezekiel reminds us of the *benefits* of shame in shaping the identity of a people. Where appropriate, feeling ashamed of past actions is vital to authentic self-knowledge and the integrity of moral agency. Acknowledging shame (over slavery or the response to Katrina, for example) is not a sign of weakness, but of strength and bona fide self-understanding.

Most of the elites Ezekiel excoriates throughout the book, the ones who have abused power and exploited the powerless, are political leaders, there being very little distinction between political and religious life in ancient Israel. Apparently, in ancient Israel, as elsewhere, political leaders were loathe to remember the past, and certainly did not frequently acknowledge shameful actions in the past—at least not voluntarily. Soon, it appears, it will become even easier for us to forget the past. Scientists are now refining a drug (using the substance PKMzeta) that can erase memories of the past from our brains. We will have the capacity to forget our most painful memories. Certainly there would be benefits: the memories powering certain behaviors could be blocked, thus aiding those struggling with addiction. Yet, as *The New York Times* reports, a substance that can erase selective memories poses troubling ethical questions because "any such drug . . . could be misused to erase or block memories of bad behavior, even of crimes. If traumatic memories are like malicious stalkers, then troubling memories—and a healthy dread of them—form the foundation of a moral conscience."[18] Often collective political memories, not only those of leaders but of the citizenry as a whole, do not require any drugs to be erased; they are just conveniently forgotten. Ezekiel derides this lack of memory and shame—this lack of self-knowledge—as fatal to the health of the nation.

In short, genuine self-knowledge is in short supply, now as in Ezekiel's time. The result for Israel as for us, is violence and the exploitation of the poor. If Christians are to witness to Christ in service to the world, we would do well to seek a deeper knowledge of ourselves—of the ways we are implicated in oppression and violence, for example, ways that are normally hidden from us. The church as an institution plays a vital role in preserving the memories critical to self-knowledge. The Reformers put special emphasis on the task of self-knowledge: In Luther's idiom: "The first step in Christianity [after the preaching of repentance] . . . is the knowledge of oneself."[19] And John Calvin famously begins his Institutes: "Nearly all the wisdom we possess . . . consists of two parts: the knowledge of God and of ourselves."[20]

Lastly, the *form* in which Ezekiel chooses to articulate the problem Israel faces in the sixth century may be instructive. Ezekiel's book is no intellectual treatise on moral agency; it's not a position paper. Rather, it's a passionate appeal to the people to embrace the vision of the future that he holds out to them. In short, he does not attempt to address the problem at the intellectual level alone, or even primarily, but rather invites the hearers to become engaged in re-envisioning society with their whole selves.[21] He tells a different story from the one to which they have become accustomed; it is a story of hope and renewal, no longer based on the old assumptions of continual human failure, but premised on God's commitment to a vision of human beings thriving together in community. To change people's hearts and minds one does not offer counter-arguments, it seems, but a counter narrative—a story so compelling that it shifts our understanding of who we are and who we might become. The church, empowered by the counter narrative of the Gospel, can play a unique role in helping to craft a new narrative for a new time.

Endnotes

1. Fishbane, "Sin and Judgment in the Prophecies of Ezekiel," 150.
2. Romans 2:24 seems to allude to Ezek 36:22; Rom 10:5 and Gal 3:12 to Ezek 20:11; and possibly 2 Pet 3:4 to Ezek 12:22.
3. The allusions to Isaiah are too numerous to mention here. The presence of Jeremiah

The Genius of the Mad Prophet

has been seen especially in Matthew and 1 Corinthians. See, for example, Knowles, *Jeremiah in Matthew's Gospel*.

4. The five texts are: Ezek 2:1–7; 17:22–24; 18:1–32; 33:1–11; 34:11–24. Interestingly, Ezekiel 1 does not appear at all.

5. For a thoughtful reflection on divine anger, see Fretheim, "Theological Reflections on The Wrath of God in the Old Testament," 1–26.

6. Zimmerli, "Knowledge of God according to the Book of Ezekiel," 29–98.

7. Odell, *Ezekiel*, 103–11. Contrary to most scholars, Odell understands these practices to be Yahwistic, albeit misguided due to the use of idols as intermediaries.

8. Several studies focus on the pornographic nature of the sexual imagery in Ezekiel 16 and 23, and the ethical implications for modern interpretation. See Exum, "The Ethics of Biblical Violence against Women," 254–56; Darr, "Troubling Texts," 97–117; Carroll, "Whorusalamin: A Tale of Three Cities as Three Sisters," 67–82; Dempsey, "The 'Whore' of Ezekiel 16: The Impact and Ramifications of Gender-Specific Metaphors in Light of Biblical Law and Divine Judgment," 57–78; and Weems, *Battered Love*, 58–67.

9. Significant instances of the language of remembering and forgetting appear in Ezek 6:9; 16:61–63; chapter 20 (amnesia is implied); 20:43; 22:12; 23:27, 35; 29:16; and 36:31. Shame often appears in similar contexts (Ezek 6:9; 16:52, 54, 61, 63; 20:43; 32:24, 25, 30; 36:31–32; 39:26; 43:10–11; 44:13).

10. For an extensive treatment of memory and shame in Ezekiel see Lapsley, *Can These Bones Live?* esp. 126–58.

11. Harland, "What Kind of 'Violence' in Ezekiel 22?" 112–13.

12. Ibid., 113.

13. Haag, "ḥamas," 482.

14. Harland, "Bs': Bribe, Extortion or Profit?" 310–22.

15. Ibid., 316–17.

16. See Newsom, *The Self as Symbolic Space*.

17. Walzer, *Thick and Thin*, 47.

18. Carey, "Brain Researchers Open Door to Editing Memory."

19. Luther, "Commentary on St. Paul's Epistle to the Galatians," 169.

20. Calvin, *Institutes of the Christian Religion*, 1.1.1.

21. On the importance of form in moral change, see Walzer, *Thick and Thin*.

8

Building Hope upon the Ruins in Jeremiah
KATHLEEN M. O'CONNOR

When I look to the prophet Jeremiah for the roots of a different biblical ethic than that of the apocalyptic literalism that has been propounded over the past decade in the United States, I discover both a process for building hope and a vision for the moral rebuilding of society. Apocalyptic literalism is easier. Its proponents hold that the Bible gives us the blueprint for life and all we have to do is apply the text like a coat of paint upon the world. In such a vision, the Bible is inanimate, requiring from us a giving away of mind and a fateful obedience to what is written, as if the ancient writers already knew everything to happen in the millennia ahead. Interpretation involves a dramatic leap of faith, but not any painful openness to the Spirit at work in the world, to the struggles and conflicts of discernment, and to a discipleship of alert awakeness to the God who does a new thing among us today.

Jeremiah calls us into covenant communion with the God of new things, and to continued conversion, a conversion guided by the cry of the hopeless, a conversion rooted in the life of worship and union with God's own self.[1]

The historical situation of Jeremiah's first audiences does not resemble in any *literal* way, the present political, economic, or religious circumstances in the United States of America in the early twenty-first century. Although we have had our share of trauma and tragedy—the 9/11 attacks in New York, Katrina in New Orleans and the Gulf Coast, the floods in Cedar River, in addition to a life-altering economic slide in the wake of our military adventurism—even so, these painful events give us only a glimpse of the catastrophe facing Judah in the onslaught of the Babylonian Empire. Those events in the sixth century BCE—three invasions, deportations, and some forms of military occupation or control—disrupted the nation of Judah down to its roots, overturned the government, interfered with the economy, upended daily life, and set in serious doubt Judah's relationship with its God. The United States may be in crisis, indeed, we currently face a number of them, but we are not a destroyed people without a future.

Conditions facing Judah, by contrast, qualify as a disaster. A disaster involves violent disruptions for which a community is not equipped to cope, for which it lacks economic, political, and spiritual resources.[2] It is to such a seriously decapitated society that the book of Jeremiah speaks. Every word in it addresses the disaster, provides language to speak about it, portrays its effects upon the community, and offers hope for survival.

Although we are not suffering from vast such destruction as a nation, we, too, require hope for our future. Our religious rhetoric has been co-opted by those who promote fear, advocate authority and submission, and hatefully dismiss those who disagree on matters of bodies, health, and economic well-being, and on who is to be included in our body politic. We know the hopelessness of the rich, the emptiness of consumerism, and grief over lost loved ones in wars and lost honor in our political, economic, and even religious leaders. We carry weighty fears that the future of the U.S. is under attack as much from insiders as from enemies elsewhere. And then there is the seeming dullness of our faith compared to the passionate expressions of joy and hope among Christians in the two-thirds world. There is Christianity's decline in the West compared to its vibrant expansions among the global poor. Perhaps we wonder if there is hope for us in the midst of our greed, power, and wealth, albeit more limited, tarnished, and weakened than we imagined.

A Process of Hope-Building

From the book of Jeremiah, we can learn a process of hope-building involving four interrelated components:

I. In the midst of the ruins, Jeremiah names reality as a work-of-art rather than as statement of fact;

II. Jeremiah names God in the context of that ruined reality;

III. Jeremiah imagines God of the Future on the Basis of Past Traditions;

IV. Jeremiah calls people to radically different social arrangements and to covenant communion with God.

This process resembles closely the work of preachers and theologians, and, of course, of poets, musicians, storytellers, and artists.

Naming Reality with Artistic Speech

Even a quick glance at the book of Jeremiah reveals a world of confusion and chaos. And although interpreters emphasize predictive aspects of Jeremiah's prophecy, the book's audience lives in the fulfillment of prophecy, in the wake of the nation's collapse. They live in a world destroyed. We know this from the superscription: "These are the words of Jeremiah . . . to whom the word of the LORD came in the days of King Josiah . . . until the captivity of Jerusalem in the fifth month" (Jer 1:1–3). Jeremiah's readers are survivors of catastrophe. Recognizing their predicament provides one key for interpreting the book.

Jeremiah names the disaster repeatedly across the book, but not in a literal way.[3] The book's naming of the disaster is potent, poetic, symbolic imagining. It lifts the reality of the destroyed nation into literary worlds where people can see their lives outside themselves. Across the book's first twenty chapters, for example, one thing or another breaks down or collapses: God's marriage to wives Israel and Judah falls to pieces (Jer 2:1—4:2); creation comes undone (Jer 4:23–26); the covenant is broken (Jer 11:1–18); Jeremiah's loin cloth disintegrates (Jer 13:1–11); the divine Potter destroys the clay pot (Jer 18:1–11); Jeremiah smashes the earthenware jug before the elders (Jer 19:1–15).

Similarly, Jeremiah speaks of the Babylonian invasions but barely touches upon literal events. It is not Babylon that invades Judah, but the mythic "foe from the north" who "eats up your harvest and your food," your " vines and fig trees" (Jer 6:15–17). Nor does the foe attack the city

Building Hope upon the Ruins in Jeremiah

of Jerusalem but the city personified as a woman, the Daughter of Zion. These poems about war re-enact the terrors of approaching armies and touch upon massive destruction in short bites and glimpses. They tell of the nation's fall in microcosmic form, as a slice of the trauma, as if it were happening on a stage to someone else; Jeremiah transforms pain into art.[4] That is how the book names reality and makes it approachable. Reality is simplified, yet emotionally the poetic images evoke the whole thing.

People who have experienced disaster or trauma often lose their capacity to speak about these events because violence destroys speech.[5] If victims encounter events again too directly, the violence repeats itself, re-traumatizing them in looping reiterations of pain that refuse to heal. To set the ruins into a poetic world creates distance. It makes it possible for people to face violent experiences indirectly and to begin to reframe them, to integrate them into their larger story as a people, to build hope.

Such transformation of ruins into artistic language is the opposite of much of our political and religious speech. We often name our world with literalizing reductions of reality to its crudest, most self-serving essentials, to media bites that obscure more than reveal and usually fail to capture the imagination or touch the best in our collective spirit. Walter Brueggemann, profound poet himself, once spoke of our prose-flattened world.[6] And with the rapid disappearance of the humanities in our schools, I wonder who can name our reality and put it before us to see, address, and engage.[7] To reconstitute ourselves as a people of hope, we might learn from Jeremiah how to name and rename reality more evocatively.

Jeremiah Renames God in the Midst of that Reality of Ruins

A second component of Jeremiah's process of hope-building is to name God as the dispenser of fire and brimstone, as the Author of War and Violence. The counterintuitive nature of my claim is compounded by the ways fire and brimstone God has been co-opted among us in the most literal of ways. The God who punishes sin has been used in some contemporary religious circles to create scapegoats. And this portrait of God is also the whipping post of the new atheists who reduce the biblical God to the Punishing One.[8] When used by outsiders to explain tragedies like 9/11 and the devastations following Katrina, such theology is hateful. It accuses "sinners" in New York and New Orleans of bringing on their own suffering.

Fire and brimstone theology is two-pronged: first, human sin causes the disaster, and, second, disaster is God's punishment upon the people for their offenses. Although this twinned theology is very difficult for many modern Western readers to accept, even with critical cautions, it is crucial for Judah's survival and the healing power of the book. To show this, I look at the worst example of such fire and brimstone texts, the rape poem.

The Rape Poem (Jer 13:20–27). The rape poem (Jer 13:20–27) is the last of a series of poems with war at its center (Jer 4:5–6:30, and also 16–17; 10:17–22). In them, divine fury sweeps away everything and everyone that make life worth living (Jer 6:11–12).

> See, a people is coming from the land of the north,
> a great nation is stirring from the farthest parts of the earth.
> They grasp the bow and the javelin,
> they are cruel and have no mercy,
> and their sound is like the roaring of the sea;
> against you, O Daughter of Zion. (Jer 6:22–23)

Any remnants of God's past love for the Daughter of Zion turns to horror here. God commands her: "Lift up your eyes and see those who come from the north" (Jer 13:20). And when she wants to know, "Why have these things come upon me?" when she wants explanation, the answer is clear: "It is for the greatness of your iniquity that your skirts are lifted up and you are violated" (Jer 13:22). The "lifting of skirts" may be a euphemism for rape, but the second clause makes rape certain, "you are violated."[9] The violator, unnamed in verse 22, is God in verse 26: "I myself will strip off your skirts over your face" (Jer 13:25–26, my translation). God's anger at the Daughter of Zion interprets the war. With arresting speech, the rape names the violence of the Babylonian invasions, and it defends God. God's anger means that God is not powerless and that cause and effect are at work in the world where chaos and godlessness seem to rule.

By shrinking vast assaults by an army into an attack upon one woman, the rape poem reduces the scope of the violence. Female rape is a familiar metaphor for war in the Old Testament and a common weapon of war throughout history. It is an apt metaphor because rape brutalizes in the most intimate and terrifying of ways.[10] For many among us, of course, God's rape of Zion is appalling and unbearable. It turns military attack into violence against a woman, makes women scapegoats for the nation's fall, sees sexual assault as suitable punishment, and it locates hideous actions within God. It is utterly unacceptable God-talk.

But unacceptability is surely the point of this poem! To be victims of invasion *is* appalling, unbearable, unspeakable, and unacceptable, a ripping apart, a destruction of life.[11] The rape poem gives the people back their story and brings to speech the profound terrors of Babylonian assaults. Because war is rape on a national scale, the poem "reproduce(s) the difficulty of the world itself."[12] Rape is what happened to them, their lives rendered symbolically, and their traumatic memories drawn into a narrative, into new speech for a speech-destroying disaster.

That God's rape is a "text of terror"[13] is central to its purpose and its capacity to defend God. It keeps God alive. Defeat by Babylon surely meant theologically that Judah lost the war to superior deities, to Marduk and his pantheon and that Judah's God is ineffectual, effete, and has "been disappeared." But if God authored this terror, God is not disappeared, not a defeated lesser being, not diminished. Babylonian deities have not triumphed, nor has ungoverned Fate propelled events.

Like all efforts to name God, Jeremiah's fire and brimstone is a provisional effort to make sense of reality, to cling to the Creator in the midst of the ruins. It is a poetic offering arising from within the experience of violence, articulated by an insider who contributes it to the work of interpretation, of making sense of the senseless. God's punishing violence gives the disaster predictable causes, orderly structure, direction, and purpose that extend beyond the visible world. It helps the people integrate the disaster into the long stream of the nation's existence, into its long narrative memory.[14]

Jeremiah Imagines God of the Future on the Basis of Past Traditions (Jeremiah 30–31)[15]

Words of explicit hope trickle across the book, but readers are simply not prepared for the explosive, interrupting beauty of the "Little Book of Consolation" that bursts upon us just after the book's center (Jer 30–31).[16]

A yawning gap exists between the present ruins and the future imagined here, but past and future are both united in God. The future world of joy, salvation, and beauty will interrupt the present weariness and despair without causal explanation.

The future is an act of God. Even though Jeremiah uses the past to tell of the future, that future does not evolve from what has gone before.[17] Jeremiah's future is utopian; that is, in its perfection, it does not exist. Neither past nor present causes the future. It is a promise, a world to be struggled for, a call to lead the people forward into a new reality. In this future, God satisfies the weary and nourishes the faint (Jer 31:25), ransoms Jacob and redeems him "from hands too strong for him" (Jer 31:11). God recreates the covenant and makes new faithful creatures by writing Torah in their hearts (Jer 31:31). God promises fidelity until all the mysteries of cosmos are revealed (Jer 31:35-37).

The future does not emerge from the past, but Jeremiah conjures the future on the basis of the past. He respins the tradition. Reinventing the tradition is a necessary survival strategy. If the nation is to be revived, then it can only do so by keeping continuity with the God of their history. Jeremiah does not start from scratch. Like politicians in the United States who appeal to speeches of Abraham Lincoln or George Washington, Jeremiah reclaims traditions, finds authority in them, and reapplies them to the new situation.

Jeremiah has to reinvent the tradition. He cannot simply repeat the old words, old stories, and the old beliefs because disasters shake the very foundations of a people's faith, and trust. They undermine confidence in God and bring traditions to a dead end. The fundamental problem facing Jeremiah is whether or not the God of their ancestors can survive the disaster. All that formerly supported the world fell apart with the nation. If the people of Judah are to remain themselves, they must reframe their lives in continuity with that past. Traditional language integrates the disaster into their larger existence.

Jeremiah Calls People to Radically Different Social Arrangements and to Covenant Communion with God

In Jeremiah's Little Scroll of Consolation (Jeremiah 30-31), the God of the Future is Author of a society reconstituted on different moral grounds.

God calls the people of Judah to a political, economic, and spiritual renewal. For a people of grievous wound and incurable pain, any future at all is a surprise, of course, let alone the possibility that they will be healed and renewed (Jer 30:27; 31:13-14).[18] Against historical probability, Zion/Jerusalem will be rebuilt, the community reorganized, the household of Jacob will be re-established. The contours of this vision challenge Christians in the United States who seek to live as disciples in the midst of our present economic and social realities.

Safe Place in a City Rebuilt. The first requirement for renewed life for Judah, for anyone, is physical safety and protection. God will rebuild the city of Jerusalem, their traditional holy place, here called "Zion" (Jer 30:17; 31:6, 12) or "the holy hill" (Jer 31:23), a name "hallowed by ancestral traditions."[19] Arising from the ruins, the city will be a habitat of safety and protection for all the people:

> I am going to restore the fortunes of the tents of Jacob,
>   and have compassion on his dwelling:
> The city shall be rebuilt upon its mount
>   and the citadel set on its rightful site. (Jer 30:18)

To a people forced out of their homes, displaced, deported, and living under foreign control, God promises a safe haven, a citadel in its rightful place. The rebuilt city fulfills the yearning of the homeless and grants them dignity as God's people. They will live there together in safety (Jer 30:18-20).

We have claimed in the United States to be this city built upon the hill, the new Jerusalem, the place where God lives among us and from which sends us to go out to the world to civilize those others and to bring them the truth and the light. But in Jeremiah, the city built upon the hill is neither the place of triumphant righteousness nor of imperial aggrandizement. It is the home of the needy and the wounded. The safe place is only the beginning of new life and less important than the transformation of the community to be formed there.[20]

Call to Return Home. Jeremiah proposes a great social upheaval. Among those returning to Zion (Jer 31:1-14), social renewal begins where it is least expected, among the feeble and the vulnerable, the lowly and the wounded.[21] The ones God calls home are the same ones who cried out in panic, had no peace, lived in distress, and endured terrors (Jer 30:5–7). They are the ones freed from bondage, whose hurt is incurable, the ones without medicine, without healing, the ones plundered and preyed upon who cry out in endless pain (Jer 30:12–17). These are the root and the beating heart of the restored society.

> See I am going to bring them from the land of the north,
>   and gather them from the farthest parts of the earth,
> Among them the blind and the lame,
>   those with child and those in labor, together;
> a great company they shall come. (Jer 31:8)

Returning to Zion is a parade of the forgotten, the disabled, and the vulnerable, the least in the society. The blind and the lame are physically different, weak, deemed deficient in the ancient world, stigmatized, and perhaps despised.[22] Pregnant women are lowly of public stature and holders of little political power, but together these people have the astonishing capacity to give birth to new life. For a nation seemingly doomed to extinction at the hands of Babylon, they are bearers of the future.

These—not kings, queens, or warriors, not the healthy, the wealthy, and the ruddy, but the wounded and disabled, the previously enslaved, survivors of destruction all—they are the new community. They are limping home to Zion to be reincorporated as the people of God. But how can the blind and the lame lead and how can the pregnant and those in labor march to Zion? Jeremiah's proclamation of return fundamentally reverses human expectations and reveals God as one who stands with history's victims. The broken and weak are the ones God calls fertile. This vision, too, is a survival strategy, a partial, provisional "stay against confusion,"[23] a revelation of the divine.

At this conference, where we are lifting up alternative biblical visions to our recent religio-political rhetoric, Jeremiah's rebuilt society reminds Christians who we are called to be. It names us as a people able to imagine and create a differently constituted community. Jeremiah offers no blueprint for life in any nation. The text is not a map but a call to faith in a God who stands with the vulnerable. And it is, first and foremost, a call to live differently within our own religious communities. It provides resources and processes for contributing to a more hopeful and just society in the United States and in our relations to the two-thirds world.

Jeremiah's rebuilt community makes an astonishing claim upon us. In it, the poor and the different are not simply included, allowed in through the back door and sent into servant's quarters in the basement or out into the fields to pick tomatoes. They are the foundation, the building stones, the fertile womb of the new community. Jeremiah's list of people who are called home signify the very people we debate about including and about how to include them in our society today. They are the disregarded, the homeless, the mentally ill, the sexually different, the immigrants upon whose back rides so much of our farming, cleaning, and care giving. They are the uninsured who have no medicine and no healing. They are peoples in the two-thirds world from whose labors and resources we benefit so much. And, as in Jeremiah's vision, they are the hope of the future, the creative ones, the fertile thinkers, the hard workers and builders, often embodying faith that can re-inflame our own.

For Christians, Jeremiah's new society evokes and anticipates Jesus' teachings about the poor and the lowly, his practices of welcoming and eating with tax collectors and sinners, of healing the sick and raising the dead. These are God's people, the bedrock and primary inhabitants of the Kingdom of God. Jeremiah tells the believing community who matters to God, who are the creative contributors to the future, who are the salt of the earth. These are the ones who anticipate Jesus' revelation of God in his own body, broken for us.

Call to Worship. Jeremiah's rebuilt community will be a gathering of worshippers. The new society is not simply a secular vision of democratic or egalitarian justice. At its heart, the new community exists to live in right relationship with God of which a just social arrangement is an expression. Gratitude, praise, and thanksgiving arise from the mouths of the vulnerable: "Out of them shall come thanksgiving and the sound of merrymakers, and I will make them many and not few, and I will make them honored and they shall not be disdained" (Jer 30:19).

These worshippers will be a community of mutual respect and honor, thankful for life together, for life at all, for survival from the ashes. Recognizing God's care of them, knowing God has brought them home, the very identity of this wounded and vulnerable people is that they are worshippers of God for "their congregation shall be established before me; and I will punish all who oppress them (Jer 30:20).

Call to Economic Well-Being for All (Jer 31:10–14). Flowing from their worshipping identity, because they worship a God of the wounded and the vulnerable, they will form a community of economic well-being for everyone.

> They shall come and sing aloud on the heights of Zion,
>> and they shall be radiant over the goodness of the Lord,
>
> over the grain, the wine, and the oil,
>> and over the young of the flock and the herd.
>
> Their life shall become like a watered garden . . .
> Then the young women shall rejoice in the dance,
>> and the young men and the old shall be merry . . . "
>
> I will give the priests their fill of fatness,
>> and my people shall be satisfied with my bounty. (Jer 31:12–14)

God's restored community is a place of abundance, not lack. There is enough for everyone, there is food for everyone. It is not an oasis for the wealthy few or even the comfortable many, as we must describe our society as being.

Jeremiah's social world imagined here is the consequence of a theological vision, an expression of divine love, revealed in the midst of the displaced, the broken, and the comfortless. Jeremiah imagines these themes somewhat differently in a series of poetic pieces about God's broken family.

Call to Family Reunion (Jer 31:15–34). When God casts off wives Judah and Israel toward the beginning of the book (Jer 2:1–4:2), Jeremiah tells the story of the nation's fall as the collapse of a marriage and a family, a story that begins in Hosea (Hosea 1–3).[24] Here Jeremiah revives the story in a family reunion. Poetic figures, drawn from tradition, Jacob, Rachel, and their grandson Ephraim are ancestors who signify the whole nation, now reunited as in the days of old. They personify and gather up the destroyed community and connect them with the larger story of their past.[25]

When God reconvenes the family, there are no exclusions,[26] only announcements of love. "I have loved you with an everlasting love, therefore I have continued my faithfulness to you" (Jer 31:3b). Mother Rachel is weeping bitterly (Jer 31:15–34), unable to recover from the loss of her children (Jer 31:15). God speaks to her directly and comforts her, seeks to dry her tears, and promises her a heart-stopping gift. The children she believed to be dead are alive and will return to her. "They shall come back from the land of the enemy; there is hope for your future" (Jer 31:16–17).

Using language of worship, child Ephraim begs to be brought back into the family, "for you are the LORD my God" (Jer 31:18–19; 31:6; cf. 3:22).[27] God had never forgotten him and delights in the child and his name (Jer 31:20). As the family of old is reviving, comes a mysterious announcement, "The LORD has created a new thing on the earth, a woman encompasses a man (*geber*)" (31:22). Who are the woman and man and what does this reversal of social roles mean?

Subsequent verses amplify rather than limit possibilities of meaning: the woman may signify the land itself, protecting, encompassing, and welcoming back the displaced and the exiled (Jer 31:21–26). She may be the women of Judah encompassing men sexually to provide offspring for the nation and to augur new generations for the destroyed peopled (Jer 31:27–28). Or she may be mother Rachel, embracing her returning son, the whole people in solidarity of responsibility, no longer divided by generations (Jer 31:29–30).

But no matter who these figures represent, family life will be greatly altered in the newly inaugurated covenant. The covenant is the "new thing," God is doing and it describes life in the restored family of God.

New Life in the Family (31:31–34). In Jeremiah, covenant renewal is cast in terms of the broken family metaphor. God announces that the people broke covenant with me even though I was "their husband."[28] God's covenant with Israel is like a marriage, and they broke it by their adulterous idolatry, but nowGod will restore them and renew the family in a divine recommitment to the family.

Jeremiah again uses the ancient tradition to imagine hope for the future. With the Babylonian invasions, the covenant tradition came to a halt. God abandoned them to the more powerful gods of Babylon and their relationship was ruptured beyond repair, or so it seemed. But the new covenant asserts something different. The new covenant is the old covenant, internalized, revivified, gathering in the whole family, and reuniting them with the God of their past. "The days are surely coming says the LORD when I will make a new covenant with the house of Israel and the house of Judah. It will not be like the old one that I made with their ancestors when I took them by the hand to bring them out of the land of Egypt, a covenant they broke, though I was their husband" (Jer 31:31–32). Again Jeremiah names the present condition of the community. They live in a broken covenant, a shattered relationship, despite all God did for them in the past, rescuing them from slavery in Egypt. Like the old covenant, the new one also involves rescue from an enslaving nation, this time Babylon.

The new covenant is a highly conservative theological assertion, the old made new. Its newness saves the original covenant, but it reframes their present spiritual brokenness in light of their larger story. And set in terms of the marriage of God to Israel and Judah, it sets their relationship with God on a new footing.

God restores life in the family on more intimate and vibrant terms. "I will put my law within them and write it on their hearts." It is the same covenant expressed with the same covenant formula, "I will be their God and they shall be my people" (Exod 19:1–6). It is the same torah, but now the law will be part of them, internal to their beings, no longer written on tablets as a law set outside them demanding obedience. It is an internal law, part of their very being. The new covenant is a new mode of life, a deeper, revivified relationship with God that affects relationships in the community. No longer shall they teach one another or say to one another, "know the LORD, for they shall know me, from the least of them to the greatest, says the LORD for I will forgive their sins" (Jer 31:34).

The Hebrew language of knowing (*yādaʿ*) conveys intimacy, sexual knowledge, and mutuality; it has consequences for the life of this poetic family. This intimacy identifies Judeans as a people who know God, live with God, and experience the presence of God. This re-enlivened relationship alters their identity, makes of them what some Christians might call a "contemplative community." They are a people focused on the divine, breathers of God's life, one with God. The new covenant is a call to a spiritually grounded way of life, to intimate knowledge of God's presence in the heart of every one, within them and among them. The knowledge of God is the divine life, glimpsed provisionally, experienced in community, and expressed in language that cannot fully express this good news.[29] Those without hope are drawn back, reunited, and made whole as a reborn and forgiven people.

The new covenant is a profoundly egalitarian vision. It grants superiority to no one or to no group in the community; "from the least to the greatest, all shall know me." Among members of God's family there is equal dignity and equal participation in God's life.

The new covenant passage calls Christians to know God with more than our minds and wills, but with our full humanity. It makes us a people who are seeking and moving toward what James Fowler called the upper stages of faith development, faith not as law external to us, but as an intimate knowing of God. And from such movement flows consequences for our life together and for our ways of building our national society. Life with God that finds no expression in the world is dead, just as action itself can become warped by selfishness, manipulation, and control without contemplative living.

Jeremiah's vision of hope enflames possibility and awakens yearning for a better world. It challenges the present reality by insisting on divine power as the enacting agent of return. It calls to us to renew intimacy with God, to seek to live in open, wounded awakeness to God's revelation among us, ever ancient, ever new. Jeremiah's vision urges us to reflect and to struggle toward social relations that ensure safety, food, dignity to the weak and vulnerable, the old, the young, the ill, and the different. It calls us to know ourselves as weak and vulnerable and to know that everyone from the least to the greatest may teach us of God, if only we could listen. It urges us to a life of worship and to political and economic arrangements that provide for well-being of everyone.

Jeremiah's utopian vision is what Marin calls "a type of praxis,"[30] a work of imaginative transformation that critiques the reigning inertia and despair and unleashes energy for new forms of life. In Jeremiah, the process of hope-building and the vision of a rebuilt community receives its origin in God, the interrupting energy who transforms the world. The people of Judah cannot achieve their promised, incandescent future on their own. Only the God of the ancestors can bring it to birth in the new life that lies just over the horizon.[31]

Endnotes

1. I am grateful to Luce Foundation for a Henry Luce III Fellowship for the study of Jeremiah using trauma and disaster studies.
2. See Smith-Christopher, *A Biblical Theology of Exile*, 79.
3. The closest we come to the literal depiction of invasion, or at least to historical reporting, is chapter 39 and chapter 52, the latter parallel is arguably borrowed from 2 Kings 25.
4. Stulman and Kim, *You Are My People*, 8–11.
5. Sebald, *On the Natural History of Destruction*, 1–32; and see extensive studies of the effects of trauma in Scary, *The Body in Pain*; and Herman, *Trauma and Recovery*.
6. Brueggemann, *Finally Comes the Poet*.
7. Slouka, "Dehumanized," 32–40.
8. See Wood, "God in the Quad," 75.
9. The Hebrew reads, "your heels undergo violence," heels being "private parts." See Lundbom, *Jeremiah 1–20*, 686. It is well known that rape is a persistent weapon of warfare. See Gordon and Washington, "Rape as Military Metaphor," 308–25. Throughout history unto this day women are assaulted and sexually violated in ways that not only harms them horribly, if they survive, but also shames their men who cannot protect them.
10. Lundbom, *Jeremiah 1–20*, 686, discusses the Hebrew of these verses and understands the assault as public shaming by exposure, though he also connects the verses to the sexual assaults against women common in war (Amos 1:13; Isa 3:17; Ezek 16:39–40).
11. On rape's horrors and survival, see Brison, *Aftermath*, 1–24. On shame in Jeremiah, see Kalmanofsky, *The Rhetoric of Horror in the Book of Jeremiah*, 65–68.
12. See Brison, *Aftermath*.
13. Language about the *Iliad* in White, *When Words Loose Their Meaning*, 87.
14. A term made part of the interpretive lexicon by Phyllis Trible in Trible, *Texts of Terror*.
15. Tal, *Worlds of Hurt*, 6.
16. Fretheim, *Jeremiah*. Most likely chapters 30–33 address exiles, as many interpreters recognize, for they promise a journey home. Interpreters think this section of Jeremiah comes late in the book's production, added by writers who borrow from Jeremiah's earlier poetry to re-imagine the future. Trauma and disaster studies confirm such a late view of this material but for different reasons. Recovery from cataclysm often involves a long, arduous process, risings and fallings, starts and stops, zigzaggings from despair to hope. And perhaps it is this zigzagging path of recovery that causes the setting of the book of consolation in the middle and not at the end of the book. Martin Kessler (Kessler, "Jeremiah 26–45 Reconsidered," 81–88) noted years ago that new life is still far off for the book's readers, so that may be why the composers set hope in the midst of continuing gloom and desolation.
17. The book of consolation is variously identified as chapters 30–31 or 30–33, but chapters 32–33 continue in the prose narrative style of chapters 26–29. See, *Jeremiah*, 257–85; Allen, *Jeremiah*, 33; and Holladay, *Jeremiah*, 155–56.
18. Boer, *Novel Histories*, 120.
19. Brueggemann, "Prophetic Ministry," 159–60.
20. Collins, "Models of Utopia in the Biblical Tradition," 67.
21. Schweitzer, "Reading Utopia in Chronicles," 29–64.

22. Ibid., 150; Marin, *Utopics*, 84; Schweitzer, "Reading Utopia in Chronicles," 4.

23. See Olyan, *Disability in the Hebrew Bible*.

24. Robert Frost's words about poetry in Benfey, "The Storm over Robert Frost," 50.

25. Diamond and O'Connor, "Unfaithful Passions," 387–403.

26. Israel/Jacob is father of the twelve tribes and the patronymic ancestor of "all the families of Israel" (Jer 31:1), and Rachel (Jer 31:15), Jacob's most beloved wife, is quintessential mother of all Israel, and Ephraim is her (grand)son.

27. See Bozak, "Life Anew." Bozak also attends to variations in addresses between masculine and feminine in chapters 30–31.

28. Reunion of father and child complete the scene of return begun in Jer 3:22–25.

29. Or "their master," Holladay, *Jeremiah*, 198.

30. For different interpretations of this passage, see Brueggemann, *A Commentary on Jeremiah*, 293–95.

31. Marin, *Utopics*, 81–82.

9

Jesus, the Poor, and Mammon: A Look at Values from Luke-Acts

DARRELL L. BOCK

It is hard to enter into a short essay on this topic without two things getting in the way almost immediately. They are the historical Jesus debate and our own ideological-political commitments. So let me clear ground by starting here briefly.

Introductory Issues

Working Backward to the Roots

First, the nature of Jesus' ministry produced early communities with many people of rather everyday origin. This is not really debated among New Testament scholars (perhaps one of the few areas where this is so!). First Corinthians 1:26–29 says it most clearly: "Think about the circumstances of your call, brothers and sisters. Not many were wise by human standards, not many were powerful, not many were born to a privileged position. But God chose what the world thinks foolish to shame the wise, and God chose what the world thinks weak to shame the strong. God chose what is low and despised in the world, what is regarded as nothing, to set aside what is regarded as something, so that no one can boast in his presence."[1]

Second, the community described in Acts spent some of its time raising money to help those in their community (the widows controversy of Acts 6; the pooled resources of the community noted in Acts 2:44–45 and 4:32–37).[2] They also had money raised outside to help them later (the collection of Paul for the Church in Judea). Such actions suggest roots connected to people having basic needs. This lays groundwork to suggest that although many of the texts I will discuss from Luke-Acts are unique to the book, the themes fit the kind of community that emerged. Third, Jesus' teaching on this topic does not represent a large deviation from aspects of second temple Jewish culture because the sensitivity to the poor we see in Jesus parallels nicely themes about alms and concern for those in need from that period.[3] Fourth, the concern of Jesus here fits with his attention to others on the fringe of society, a theme multiply attested in the gospels.[4] Finally, the very locale of the core of Jesus' ministry around the Galilee would point to such a context, especially given that he is not associated strongly with the larger settlements of Sepphoris or Tiberias. In other words, there is no good reason to drive a wedge between the historical Jesus and the portrait of him in the gospels on this topic. So we can come to this Jesus material with some confidence what we are hearing does reflect Jesus.

Allowing Jesus to Speak

As for our own ideological or political commitments, I simply say that whatever explanations one may have about why poverty exists or the best way to socially and politically deal with it does not absolve us of responsibility for coming to grips with how Jesus engaged the question in his time, even if we understand our times are not his. In particular, it will be important to see how Jesus views the value of meeting human needs, since Jesus himself did not posit any explicit political answers to such dilemmas.

So with these initial observations clearing the brush, I now turn to consider how Luke portrays Jesus' approach to the poor and money, as well as how the community in Acts also may reflect such concerns. Normally when this topic has been taken up in theological discourse or in biblical theological treatments, there is an affirmation of Jesus' preference for the poor. Such a preference is perhaps most well known in liberation theologies of the two-thirds world.[5] I will argue something slightly different is going on—a sensitivity to the poor alongside an awareness of how money and possession with their accompanying power risk distorting a sensitivity to others in need.

Two Key Lucan Texts Introduce Our Theme

Luke's infancy material and John the Baptist's teaching set up much of what Jesus says about money, power, and the poor. Both of these texts are unique to Luke's gospel, reflecting his concentration on this theme. In Mary's hymn praising God's kindness to her, there is a turn in Luke 1:50 to how the deity treats people in general. God is merciful to those who fear him. In the context of God's covenant with Israel (Luke 1:54), he has acted by demonstrating "power with his arm; he has scattered those whose pride wells up from the sheer arrogance of their hearts. He has brought down the mighty from their thrones, and has lifted up those of lowly position; he has filled the hungry with good things, and has sent the rich away empty (Luke 1:51–53). Here the hymn warns of the danger of power; it can produce arrogance. The text proclaiming a future judgment and a resulting reversal of fate shows what values God honors. God sees and cares about the need and the needy, rewarding them with an eternity of benefits that extend long beyond the earthly period of their suffering. The passage issues a warning not just about the future; it also is a statement about resources. They are not to be used selfishly; they are to be used as resources of ministry. Jesus will restate this value just as emphatically later.

In Luke 3:14, John the Baptist makes a point about the value of living modestly with contentment, while being careful not to abuse power. When soldiers ask John about repentance and what it looks like for them specifically in light of the new era and reform, John the Baptist says, "Take money from no one by violence or by false accusation, and be content with your pay" (Luke 3:14). Once again the summary could well be, "Do not abuse power, but be content with a quality of life that allows you to have basic needs."

Neither of these texts has any secrets tucked away in the Greek. They are like an overture at the beginning of a symphony that sounds notes to be playing again and again in various keys as the Gospel and Acts proceed. God cares about how we treat others and how we use what God gives us. When John the Baptist's ministry was introduced in

Jesus, the Poor, and Mammon

Luke 1:16-17, this prophet was not only said to be calling people to turn to God, but he would also call for a reconciliation where fathers and children would come together, as would the disobedient be reconnected to those who were just and lived wisely. This note introduces an ethical core that was to be the goal of the new era John was announcing. Turning to God meant treating others in a way that honored God and brought a reconciliation that was healthy for all, yielding both righteousness and peace. The righteousness we see in how John addresses the soldiers and in God's admonition that judgment will reverse wrong. There is accountability to God that will uphold what is right. However we should not have to wait for righteousness. Responding to it now makes for a better world and reflects a commitment to truly follow God.

The Teaching of Jesus: Eleven Texts

Surveying the Teaching of Jesus

Jesus' teaching on this combination of themes appears in twelve units in the gospel (the asterisk means uniquely Luke; parallels, if they exist, are noted in brackets): *Luke 4:18; *6:20 and 6:24 [with unique emphasis, but see Matt 5:3]; 7:22 [Matt 11:5]; 8:14 [Mark 4:18; Matt 13:22]; *12:16 and 12:21; 12:33 [Matt 6:20]; *14:12, 13, 21; 16:13 [Matt 6:24]; *16:19-22, *16:27, *16:30; 18:22-25; Mark 10:21, 10:25; Matt 19:21-24; *19:2, 19:8; 21:13 [Mark 12:41-44]. Other uses of the term "money" are merely descriptive and as such do not contribute to this topic (Luke 9:3; 10:4; 14:28; 16:1, 14; 19:15, 23; 22:5; 22:35-36). We proceed through these texts in their Lucan sequence, so we can also see how Luke's portrait of Jesus' teaching builds. In some cases we shall cluster discussions of some texts together, because they build off of one another. In addition to these twelve units, we shall consider one brief narrative example of someone who uses resources well.

Luke 4:18; 6:20, 24; and 7:22

So we begin with Luke 4:18, 6:20, 24; and 7:22, because they are very related, as we shall see. Luke 4:18-19 is part of a short address Jesus made in the synagogue in Nazareth. He reads from a combination of Isa 61:1-2 and 58:6. Most of the passage is from Isaiah 61, but the line about freeing the oppressed is from Isa 58:6. He makes this association of the texts through words these two passages and their context share: forgiveness, to send, and acceptable. *Here is Luke 4:18-19:* "The Spirit of the LORD is upon me, because he has anointed me to proclaim good news to the poor. He has sent me to proclaim release to the captives and the regaining of sight to the blind, to set free the oppressed, to proclaim the year of the LORD's favor."

Jesus says to those present that this text is now fulfilled. The verb "proclaim" is used three times because Jesus is announcing an era of comprehensive Jubilee (the year of the Lord's favor). This is good news. Jubilee is when all debts were forgiven (Lev 25:8–17). Jesus has turned a social practice into a metaphor of his work. In particular, Jesus' ministry is focused on the poor, the captives, the blind, and the oppressed. As we shall see, these terms are simultaneously religious and social. Part of this combined meaning is seen in the comparison Jesus makes to Elijah and Elisha later in this passage (Luke 4:24–27). Part of it comes from the context of Isaiah 61 and 58 where the prophet calls Israel back to a spiritual renewal that also brings a tangible change in relationships. In fact, Isaiah 58 is alluded to because in it Israel is rebuked for failing to offer the true spiritual fast of response to God that he had called them to perform. Jesus now says he will do what the nation had failed to do. In this text, Jesus presents himself as the fulfillment of this promise as he both announces and effects the release God is bringing. It is clear Jesus focuses on those in need (poor, blind) and those society has either persecuted or rejected (captives, oppressed).[6] The anointing looks back to the divine endorsement Jesus received at his baptism in Luke 3:22.

Who are the poor in this text? It is best to see them as equivalent to the humble of Luke 1:52, but in saying this we are not spiritualizing the reference to remove the idea that the poor are addressed. This is because the poor reappear in Luke 6:20. There beatitudes are announced for groups that include a reference to the poor. They are contrasted to the rich of Luke 6:24-26, for whom Jesus issues a series of woes. The spiritual dimension of the title is seen in its background from Isaiah and the Psalter, as well as from the description in Luke 6:22, where the note is made that the prophets were treated just as the poor are and where the response to the Son of Man is part of the point. Meanwhile in Luke 6:26, the rich are compared to false prophets, that is, they reject the message and the way of God. These descriptions are generalizations. They refer to tendencies each group has: the poor tend to be open to God while the rich see themselves as more self-sufficient and thus less responsive.

The scriptural background for the concept of the poor refers to the pious poor, those whose response to God has left them exposed to injustice in the world (Exod 22:25–27; Deut 15:7–11; Pss 14:6; 22:24; 25:16; 34:6; 40:17; 69:29; Isa 3:14–15; 10:2).[7] Isaiah 3:14–15 has a clear use of this sense of the term in a rebuke to the rich, "The LORD comes to pronounce judgment on the leaders of his people and their officials. 'It is you who have ruined the vineyard! You have stashed in your houses what you have stolen from the poor. Why do you crush my people and grind the faces of the poor?' The sovereign LORD who commands armies has spoken." The references to the vineyard and "my people" show the spiritual dimension of the term, while the rebuke shows that the poor cannot be spiritualized to remove the sociological dimension in the term. God's rebuke shows the values: do not take advantage of or exploit the poor to enhance one's own status. The fact that Luke 6 goes on to call the poor, the hungry, those who weep, and the hated shows their social condition and status.

Putting Luke 4 and 6 together, we see Jesus' sensitivity to the poor and his concern that they not be neglected, taken advantage of, or exploited. They are seen as sensitive to the dependence they have in life. Jesus' beatitude in Luke 6:20 reads, "Blessed to you who are poor, for the kingdom of God belongs to you." It might well be paraphrased, "Blessed are you materially poor, who nonetheless look to God and his promise, for the kingdom of God belongs to such as you."

Luke 7:22 has Jesus tell John the Baptist that Jesus as "the one who is to come" preaches the good news to the poor. In other words, what Jesus announced he was called to do and did in the synagogue in Nazareth, Jesus has done throughout his ministry.

Luke 8:1–3

This passage combines two Lucan themes in his gospel. It is one text where Jesus does not teach, but simply presents an example. It is an example we will see replicated in the community of Acts. The themes involve an affirmation of the role of women and how to use resources positively. Three women are noted: Mary Magdalene, the beneficiary of an exorcism by Jesus; Joanna, the wife of Herod's steward, Chuza; and Susanna. These three are said to have contributed to the support of the ministry with their resources. The presence of Joanna is important because it shows that the wealthy or those of status are not ignored.

Luke 8:14

The threat of riches to spiritual and community well-being comes up in the key kingdom parable of the soils that picture different responses to Jesus' message of the new era. As is well known, the seed of the word falls on the road, on rocky ground, among the thorns, and in good soil. The thorns in Luke are said to represent the worries of life, riches, and the pleasures of life that choke the ability of God's way and values to become evident in our lives. Exactly how this works is seen in some of the parables Luke tells. This is one of the few passages on our theme that both Matthew and Mark also include. So this warning about the dangers of the distraction of the pursuit of riches runs deep in early Christian tradition.

Luke 12:13–21

Our next passage is a parable. A brother has asked Jesus to intervene in a familial dispute about the family inheritance. Jesus refuses and warns about the danger of greed, noting that life does not consist of an abundance of possessions. Whenever I come to this text, I am reminded of the bumper sticker I used to see: "The one with the most toys wins." This parable says that is the attitude of a loser in life.

The parable is simple. A rich man grows a huge crop. There is nothing wrong with his being fortunate. The issue stems around what he does with what he is given. Here is how Jesus tells the parable:

> The land of a certain rich man produced an abundant crop, so he thought to himself, "What should I do, for I have nowhere to store my crops?" Then he said, "I will do this: I will tear down my barns and build bigger ones, and there I will store all my grain and my goods. And I will say to myself, 'You have plenty of goods stored

up for many years; relax, eat, drink, celebrate!'" But God said to him, "You fool! This very night your life will be demanded back from you, but who will get what you have prepared for yourself? So it is with the one who stores up riches for himself, but is not rich toward God."

This man is already rich. He has what he needs to live. Notice how his focus is on the crops as his and sees the use of these resources as something that is only to benefit him. This is stressed by the excessive use of the first-person pronoun and other self references in the parable—twelve times in four verses. This crop is his. He thinks of nothing other than how the crop can benefit him. He longs only to relax and enjoy what is his. This kind of tunnel vision focused on the self is one of the dangers riches produce if one is not careful. The application of the text comes at the end. The rich man is called out of this life. The question Jesus raises—Who will get what you have prepared for yourself?—is a good one because there is one person who will not get it, the rich fool. To only look to the self and not God (and what he asks of us) is to live a foolish life.

This passage reinforces something we saw earlier. Jesus' teaching on this topic is not a mere journey into secular political philosophy and theory. At the core of who we are as people comes our relationship to God and how we think about what he gives us in life. It is not the one with the most toys who wins, but the one who seeks and responds to God with values that reflect why he created us. There is a personal sense of accountability to God, a humility our first passage in Luke 1 noted that is important here. We are never alone in the world. We not only have neighbors, we have a God who cares what we do with the life and resources he gives us.

Luke 12:33

This passage serves as a contrast to the rich fool. Where the parable gave the negative example *not* to follow, here we have the example *to* follow. What is said here will be nuanced by passages to come later. Still this exhortation comes in a section on being a disciple. It says, "Sell your possessions and give to the poor. Provide yourselves purses that do not wear out—a treasure in heaven that never decreases, where no thief approaches and no moth destroys." Everything here is the reverse of the earlier passage. We are to give our resources for the benefit of others, including the poor. This produces a reward that comes with us to heaven and never wears out. The picture of an acceptable heavenly reward is a way of affirming the value of this kind of generosity. Where the rich man hoarded what came to him, disciples are to share what God gives them.

I have not made any explicit application to our time and setting yet, but here I must. One of the values of Western culture is individual freedom and ownership. These are core Western values. There is, however, a danger that a core value can become almost like a god, an idol. This is why some New Testament texts equate greed with idolatry (e.g., Eph 5:5). It risks turning us into thinking we are our own gods, an allusion that is so destructive to community. I often hear political debates on money and resources and hear the cry that the money I earn is mine. I understand this confession because I was inculcated with these values and expectations myself. However these texts warn me to be careful here on how much and how inviolate I view the possessions God gives to me. As Jesus sees them in these texts, money and resources are tools for service, not rewards for self-indulgence. Used well, these resources can serve and help people, but hoarded and handled selfishly they can become weapons of unrighteousness. It is too easy, given our cultural grounding, to think that ownership has such privileges that our possessions should be untouchable. Jesus calls us to give, not to hoard.

Luke 14:12–14

This short exhortation comes in the midst of a meal where Jesus is watching how people are jockeying for social status. He has just called for humility when: "He said also to the man who had invited him, 'When you host a dinner or a banquet, don't invite your friends or your brothers or your relatives or rich neighbors so you can be invited by them in return and get repaid. But when you host an elaborate meal, invite the poor, the crippled, the lame, and the blind. Then you will be blessed, because they cannot repay you, for you will be repaid at the resurrection of the righteous.'"

This text is laid out in a common Semitic "not X, but Y" format. So God desires mercy, not sacrifice. This often is not to be taken literally as not X but Y. Rather, it is a way of saying Y is more important than X. So

Jesus, the Poor, and Mammon

Jesus is saying to be sure and include the poor, crippled, lame, and blind. Note how this list parallels the list Jesus gave in Luke 7:22. He will parallel the list here in the parable that follows in Luke 14:21. The poor, crippled, blind, and lame are invited to feast at God's table in the end. The key is to respond to the invitation to come. Note again how the value is affirmed by saying that God will reward in the world to come the one who is so open with his invitations. These acts parallel what God will do in the world to come and does now. They show us to be a child of God.

We have seen these themes before. Jesus is emphasizing the point by repetition. Jesus is calling for an inclusiveness that honors the human integrity of each individual, even those the world often forgets. He is asking that we show the love of God by how we relate to those in need. He is teaching that this is what disciples are to do and be.

Luke 16:13

This passage is better known in its form in the Sermon on the Mount. In fact, most people know this verse whether they have been to church or not. It is a text that raises a question about ultimate loyalty. Is it to God or mammon? Jesus said, "No servant can serve two masters, for either he will hate the one and love the other, or he will be devoted to the one and despise the other. You cannot serve God and material possessions." There are moments of truth when values surface and the choice of ultimate allegiance is clear. That is what Jesus raises here. What will one serve: what earns one the most money or what honors God? The fascinating thing to note about the passage is how money is personified here as a master, one that competes with God. Here a thing takes on a role of controlling power. It is a distortion for this to happen, but happen it does. Jesus simply raises the point and moves on.

Luke 16:19–31

The parable of the rich man and Lazarus is one of the most important texts for our study. The core story is well known. There is a rich man who has purple undergarments and banquets daily, pictures of a sumptuous life. In contrast, Lazarus is hungry, covered with sores, and is licked by the unclean dogs that roam the street. In later Jewish tradition of the

Talmud, it was said that a man who depended on another man's table, had a body full of sores, and was ruled by his wife had no life (*b. Beṣah* 32b). Lazarus has two out of three. When they die, Lazarus ends up in blessing with Abraham while the rich man is below. The rich man appeals for relief, asking that Lazarus be sent to him with some water. This request is denied, as is a subsequent request to warn his brothers not to repeat the rich man's error. The rich man is told Moses and the prophets are enough. Anyone who does not listen to them will not listen to someone who comes back from the dead.

Most people think this text is about the hope of resurrection and the lack of responsiveness some will have to it, since that is where the parable ends. However, the core of this parable is about the rich man's utter lack of concern for Lazarus in contrast to the perspective of God. The parable pictures the eschatological reversal of the rich and humble described in Luke 1:52–53. In the end, Lazarus ends up in heaven and the rich man is cast down. Although Lazarus never speaks in this parable (the poor often get no voice), how he is responded to and what happens to him is a key to the story. The text warns that wealth is not a guarantee of blessing and calls for avoiding the kind of self-indulgence the rich man chose for his lifestyle, a self focus that caused him to be callous to a man in need right outside his own house. In many ways, this parable summarizes themes we have already raised.

The key part of the passage revolves around a peculiarity in the parable, namely that the name of one of its characters is given. Of all the parables of Jesus, this is the only one where an internal character has a name. The peculiarity yields many points. First, when the rich man dies and goes to the place of torment, he cries out to Abraham to send Lazarus to bring him some water for relief. The fact that the rich man knows Lazarus's name means that the rich man knew Lazarus had been sitting at his gate wanting only the crumbs the rich man could have provided. The rich man knew who Lazarus was. The rich man had given him nothing, even though it was possible and would have been simple for him to do so. Second, the calling out of Lazarus by name to "serve" him also points to another tendency wealth can engender. It is to see people for what they can do for me and as having a status to serve me. Even though their fates had changed in the afterlife, the rich man still saw Lazarus as someone who could be at the rich man's beck and call. A third key point in the passage is that once again the pictures of the afterlife, judgment, and reward are used to present the values Jesus affirms or challenges. A fourth point comes from one of the key ironies of the text. In the parable after the rich man has given up his quest for relief, he asks that someone be sent from the dead to warn his brothers. In the parable this request is refused. No one will be sent from the dead to warn his brothers. However, what the story denies, the story performs in its narrative. We as participants in the parable are hearing a warning from the afterlife and heaven. The account gives us a glimpse of values God honors. This fourth point needs development because the answer given to the rich man's request is that the brothers have Moses and the prophets. In fact, what the brothers are to see from these texts is God's consistent call to be sensitive to the poor. We are not to treat them as objects, only useful when they can serve us, but we are to be sensitive and responsive to their needs. Numerous texts in Moses and the prophets make this point (Deut 14:28–29; 15:1–3, 7–12; 22:1–2; 23:19; 24:7–15, 19–21; 25:13–14; Isa 3:14–15; 5:7–8; 10:1–3; 32:6–7; 58:3, 6–7, 10; Jer 5:26–28; 7:5–6; Ezek 18:12–18; 33:15; Amos 2:6–8; 5:11–12; 8:4–6; Mic 2:1–2; 3:1–3; 6:10–11; Zech 7:9–10; Mal 3:5).[8] Jesus' concern for the poor has deep roots in the sacred scripture of Israel. This ethical core drives this parable, which itself appears in a chapter of Luke dedicated to how resources are handled.

Luke 18:18–30

The story of the rich ruler is also an important passage for our theme. Here a rich man asks what he must do to inherit eternal life, an ancient way of asking how one is saved. Jesus replies by citing the second part of the Ten Commandments, a way of saying we honor God by how we treat others, a variation of the call to love God and love our neighbor. The rich ruler tells Jesus he has done all of these things. So Jesus adds one more requirement for him, "Sell all that you have and give the money to the poor, and you will have treasure in heaven. Then come, follow me." This is still part of Jesus' answer, a point often missed in discussing this passage. The man is told to sell all and give his money to the poor. The reward will be God's blessing. Then the man is to follow Jesus. The challenge is a test of the rich man's heart. Does he want God's blessing and does he seek God's way or is he married to his mammon? Does he love God or money?

The fact the man walks away shows where his heart is. Jesus explains it is hard for the rich to enter into the kingdom. This shocks the crowd and the disciples. For them, wealth was a sign of blessing. If the rich do not make it, then who can? Peter closes the scene asking if the disciples have done what Jesus had asked (even though they had not sold everything). Jesus reassures them they are headed for blessing.

This passage shows how attached we can become to our possessions, choosing these things even over that which means relationship with God. Our possessions can turn our hearts into a direction that is slow to care about others, especially others in need. Jesus exposes such a heart in this exchange with this rich man. But Jesus holds out hope. God can do with a heart what is impossible for that heart to do for itself. In addition, the disciples who were responsive to Jesus and the kind of sacrifice he called for were assured they had a new family in this life and life in the world to come. The eternal life the rich man had sought on his own terms and strength, the disciples received by humbly responding to God. So the passage ends where it began, showing that life can be attained.

Luke 19:1–10

With Luke's many notes about the dangers of wealth, one might ask if there is any hope at all for the rich. The account of Zacchaeus, the chief tax collector, answers that question by showing there is hope for the rich man who turns and learns how to be generous with what he has. The key to this passage is in Zacchaeus's response to Jesus' request that the tax collector host Jesus during his stay in Jericho. Zacchaeus on hearing the request responds, "Look, Lord, half of my possessions I now give to the poor, and if I have cheated anyone of anything, I am paying back four times as much!" The tax collector does not sell all, but half. His heart is in the right place. His possessions are resources to be shared. More than that, if he has cheated anyone, he is willing to accept the full burden of restitution the law required, by paying back fourfold. Later Jewish tradition saw it as generous to give back twenty percent of one's possessions (*b. Ketubot* 50a).

The Law required a twenty percent restitution beyond the value (Lev 5:16; Num 5:7), except in the case of rustling, where the payback became four sheep for each one or five for each ox (Exod 22:1). Zacchaeus's heart shows a willingness to repay in full, accepting his guilt in the matter. Jesus' response is that Zacchaeus is a true son of Abraham. Here is man who has becomes a generous rich man. No longer does Jesus say to him, sell all. Rather, he is to continue to use the resources God has given him in ways that also benefit others.

Luke 21:1–3

Our last passage about Jesus' teaching moves us to the other side of the social spectrum. Here a very poor widow gives two lepta to the temple. As a poor woman, she could have easily given one coin (think of a penny here) and kept one for herself, but she gave "out of her very life" as Jesus puts it when he commends her. The example here is that it is not the amount that is given that shows the dedication to God but the kind of selfless, sacrificial offering that shows the offering's quality. As Jesus said in Luke 21:3, "this poor widow has put in more than all of them."

Summary

So the gospel ends with two good examples of how to handle resources. Be generous to others and be generous to God with what he gives us. Resources are tools of service and ministry. Where your resources go show where your heart is. Or as Jesus said in an earlier passage on this theme in Luke 12:34, "For where your treasure is, there your heart will be also." Those who give to people, honor God and people. Those who hoard what they have show their love is far too selfish.

Examples from the Book of Acts

Acts 2:44–45 and 4:34–37

We note four brief examples from Acts that show the spirit of what Jesus taught. The first example involves two passages that work together to show how the community supported one another. Acts 2:44–45 shows the level of sharing in the new community. This text reads, "All who believed were together and held everything in common, and they began selling their property and possessions and distributing the proceeds to everyone, as anyone had need." This kind of community indicated a sense of kinship among the followers of Jesus. The practice was voluntary, as Acts 5:4 indicates, since Ananias had the choice to keep his property for himself. The voluntary nature of the giving is different from that which took place at Qumran, where the sharing of resources was compulsory for those who wished to join that community (1QS 1:11–12; 5:1–3; 6:2–3; CD 9:1–15). Such ethical unity was often praised in the ancient world (Philo *Good Person* 12 §86; Josephus *Antiquities* 18.20).

Generosity became a natural expression of care in the community. Acts 4:34–37 reinforces this commitment and notes the example of Barnabas. It reads: "For there was no one needy among them, because those who were owners of land or houses were selling them and bringing the proceeds from the sales and placing them at the apostles' feet. The proceeds were distributed to each, as anyone had need. So Joseph, a Levite who was a native of Cyprus, called by the apostles Barnabas [which is translated "son of encouragement"], sold a field that belonged to him and brought the money and placed it at the apostles' feet." Here the portrait of Acts 2 expands as we are told that no one had a need as the wealthy shared resources with those who lacked.

Acts 6:1–5

In this passage we see the church resolve a conflict over how to meet the needs of widows who needed care. The Hebrew widows were being cared for, but the widows of the Hellenists were not. So when the complaint came to the leadership, they asked the group making the complaint to help with the solution and appoint trusted people from their group to be sure the widows had their needs addressed. There was to be no ethnic preference in how the community would help those who needed aid.

Acts 8:9–25

Here we have another negative example that fits with the already-noted deceit of Ananias in Acts. Here Simon seeks to purchase from Peter the power of ministry that comes through the Holy Spirit. Simon is roundly rebuked. The church and ministry are not for sale to the highest bidder.

As Peter said to Simon, "May your silver perish with you, because you thought you could acquire God's gift with money!" The value here also suggests that ministering to gain wealth is not exactly in tune with the values we have seen in these two New Testament books. In fact, earlier when someone asked Peter and John for alms, they noted that they did not have gold and silver but would gladly freely give what they could to help the man as they moved to heal him.

Acts 24:17

The final example is Paul taking up a collection for the needs of the church in Jerusalem. It was as he was bringing this collection to the church there that he was arrested and found himself before Felix, the Roman representative in Israel. Paul notes that these gifts were for the poor.

Summary

These short examples show a church pooling resources and meeting one another's needs. Possessions are seen not as private property to be hoarded, but as means of serving one's neighbor. The focus of these texts from Acts involve mostly activity in the community, but the care that is represented is part of the evidence of a genuine love and care for people, especially those in need.

Concluding Observations

Our survey of key texts on possessions, the poor, and the value of Jesus is done.[9] We have seen several things. Possessions are a threat to personal well-being, not because they are bad in themselves but because of what they can do to us. They can cause us to be selfish. They can lead us to treat others as objects. They can choke out our focus on God and spirituality. Possessions are not seen primarily as private property, but resources to be used to care for needs and benefit of others. We see this vividly illustrated in the community of Acts in meeting one another's needs as they share resources. It is interesting how often Jesus commends these values by noting what God will do one day in his evaluation of our lives, a reminder of our accountability to God. Almost half of our passages made this point. Jesus calls for a generosity in how we handle resources.

A text in the Luke 16 cluster we did not discuss has Jesus call on us to make friends with our use of unrighteous mammon, so when it runs out we will be welcomed into heavenly mansions. The combination of how we use resources along with how God sees it is juxtaposed in the text from Luke 16:9, summarizing well what we have seen.

Nothing in what I have said is placed into political terms that we think of today. Jesus did not call on the state to do these things. Rather he called individuals and the believing community to think this way and live this way. I say this *not* to ask for a separation of church and state in such caring, but to highlight the point that as an ethical matter Jesus called on disciples to show sensitivity to the poor and use resources in ways that reflect generosity. It is interesting that although our country is among one of the most generous in private giving, the percentage is actually pretty paltry, hovering at a two to four percent on average.[10]

This is short of the tithe that God had built into the support of Israel as a nation in the Hebrew Scriptures. The building of healthy community seems to be grounded in part in showing a love for one's neighbor and especially for one in need. There is a solidarity that forms when people know others care about them and their need. This is something the entire Judeo-Christian tradition has stressed, as the parable of the rich man and Lazarus also showed. Jesus said that one would know what to do, if they paid heed to Moses and the prophets. In contrast, our culture's focus on private property appears to risk seriously undercutting this value, becoming an excuse to keep rather than to give. This difference is why I have focused on values. It is competing values that get in the way of following what Jesus called people to do to be at their best. As Jesus said, it is very difficult to follow God and mammon. Fortunately for us, these texts give us examples that call us to move beyond our tendency to only think about our own needs and desires.

In making these points, these texts are not the only ones Scripture raises on this theme. The pastorals in 1 Timothy 6 have much to say on this topic, including the idea that the love of money is the root of all sorts of evil (1 Tim 6:9–10) and that contentment is ultimately rooted in godliness, not resources. In fact, if we have food and shelter, that is enough, given we cannot take anything with us (1 Tim 6:6–8). In words that echo what we have seen here, the epistle in 1 Tim 6:17–19 exhorts: "Command those who are rich in this world's goods not to be haughty or to set their hope on riches, which are uncertain, but on God who richly provides us with all things for our enjoyment. Tell them to do good, to be rich in good deeds, to be generous givers, sharing with others. In this way they will save up a treasure for themselves as a firm foundation for the future and so lay hold of what is truly life." Note that once again we juxtapose what we do now with what God will honor one day.

Indeed, the book of Proverbs has much to say about how sometimes poverty is the result of a person's own foolish choices. For example, Prov 10:4 says, "The one who is lazy becomes poor, but the one who works diligently becomes wealthy." The next verse compares wealth to a fortress, while poverty is seen as ruinous. But Proverbs can also say things that fit with what we have seen from Jesus in Luke. Listen to this maxim, "There is one who pretends to be rich and yet has nothing; another pretends to be poor and yet possesses great wealth" (Prov 13:7). Or ponder this word, "The one who oppresses the poor insults his creator, but whoever shows favor to the needy honors him" (Prov 14:31). Or consider this text, "The one who mocks the poor insults his creator; whoever rejoices over disaster will not go unpunished" (Prov 17:5). Those made by God in his image deserve honor and care, whoever they are. So Prov 22:2 says, "The rich and the poor meet together; the LORD is the creator of them both." We all stand before him as his creatures, deserving of mutual care and kindness. This is part of what it really means to be pro-life, a phrase defined far too narrowly in our cultural wars.

These later passages fit nicely with the Law and the prophets which calls for us to reach out and help those in need, as we already noted. So the Judeo-Christian tradition shows great awareness of the complexity of these issues and how to treat them. Still, Jesus' evidence of sensitivity to the poor and the power of what meeting the needs of others shows argues that if we are to err, it should be on the side of generosity. After all, God is watching and waiting from heaven to see what values we each choose to exercise. And I believe he cares how we live as a corporate people, whether in our church and religious communities or in our nation.

Endnotes

1. Theissen, *Social Setting of Pauline Christianity*, 70–73.
2. Bock, *Acts*, 152–53, 213–18, 257–63.
3. Sirach 29:8; Tobit 4:6–7, 16; 12:8; 14:10–11; *T. Job* 9:7–8; m. *Abot* 5:13.
4. The poor: Q: Matt 5:3=Luke 6:20; Matt 11:4–5=Luke 7:22–23; Mark: Mark 10:21=Matt 19:21; Mark 12:41–42=Luke 21:2–3; L: Luke 4:16–19; 14:13–14, 21; 16:19–31; 19:1–10.
5. Often referred to as the third world, the two-thirds world is a more accurate term, reminding us that a majority of the world lives in these settings.
6. Carroll-Rodas, "La Cita," 61–78.
7. Guelich, *Sermon on the Mount*, 67–72.
8. Bock, *Luke*, 1375.
9. Two key monographs on this theme are Pilgrim, *Good News to the Poor*; and Johnson, *Possessions in Luke-Acts*.
10. In 2008, giving was $307.65 billion. That sounds like a large number, but it is 2.2% of the Gross Domestic Product. Statistics from "2008 U. S. Charitable Giving Estimated to be $307.65 Billion," posted by Reuters News Agency, June 10, 2009; online: www.reuters.com/article/pressRelease/idUS117166+10-Jun-2009+PRN20090610.

10

Jesus and the Renewal of Covenantal Economics
RICHARD A. HORSLEY

Confusion of National Identity

Most Americans think of themselves as a biblical people. The Pilgrims and others who settled New England were embarking on a new exodus to escape pharaoh-like tyranny of the English monarchs. The Mayflower Compact and scores of town charters created new covenant communities in which the civil government as well as the congregational churches were patterned after Israel's Covenant with God on Sinai and Jesus' Sermon on the Mount. The Revolutionary War was, again, a new exodus. The deists Thomas Jefferson and Benjamin Franklin wanted the Great Seal of the United States to portray Moses leading the Israelites through the Red Sea. And at its ratification, the Constitution of the United States was discussed explicitly as a new Covenant. As the twelve tribes of Israel had created a model of civil government on Sinai, so the thirteen states were creating another covenant, a model of civil government for all nations.[1]

Earlier generations of Americans understood the Bible to be concerned not only with religion, but also with politics and even economics. While stated in eighteenth-century language, the inalienable rights of the people proclaimed in the Declaration of Independence and protected in the first ten amendments of the Constitution are rooted in the Ten Commandments of the Covenant. "We hold these truths to be self-evident, that all men (people) are endowed by their Creator with certain inalienable rights, and that among these are life, liberty, and the pursuit of happiness." Behind Jefferson's loose paraphrase of that good Bible-reading Scottish Presbyterian John Locke's "life, liberty, and property (or in today's terms, life, liberty, and a livelihood)," we can hear the commandments resounding from Sinai: "You shall not murder, you shall not covet, and you shall not steal."

The Covenant was the basis of the people's understanding that the society as a whole had a responsibility to care for its members in basic ways, guaranteeing their rights in public safety, public health, public roads, basic education, and an economic "safety net" for the needy. As John Winthrop declared in his sermon at the founding of the covenant community of Boston in 1630, "we must be willing to abridge ourselves of our superfluities for the supply of others' necessities." The framers of the Pennsylvania Declaration of Rights wanted to include the explicit statement of economic rights that "an enormous proportion of property vested in a few individuals is dangerous to the rights and destructive of the common happiness of mankind."

A century later, as huge proportions of the national wealth were becoming concentrated in the hands of giant corporations and their CEOs, Republicans as well as Democrats appealed to the Ten Commandments as the ultimate basis for regulations to limit the predatory practices of the corporations. Both Theodore Roosevelt and William Jennings Bryan, populist advocate for farmers and workers, accused the immensely wealthy (Republican) CEOs of blatant, systematic stealing, in violation of the commandment, "Thou shalt not steal." And when Roosevelt's friends on Wall Street and in the Republican Party accused him of attacking free-enterprise capitalism, he replied that "most of what I preach you can find in the Ten Commandments."

From early on, however, Americans established another identity: America as the New Rome. From the presidency of George Washington on, enthusiastic leaders declared that, in contrast with all former empires that were built on "conquest, blood, and usurpation," America would build an "empire of freedom" that other lands would embrace. The United States proceeded to clear the land of Native American peoples, take away half of the territory of Mexico, and seize Cuba and the Philippines.

Lest we think that the evangelical Christian Right of the past few decades is a new departure in American Christianity, it is well to remember that mainline church leaders were some of the most vocal cheerleaders of American "Manifest Destiny" throughout the nineteenth century. No figure was more influential than Josiah Strong, a leader in liberal theology and the nascent social gospel movement. In his widely read tract *Our Country*, a fund-raiser for home missions, he declared that God had commissioned the United States, the "Western Empire," which had already reached the highest degree of Anglo-Saxonism and true Christianity, "to dispossess the many weaker races, assimilate others, and mold the remainder."

Less noticed in our history books than U.S. expansion by blood and conquest was how America as the new Rome quickly became an economic empire of rapidly expanding commerce, burgeoning industry, and large corporations. Most Americans, including church leaders and political leaders, were eager supporters of U.S. economic imperialism, which became suffused with Christian rhetoric. As the U.S. Navy took over Cuba and the U.S. Army fought a four-year war of counter-insurgency in the Philippines, Sen. Albert J. Beveridge of Indiana, staunch Presbyterian and Progressive reformer who worked tirelessly for meat inspection, railway regulation, and the eight-hour work day for exploited workers, proclaimed that as part of "the Almighty's plan, Americans should follow the instinct of empire." "We shall establish trading-posts throughout the world as distributing points for American products. . . . We shall build a navy to the measure of our greatness . . . Our institutions will follow our flag on the wings of our commerce."[2]

Dwight D. Eisenhower is famous for having warned the country to beware of the growth of the military-industsrial complex. Under Eisenhower, however, the CIA toppled the democratically elected government of Prime Minister Mosadegh in Iran and the U.S. Army overthrew the elected government of President Arbenz in Guatemala. Why? As was evident then, and has been well documented since, it was to gain control of oil for U.S. companies in Iran and at the behest specifically of the United Fruit Company in Guatemala, and supposedly more broadly to secure the American supply of energy and food from around the world. And what lay behind the recent "preventive war" invasion of Iraq that has turned into the most disastrous U.S. foreign policy mistake in history? To secure the dwindling supply of oil for the huge U.S. oil companies and for the high-powered SUVs that bolster our dwindling sense of personal power.

There are two further major stages in the history of America as the new Rome. One of the most important moves in American history, rooted in the Covenant commandment tradition in the formation of the

U.S., to which figures such as Rev. Josiah Strong, Senator Beveridge, and President Teddy Roosevelt contributed, was regulation. Not only was there trust-busting, but in the Progressive Era, in the New Deal and again after World War II, there was a whole range of legislation and government watchdog agencies engaged in regulation of excessive profits, manipulation of markets, and consolidation of wealth and power in a few huge corporations. Limits were placed on compensation for corporate managers, progressive income tax, and estate taxes distributed the cost of public services more justly, workers were finally granted the right to organize and bargain for just wages.

The Reagan administration, however, followed by all subsequent administrations, brought massive deregulation. The cry was "free enterprise," but of course that meant mainly freedom from regulation and, in fact, the backing of the U.S. government for the enhancement of profits. The huge megacorporations were now calling the shots, including shaping government policy, such as the imposition of the North American Free Trade Agreement (NAFTA), which meant the export of jobs from the U.S. and the ruin of a million and half small corn farmers in Mexico, who then came across the border looking for any work they could find. The effect worldwide, as the now multinational corporations expanded their power, was the emergence of global capitalism, under the military umbrella of the U.S. as the sole superpower and world policeman. This meant that a whole network of transnational corporations, too wealthy and powerful to be regulated by any nation, including the U.S., dominated the economy of virtually all countries.

The actions of the Bush administration in the past eight years provide vivid illustrations of deregulation, globalization, and their effects. The massive tax cut for the very wealthy and invasion of Iraq left a huge national budget deficit, while government regulatory agencies were trimmed of their staff and instructed not even to enforce the regulations that still existed. Companies such as Enron manipulated energy supplies and prices, as well as their own stock prices, resulting in the virtual bankrupting of the state of California as well as the embezzlement and utter loss of many people's life savings. The big banks, greedy for a further killing, encouraged brokers to manipulate people into taking sub-prime mortgages with hidden clauses, and then sliced and diced the mortgages into high-yield securities, while brokers gambled away people's retirement savings in credit-default swaps. But these are only the tip of the iceberg of the devastating effects in loss of jobs, life savings, retirement, homes, and housing values on hundreds of millions of people in the U.S. and billions of people in the rest of the world. It is now commonly agreed that it was the greed of the huge U.S. banks and investment houses and their CEOs that were "too big to fail," that led to the current global economic crisis. Centralization of wealth and power, and deregulation, with the U.S. government doing the bidding of the megacorporations, were responsible. America played the part of the new Rome, center of the deregulated global capitalist empire.

Might the Bible have some implications for the future of America? The founding fathers and mothers clearly thought the Bible was concerned with politics and economics as well as religion. And only a century ago, presidential candidates were attacking large corporations for violating the commandment, "Thou shalt not steal." Since the United States was, in its origins, a covenanted society, I want to focus our attention on the Covenant that was made between God and the people of Israel on Mount Sinai and renewed among Galilean villagers by Jesus. And since this is a book for people in the thousands of covenanted communities in the U.S., most of whom see special importance in the Christian Gospel and the mission of Jesus, I want to focus particularly on Jesus' renewal of the Covenant, which stands at the center of the Gospel.

Israel's Covenant with God as the Background and Basis of the Gospel Story

We have become accustomed to reading the Gospel and the rest of the Bible one verse or one paragraph at a time, focusing on individual sayings of Jesus or on the Gospel reading for our weekly worship. Those are time-honored and important for devotional reading and mediation, for personal and group Bible study, and for worship and preaching in a way that provides coverage of several Gospels in a three-year cycle. But the Gospels are also, and were originally, whole stories of Jesus' mission, his crucifixion by the Romans, and his vindication by God. The Gospel story, moreover, does not begin only with Jesus' birth and baptism. The Gospel is a continuation of the story of Israel, indeed it claims that Jesus is engaged in the renewal of Israel, the fulfillment of the people's longings for a life of justice and peace, free of oppression by the wealthy and powerful, especially the overwhelming power of foreign empires such as Rome.

We all know the larger story from our Bibles. Early Israel got its start as a band of fugitive slaves whom Moses led out of hard bondage in the ancient Egyptian empire headed by the pharaoh. Under Joshua, the loose confederation of Israelites had to fight for their freedom against wealthy and powerful Canaanite kings who taxed them heavily to support the military forces that kept them in power.

Once the people gained their independence, they made a Covenant with God and each other at Sinai, which became the constitution of the twelve tribes of Israel.[3] The Ten Commandments or principles of the Covenant did two major things as a model of civil government. The first two commandments of the Covenant declared that the people were to maintain exclusive loyalty to the Force of Deliverance, who had taken compassion on the oppressed and led them out from under their hard service. The people's exclusive loyalty to God was not just religious, but political and economic as well. The second commandment is not merely about "false idols." It says explicitly, "You shall not bow down and serve," with your hard labor and your produce, any of those fearsome Powers such as Storm-kingship or Irrigation or River Nile (that brings fertilizing water), that is, the gods of the Egyptian or any other imperial system of centralized political-economic power. That was what YHWH had just liberated them from. The Force of Freedom, demanded service, exclusive service, in the form of first fruits brought to the altar. But there were (to be) no high priestly CEOs who kept a high percentage of the "take" as their own exorbitant compensation. Rather, the God of the Covenant had the offerings distributed to the poor, an economic safety net for subsistence farmers in a fledgling agrarian economy (Deut 26:1–11).

The majority of the commandments, or principles of social-economic interaction, governed relations among the covenanting people. The commandments "You shall not murder," "You shall not covet (i.e., scheme to take control of) your neighbor's house and field and livestock and family members," and "You shall not steal" declared that the people were not to infringe upon each others' rights to life, liberty, and property. Following these commandments would supposedly prevent a small number of people from consolidating economic and then political power by coveting, i.e., scheming to gain control of, and stealing other people's

Jesus and the Renewal of Covenantal Economics

produce and even their land. The land was understood as held in common by the whole people as a gift from God, its ultimate owner, who had parceled out some land to every family as its inalienable possession, the basis of its livelihood (Lev 25:23). The implications and implementation of these principles were further spelled out in covenantal laws and devices to protect people's rights to a secure livelihood, a kind of economic safety net of mutual sharing and cooperation for an agrarian society. The people were encouraged to lend to those who fell into economic difficulty but were prohibited from charging interest (Deut 15:7–8; Exod 22:25; Lev 25:35–37). They were further prohibited from taking advantage of those who fell into debt. Debts were to be cancelled every seventh year. Any members of indebted families who had been sent out to work for the creditors to pay off the debt were to be released every seven years. And if all else failed, every fifty years an amnesty on debts and release of debt-slaves was declared so that the destitute people were restored to their ancestral family land (Deut 15:1–2, 12–15; Lev 25:9–10).

We also all know the next stage of the biblical history: the people with wealth and power used it to take advantage of other people, mainly to get them into debt, and thus to gradually expand and consolidate wealth and power. In the advanced capitalist system, those who gain economic power are able to exercise political power as well. In the ancient world it was the other way around, as the kings and their officials used their political power to gain economic power as well. When subsistence farmers were unable to feed their families after yielding up the portion of their crops taken as tithes, taxes, and offerings to the Temple and the king, they borrowed from the wealthy who had a surplus. Taking advantage of their desperation, however, the wealthy charged high rates of interest, which only brought the poor further into debt. When the families were utterly unable to repay the spiraling debts, the wealthy creditors seized family members as debt-slaves and as the debt increased, seized the debtors' fields, ancestral land, and houses that were supposed to be inalienable. Wealthy figures were thus able to take control of large tracts of land and to turn those whose fields they seized into their tenants, cheap labor to raise the crops that the wealthy then exported in trade for luxury goods.

The prophets Amos, Micah, and Isaiah pronounced God's judgment against the wealthy and powerful for exploiting the people in violation of the covenantal principles meant to protect the people's right to a livelihood.

> The LORD enters into judgment against the elders and officers of his people:
> You have devoured the vineyard;
> The spoil of the poor is in your houses. (Isa 3:13–15)

> Woe to you who join house to house,
> Who add field to field.... (Isa 5:8)

> Woe to those who devise schemes... since they have the power.
> They covet fields, and seize them; houses and foreclose on them,
> people and their inheritance. (Mic 2:1–2)

The prophets declared that the Lord was about to destroy the wealthy and powerful elite of the monarchy and the Temple because they were violating the covenantal commandments. They interpreted the Babylonian destruction of Jerusalem and the Temple as God's enforcement of the Covenant the people had made with God and each other.[4]

The next step of the story of Israel that leads up to the Gospel story of Jesus we often miss or misunderstand. The books of Ezra and Nehemiah and Haggai and Zechariah say that not the whole people, but only the previously deported ruling class returned from exile in Babylon to rebuild the Temple, under the sponsorship of the Persian Empire. The people could now again worship the God of their ancestors in the Temple. But the temple-state was also a local branch of the imperial administration, with the new priestly ruling class responsible to maintain order for the Persian imperial regime and to collect the tribute to be sent to the Persians as well as collect tithes and offerings to support themselves.[5]

The restored ruling class turned out to be so oppressive of the ordinary Judeans that the Persians had to send Nehemiah as their governor to impose regulations. If we look closely at the books of the Bible that were composed to legitimate the temple-state headed by the high priestly aristocracy, what we see is a sacred political-economic system in which power and wealth are centralized as part of a wider imperial system. The books of Exodus, Leviticus, and Deuteronomy, however, included covenantal law-codes to limit the exploitation of the people by the wealthy and powerful.

Jesus and the Renewal of Covenantal Economics

Centuries later the Romans conquered the Judeans and Galileans demanded payment of tribute from the people. The Romans kept the Temple and high priesthood intact as their local client rulers, and imposed yet another layer of client rulers in the Herodian kings. The people thus now had demands from multiple layers of rulers for tribute, taxes, and tithes and offerings. This is the context in which Jesus carried out his mission.[6]

The Gospel Story: Jesus' Renewal of Israel

The Gospel tells the story of Jesus' renewal of Israel over the Jerusalem and Roman rulers. Since we are focusing on the Gospel of Mark this year in the lectionary, let's focus here also on Mark's story, but check on some of Jesus' covenantal teaching in Matthew and Luke as well.[7] While reading the summary of the story, keep in mind that in the ancient world there was no separation between religion and politics and economics, from Caesar and the Temple at the top to the villages of Galilee at the bottom. Caesar was not only the emperor but also the widely worshipped Savior who brought Peace and Security, at least to the wealthy. The Temple was the political capitol complex and bank as well as the place where sacrifices were offered to God (along with some for Rome and the emperor as well). The high priests in Jerusalem not only presided at sacrifices in the Temple, but were the Romans' client rulers of Judea, appointed by the governor and responsible for collecting the tribute to Caesar. Among the ordinary people, note that the prayer Jesus teaches his followers, "Our Father, who art in heaven . . . ," is mainly about economic subsistence: "give us enough bread to eat, day by day, and cancel our debts, as we herewith cancel the debts of our debtors."

Jesus announces the main theme as he begins his mission in Galilee: "The kingdom of God is at hand!" It quickly becomes clear that what he is saying and doing as manifestations of the kingdom constitutes a renewal of the people of Israel, over against the rulers of Israel.

Through much of the story, Jesus appears as a new Moses and Elijah. He recruits protégés to assist in his mission, just as Elijah had recruited Elisha (Mark 1:16–20; 1 Kgs 19:19–21), and he appoints twelve disciples, representative of the twelve tribes of Israel, just as Elijah had made an altar of twelve stones representing the twelve tribes (Mark 3:13–19; 1 Kgs

18:30–32). He does not preach to no one in particular or minister just to individuals. He preaches and heals in village communities, which were the basic social-economic form in which the people lived and worked, and sometimes in the synagogues, the local gatherings of the people in village communities for prayers and discussion of common problems, like town meetings in small towns today. When he sends out the disciples to expand his work, he sends them also into village communities, to stay in local households and to work with the people, preaching and healing (Mark 6:6–24; cf. Luke 10:2–16).

In the middle section of the story Jesus performs two series of "acts of power," including sea-crossings and wilderness feedings like Moses in the exodus, and healings, as in Elijah's mission of renewal of the suffering and oppressed people (Mark 4:35—8:26). Sandwiched into these events is the episode where Jesus accuses the scribes and Pharisees, representatives of the Jerusalem rulers in the Temple, of preventing the people from keeping the basic commandment(s) of God by urging them to devote so much of their produce to the Temple that there was nothing left to feed their elderly parents (Mark 7:1–13). At the end of the ensuing middle section, in what appears to be the consolidation of his mission in the villages of Galilee and beyond (Mark 10:2–45), Jesus sets forth a renewal of the Covenant in a series of dialogues. He gives the greatest attention to economic relations (Mark 10:17–31), quoting most of the Ten Commandments, in the dialogue that includes his declaration that "it is easier for a camel to go through the eye of the needle than for someone who is rich to enter the kingdom of God" (Mark 10:25).

Having set in motion a renewal of Israel as the implementation of the coming kingdom of God, Jesus then marches up to Jerusalem, the capital of Judea, for a sustained confrontation with the rulers at the time of Passover, the annual celebration of Israel's historical liberation from foreign imperial rule (Mark 11–12). He carries out a highly provocative, forcible demonstration in the Temple. This is misnamed and misunderstood as a "cleansing." There is nothing in the episode about cleansing. Jesus blocks the basic business of the Temple. The framing by the cursing of the fig tree indicates clearly that this is a prophetic demonstration that symbolizes and pronounces God's imminent destruction of the Temple—and destruction of the Temple is precisely what he is accused of threatening at his trial and again when he is hanging on the cross. He then tells a prophetic parable against the high priests that suggests that God is about to destroy them. When the Pharisees and Herodians attempt to entrap him with the question of whether it is lawful to pay tribute to Caesar, Jesus wriggles out of the trap by suggesting the people do not owe the tribute but without saying explicitly, 'no, don't pay it.' In the last episode of confrontation, Jesus accuses the scribes of desiring the places of honor and of devouring widows' households/livings, an accusation immediately illustrated when the impoverished widow gives away the last copper of her livelihood to the Temple, which Jesus then prophesies is about to be destroyed.

It is not surprising that the high priests and scribes are desperate to arrest and kill him (Mark 14). Before his arrest, however, at the Passover with his disciples in celebration of the historical liberation of the people, Jesus enacts a covenant renewal in his words over the cup: "this is my blood of the covenant poured out for many" (Mark 14:12–25). As the disciples betray, abandon, and deny Jesus, he is arrested and tried before the high priestly council (Mark 14:43–72). Finally the Roman governor ordered that Jesus be crucified, the Roman method of slow execution specifically for rebel leaders in the provinces—hence the mocking inscription on the cross, "Jesus of Nazareth king of the Judeans" (Mark 15:1–32). But the story has a strange open ending, with the empty tomb and the figure in white telling the women that Jesus "is going ahead of you back up to Galilee, where you will meet him" (Mark 16:1–8)—evidently to continue the movement he had started, and a clear signal to us hearers of the story to do the same.

Jesus' Prophetic Pronouncement of God's Covenantal Justice[8]

Just as the Covenant was, in effect, the very constitution of the people of Israel, so in the Gospel story the renewal of the covenant is central in Jesus' renewal of Israel over against the rulers of Israel. This has always been most obvious in the Sermon on the Mount in Matthew, when Jesus goes "up on the mountain" and delivers a renewed covenant, complete with the intensified commandments. But it is central throughout Mark's story (and in Luke), from the appointment of the Twelve as representatives of Israel undergoing renewal, the quotation of the commandments in several episodes, and Jesus' word over the cup at the Last Supper.

Indeed, Jesus' basic proclamation of the kingdom of God means God's direct rule of the people according to the commandments of the Covenant. The Covenant commandments are thus also the basis on which Jesus pronounces God's condemnation of the Temple and high priests and speaks against the tribute to Caesar. Once we no longer project the peculiar modern western separation of religion from politics and economics onto the Gospel story, it is clear that Jesus' renewal of the Covenant was about political-economic life in ways inseparable from loyalty to God.

We begin at the broadest level. Jesus' basic proclamation that the kingdom of God is at hand, that the time has come when God is to rule the people directly, was a direct challenge to Roman imperial rule. The whole Mediterranean world, including peoples of the Middle East such as the Judeans and Galileans, had been subjected to the kingdom of Caesar. Rome had conquered Galilee and Judea with horribly destructive "shock and awe": destruction of villages, slaughter and enslavement of the people, crucifixion of any leaders of resistance along the roadsides as warnings to the subject people not to resist Roman rule. Then the Romans installed the Herodian kings and the Jerusalem high priests as their client rulers, and demanded tribute from the subject people, which was collected by the client rulers, in addition to the taxes, tithes, and offerings they already paid to Herod and the Temple.

The Gospels of Luke and Matthew make the irreconcilable conflict between the rule of God and the political-economic-religious rule of Caesar even clearer at the beginning of the Gospel story. In Luke, the decree by Caesar Augustus, the Savior of the world, that all the world must be enrolled to render tribute is what forces Joseph and Mary to journey to Bethlehem, where Jesus is born as the alternative Savior (Luke 2:1-20). In Matthew, when the Roman client king Herod learns of the birth of a new king, he sends out his special counter-insurgency forces to nip the supposedly nascent insurrection before it can get started (Matt 2:1-18).[9]

Judeans and Galileans, among them Jesus and his followers, were faced with an impossible conflict by the Roman demand for tribute. Caesar was not just "worshipped" but honored and served as the divine Lord and Savior by his subjects all around the empire. Why? Because by conquering and controlling the world Caesar had become the most dominant powerful Power in the people's lives, like the chief god in ancient Near Eastern civilizations, Lord Storm, called Enlil/Marduk in Babylon,

Jesus and the Renewal of Covenantal Economics

and Ba'al in the Canaanite and Phoenician kingdoms. As in previous empires, tribute was the service demanded of conquered peoples.

The resources taken in tribute steadily increased the wealth and power of the Roman elite. But they also enhanced the lifestyle of ordinary Roman citizens, who could thus enjoy the famous "bread and circuses," the ancient equivalent of a comfortable home, cheap imported food and other goods, and a rich array of entertainment spectaculars in the arenas. The Romans treated non-payment as tantamount to rebellion and sent in the Roman legions to take vengeance on recalcitrant people.

The Galileans and Judeans, however, were required by the first two commandments of the Covenant to serve God alone as their Lord and master, and not to bow down and serve any other Lord with their produce and labor. It was not lawful, not covenantal, to pay the tribute to Caesar. This fundamental conflict over payment of the tribute to Rome came to a head when Jesus was a boy. Some scribal and Pharisaic leaders, who were experts in covenantal law, but who would supposedly enforce the orders of the high priests for whom they worked, organized a resistance to paying the tribute. They eventually backed down, perhaps realizing that sustained resistance would have led to another devastating Roman conquest like the one ten years earlier (at the time of Jesus' birth).

It should thus be clear that the attempt to entrap Jesus with the question about tribute to Caesar in the Gospel (Mark 12:13–17) is seriously misunderstood when interpreted according to the separation of church and state assumed in the U.S. There was no such separation in ancient Judea and the Roman Empire. The Pharisees who posed the question, experts on covenantal law, knew better than anyone that payment was not lawful. But if they could trick Jesus into saying just that, they would have grounds to arrest him for fomenting revolt. Jesus first forced them to show their hand: they were carrying a Roman coin with the image of Caesar inscribed. Then he gave his carefully crafted answer that avoided culpability but stated the basic covenant principle that all Judeans and Galileans would have understood immediately: "Give to Caesar the things that are Caesar's, and to God the things that are God's." The key is "the things that belong to . . ." What belonged to Caesar, according Covenantal principle? Nothing. Because all belonged to God. Jesus was restating the fundamental covenantal principle that the people did not owe and should not be required to pay the tribute—but without saying explicitly 'do not pay it.'

The dominant conflict in Mark as in the other Gospels is between Jesus (as God's prophet) and the Temple and high priestly aristocracy who operated it. As in its establishment under the Persian Empire, so under the Romans, the Temple and high priesthood were the local representatives of the imperial system, the very face of Roman rule in Judea. At the time of Jesus the high priests were the descendants of families installed by Herod the Great, now appointed by the Roman governor, and collectively responsible to the Romans to maintain order and gather the tribute.

The Temple, of course, was also the sacred center of Judean society, where the priests offered sacrifices to God. As the representatives of the people to God and of God to the people, the high priests insisted, in time-honored tradition, that the people must bring sacrifices and offerings to God in the Temple, and they controlled the tithes that the people owed to support the priests. Toward the time of Jesus they also developed other devices to extract further resources from the people, such as *korban*, in which people "devoted" some of their family resources to the Temple.

The Temple, which dominated the economy in Judea, was thus also the central bank, where the rich deposited their excess wealth, which became the basis of further exploitation of the people. The centralization of wealth and power in the Temple and high priestly oligarchy was supposed to operate under the regulations included in the Law, in the books of Exodus, Leviticus, and Deuteronomy. But under Herod and the Romans the operations of the Temple and high priests became, in effect, "deregulated." The wealthy creditors felt free to ignore the laws against taking interest, the seventh year cancellation of debts, freeing of debt-slaves, and the right of redemption of family land. As excess funds piled up in the Temple, wealthy figures made loans to needy families at high rates of interest. And when families became hopelessly indebted, the wealthy creditors foreclosed on their houses and ancestral lands.[10] There are numerous passages in rabbinic literature and in the histories of the Judean historian Josephus, himself a wealthy priest, that document the predatory practices of priestly aristocracy at the time of Jesus.[11]

In an economy such as the Roman Empire or the Judean temple-state, the centralizing institutions such as the imperial family and the high priestly aristocracy, far from contributing productively to the economy, siphoned the produce and resources from the people to support their lavish lifestyle in urban mansions, gated-fortresses, and country villas staffed by slaves and servants. But they had the power, not only to compel the payment of tribute and taxes, but to extract even more from the people through high interest on loans and then seizing the property of those who fell deeply into debt.

The Covenant and its commandments are also the basis of Jesus' prophetic demonstration of God's judgment of the Temple and his prophetic parable against the high priests (Mark 11:25–27; 12:1–12). The reasons for God's condemnation of the Temple, says Jesus in reference to Jeremiah's prophecy against the earlier Temple (Jer 7:26), is that it has become "a bandits' stronghold." That is, the high priests plunder the goods of the people all the while trusting that they will be safely protected in the sacred precincts of the Temple. Having been entrusted by God to be the caretakers of the vineyard of his people, the high priestly tenants have horded the produce of the vineyard for their own lavish lifestyle, and have even killed the messengers God sent, i.e., the prophets. Matthew and Luke include yet another statement of God's judgment in Jesus' prophetic lament over the Jerusalem ruling house in which Jesus speaks as the voice of a very protective mother-like God:

> Jerusalem, Jerusalem!
> The city that kills the prophets
> and stones those who are sent to it!
> How often have I desired to gather your children together
> as a hen gathers her brood under her wings,
> and you were not willing.
> See, your house is a desolation. (Matt 23:37 // Luke 13:34–35)

The covenantal commandments are also the basis of Jesus' accusations against the scribes and Pharisees for facilitating the exploitation and impoverishment of the people, in two episodes in particular. In the first (Mark 7:1–13), Jesus charges them with rejecting and violating the basic commandment of God. He purposely picks "honor your father and mother," the most sacred of filial duties. Violation of this commandment was the effect of their pressuring the people to "devote" (*korban*) the produce of some of their land to the Temple, because they would thus be left without enough to support their parents and other family members. In a later episode (Mark 12:38-44), part of his sustained confrontation in the Temple, Jesus charges the scribes with "devouring widows' households," i.e., livelihoods. And sure enough, a widow comes along and (presumably having been pressured by the scribes) gives away that last of her livelihood to the Temple, leaving her now utterly impoverished, destitute, thus illustrating Jesus' charge.

In both cases the Pharisees and scribes were just doing their job as representatives of the Temple and high priests, trying to extract resources from the people in support of the centralization of goods and wealth in the Temple.[12] As prophetic spokesperson for the people, however, Jesus charges the scribes and Pharisees with inducing the people to yield up the very resources that they needed to take care of themselves and their aging parents, to yield up the livelihood to which they supposedly had an inalienable right, as protected by the Covenantal commandments.

Jesus' Renewal of Covenant Community

In addition to prophetic pronouncements against centralization of wealth by the Roman rulers and their clients based in the Temple, Jesus renewed the Covenant among the people in their local communities and among the people as a whole. Jesus' covenant renewal, in which he often recited the commandments, focused mainly on mutually supportive and non-exploitative social-economic relations among the people. He also insisted that cooperative, non-exploitative economic relations were the way of being loyalty to God. We focus on four key passages.[13]

First, in celebration of the people's liberation at Passover just before he was arrested, he transformed the meal into a renewal of the people's Covenant with God and each other (Mark 14:22-25). Alluding to Moses' sprinkling the blood over the people and the altar, binding the people and God in the Covenant, Jesus declared solemnly "this is my blood of the covenant poured out for many. Jesus' last supper became the prototype for the Lord's Supper as the ceremony of covenant renewal of God's people in an international, interclass, multi-ethnic, and multi-cultural association who took on the heritage and the principles and commitments of the original Covenant.

Second, at several points earlier in Mark's gospel story, but particularly in the series of dialogues that constitute a covenant renewal speech

(Mark 10:2–45), Jesus insisted that the people recommit to the basic principles of the Covenant in their common life, with emphasis on economic relations (10:17–31). The young man serves as a foil, a negative example of what not to do. From the outset we can tell that he was rich from the question he asked Jesus: "What must I do to inherit eternal life?" He was obviously not one of the villagers among whom Jesus was working, who were worried instead about where the next meal was coming from. Jesus replied, "you know the commandments," and recited the second six, except that instead of "You shall not covet" he said "You shall not defraud." The man replied that he had kept all these from his youth. When Jesus responded, "Then, give all you have to the poor and come join my movement," the man was shocked and left, for he was too deeply attached to his great wealth.

Do we "get it"? The clue is Jesus' rephrasing of the commandment "You shall not covet" to "You shall not defraud." The original meaning of the Hebrew word was stronger than "covet," more like "You shall not covet and strive to take control of your neighbor's house and fields, etc." How did someone become wealthy in ancient agrarian society? By charging interest on loans, which was forbidden by covenant law: "If you lend to my people, to the needy among you, you shall not deal with them as a creditor; you shall not exact interest from them" (Exod 22:25). And no wonder the creditors who made loans were able to "grow their wealth" rapidly, since they charged high rates of interest, as we know from Jesus' parable of the "dishonest manager" (Luke 16:1–9). When he told his master's debtors to change their bill from 100 measures of grain that they owed the master to eighty, that indicates that when they took out a loan of 80 measures of grain, the wealthy creditor had insisted they write down 100 measures, that is 20 percent interest, which was a fraudulent promissory note, since it was illegal by covenant law to charge interest. To drive home the point of his covenantal renewal teaching, Jesus declared that "it will be easier for a camel to go through the eye of a needle than for someone who is rich to enter the kingdom of God" (Mark 10:25).

Third, Matthew and Luke have other covenantal teaching of Jesus that makes the same point. Those who are busy "growing their wealth," which they could do only by taking advantage of others' by charging interest, in violation of covenant law, were in effect serving another god, called "Mammon," "Wealth." And, Jesus declared, you cannot serve two masters, you cannot serve God and Wealth" (Matt 6:24 // Luke 16:13). According to the Covenant, *the way* of being loyal to God in social-economic life is to *not* take advantage of others by charging interest, but to cooperate with one another in mutual support, according to the traditional covenantal principles. Jesus says basically the same thing in his response to the scribe's ridiculous question, "which commandment is the greatest?" (Mark 12:28–31). Jesus replies by summarizing the Ten Commandments in two equivalent principles: "Love God, and love your neighbor," that is, the way you manifest your love of God is by taking care of rather than exploiting your neighbor.

Fourth, the most important covenant renewal speech we have from Jesus, known as the Sermon on the Mount (Matthew 5–7), paralleled by the Sermon on the Plain (Luke 6:20–49), suggests how the covenant renewal worked to revive mutual social-economic assistance and cooperation in community life, and thus strengthened the people's ability to resist further disintegration of family and community by the predatory pressures of the wealthy and powerful. These are parallel covenant renewal speeches, with many references and updating of covenantal laws and teaching, especially in the set of sayings that begins with "Love your enemies."[14] The best known may be "if someone seizes your cloak give him your shirt as well," which is a direct reference to the law about borrowing and lending in the Covenant Code: "If you take your neighbor's cloak as (symbolic) collateral (for a loan) you shall give it back before sunset, for it may be his only covering when he sleeps at night" (Exod 22:26–27). These parallel speeches in Matthew and Luke also have the traditional covenantal structure, with the declaration of God's deliverance preceding the statement of God's demands. In the original Covenant given on Sinai, the declaration was God's deliverance at the exodus and the demands were the Ten Commandments. In Jesus' covenant renewal speech, the declaration of God's new deliverance comes in the beatitudes and woes, as Jesus declares that the kingdom of God is for the poor and hungry, while pronouncing God's judgment on the wealthy. On the basis of God's new deliverance, Jesus makes renewed covenantal demands, beginning with the thematic "Love your enemies." And the covenantal demands of Jesus are, like the commandments of the Covenant on Sinai, about common economic life. The context that Jesus' covenantal demands address are indicated in the content of what he says. This is clearer (I think) in the simpler and almost certainly earlier version in Luke 6. "Love your enemies, do good... If someone strikes you on the cheek, offer the other also; and someone seizes your cloak, give him your shirt as well. Give to everyone who begs from you... Love your enemies, do good, and lend, expecting nothing in return... Be merciful as our Father is merciful" (Luke 6:27–34).

The enemies here are not foreign soldiers, the Romans. The context is the local community in which people have been borrowing from and lending to one another, and the person who has made the loan now needs it back to feed his own family and is symbolically seizing the debtor's cloak, slapping the neighbor on the cheek in anger, and refusing to lend any more to others in need. Jesus is saying bluntly, cut it out! Quit quarreling with one another and being divided among yourselves. God is bringing you the kingdom. So now you all can get back to the covenantal basics of community cooperation, of mutual aid in time of difficulty, of sharing what you have so that you can all make it through the difficult time. This renewal of common life according to traditional covenantal principles not only revived cooperation among the members of village communities, but enabled both the community and its component families to resist the disintegrating effects of becoming indebted to the wealthy and powerful who were eager to become wealthier by gaining control of their land and labor.

The Implications of Jesus' Renewal of the Covenant for America as the New Rome

The Gospel is a story about Jesus' renewal of Israel, addressed to (other) people subject to Rome. But America has long since become the New Rome, enjoying bread and circuses derived from its domination of the rest of the world. So the Gospel story is not addressed to America and certainly does not belong to Americans. That is an obvious conclusion to draw, at least at one level. But the situation in America today is more complicated, as it was in the ancient Roman Empire as well. The population of ancient Rome included the descendants of people brought in as slaves, other immigrants from various countries who did the most menial jobs, and those who had been pushed off their family farms by the ancient Roman military-agribusiness complex. These were among the poor, ordinary people who heard the Gospel story and joined new local covenantal communities (churches) of the international, intercultural movement that became known as Christians. Thus at another level the Gospel story is indeed addressed to those Americans who, like the vast majority in ancient Rome, are subject to the power of the wealthy and powerful who have come to control the economy.

Since the new unregulated globalized economy is run from the top, just as the Roman Empire was run from the top, let's start there. At the top in the ancient Roman Empire, Caesar had become the divine Power that dominated people's lives and insisted on being served, demanding that subject peoples pay tribute, even if it meant that they no longer had an adequate livelihood. What today corresponds to Caesar as the Power or Force that most determines our lives and demands our service? Isn't it capital? What determines whether we have a good economy? Whether capital is growing, enhanced with more profits, as measured in the daily stock market reports. The economy must always grow, by rendering interest to capital, no matter what happens to the environment or people's lives. Like Caesar demanding tribute, capital demands a certain percentage of the value of what workers produce, so that the corporation can make a profit to return to the investors of capital. But in consumer capitalism, industry in which capital is invested produces not just what we need, but all sorts of things that we do not really need but are induced to buy, so that capital can grow with more returns on more investment. Thus we are induced to serve capital in yet another way when we use credit cards, and are charged 18 percent or more on our purchases. Insofar as all of our savings, including our resources for retirement, have become bits and pieces of capital, we are all held hostage to the stock market in which capital must grow. In contrast to Caesar in the ancient world, however, it is often hidden from us that we are serving capital in most of our economic activities.

According to the first two commandments of the Covenant the people are not to serve a Power other than God. Exclusive loyalty to the God of justice is maintained by observing the other commandments that keep some people from acquiring wealth by taking advantage of other people, by coveting, stealing, and making loans at interest. Jesus declared, in his crafty subtle way, that the people do not owe, and really should not pay tribute to Caesar. Moreover, as Jesus warned, if we listen to the ads from banks and investment houses and are concerned to "grow" our wealth (laying up treasure), then aren't we serving Mammon rather than the God concerned that all have an adequate livelihood? Did we lose our soul long before we lost our shirt in the recent economic crash of those banks and investment houses?

Jesus announced, in a prophetic demonstration and a prophetic parable, that the Temple and its CEOs stand under God's condemnation —for draining upward, into centralized control, the resources that belonged to and were needed by the people for their own livelihood, in violation of covenantal commandments and principles. What and who, today, correspond to the Temple and the wealthy high priestly managers who, first, demand a certain percentage of what people produce; second, give themselves exorbitant compensation for their management; and then, third, lend out the resources they control at high rates of interest, bringing the borrowers into spiraling debt? Aren't the equivalents in today's economic system the banks, insurance companies, and their CEOs, COOs, and high management? In our global capitalist system, wealth demands a return on investment, a certain rate of interest. The officers of the banks and investment firms, first, control the investment and collect the interest. Second, through their boards, they award themselves huge, recently obscene, compensation in multimillion dollar salaries and stock options (while cutting workers' wages). Then, third, they further "grow their wealth" by devising such instruments as credit cards, which they send to people who do not even ask for them, charge high rates of interest, 18 or 25 percent or more with penalties for late payment, manipulating many into spiraling indebtedness from which they cannot hope to recover. More recently they pushed sub-prime mortgages with escalating interest rates and other devious devices in the fine print, eventually forcing people to forfeit their homes to foreclosure, which in turn drives down the value of others' homes in whole neighborhoods. The banks and insurance companies and their CEOs have been able to do all this because of deregulation. In all of this exploitative business, "the finance industry " ("Wall Street") and its management not only do not contribute to the productivity of the economy, but are parasites on the economy, siphoning off into their own control the value that is produced by farmers and workers, etc. A century ago, Teddy Roosevelt and William Jennings Bryan called what the big banks and the captains of industry and their cartels were doing a blatant violation of the commandment, "Thou shalt not steal." Corporate exploitation on a massive scale has only escalated many times over into a now global imperial system, especially in the past three decades.

Next, what and who today correspond to the scribes and Pharisees who pressured the people to yield up not only tithes and offerings to centralization of wealth, but to devote even more of the resources they needed for basic livelihood to the centralized wealth in the Temple? Isn't this the role played in a consumer-capitalist society by marketing and advertising? The psychologists and graphic artists on "Madison Avenue" devise ingenious ways of channeling our desire with images of the good life, so that in order to possess those images, we buy products, many of which are not necessary for our livelihood. This is often how people are manipulated into credit card debt. Advertising, creating images of false values, induces us today to covet, to desire and acquire possessions, thus again to bow down and serve the Power—capital—that those idols represent.

Jesus' renewal of the Covenant focused on covenant communities in the villages of Galilee. Presumably what today corresponds to those covenant communities are the tens of thousands of local covenant communities and larger national and international denominations and associations of covenant communities who see themselves as standing in continuity with and faithful to Jesus' renewal of the Covenant. Moreover, as discussed at the outset, in the very origins of the United States, Americans thought of themselves as a covenant community. Members of churches (and synagogues and mosques) are thus involved in two or more overlapping covenantal communities, their local covenanted community, along with a larger church denomination or association, and American civil society—and their membership in the one may strongly influence their participation in the other(s).

Covenantal communities then and now, however, occupy dramatically different situations in the dominant political-economic power relations. The covenant communities that responded to Jesus' mission had a degree of local autonomy, but little room to maneuver vis-à-vis the powerful institutions and forces that dominated their lives. Often the early assemblies of Christ were persecuted, arrested, and even executed for any moves that seemed suspicious to the holders of power. Today the situation is strikingly different. Although political power has been co-opted by powerful economic institutions and interests as economic power has been increasingly centralized, Americans (including church members) still have the vote and enjoy certain civil liberties, such as the right to organize. And although the churches have been increasingly marginalized as political-economic power has been centralized, and although churches have assimilated to the dominant culture, they are some of the principal voluntary associations still operating and one of the only potentially alternative voices. Despite the differences in respective political situations, the biblical Covenant and Jesus' covenant renewal have significant implications for churches today, for America as a covenant people, and for the relations between them.

First, American Christians could themselves renew the long tradition of the churches being economic as well as religious communities. Wealthy elite in the Roman Empire who despised the early Christians often scoffed at them for taking care of each other economically. Churches in the United States continued the early church tradition of being economic as well as religious communities. The minister and/or a church committee usually had a fund that could be used to aid families in an emergency. Catholic churches consisting largely of immigrants were also, in effect, credit unions in which people provided mutual economic support and protection from exploitation by banks and loan sharks. Churches acted economically beyond the local parish as larger denominations, for example, in disaster relief and provision of health care.

Second, acting like the covenantal communities Jesus renewed, covenantal communities today could act cooperatively to provide aid to neighbors hard hit by the economic crisis, from loss of jobs, home foreclosures, loss of health care, loss of retirement funds. The government still has some safety net programs, but those have been cut back to pay for the tax cuts for the wealthy and the pre-emptive invasion of Iraq, which has devastated that country and its people.

Jesus' demand to "love, do good, and lend" can be adapted to today's complicated circumstances. Two recent examples: In Flint, Michigan, an association of church members and others started a land-bank, buying up foreclosed houses and placing needy people in the houses who would take care of them, preventing further decline in value and thus beginning to rebuild whole neighborhoods. In Tucson and Los Angeles and elsewhere, church leaders along with church-related agencies organized thousands whose houses were being foreclosed and held workshops in local churches in which information and expertise was available to help people keep their homes. In these actions the foreclosing mega-banks were sufficiently embarrassed by the publicity that they sent representatives to the workshops authorized to renegotiate mortgages.

Third, American Christians might learn from an important effect of Jesus' covenant renewal of local communities: to strengthen local cooperation so that the whole community as well as individual families could resist the pressures from powerful institutions to yield up resources needed for local livelihood. Some church leaders are suggesting that people can take cooperative action to check the practices of huge banks taking the resources we deposit away from the community, investing them elsewhere, and consolidating the profits on Wall Street. In coordinated collective action, people could simply stop depositing and otherwise cooperating with the "zombie banks" and other megacorporations that impoverish local communities, and instead do business with (or re-establish) local banks, credit unions, and other locally based businesses—but with covenantal arrangements to make sure they are not then gobbled up by megacorporations.

Fourth, churches and church leaders could again take up their traditional prophetic role of "speaking truth to power" in defense of the powerless against the wealthy and powerful, bringing covenantal principles to bear on centralized economic power and its abuses. Mainline churches, having lost membership when they spoke out more boldly in favor of civil rights for all and against the Vietnam War, backed away from their traditional prophetic role. Perhaps the combination of economic and ecological crisis is now sufficiently serious that mainline churches will regain their courage and join with the more progressive Evangelical churches in insisting publically on at least a modicum of economic justice.

Fifth, government in the U.S., as the political arm of the covenanted civil society, is supposedly set up both to provide for the common good in ways that individuals and small local communities cannot (public safety, clean water and air, public education, public roads, public health, etc.) and to protect the citizens' rights to life, liberty, and a livelihood, etc. Abraham Lincoln articulated what we supposedly have in America—a government of the people, by the people, and for the people. But with election campaigns funded largely by huge corporations, who also hire thousands of lobbyists, with industries so powerful that they can block legislation they do not want and are even invited to formulate public policy, we have come to have a government of, by, and for those huge corporations. It is now widely agreed among economists as well as world public opinion, however, that American deregulation went much too far, that it is essential to again institute regulation of super-powerful corporations and their CEOs. Yet because corporate power will block their (re-)election, presidents and senators have very limited scope within which they can take the lead. They must be pushed hard by the public, which leads directly to the overlap, the dual membership that Christians and others have in two or more covenant communities.

Sixth, re-regulation of megacorporations will not happen unless the people push hard. Reorientation to the public good will not happen unless the public insists. The founding American fathers and mothers used to think of the churches as the schools of democracy, where people learned to work together for the common good, hence learned how to be active as citizens. The churches can again be bases from which the people can organize cooperative action to again make their government responsive and accountable to the people.

Finally, let's come back around to America as the New Rome and focus on Americans as the new Roman citizens living at the center of the new Empire of global capitalism. The wealthy elite who controlled the Roman Empire used some of the resources they took from the Empire to provide Romans citizens with a high level of consumption, both of food and of spectacular entertainment all year-round, the famous "bread and circuses." In the New Rome, Americans, joined in recent decades by Western Europeans and the Japanese, have an inordinately high level of consumption relative to the rest of the world from which many of the goods consumed are taken. As noted before, Jesus declared that it was not lawful, according to the covenantal commandments of God, for Galileans and Judeans to yield to Caesar the resources and produce that belonged to God, who in turn granted them to the people for their livelihood. It seems to be diametrically counter to the covenant commandments that American Christians consume twenty or thirty times more resources than the poor peoples of the world, whether fossil fuels for high-powered gas-guzzling SUVs or high-calorie fast foods or a thousand and one products that are far from necessary and can hardly be justified when measured by covenantal principles.

There is general agreement among professional economists that it will be necessary for U.S. consumers to buy and consume less and save more. But even that level of consumption will still be not only far above the average in the rest of the world, but utterly unsustainable. Even reduced consumption in the U.S. will continue to exacerbate climate change and the exhaustion of resources and the pollution of the world that Christians, Jews, and Muslims believe is God's creation, of which humans are the custodians. Thus both to keep the covenant commandments and to be custodians of God's creation, American Christians will be required to drastically reduce their consumption of the world's resources. There is no reason to think of this in terms of a reduction in the level of lifestyle. It can be rather a conversion to covenantal cooperation. Instead of constantly consuming more goods and resources, American Christians could commit themselves to creating community and caring for the creation, other people, and the common life.

When Joshua presided over the renewal of the Covenant at Shechem, he challenged the people of Israel to choose which god they would serve, the gods of the centralized imperial system of Babylon and Egypt, which offered security in service of the system, or the Lord, who had just delivered them from that hard bondage but now demanded that they take responsibility for maintaining just social-economic relations according to the commandments. In his renewal of the Covenant, Jesus challenged the people to choose between the service of Mammon, the god of security through acquisition of greater wealth (through the exploitation of others), or God who was taking new action of deliverance and calling the people to renewed economic cooperation and commitment to the common good. Jesus' renewal of the Covenant among the people living under the old Rome now poses a challenge and some hard choices for covenantal people living under the new Rome of American-based deregulated global capitalism.

Endnotes

1. On the influence of the Bible, particularly of Israel's exodus and Covenant, in the formative history of the United States, the rival American identity as the new Rome, the distinctive American sense of "Manifest Destiny," and concentration of economic power in large corporations, see further Bellah, *The Broken Covenant*; Jewett, *Mission and Menace*; Stephanson, *Manifest Destiny*; and Horsley, *Covenant Economics*, "Introduction."

Jesus and the Renewal of Covenantal Economics

2. Stephanson, *Manifest Destiny*.

3. For further exploration of Israel's Covenant with God, the centralization of power in the monarchy, and the response of the prophets, see further Horsley, *Covenant Economics*, chaps. 2-5, on which the following sketch depends.

4. On the exploitation of peasants under the monarchies in Israel and Judah, and the prophets' condemnation, see further Chaney, "Bitter Bounty, 365-75; Chaney, "Whose Sour Grapes?" 105-22.

5. Fuller exploration of the foundation and history of the Judean temple-state and its legitimation and regulation in books that were later included in the Hebrew Bible, see Horsley, *Scribes, Visionaries, and the Politics of Second Temple Judea*, chaps. 1 and 6.

6. On the Roman conquest and rule of Galilee and Judea, see detailed and documented critical investigation in Horsley, *Galilee: History, Politics, People*, chaps. 2, 3, and 5; and the more recent survey in Horsley, *Jesus and Empire*, chap. 1.

7. For a fuller exploration of the Gospel of Mark as a complete story, see further Horsley, *Hearing the Whole Story*, especially chaps. 1 and 5.

8. For more extensive investigation of Jesus' pronouncements of judgment on the basis of the Covenant, see Horsley, *Covenant Economics*, 125-32; Horsley, *Jesus and Empire*, chap. 4; and Horsley, *Jesus and the Spiral of Violence*, chap. 10.

9. On the infancy narratives in Matthew and Luke, see further the historical contextual analysis and interpretation in Horsley, *The Liberation of Christmas*, chaps. 2 and 3.

10. See further Broshi, "The Role of the Temple in the Herodian Economy," 31-37; Goodman, "The First Jewish Revolt," 422-34. According to the Judean historian Josephus (*War*), when the people finally erupted in revolt in the summer of 66, they attacked both the mansion of the high priest Ananias and the archives, where they tried to destroy the records of the debts that were dragging them into destitution and dependency.

11. Pointing out these historical relationships is in no way a support for the anti-Judaism that has tragically been part of Christian biblical studies in the past. Jesus is one among the many contemporary popular and scribal leaders who headed movements of renewal of Israel that opposed the high priestly rulers as well as the Roman rulers in the decades just before and just after Jesus' mission. Many late second-temple Judean texts, such as Daniel 10-12, the Damascus Document, *Psalms of Solomon* 2, and *1 Enoch* 94-104 also sharply criticize or condemn the incumbent high priests. An idealized Temple became prominent in rabbinic literature after its tragic destruction by the Romans in 70 CE.

12. See further the discussion in Horsley and Draper, *Whoever Hears You Hears Me*, chap. 9; and Horsley, *Covenant Economics*, 279-83.

13. For fuller investigation of Jesus' renewal of covenant community in the villages of Galilee, see Horsley, *Covenant Economics*, chaps. 7, 8, 10; Horsley, *Jesus and Empire*, chap. 5; and Horsley, *Hearing the Whole Story*, chap. 8.

14. More extensive analysis in Horsley and Draper, *Whoever Hears You Hears Me*, chapter 9; and Horsley, *Covenant Economics*, chap. 7.

11

Divine Violence in the Christian Bible
JOHN DOMINIC CROSSAN

Prologue

I hold these truths to be self-evident: *That* the United States of America is an empire. *That* the imperial virus came—as did so many other lethal pathogens—on the first ships from Europe. *That* American imperialism advanced with gathering speed from continental to hemispheric to global hegemony. *That* from the beginning until now, our American Empire proclaimed itself as the new Roman Empire and not, of course, as the new British Empire! *That* America-as-Empire no longer operates by conquering alien peoples and acquiring foreign territories, but by controlling economic institutions and securing military bases. *That*, as in so many recent imperial demises, our own obituary may leave the imperial homeland in comfort but the colonial periphery in discord. *That*, finally, we are a very modern *democratic republic* which serenely ignores two very ancient warnings, namely, that Greece invented *democracy* but found you could have either democracy or empire but not both at the same time—for long; and that Rome invented *republic* but found you could have either republic or empire, but not both at the same time—for long.[1]

All of that is my ongoing concern but not my present focus. That focal point concerns the Biblio-Christian basis for the violence of our imperial injustice. Is not the God of the Christian Bible violent? Is not that God's final solution to the problem of evil the extermination of all evildoers? Is

Divine Violence in the Christian Bible

not that violent Biblio-Christian God our model for Manifest Destiny, our paradigm for imperial vocation, and our invitation to participatory and collaborative violence? My present focus, then, is on this single question: Is the God of the Christian Bible violent, nonviolent, or some transcendental combination of both violence and nonviolence to be mixed and matched according to one's religious tradition or theological taste?

Some prefatory comments: First, I speak here exclusively of the Christian Bible, of that canonical collection that starts with Gen 1:1 and ends with Rev 22:21. Second, I understand its distinction of "Old Testament" and "New Testament" *not* with modernity where the new supersedes and displaces the old, but with antiquity where the new is the old re-newed, completed, climaxed, and consummated. Third, I emphasize that my inaugural question involves a *Christian* theology of the *Christian* Bible. Fourth, and finally, I reject absolutely any response to that problem that even hints that the God of the Old Testament is a God of violence, punishment, and vengeance but the God of the New Testament is a God of nonviolence, forgiveness, and love. That ancient libel will only work if one never reads the Christian Bible through to its final book—Revelation or Apocalypse—that most consistently and relentlessly violent text in all the canonical literature of all the world's great religions.

Finally, I recognize the magnificent terminal vision of "a new heaven and a new earth" in Rev 21:3-4 where "the home of God is among mortals," where God "will dwell with them as their God," where God "will wipe every tear from their eyes," and where "death will be no more; mourning and crying and pain will be no more, for the first things have passed away."

But, and this is the problem, one gets to that climax by wading through blood "as high as a horse's bridle, for a distance of about two hundred miles" (Rev 14:20). So, our constitutive question could also be rephrased like this: Does the end—even for the biblical God—justify the means?

My strategy for facing that question of whether the God of the Christian Bible is violent, nonviolent, or both, is to conduct probes into two major themes or textual swaths that cut across that collection from one end to the other: first *Justice*, then *Eschaton*, and finally *Parousia*. In all cases, I find a struggle of Gods, a clash between a nonviolent and a violent God. I could have said a conflict between opposing *visions* of God but those visions claim alike to speak for the same God to reveal the same God.

Once that dichotomy is established, the subsequent question is obvious. If, from Genesis through Revelation, the God of the Christian Bible is both nonviolent *and* violent in resistance to evil, how do we Christians respond to that duality? Are we ourselves to be nonviolent, violent, or both, in our own resistance to evil? Are we to "beat our swords into plowshares, and our spears into pruning hooks" with Isa 2:4 and Mic 4:3 or to "beat our plowshares into swords, and our pruning hooks into spears" with Joel 3:10? It is, by the way, hard to obey both those injunctions at the same time. Are we to be nonviolently or violently "holy as I am holy" in response to that divine challenge from Lev 19:2 and 1 Pet 1:16?

Justice

If God is a God of justice and righteousness—equal terms, by the way, for the same divine quality—is that about nonviolent distributive justice and restorative righteousness or about violent retributive justice and punitive righteousness? Or, of course, about both? It would seem clearly to be both—just follow these two mighty and divergent streams flowing outward from the Torah itself.

The God of Nonviolent Distributive Justice

The sign of that nonviolent God is the Sabbath and we will follow that theme in the Priestly Code from Sabbath Creation, through Sabbath Day and Year, to Sabbath Jubilee.[2] That sequence is for presentation here and does not presume any chronological sequence or genetic development.

Sabbath Creation. That magnificent parable of creation in Gen 1:1—2:4a images God as the Divine Architect who first drafts and builds the World-House in the first three days (Gen 1:3–13) and then furnishes and fills it in the corresponding next three days (Gen 1:14–31). You recognize immediately that each component gets ritually similar language: The units begin with, "God said, 'Let there be...'" and moves through "And it was so," or "And God saw that it was good" to close with "And there was evening and there was morning..."

Divine Violence in the Christian Bible

But as soon as you notice those repetitive phrases and frames, you also see clearly the composition's intentional purpose and deliberate climax. Creation has eight units, components, or chunks of stuff, but they have to be squeezed into six days. Thus, while Days 1 and 2, Days 4 and 5, each get one set of those stereotyped expressions, Days 3 and 6 have two of the openings, "And God said, 'Let . . .'" (Gen 1:9, 11 and 1:24, 26), but, of course, only one of the closing, "And there was evening and there was morning . . ." (Gen 1:13 and 1:31).

We humans are not the climax of creation. We are the work of a late Friday afternoon and no one does one's best work on a late Friday afternoon—possibly not even God? No, the climax of creation is the Sabbath, when "on the seventh day God finished the work that God had done, and God *rested* on the seventh day from all the work that God had done. So God *blessed* the seventh day and *hallowed* it, because on it God *rested* from all the work that he had done in creation" (Gen 2:2–3).

Notice two striking aspects of that powerful and visionary parable. First, Genesis never says that God created the Sabbath. It is almost as if the Sabbath is equiprimordial with God so that God must (as it were) make sure that "the heavens and the earth were finished, and all their multitude" (Gen 2:1) by dusk on that inaugural Friday. Indeed, as we shall see, the Sabbath is about the just distribution of God's creation to all God's creatures so Sabbath-as-Justice is, indeed, the very character of God as externally revealed. Second, in that all-perfect dawn-world, no blood is ever to be spilt upon the sacred earth of creation: "God said [to humans], 'See, I have given you every plant yielding seed that is upon the face of all the earth, and every tree with seed in its fruit; you shall have them for food. And to every beast of the earth, and to every bird of the air, and to everything that creeps on the earth, everything that has the breath of life, I have given every green plant for food.' And it was so" (Gen 1:29–30). Humans—and even animals—are to be vegetarians. It is easy to mock lettuce for lions, pesto for panthers, and tofu for tigers. But, still, it is a vision of a nonviolent earth given to us as a parable to ponder.

Sabbath Day. As crown of creation, the Sabbath Day is not about rest-*for*-worship but about rest-*as*-worship. It is a weekly reminder that, since all God's creatures have rights to equal rest, they have equal rights to all of God's creation. The Sabbath Day subjects time itself to nonviolent distributive justice. To observe it is a commitment to that meaning. Listen: "Six days you shall do your work, but on the seventh day you shall rest, *so that* your ox and your donkey may have relief, and your home-born slave and the resident alien may be refreshed" (Exod 23:12). "Observe the Sabbath day and keep it holy, as the Lord your God commanded you. Six days you shall labor and do all your work. But the seventh day is a Sabbath to the Lord your God; you shall not do any work—you, or your son or your daughter, or your male or female slave, or your ox or your donkey, or any of your livestock, or the resident alien in your towns, *so that* your male and female slave may rest as well as you" (Deut 5:12–14). Notice especially how my italicized *so that* gives the purpose of the Sabbath Day—so animals, slaves, and children may all rest. The command is, therefore, addressed to those left unmentioned, to the mothers and fathers, the parents and householders of Israel.

That second version appends another reason or argument: "Remember that you were a slave in the land of Egypt, and the Lord your God brought you out from there with a mighty hand and an outstretched arm; therefore the Lord your God commanded you to keep the Sabbath day" (Deut 5:15). Bereft of the Sabbath Day, Israel becomes Neo-Egypt.

Sabbath Year. Time is subject to justice and that hallowing of temporality extends representatively from one day every seven days to one year every seven years: "For six years you shall sow your land and gather in its yield; but the seventh year you shall let it rest and lie fallow, so that the poor of your people may eat; and what they leave the wild animals may eat. You shall do the same with your vineyard, and with your olive orchard" (Exod 23:10–11).

> When you enter the land that I am giving you, the land shall observe a Sabbath for the Lord. Six years you shall sow your field, and six years you shall prune your vineyard, and gather in their yield; but in the seventh year there shall be a Sabbath of complete rest for the land, a Sabbath for the Lord: you shall not sow your field or prune your vineyard. You shall not reap the aftergrowth of your harvest or gather the grapes of your unpruned vine: it shall be a year of complete rest for the land. You may eat what the land yields during its Sabbath—you, your male and female slaves, your hired and your bound laborers who live with you; for your livestock also, and for the wild animals in your land all its yield shall be for food. (Lev 25:2b–7)

Divine Violence in the Christian Bible

The concern is not for proper agricultural maintenance or the better rotation of crops but for the land itself, for the wild animals, and for the poor. Indeed, just as the corners of the fields and the gleanings of the harvest belong by divine decree to the poor (Lev 23:22), so the produce of those Sabbath Years belongs by right to all—animals and humans alike.

On the one hand, the *letter* of those laws may be totally ideal and utopian in their details and even be a recipe for agricultural starvation and economic disaster in their specifics. But, on the other, the *spirit* of attempting fair distribution of a world we did not create lies at their heart and challenges us to better details and other specifics if those do not work.

Furthermore, every seventh year all debts were to be liquidated and all those held in debt-slavery were to be freed: "Every seventh year you shall grant a remission of debts. And this is the manner of the remission: every creditor shall remit the claim that is held against a neighbor, not exacting it of a neighbor who is a member of the community, because the LORD's remission has been proclaimed" (Deut 15:1-2). "When you buy a male Hebrew slave, he shall serve six years, but in the seventh he shall go out a free person, without debt" (Exod 21:2).

Deuteronomy goes even further and commands that debt-slaves so freed are to be provided liberally from their owner's "flock, threshing floor, and wine press ... because for six years they have given you services worth the wages of hired laborers" (Deut 15:12-18).

Sabbath Jubilee. The fiftieth year, the year after the passage of seven Sabbath years, was especially holy. All dispossessed rural property was to return to its original familial owners:

A) It shall be a *jubilee* for you: you shall return, every one of you, to your property and every one of you to your family.

    B) That fiftieth year shall be a *jubilee* for you: you shall not sow, or reap the aftergrowth, or harvest the unpruned vines.

    B´) For it is a *jubilee*; it shall be holy to you: you shall eat only what the field itself produces.

A´) In this year of *jubilee* you shall return, every one of you, to your property. (Lev 25:11-13)

Once again, and especially here, the *letter* of the Sabbath Jubilee would probably kill the agricultural economy, but its *spirit* would hopefully enliven a just and nonviolent redistribution of rural property.

"The land," says God, "shall not be sold in perpetuity, for the land is mine; with me you are but aliens and tenants" (Lev 25:23). You cannot sell property that does not belong to you as a tenant farmer or resident alien on the land of another. And neither could that land be permanently alienated by foreclosure. But, in reality, "Ah, you who join house to house, who add field to field," said the prophet Isaiah, "until there is room for no one but you, and you are left to live alone in the midst of the land" (Isa 5:8).

The God of Violent Retributive Justice

A very basic locus for the vision of God as a God of retributive justice and punitive righteousness is in Deuteronomy 28 and that understanding of God continues as the constitutive basis for the historical books that follow it.

My point is not, emphatically not, that you find *only* distributive justice in that preceding Priestly tradition and *only* retributive justice in the Deuteronomic one. You find both in each as indeed you find both in the prophetic tradition where maldistribution begets retribution My point is simply to emphasize two divergent swaths that cut across the entire Bible from one end to the other.

First, and on the one hand, Deuteronomy 28 promises that, "if you will only obey the LORD your God, by diligently observing all his commandments . . . all these blessings shall come upon you and overtake you, if you obey the LORD your God" (Deut 28:1–2) and the next twelve verses specify fertility and prosperity of farm and family along with security from or victory over enemies. "The LORD will cause your enemies who rise against you to be defeated before you; they shall come out against you one way, and flee before you seven ways" (Deut 28:7).

Second, and on the other hand, Deuteronomy 28 warns that "if you will not obey the LORD your God by diligently observing all his commandments and decrees . . . then all these curses shall come upon you and overtake you" (Deut 28:15). Once again, fertility from within and victory from without are stressed but in the reverse direction: "The LORD will cause you to be defeated before your enemies; you shall go out against them one way and flee before them seven ways. You shall become an object of horror to all the kingdoms of the earth" (Deut 28:25). Still, despite some symmetry between blessings and curses, the former got only fourteen while the latter got fifty-four verses.

If you read over *all* of that chapter a few times, one very pressing question arises. Is it true? Is it—in any way, shape, or form—actually true? All those blessings and curses are earthly sanctions, empirically open at least to counter-factual meditation. If, for example, all the people of Israel had been saints and spent all their time on their knees in prayer, what would have happened differently? Nothing. Nothing at all. Why?

First, tiny Israel was geopolitically positioned as the hinge of the three known continents of its time—Europe, Asia, and Africa. When the axis of empire was mainly north and south between Mesopotamia and Egypt, Israel was in the middle. When the axis shifted to west and east, with Macedonians and Persians, Romans and Parthians, Israel was still in the middle. Were they all saints, the only difference is that they would have died—be it from regular invasion or occasional drought—on their knees.

Second, there is already doubt cast on that Deuteronomic theology of blessings and curses, rewards and punishments, by its failure to explain why a "good" southern king like Josiah died too soon or a bad northern king like Manasseh lived too long. In those cases history had later to be adjusted to preserve the integrity of that Deuteronomic theory. Here are the details.

The earlier account of Josiah is straightforward: "Pharaoh Neco king of Egypt went up to the king of Assyria to the river Euphrates. King Josiah went to meet him; but when Pharaoh Neco met him at Megiddo, he killed him. His servants carried him dead in a chariot from Megiddo, brought him to Jerusalem, buried him in his own tomb" (2 Kgs 23:29–30). But, the later version explains his death as divine punishment:

> King Neco of Egypt went up to fight at Carchemish on the Euphrates, and Josiah went out against him. *But Josiah would not turn away from him, but disguised himself in order to fight with him. He did not listen to the words of Neco from the mouth of God, but joined battle in the plain of Megiddo*. The archers shot King Josiah; and the king said to his servants, 'Take me away, for I am badly wounded.' So his servants took him out of the chariot and carried him in his

> second chariot and brought him to Jerusalem. There he died, and was buried in the tombs of his ancestors. (2 Chr 35:20–24)

That italicized material is not new archival information but simply an attempt to fit Josiah back into Deuteronomic theology and explain why one of Israel's few "good" kings ended up dead by Egyptian archers.

The opposite problem arose with Manasseh who "was twelve years old when he began to reign; he reigned fifty-five years in Jerusalem. His mother's name was Hephzibah. He did what was evil in the sight of the Lord" (2 Kgs 21:1–2). His "evil" is then specified in very great detail (2 Kgs 21:3–16) and this version concludes: "Now the rest of the acts of Manasseh, all that he did, and the sin that he committed, are they not written in the Book of the Annals of the Kings of Judah? Manasseh slept with his ancestors, and was buried in the garden of his house, in the garden of Uzza. His son Amon succeeded him" (2 Kgs 21:17–18).

That is, of course, an extraordinary long reign for a poster-boy of a "bad" king. Once again, the later account of the Chronicler adapts history to fit with Deuteronomic theology. The account begins with the same opening data: "Manasseh was twelve years old when he began to reign; he reigned fifty-five years in Jerusalem. He did what was evil in the sight of the Lord" (2 Chr 33:1–2). Next follows a shortened list of his "evil" deeds (2 Chr 33:3–10). But then comes this revisionary addition:

> Therefore the Lord brought against them the commanders of the army of the king of Assyria, who took Manasseh captive in manacles, bound him with fetters, and brought him to Babylon. While he was in distress he entreated the favor of the Lord his God and humbled himself greatly before the God of his ancestors. He prayed to him, and God received his entreaty, heard his plea, and restored him again to Jerusalem and to his kingdom. Then Manasseh knew that the Lord indeed was God. (2 Chr 33:11–13)

Finally, his post-conversion "good" actions are detailed (2 Chr 33:14–17), and it concludes with this summary:

> Now the rest of the acts of Manasseh, *his prayer to his God, and the words of the seers who spoke to him in the name of the Lord God of Israel*, these are in the Annals of the Kings of Israel. *His prayer, and how God received his entreaty,* all his sin and his faithlessness, the sites on which he built high places and set up the sacred poles and the images, *before he humbled himself,* these are written in the

Divine Violence in the Christian Bible

> records of the seers. So Manasseh slept with his ancestors, and they buried him in his house. His son Amon succeeded him. (2 Chr 33:18–20)

My italics emphasize the expansions in that version over the one just seen in 2 Kgs 21:17–18.

Third, maybe Josiah and Manasseh were simply exceptions that proved the Deuteronomic rule, exceptions one might not have noticed were it not for the somewhat crude theological revisionism of the Chronicler? Should we then explain the book of Job as just one more exception or is it a repudiation of Deuteronomic orthodoxy within the Old Testament itself?

It is, first of all, an extraordinary book. The author lets the reader in on the truth from the very beginning, but Job never learns it even by the end of the story. At the start, God announces immediately that "there is no one like Job on the earth, a blameless and upright man who fears God and turns away from evil" (Job 1:8). Job is, by divine assertion, completely holy and totally blameless. For the reader that is—from the very start—a divinely proclaimed fact.

Satan responds that Job is only blamelessly holy because God has "blessed the work of his hands, and his possessions have increased in the land" (Job 1:10). Were Job to lose everything, says Satan, he would surely "curse" God (Job 1:11). For, if rewards and punishment are promised for virtue and vice, how does one know who would be good or bad even without those sanctions? And so begins the testing of Job. Is he or is he not simply a calculating Deuteronomist?

Then come the Friends—first three (Job 2:11–31:40) and then a fourth (Job 32:1—37:24). They are all absolutely sincere, all Deuteronomic fundamentalists, and all totally wrong—and the reader knows they are wrong before they open their mouths. Remember that the author could have kept the reader in the dark about what had happened in heaven by starting with, say, Job 2:7. Then the reader would be wondering chapter after chapter—along with those Friends—what Job could have done to deserve such ghastly retribution from God.

But the author forces us relentlessly to hear over and over again that Deuteronomy-based explanation that Job must have done something for which God is punishing him and, if he will but admit and repent, God will surely forgive him. And, from start to finish, we know they are wrong.

We also know that, despite some transcendental bluster that reduces Job to silence (Job 38:1—42:6), God never tells Job the truth.

Still, of course, the Friends and their Deuteronomic theology are certainly wrong. "The LORD said to Eliphaz the Temanite: 'My wrath is kindled against you and against your two friends; for you have not spoken of me what is right, as my servant Job has'" (Job 42:7). On the one hand, then, the book of Job offers no overall explanation of human suffering—the case of Job is too unique to be generalized. But, on the other, it constitutes—I would argue—a repudiation of Deuteronomic theology within the Old Testament itself. Unfortunately, however, it created not even a speed bump on the Deuteronomic roadway through the Christian Bible and later Christian tradition.

Here, however, is my heuristic conclusion-as-challenge from those discordant texts. There is no proof—apart from reiterated claims—that the biblical God ever punishes anyone, anywhere, ever. But there is, let it be said with fear and trembling, terrible human consequences for what we do—for our injustice, for our oppression, and for our violence against God's world and God's people. Let me be very clear about my language. I distinguish constitutively between *consequences* as derived internally—a drunk driver hits a tree and is killed—from *punishments* as added externally—a drunk driver hits a tree and is fined.

An historical example: On *Kristallnacht*, or "Night of Shattered Glass," between Wednesday and Thursday, November 9–10, 1938, the largest and most beautiful synagogue in Germany, high above the river Elbe in Dresden, capital city of Prussian Saxony, was deliberately set on fire by paramilitary brigades who forced the firefighters to let it burn to the ground.

On the night between Shrove Tuesday and Ash Wednesday, February 13–14, 1945, the first of four Allied air raids deliberately created a perfect firestorm with a lethal mix of sixty percent explosive and forty percent incendiary bombs centered on Dresden's Old City. That second fire was a human consequence and not a divine punishment for the first one.

Think of our evolutionary world as the incarnate revelation of God's distributive justice and restorative righteousness. Our oppression, injustice, and violence against that world and its God have inevitably necessary earthly consequences and it is simply bad and dangerously trivializing theology to call them heavenly punishments.

Eschaton

The biblical tradition's *faith* proclaimed a God of justice and righteousness who owned the earth by right of creation. But the biblical tradition's *experience* was that God's earth was suffused with injustice and unrighteousness and that God's own people had far more than their fair share of that evil and injustice, oppression, violence, and war. If neither faith nor experience could be denied, how could they be reconciled?

The Great Divine Cleanup of the World

The answer to how they could be reconciled was *eschatology* from the Greek word "eschaton" meaning "the end" or "the last." The word is quite ordinary—used, for example, in the "first will be *last*, and the *last* will be first" (Mark 10:31). The meaning of "eschaton" depends, in other words, on context—the "last" or "end" of what?

Biblical eschatology was not about—emphatically not about—the "end" of the world, the "last" of the earth. The KJV, for example, translates the Greek expression *synteleia (tou) aiōnos* as "end of the world" in Matt 13:39, 49; 24:3; 28:20; but the NRSV more correctly translates it as "end of the age." Note, also, that the term used is not *eschaton* but *synteleia*, which means consummation, perfection, completion, fulfillment.

Whether with *synteleia* or *eschaton*, the focus is on the end or last of evil, injustice, war, and violence here below upon an earth transfigured, transformed, perfected, consummated, and restored to God's creational vision of equity and peace. In my own language, eschatology is about the Great Divine Cleanup of the World.

There is a classic example of this cosmic transfiguration in *Sibylline Oracle* 3 from Egyptian Judaism around 150 BCE.[3] It imagines an earth perfected in its physical, animal, and social dimensions.

The physical or material world will "give the most excellent unlimited fruit to mortals, of grain, wine, and oil and a delightful drink of sweet honey from heaven, trees, fruit of the top branches, and rich flocks and herds and lambs of sheep and kids of goats" (*Sib. Or.* 3:744–748). And the animal world will be no longer feral: "Wolves and lambs will eat grass together in the mountains. Leopards will feed together with kids. Roving bears will spend the night with calves. The flesh-eating lion will eat husks at the manger like an ox, and mere infant children will lead them with ropes. For he will make the beasts on earth harmless. Serpents and asps will sleep with babies and will not harm them, for the hand of God will be upon them" (*Sib. Or.* 3:788–795). You will recall that Isa 11:6–9 had imagined a similar ecstatic prospect 600 years earlier. Even if one dismissed those visions for the physical and animal worlds as wildly impossible, these for the human and social world are not so easily discarded:

> There will be no sword on earth or din of battle, and the earth will no longer be shaken, groaning deeply. There will no longer be war or drought on earth, no famine or hail, damaging to fruits, but there will be great peace throughout the whole earth. King will be friend to king to the end of the age. The Immortal in the starry heaven will put in effect a common law for men throughout the whole earth ... Prophets of the great God will take away the sword for they themselves are judges of men and righteous kings. There will also be just wealth among men for this is the judgment and dominion of the great God. (*Sib. Or.* 3:751–758, 781–784)

None of that is about the destruction but rather the perfection of our earth. It is not about a heavenly evacuation but an earthly transformation.

One other word also requires close attention. An *apocalypse* (from the Greek) is a *revelation* (from the Latin) and *apocalyptic eschatology* concerns claims to special revelation about that Great Divine Cleanup of the World. Strictly speaking, the content of such a claim could be anything relevant about the eschaton. But in the heightened tensions of that first-century CE Jewish homeland where 500 years of imperial oppression had climaxed with Rome as the most powerful empire of them all, the focus of any apocalyptic eschatology was on time: When? How soon? Any day now? In our lifetime? How imminent was God's Great Cleanup of the World?

In any case, be that advent distant or imminent, there was this obvious question: Come the eschaton, what about the Gentiles? It was not some general question about non-Jews (the Irish, for example) but a very specific one about the Gentiles they knew best, about those all-powerful and conquering imperialistic Gentiles. Since they were God's problem, what would be God's solution—on that day when creation would shine again in the just splendor of its first dawning?

Divine Violence in the Christian Bible

Put bluntly: How would God put an "end" to the Roman legions? And, by now, it should not be a surprise that the biblical tradition has two contradictory answers—one violent and one nonviolent—to that problem and that question. Furthermore, just as with justice, so also with eschaton, those two contradictory responses flow through the entire Christian Bible from one end to the other. Indeed, they are often found in the same book, even in the same chapter, and sometimes even in the same verse.

A Violent or Nonviolent Eschaton

I am accepting and following here a distinction emphasized by Paula Fredriksen almost twenty years ago.[4] What that earlier article distinguished as a "negative extreme" *versus* a "positive extreme," a later book spoke of as "less generous speculations" *versus* "inclusive traditions." I rephrase that distinction as "violent eschaton" *versus* "nonviolent eschaton," but, by whatever name or term, it is exactly the same content and meaning.

Take, for example, Micah, from the eighth century BCE, within that basic distinction. He imagines God's violent eschaton like this:

> In anger and wrath I will execute vengeance on the nations that did not obey . . . Then my enemy will see, and shame will cover her who said to me, "Where is the LORD your God?" My eyes will see her downfall; now she will be trodden down like the mire of the streets . . . The nations shall see and be ashamed of all their might; they shall lay their hands on their mouths; their ears shall be deaf; they shall lick dust like a snake, like the crawling things of the earth; they shall come trembling out of their fortresses; they shall turn in dread to the LORD our God, and they shall stand in fear of you. (Mic 5:15; 7:10, 16–17)

But, earlier in that very same book of Micah, the eschatological consummation was imagined as a nonviolent and even antiviolent eschaton:

> In days to come the mountain of the LORD's house shall be established as the highest of the mountains, and shall be raised up above the hills. Peoples shall stream to it, and many nations shall come and say: "Come, let us go up to the mountain of the LORD, to the house of the God of Jacob; that he may teach us his ways and that we may walk in his paths." For out of Zion shall go forth instruction, and the word of the LORD from Jerusalem. He shall judge

> between many peoples, and shall arbitrate between strong nations far away; they shall beat their swords into plowshares, and their spears into pruning hooks; nation shall not lift up sword against nation, neither shall they learn war any more; but they shall all sit under their *own* vines and under their *own* fig trees, and no one shall make them afraid; for the mouth of the LORD of hosts has spoken. (Mic 4:1–4; italics added)

That magnificent vision is, of course, repeated verbatim from "in days to come" down to "war any more" in the contemporary prophecy of Isa 2:2–4.

Notice, by the way, that, while all will have their own vines and figs, they will not all have their own Gods. Those other Gods, so well known to the people of Israel, had usually justified this or that imperial oppression, so, no, all would eventually have the same God of nonviolent distributive justice. The Gentiles would be converted, not to the nation of Israel but, yes, to the God of Israel:

> Thus says the LORD of hosts: Peoples shall yet come, the inhabitants of many cities; the inhabitants of one city shall go to another, saying, "Come, let us go to entreat the favor of the LORD, and to seek the LORD of hosts; I myself am going." Many peoples and strong nations shall come to seek the LORD of Hosts in Jerusalem, and to entreat the favor of the LORD. Thus says the LORD of hosts: In those days ten men from nations of every language shall take hold of a Jew, grasping his garment and saying, "Let us go with you, for we have heard that God is with you." (Zech 8:20–23)

Another way of expressing that same distinction of violent *versus* nonviolent eschaton is to speak of The Great Final Battle *versus* The Great Final Feast. We just saw an example of The Great Final Battle in Mic 5:15 and 7:10, 16–17 above. Here is a classic example of The Great Final Feast:

> On this mountain the LORD of Hosts will make for all peoples a feast of rich food, a feast of well-aged wines, of rich food filled with marrow, of well-aged wines strained clear. And he will destroy on this mountain the shroud that is cast over all peoples, the sheet that is spread over all nations; he will swallow up death forever. Then the LORD God will wipe away the tears from all faces, and the disgrace of his people he will take away from all the earth, for the LORD has spoken. (Isa 25:6–8)

Divine Violence in the Christian Bible

Those to disjunctive eschatons are also symbolized by two different mountains in later tradition. The Great Final Feast takes place on Mount Zion and the Great Final Battle occurs in the shadow of Mount Megiddo—the infamous Armageddon.

Parousia

First-century Jews who had expected a violent eschaton and so, presumably, a violent messianic intermediary, must have been surprised if not exasperated with Jesus of Nazareth. In considering the various and divergent messianic figures in ancient Jewish literature, for example, John J. Collins concludes that "the typical profile of the Davidic messiah" as "first of all, a warrior prince, who was to defeat the enemies of Israel . . . a warrior king who would destroy the enemies of Israel and institute an era of unending peace" was "the common core of Jewish messianism around the turn of the era." He contrasts that popular consensus with the New Testament's vision of Jesus of Nazareth as Davidic messiah that "does not fit the typical profile of the Davidic messiah.[5]

In my own words, that contrast is between a violent *versus* a nonviolent messianic eschaton. But that is based on an even deeper and more fundamental contrast between the messianic eschaton as *a present process of bilateral divine-human cooperation rather than as an imminent instant of unilateral divine intervention*. In other words, Jesus of Nazareth represents Messianic/Christian-Judaism as a paradigm shift[6] or tradition swerve within standard messianic, apocalyptic, eschatological Judaism itself.[7]

Once Messianic/Christian-Judaism imagined eschaton as a process of collaboration rather than as an instant of intervention, one very obvious question arose immediately: How would that process end? If eschatological *initiation* was nonviolent rather than violent, what about its *consummation*? Would it be nonviolent or violent? It was actually portrayed, first, as nonviolent—with Paul of Tarsus—and then as violent—with John of Patmos.

Paul of Tarsus and a Nonviolent Eschatological Consummation

Paul proclaimed—in my terms—a *collaborative eschatology* in which all Christians "with unveiled faces, seeing the glory of the Lord as though reflected in a mirror, *are being transformed* into the same image from one degree of glory to another; for this comes from the Lord, the Spirit" (2 Cor 3:18). But he also presumed—incorrectly, of course, as we now know—an early end to that collaborative process.

From 1 Thessalonians, where he speaks of "*we* who are alive . . . will be caught up in the clouds . . . to meet the Lord in the air" (1 Thess 4:17), through 1 Corinthians, where "the impending crisis" means that "the appointed time has grown short" so that "the present form of this world is passing away" (1 Cor 7:26–31), to Romans where he could still maintain that, "salvation is nearer to us now than when we became believers; the night is far gone, the day is near" (Rom 13:11–12), Paul thought that the eschatological consummation would occur not only in his generation but even in his own lifetime.

Leaving aside for now that mistake about the *time*, what does Paul imagine as the *content* of the eschaton's conclusion? What is this Coming of Christ to do and will it be done nonviolently or violently? What metaphor or model controls his expectation? To understand Paul's vision of eschatological consummation, I focus on two messages from his seven authentic letters—first from 1 Thess 4:15–17 and then from 1 Cor 15:20–28.

When Paul first arrived in Europe, he was forced to flee from the Roman province of Macedonia to that of Achaia. In Macedonia, he was accused, at Philippi, of "advocating customs that are not lawful for us as Romans to adopt or observe" (Acts 16:21) and, at Thessalonica, of "acting contrary to the decrees of the emperor, saying that there is another king named Jesus" (Acts 17:7). He was ultimately forced to flee to Athens from which he sent Timothy back to Thessalonica to find how the community had fared under persecution (1 Thess 3:1–7). Timothy returned with news that, as Paul sums it up from Corinth: "You became imitators of us and of the Lord, for in spite of persecution you received the word with joy inspired by the Holy Spirit, so that you became an example to all the believers in Macedonia and in Achaia. For the word of the Lord has sounded forth from you not only in Macedonia and Achaia, but in every place your faith in God has become known, so that we have no need to speak about it" (1 Thess 1:6-8). But the community had one very human and very pastoral question. Paul had warned them of possible persecution, but he had also promised them an imminent eschatological consummation. When that happened to the living, would not the dead be at a disadvantage? What about their persecuted and executed members?

In answer, Paul, dancing theologically as fast as he can, uses a magnificent metaphorical model to reassure them that their honored dead, far from being at a disadvantage, would be very much at an advantage when the imminent consummation occurred. His model is evidenced by the twin key and—in context—technical terms that he uses in 1 Thessalonians:

> For this we declare to you by the word of the LORD, that we who are alive, who are left until the coming of the LORD (*eis tēn parousian tou kuriou*), will by no means precede those who have died. For the LORD himself, with a cry of command, with the archangel's call and with the sound of God's trumpet, will descend from heaven, and the dead in Christ will rise first. Then we who are alive, who are left, will be caught up in the clouds together with them to meet the LORD (*eis apantēsin tou kuriou*) in the air; and so we will be with the LORD forever. (1 Thess 4:15-17)

Those twin Greek expressions represent the two parts of an official imperial visitation—coming and greeting, advent and reception.

Think, for example, of those two terms as used of Alexander the Great by Josephus in his *Jewish Antiquities*—a story, by the way, more parable than history. In November 333 BCE, having defeated Darius of Persia at Issus in northwestern Syria and devastated both Tyre and Gaza for their resistance, Alexander turned his army toward Jerusalem. The Jewish high priest Jaddus "was in an agony of fear not knowing how he could meet (*apantēsai*) the Macedonians" (*Jewish Antiquities* 11.326), "so he sacrificed for deliverance and, God spoke oracularly to him in his sleep, telling him to take courage and adorn the city with wreaths and open the gates and go out to meet them [literally: make the *hypantēsin*], and that the people should be in white garments ... And, after doing all the things that he had been told to do, [he] awaited the coming (*parousian*) of the king ... And making the reception (*hypantēsin*), sacred in character and different from all other nations, met him" (11.327, 329).

In the context of Alexander's imperial plans, those technical terms for *visitation* and *reception* have—despite Josephus's parabolic propaganda—an aura of force, war, and violence. But under the Pax Romana, the Thessalonians would immediately envisage such an imperial advent as nonviolent. The emperor—or his official legate—would come in peace with feasting, celebration, patronal gifts, and maybe even urban renewal projects but also—as documents indicate—with some added taxes so that the city could pay for the privilege of imperial presence.[8]

Furthermore, as the imperial cortege approached the wide-open city gates, the first citizens to greet them would be in the tombs of the honored dead. Before the living dignitaries at the city gate ever greeted the imperial cortege, those dead dignitaries would have confronted it. Think, for example, of those tombs that would have greeted an imperial visitor approaching, say, Hierapolis on its great north road. So, argues Paul, the martyrs, the honored dead of the Christian community, would rise first to greet Christ and then "we who are alive, who are left" (*hoi perileipomenoi*) would come second. If one wishes, by the way, to speak of the "left behind," there they are—mentioned twice—but they include all living Christians (1 Thess 4:15, 17).

Finally, that advent/reception sequence does not intend to return with the Visitor whence he came, but he led him joyfully into their city. So also with eschatological consummation. The logic of the metaphorical model means that after Christians meet Christ "in the air" above the earth, they all return with Christ to that already-transfigured earth. In other words, Christ is not coming to do for us a project at which we have failed, but to rejoice with us on one at which we have succeeded.

That understanding is confirmed by what Paul says in 1 Corinthians 15. At the end of the chapter, still presuming an imminent consummation and being alive for it, Paul says: "Listen, I will tell you a mystery! *We* will not all die, but *we* will all be changed, in a moment, in the twinkling of an eye, at the last trumpet. For the trumpet will sound, and the dead will be raised imperishable, and *we* will be changed" (1 Cor 15:51–52). At the end, the dead will need to be raised but the living will only need to be changed—all into immortality.

Earlier in that same chapter he described the "coming" (*parousia*) of Christ like this: "Then comes the end, when he hands over the kingdom to God the Father, after he has destroyed every ruler and every authority and power. For he must reign until he has put all his enemies under his feet" (1 Cor 15:24–25). Once again, for Paul, the *parousia* of Christ is not to do by unilateral intervention what Christians have failed to do in bilateral collaboration. The "coming" (*parousia*) of Christ is to consummate and celebrate the Kingdom of God established on a transfigured earth and therefore ready to be handed over "to God the Father . . . so that God may be all in all" (1 Cor 15:24, 28).

John of Patmos and a Violent Eschatological Consummation

There are major agreements and even more important major disagreements between Paul of Tarsus and John of Patmos on the expected consummation of the eschaton. Consummation, I repeat, meant the end and not the beginning of the divine-human collaborative transformation of the earth proclaimed by Jesus.

Paul and John agree that something climactic would happen soon. We have already seen that Paul presumes that he (recall his use of "we") would live to see this event of eschatological consummation take place. In the book of Revelation or the Apocalypse, the final book of the Christian Bible, John's presumption is even more emphatic.

He announces his volume as: "The revelation of Jesus Christ, which God gave him to show his servants what must soon (*en taxei*) take place" (Rev 1:1) and Jesus warns some in the Pergamum community that "I will come to you soon (*taxu*) and make war against them with the sword of my mouth" (Rev 2:16). Thereafter, "I am coming soon" (*erchomai taxu*) is repeated by Christ from Rev 3:11 to its triadic crescendo in Rev 22:7, 12, 20.

Paul and John agree—at least in English translation—to describe that eschatological climax as the "Coming" of Christ. But while Paul uses the Greek word *parousia* for that event—as we just saw in 1 Thess 4:15 and 1 Cor 15:20 and can also see in 1 Thess 2:19 and 5:23—John uses the ordinary Greek verb "to come" (*erchomai*). In other words, John's terminology does not reflect the nonviolent imperial visitation characteristic of that first-century Pax Romana.

Furthermore, and following that divergence in language, the Coming of Christ in John is *not to celebrate success but to redeem failure*, not to rejoice at the successful completion of a divine-human collaboration but to redeem its failure by a unilateral divine intervention. Finally, and above all else, that intervention will be *incredibly violent*, will make Revelation the most relentlessly violent book in all the canonical literature of the great religions of the world.

If Paul uses the metaphorical model of *nonviolent imperial visitation* for Christ's Coming, what metaphorical model controls John's alternative vision of Christ's Coming as punitive cosmic slaughter? It is, ironically, that of *violent imperial visitation*. But how, within the time and place of the Pax Romana, is that a credible, viable, or even possible model? What paradigm gave John his terrible vision of the Great Final Feast as one for "all the birds who fly in midheaven . . . to eat the flesh of kings, the flesh of captains, the flesh of the mighty, the flesh of horses and their riders—flesh of all, both free and slave, both small and great"? (Rev 19:17–18). What would the rich cities of the rich Roman province of Asia know about violent imperial visitation? How could that be a successfully convincing model and metaphor for the Coming of Christ?

The Emperor Nero. It is not uncommon in human history for very popular leaders who depart this life under unusual or mysterious circumstances with their lives unfulfilled and their projects unfinished to be allegedly hidden away somewhere pending eventual return as future saviors. That happened—surprisingly so—to the fifth emperor of the Julio-Claudians, the final emperor of Rome's first imperial dynasty.

Nero was two months short of his seventeenth birthday when, on October 13, 54 CE, he succeeded Claudius amid high hopes and extravagant praise. The poet Calpurnius Siculus announced that, "The golden age is reborn with untroubled peace . . . while a god himself rules the peoples" (*Eclogues* 1.42, 46).[9] But all of that had turned to dust and ashes when, on June 9, 68 CE, Nero committed suicide to escape assassination. He left behind a reputation for crimes so monstrous that the senatorial and aristocratic classes of Rome had clearly rejected even his memory. But he also left behind a very different reputation among the lower classes of Rome and even among upper classes in the east. A Roman emperor who competed with others by performing on his lyre and racing in his chariot was popular precisely among those groups. And it was there that the legend of Nero *redivivus* was born and survived—even to the time of Saint Augustine over 300 years later.

Divine Violence in the Christian Bible

***The Legend of Nero* Redivivus.** Roman historical writers record a belief that Nero had not died but had fled eastward beyond the Euphrates. From there he would soon return at the head of Parthian imperial armies to destroy the Roman Empire. Those not only mention that belief, they also cite pretenders who claimed to be Nero *redivivus*.

Tacitus (c. 56–120) notes that, "About this time [summer, 69 CE] Achaia and Asia were upset by a false alarm. It was rumored that Nero was on his way to them. There had been conflicting stories about his death, and so numbers of people imagined—and believed—that he was alive (*Histories* 2.8).

Suetonius (c. 69–150) adds that, "There were some who for a long time decorated Nero's tomb with spring and summer flowers, and now produced his statues on the rostra in the fringed toga, and now his edicts, as if he were still alive and would shortly return and deal destruction to his enemies" (*The Lives of the Caesars: Nero* 57).

In the Jewish *Sibylline Oracles* 10 that legend is repeated not because they particularly liked Nero—they did not—or particularly liked the Parthians—they did not—but because it imagined the (imminent?) demise of the Roman Empire which had destroyed their temple and devastated their homeland in the terrible war of 66–74 CE. An eastern vengeance on western imperialism seemed divinely appropriate—even if led by a Nero *redivivus*.

Oracles dated between 80 and 100 CE identify Nero as killing his own mother (*Sib. Or.* 4:121; 5:142), attempting to build the Corinthian canal (5:139), and "playing at theatricals with honey-sweet songs rendered with melodious voice" (5:141–142). He is "a great king of great Rome, a godlike man" (4:119; 5:138); he is begotten of Zeus and Hera (5:140); but he is still "a savage-minded man, much bloodied, raving nonsense" (5:96).

This Nero fled "from Italy like a runaway slave unseen and unheard over the channel of the Euphrates" (*Sib. Or.* 4:119–120); he went "beyond the Parthia land" (4:123); he escaped "to Babylon, a terrible and shameless prince" (5:143). And from there he will return leading Parthia to destroy Rome: "Then the strife of war being aroused will come to the west, and the fugitive from Rome will also come, brandishing a great spear, having crossed Euphrates with many myriads" (*Sib. Or.* 4:137–139).

The coming of Nero *redivivus* will be far from the nonviolent imperial visitation of the Roman peace. It will be the violent imperial visitation of the Parthian revenge.

John of Patmos and Nero Redividus. Granted, then, that the legend of Nero *redivivus* was used in those Jewish *Sibylline Oracles* in prophetic warning of Rome's ultimate fate, what does that have to do with John of Patmos, the book of Revelation, and the Coming of Christ?

First, John announces the imminent destruction of Rome, the city set on seven hills (Rev 17:9). Babylon had destroyed Israel's First Temple and Rome did the same to the replacement Second Temple. So John calls Rome "Babylon" (Rev 14:8; 16:19; 17:5) and gleefully proclaims its destruction in a climactic triple assertion (Rev 18:2, 10, 21). Second, whenever he mentions or counts out the emperors who incarnate and personify Rome, Nero—precisely as *redivivus*—gets special attention. He is that one who "seemed to have received a death-blow, but its mortal wound had been healed" (Rev 13:3, 12). He is "the beast that had wounded by the sword and yet lived" (Rev 13:14).

That series in Revelation 13 concludes with a mysterious identification which invites the hearers or readers to think about it: "This calls for wisdom: let anyone with understanding calculate the number of the beast, for it is the number of a person. Its number is six hundred sixty-six" (Rev 13:18). The title "Nero Caesar" is *NERŌN KAISAR* in Greek and *NRON KSR* in Hebrew. Using Hebraic *gematria*, where letters of the alphabet also indicate numbers, those seven letters translate numerically as: $50+200+6+50+100+60+200 = 666$.

Nero *redivivus* is identified as, "the beast that . . . was, and is not, and is about to ascend from the bottomless . . . And the inhabitants of the earth . . . will be amazed when they see the beast, because it was and is not and is to come" (Rev 17:8). Finally, once again, a mysterious identification invites the hearers/readers to think about it: "This calls for a mind that has wisdom: the seven heads are seven mountains on which the woman is seated; also, they are seven kings, of whom five have fallen, one is living, and the other has not yet come; and when he comes, he must remain only a little while. As for the beast that was and is not, it is an eighth but it belongs to the seven, and it goes to destruction" (Rev 17:9–11). However one identifies that entire series of seven emperors, Nero *redivivus* is the beast "that was," who "belongs to the seven," but "is not" now, only to reappear as "an eighth."

But why is John of Patmos so fascinated and focused not just on Nero as, say, the first great imperial persecutor of Christianity but on Nero precisely as Nero *redivivus*, precisely as the one who would return, as it were, from the dead to destroy the Roman Empire?

The answer is sad if not tragic. Rome will be destroyed imminently, announces John, but not by Nero *redivivus*. It will be destroyed by Christ *redivivus*. Not Nero backed by the Parthians but Christ backed by the angels will come—and come soon—to destroy Rome. In that transfer from Nero to Christ, the eschatological consummation retains all the violent imagery of imperial warfare. It is the counter-violence of Christ-as-Nero whose Coming will destroy the violence of the Roman Empire. That is the model and metaphor that controls the Revelation from Patmos.

Eschatological consummation will indeed be a Great Final Feast but only for carrion crows and vultures: "Come, gather for the great supper of God, to eat the flesh of kings, the flesh of captains, the flesh of the mighty, the flesh of horses and their riders—flesh of all, both free and slave, both small and great . . . and all the birds were gorged with their flesh" (Rev 19:17, 18, 21).

Incarnation

The conclusion to all of those preceding probes—from the Justice of God to the Coming of Christ—is that two divergent visions of God appear from one end of the Christian Bible to the other. The Christian Bible is not, *emphatically not*, an Old Testament of violence and a New Testament of nonviolence. It is not an (auto)biography whereby divine maturation moves through violence to nonviolence—just compare Genesis 1 with Revelation 19.

The Christian Bible is a struggle between two visions of God, between a God of nonviolence making us in that God's image and a God of violence we are making in our own image. That is the value and power, the dignity and integrity, the inspired struggle between the Word of divinity in the words of humanity that makes our Christian Bible what it now and forever is.

But how, then, do we decide between those discordant images, between a God who establishes justice by violence and one who establishes justice by nonviolence? Do we simply prepare a transcendental cocktail of so many parts violence and so many parts nonviolence, mix according to spiritual taste or religious mandate, and sip carefully or drink heavily according, once again, to individual or denominational tradition. What, in other words, is the *Christian* theology for our *Christian* Bible?

The answer is profoundly obvious. Which of those two divine visions is incarnated in the Nazarene, that same person known to reason and research as the Jesus of history *and* to revelation and religion as the Christ of faith? *It is that nonviolent God who is represented on earth by Jesus of Nazareth.* You will also recall that Jesus justified nonviolence resistance to injustice by appealing to the very character of God who "makes his sun rise on the evil and on the good, and sends rain on the righteous and on the unrighteous" (Matt 5:45).

The primary New Testament witness to the nonviolent resistance that characterized Jesus is Pontius Pilate himself who, on the one hand, legally, publicly, and officially crucified Jesus and, on the other, made no attempt to round up his companions.[11] That was the Roman method with *nonviolent* resistance—execute the leader and ignore the followers—and, if necessary, do it again and again with successive leaders.

The nonviolence of Jesus is the heart of two superb *parabolic* scenes concerning him and Pilate in Mark and John. In the dramatic parable of Mark 15:6–9 Pilate is shown as clearly recognizing the difference between Barabbas and Jesus. As a *violent* revolutionary, "Barabbas was in prison with the rebels who had committed murder during the insurrection" (Mark 15:7). Pilate arrested him along with those of his followers he could capture. But Jesus was a nonviolent revolutionary so Pilate made no attempt to round up his companions. Both Barabbas and Jesus opposed Roman injustice in the Jewish homeland but Pilate knew exactly and correctly how to calibrate their divergent oppositions.

In John 18:36—in, once again, correct history summarized as dramatic parable—Jesus confronted Pilate with the famous claim that, "My kingdom is not from this world. If my kingdom were from this world, my followers would be fighting to keep me from being handed over to the Jews. But as it is, my kingdom is not from here" (18:36). It all comes down to that basic difference. The kingdom of Rome is based on fighting

Divine Violence in the Christian Bible

and maintained by violence. The kingdom of God is based on not fighting and maintained by nonviolence. Nonviolent resistance to violence is what God wills (*Deus vult*).

We Christians are not primarily the People *of* the Book; we are primarily the People *with* the Book. We are not fundamentally the People of the Inscribed Word of God; we are fundamentally the People of the Incarnate Word of God. If our faith demands a *sola* it is *sola incarnatio*. Does John 3:16 say that "God so loved the world that he gave us a Book"? Christ, as the incarnate revelation of the nonviolent God, is rule, norm, standard, and criterion even—or especially—of the Christian Bible itself. In other words, the nonviolence of the Incarnation negates the violence of the Apocalypse.

The great and sweeping *parabolic story* of the Christian Bible is therefore an extraordinary or maybe even a unique one because its meaning is in the middle, its climax is in the center. That central core is Jesus of Nazareth who is confessed by faith as Christ the Lord. His nonviolent resistance to violent injustice judges all that goes before that life and after it as well—in the book and in the world. That, by the way, is why Christianity counts time down to and up from the Incarnation.

Epilogue

Today it is called the Kariye Muzesi or Chora Museum of Istanbul. It started, however, as a small monastic church given glorious magnificence in mosaic and fresco at the start of the fourteenth century during the Palaeologian Renaissance between Constantinople's sack by the Latin Christians in 1204 and by the Ottoman Muslims in 1453. It is debated whether "Chora" (Greek for Land, Countryside, Container) was originally a geographical designation for its rural location outside the city's Constantinian walls or—as it certainly was later—a theological term for Christ Pantokrator as "The Chora/Land of the Living" and for Mary Theotokos as "The Chora/Container of the Un-Uncontainable One."[12]

Above the main entrance from outer to inner narthex is a typical Pantokrator mosaic, but Christ is only shown above the waist. His right hand is lifted with fingers separated into two—for the two natures in Christ—and three—for the three persons of the Trinity—in standard

233

Byzantine style. His left hand holds a book, the closed and clasped Book of the Gospels.

Above the main entrance from inner narthex to church proper is a full and seated Pantokrator mosaic. Theodore Metochites, the second most powerful official under the emperor, is to right of Christ offering him a model of the church he had restored between 1315 and 1321. Once again, and as usual, Christ's right hand is raised with separated fingers. Once again, and as usual, his right hand holds the Book of the Gospels closed shut and clasped shut.

Inside the church proper, toward the left side of the nave is another mosaic of Christ Pantokrator. Like those two preceding ones, he is identified as "The Land of the Living" but the style is less hieratic and more human. His right hand has the fingers divided as usual but now the left hand holds open the Book of the Gospels. It is, however, opened toward the viewer and says in Greek: "Come to me, all you that are weary and are carrying heavy burdens, and I [will give you rest]" (Matt 11:28).

In those three images, as in the other Pantokrator images in that Monastery Church of Christ Pantokrator and Mary Theotokos, and in the myriad other ones across the Byzantine tradition, *do you ever see Jesus reading the Gospel?* The Book is usually closed and, if not, it is opened to us and its voice is not its own but that of Christ. "Come to me" is not the voice of the Book but that of the Person holding it. Christ does not read the Book—be it Christian Bible, Christian New Testament, or Christian Gospel—because Christ is the norm of the Book. That is, in fact, the Christian *Gospel*—the good news that Christ as the incarnation of God's nonviolent response to human violence is the norm not only of the world but also of the Christian Bible, the Christian New Testament, and even— or especially—of the Christian Gospels.

Endnotes

1. For definitions of empire and/or imperialism see Davis and Huttenback, eds., *Mammon*, 279: "Imperialism can best be viewed as a mechanism for transferring income from the middle to the upper classes." Parenti, *Against Empire*, 1: "By 'imperialism' I mean the process whereby the dominant politico-economic interests of one nation expropriate for their own enrichment the land, labor, raw materials, and markets of another people." Maier, *Among Empires: American Ascendancy and Its Predecessors*, 7, 23, 76: "Empire is a form of political organization in which the social elements that rule in the dominant state . . . create a network of allied elites in regions abroad who accept subordination

in international affairs in return for security of their position in their own administrative unit ... Empire has a function of stabilizing inequality or, perhaps more precisely, reconciling some rituals and forms of equality with the preservation of vast inequality ... Empires are epics of entropy." For America as the New Rome see Doyle, *Empires*, 83: "Rome introduces to our examination of empire a challenging moral ambiguity—peace and material progress are now borne by the chariot of imperial domination." Ferguson, *Colossus*, 14: "[T]he United States is perhaps more like a 'new Rome' than any previous empire ... The Roman parallel is in danger of becoming something like a cliché." Lieven, *America Right or Wrong*, 41: "[T]he Roman empire ... is an image which also has a long history in American thought, and which has spread enormously in U.S. public debate as a result of America's emergence as the world's only superpower." Johnson, *The Sorrows of Empire*, 3: "September 11, 2001 ... produced a dangerous change in the thinking of some of our leaders, who began to see our republic as a genuine empire, a new Rome, the greatest colossus in history, no longer bound by international law, the concern of allies, or any constraints on its use of military force." Murphy, *Are We Rome?*, 5: "President and Emperor, America and Rome—the comparison is by now so familiar, so natural, that you just can't help yourself: it comes to mind unbidden, in the reflexive way that the behavior of chimps reminds you of the behavior of people" [and I wonder, in that comparison, who are the "chimps" and who are the "people"?].

2. For my earlier work in this area see Crossan, *Birth of Christianity*, 182-208; Crossan, *God and Empire*, 49-95. My special sources were Epsztein [or Epzstein], *Social Justice*; Fager, *Land Tenure*; Weinfeld, *Social Justice in Ancient Israel*. For this section here I am most indebted to Lowery, *Sabbath and Jubilee*.

3. On these texts in general see: Collins, "Sibylline Oracles," 317-472. On *Sib. Or.* 3, see 362-80. The quotations are from 378-79.

4. Fredrikson, "Judaism," 532-64. For example: "What place, if any, do Gentiles have in such a kingdom? We can cluster the material around two poles. At the negative extreme, the nations are destroyed, defeated, or in some way subjected to Israel ... At the positive extreme, the nations participate in Israel's redemption. The nations will stream to Jerusalem and worship the God of Jacob together with Israel" (544-45; see also 547-548). Fredriksen, *Jesus of Nazareth*, 129. For example: "[I]t is the inclusive tradition anticipating gentile participation in Israel's final redemption that sounds increasingly in intertestamental writings, in later synagogue prayers, and in rabbinic discussion. And, clearly, this is the tradition shaping the convictions and activities of the earliest Jewish Christians—James, John, Peter, Barnabas, and most especially, Paul (see Gal 2)."

5. Collins, *The Scepter and the Star*, 13, 68, 209. These are the key quotations: "Although the claim that he [Jesus of Nazareth] is the Davidic messiah is ubiquitous in the New Testament, he does not fit the typical profile of the Davidic messiah. This messiah was, first of all, a warrior prince, who was to defeat the enemies of Israel" (13); "This concept of the Davidic messiah as the warrior king who would destroy the enemies of Israel and institute an era of unending peace constitutes the common core of Jewish messianism around the turn of the era" (68). There are, however, "other messianic paradigms that are less widely attested. These are the eschatological High Priest or messiah of Aaron, who figures prominently in the [Dead Sea] Scrolls, the eschatological prophet, and the heavenly messiah or 'Son of Man'" (68); "There was a dominant notion of a Davidic messiah, as the king who would restore the kingdom of Israel, which was part of the common Judaism around the turn of the era. There were also, however, minor messianic strands

which envisaged a priestly messiah, or an anointed prophet or a heavenly Son of Man. Christian messianism drew heavily on some of the minor strands (prophet, Son of Man) and eventually developed them into a doctrine of Christology that was remote from its Jewish origins" (209).

6. Kuhn, *The Structure of Scientific Revolutions*. The term is taken from this book. Paradigm shift or tradition swerve seems to me operational not just in science but in all aspects of fundamental human change.

7. I am presuming here my proposal on Jesus' own paradigm shift or tradition swerve concerning the Kingdom of God. See Crossan, "Collaborative Eschatology," 103-30.

8. Deissmann, *Light from the Ancient East*, 368-73.

9. *Minor Latin Poets*, 220-23.

10. On *Sib. Or.* 4-5 see Collins, "Sibylline Oracles," 384-405. Quotations for *Sib. Or.* 4 are on 387 and for *Sib. Or.* 5 are on 395-96.

11. Fredriksen, *Jesus of Nazareth*, 9, 11, 240-41, 243, 253, 255, 257. On the book's opening pages, Fredriksen notes the "incontrovertible fact" that, "Though Jesus was executed as a political insurrectionist, his followers were not" (9). Again: "Our focus on the anomaly of what we know past doubting to be historically true—that Jesus was executed by Rome as an insurrectionist, but that none of his followers were" (11). Then, on the book's closing pages, she speaks of "the paradox that has driven this investigation, namely, that when Pilate moved against Jesus, Jesus was the sole one of his movement to die" (240); and later of "the core historical anomaly of the Passion stories: Jesus was crucified, but his followers were not" (255). I think that is a profoundly important insight, but that said with gratitude, I disagree very strongly with her interpretation of *why* Pilate did *what* she has correctly and programmatically summarized as his judicial act. On the one hand, "Jesus was harmless, and Pilate knew it" (241), "because Pilate knew that the message of Jesus' movement posed no threat to Roman power" (243). Furthermore, "The chief priests know what Pilate knows: Jesus himself is not dangerous. But for the first time, this Passover, the crowds who swarm around him are" (253). On the other, Jesus' "pinpointing the arrival of the Kingdom for *this* particular Passover was the spark that ignited all the rest" (257). Even on its own terms, I find that historically untenable. If that *were* actually the spark—and I do not think it was—Jesus had indeed excited the Passover crowds and was executed not just to quiet them but to punish him.

12. Underwood, *Kariye Djami*. For the history of the building, see vol. 1, 3-8. For the three mosaics, see vol. 2, 12-19, 26-29, and 186, respectively.

12

Cultured Pearls: Changing the Future of America as an Exercise in Culture-Making[1]

BEN WITHERINGTON III

> And we pray to our Lord,
> Who we know is American,
> He reigns from on high;
> He speaks to us through middlemen
> And he shepherds his flock
> We sing out and praise his name
> He supports us in war
> He presides over football games,
> And the right will prevail
> And our troubles will be resolved
> We hold faith above all,
> *Unless there's money or sex involved*
>
>   —Don Henley, "Frail Grasp of the Big Picture"

> "The first duty of a human being is to assume the right functional relationship to society—more briefly, to find your real job, and do it."
>   —Charlotte Perkins Gilman

On the Horns of a Dilemma

My Southern Baptist granny who went through the Great Depression in the 1930s had an expression for the situation we find ourselves in these days: "We are in a mell of hess" she would say, and she'd be right. And since we are there and need to do cleanup on aisle three for a while, it might be useful to ask ourselves how we got here. I will avoid dealing with the macro-answers to this question in regard to the forces of the global economy. Rather, I want to focus on the micro-answers of how we *all* have contributed to this problem. The following are only some of the factors:

1. Most of us are living beyond—and in some cases well beyond—our means. I am not talking about having a home mortgage or a car payment which we are paying for over time. I'm talking about paying for almost everything on credit, rather than paying as we go. The rise of the credit card industry in this country in my lifetime, and our love of using the plastic whether it's financially responsible to do so or not, has turned the good ole U.S.A. into a debtor nation. Never mind that we are also debtors to other world powers like China or oil-producing nations like Saudi Arabia. I am talking about each of us as individuals being prepared to abuse credit cards without hesitation, without limitation, without moral reservation. You get the picture. Our spending habits are ridiculous, and frankly quite un-Christian, as we shall see.

2. We have been conditioned to think, even by some preachers in the church, that we are entitled to success, entitled to wealth, entitled to a lifestyle of the rich and famous. Shoot, we have been trained to see this as a big blessing from God. In other words, we have completely silenced our conscience when it comes to the issue of moral responsibility in regard to what we buy, when we buy it, how much buy, and all without thinking about our obligations to those less fortunate than ourselves. That self-centered sense of entitlement is what the advertisers keep appealing to. They even have the brass to say, "You owe it to yourself to pamper yourself." Notice the word 'owe,' as if we have an obligation to shop until we drop and engage in constant self-indulgence or else we are not doing our patriotic duty to the economy!!

3. We have been led to think we can even obtain the ends we want without sacrifice, without the means. Gambling in its various forms,

including state lotteries, has been growing throughout the land like Kudzu over a giant pine forest, and of course the premise behind gambling is—'with only a little investment I could strike it big and be set for life.' Worst of all, Christians seem to increasingly have no problems with gambling. Just today I heard a minister mention the gambler's prayer: "Lord, I know I am a sinner, but make me a winner." Not, mind you, "make me quit wasting my family's money." Not "make me repent of my gambling ways." No, "help me hit the jackpot God!" The issue of commensurability of outcome based on input or hard work is not considered. We'd just like to get rich quick, and then retire. The other thing that is undermined by the whole gambling industry is "an honest day's pay for an honest day's work." The link between work and reward is severed, and instead one thinks one has found a shortcut. Maybe the prize patrol will show up this week, if I just subscribe to a few more of those tabloid magazines. Never mind that those magazines might ruin my character, and indeed so might winning such a prize as well! Somewhere in the background I hear playing the old Isley Brothers' classic—"Money, Money, Money Money!"

4. Somehow we have gotten to the point where we assume that we must spoil our children, and so money we could have spent on necessary things, on charitable giving, on ministry opportunities is instead spent on little Johnny's nose job, or Melissa's breast implants just because "image is everything." The dictionary definition of the verb "to spoil" is as follows: a: to damage seriously : ruin; b: to impair the quality or effect of; c: to impair the disposition or character of by overindulgence or excessive praise d: to pamper excessively : coddle; And as an *intransitive verb* a: to practice plunder and robbery b: to lose valuable or useful qualities usually as a result of decay. None of this is good, and we should not wish it on our worst enemies, never mind our own children. Some of this can be attributed to parents trying to live their lives vicariously through their children, getting them the things they were deprived of as children, but whatever its root causes in the human heart, the results are disastrous. It simply further feeds the engines of conspicuous consumption which leads to our being a debtor nation.

5. Entertainment is king, and luxury is desirable. If you ask most economists what most Americans do with their spare change or even their disposable income in general, many will tell you that *instead of saving*

money, we spend it on entertainment or luxuries for ourselves. The cable TV, movie, music, and iPod industries have boomed in the past half century, because "there's gold in them thar things." *We feed our desires before we even meet our needs in many cases.* Our spending priorities are totally screwed up. We've supersized our food, our cars, and ourselves. Go watch the movie Wall-E and see where all this leads.

6. The Bible has some pretty stout and stark and strong things to say about believers not lending money on interest to fellow believers. It is a sign of our times that Christians think nothing of charging other people interest, or for that matter paying obscene rates of interest so they may buy on demand on their credit cards. We hardly give it a second thought—that is, until the bills come due. I have real sympathy for people who are losing their homes during this recession because they can't pay their mortgages. But unfortunately a good deal of these wounds are self-inflicted, with people buying bigger homes than they can afford, especially in an economic downturn, and predatory lenders licking their chops over getting people to sign on the dotted line, even when the persons in question don't really know or understand fully even basic things like whether the interest rate on their mortgage is fixed or not.

7. Even when Christians do save some money, they will normally say they are saving it for their own retirement. I was disgusted the other day to see an RV with a Christian fish symbol on it, and next to it was the bumper sticker that read: "I'm spending my grandchildren's inheritance," as if this were humorous or something to celebrate. Rather, it is something to be ashamed of. And about that retirement and pension thing—the Bible says nothing about that. It does, however, talk a good deal about the community of believers taking care of each other as they grow old.

8. In a culture where the new is the true, and the latest is said to be greatest, even Christians get caught up in the fads, trends, and trajectories of frivolous fashion, foolish financial deals, and in general, indulgence beyond anything healthy, helpful, or holy. Raise your hand if you or your children are guilty!

Needless to say, I could go one with one illustration after the other, but this should suffice to make the point that what determines how most

Christians view money, lending, giving, one's economic lifestyle, the future, and a host of related matters is not the Bible, but rather cultural factors and influences. In many ways this is not a surprise in a biblically illiterate culture, indeed in a culture where even most Christians are largely oblivious to what the Bible says about money and related matters.

There is an old Pogo comic strip where the tiger comes back to report on the battle front and says this to his commanding officer, the turtle: "I have seen the enemy sir, the enemy is us!" It's true—to a very great extent, we are our own worst enemies when it comes to money and debt and the like. It is my hope, however, that perhaps through a significant injection of biblical hormones, we might actually grow a conscience about some of these things, a specifically Christian conscience.

The question I want to raise and attempt to answer in this essay is: What would happen if we approached the future from a more biblical and constructive point of view, not as despisers of culture, but as culture-makers? What if, to some extent, God has called us to take some matters into our own hands, and mold and meld things in a certain way so that we help create a culture worth saving, a culture worth living in rather than just adopting or aping the extant values of our materialistic culture, baptizing such values and calling them good?

Christ against Culture?

For reasons partially understandable, if you have ever read H. Richard Niebuhr's classic, *Christ and Culture*, a book composed in the year I was born (1951), many Protestant Christians have had something of an allergic reaction to "culture," including the mainstream culture of America. This allergic reaction has ranged from mild to severe, with Holiness, Mennonite, and Amish traditions reacting most strongly to "culture." It was OK to critique culture or be counter-cultural, but certainly *not* to be contributing to decadent culture. Niebuhr set up a paradigm for discussing culture as follows:

> **Christ against Culture.** For the exclusive Christian, history is the story of a rising church or Christian culture and a dying pagan civilization.
>
> **Christ of Culture.** For the cultural Christian, history is the story of the Spirit's encounter with nature.

> **Christ above Culture.** For the synthesist, history is a period of preparation under law, reason, gospel, and church for an ultimate communion of the soul with God.
>
> **Christ and Culture in Paradox.** For the dualist, history is the time of struggle between faith and unbelief, a period between the giving of the promise of life and its fulfillment.
>
> **Christ Transforming Culture.** For the conversionist, history is the story of God's mighty deeds and humanity's response to them. Conversionists live somewhat less "between the times" and somewhat more in the divine "now" than do the followers listed above. Eternity, to the conversionist, focuses less on the action of God before time or life with God after time, and more on the presence of God in time. Hence the conversionist is more concerned with the divine possibility of a present renewal than with conservation of what has been given in creation or preparing for what will be given in a final redemption.[2]

It was this last paradigm that Niebuhr was mostly advocating, perhaps being the clearest voice of the old liberal Protestant vision of the Christian role in society. On this showing, the Christian could go about the task of building the Kingdom of God on earth. The problem was that Kingdom of God in the Gospels is not an item on a human 'To-Do' list, in the present, it is the divine saving activity of God in our midst which changes persons. This is perhaps why Richard Niebuhr was wise enough to title his book *Christ and Culture* rather than *Christians and Culture*. But all too many have assumed since Niebuhr that what is descriptive in the Gospels should be prescriptive for us—our marching orders as Christians, so to speak. One is reminded of William Blake's famous poem on Milton that was turned into an English hymn in which he asks:

> And did those feet in ancient time,
> Walk upon England's mountains green:
> And was the holy Lamb of God,
> On England's pleasant pastures seen!
>
> And did the Countenance Divine,
> Shine forth upon our clouded hills?
> And was Jerusalem builded here,
> Among these dark Satanic Mills?

Cultured Pearls

> Bring me my Bow of burning gold;
> Bring me my Arrows of desire:
> Bring me my Spear: O clouds unfold:
> Bring me my Chariot of fire!
>
> I will not cease from Mental Fight,
> Nor shall my Sword sleep in my hand:
> Till we have built Jerusalem,
> In England's green and pleasant Land.

Blake, of course, was talking about the English vision of building the new Jerusalem in the United Kingdom, and not accidentally these verses are part of the preface to his poem about John Milton, who furthered the Puritan vision of life and society in his epic poems and writings. Alas, the Puritan experiment both in England and New England bore painful witness to the fact that even the most devout could not build the Kingdom on earth much less the new Jerusalem, not even with the fires of a hundred revivals burning bright. So while Kingdom is more a matter of an event or a happening which God produces and we can only receive, can we talk about the lesser task of culture-making, and what the Christian responsibility is when it comes to their work being part of culture making? Culture-making sounds a little less pretentious than "kingdom-building," and it is worth discussing with someone who has thought long and hard about Christians and culture making—Andy Crouch.

In his review of Andy Crouch's *Culture Making: Recovering Our Creative Calling*, Christian Smith, a professor of sociology at Notre Dame, says this: "American evangelicals in the last hundred years have found it easy to condemn culture, critique culture, copy culture and consume culture. It has been much harder for them to actively and imaginatively create culture. Andy Crouch is out to change that."[3] I like this already.

Evangelical Christians have too often been guilty of various forms and degrees of tunnel vision. One such form which I will call "missional tunnel vision" views the world as something out of which people need rescue. Ministry, then, is rescuing the perishing from a world going to Hades in a hand basket. The problem with this vision is that it not merely promotes a lifeboat philosophy about church and Christian life ("we must live within the safe haven!"), it grossly underestimates the power of God and his role not merely in the church but in the world. It also ignores entirely the creation theology which says God made the world good, and human society and human work are valued as good from the beginning.

Yes, we sing, "This is my Father's world" but we hardly mean it, or understand what that means. Some of this comes from what Niebuhr would have called either a Christ vs. culture approach to life, or perhaps a Christ beside culture (like an Amish community beside a secular one). Some of it comes from a belief that Christ transforms culture, and there is some truth in that approach as well. But what if Christ came to make all things new, what if he came to create culture, and calls us not merely to transform the culture that exists, but even to build new culture? What if it is in the DNA of the church and the original mission statement about our *work* indicates that we are supposed to be banqueting with the bad like Jesus did? What if it is true that "greater is he who is in us, than anything else in the world"? I am convinced Andy Crouch can help us gain a more holistic and wide-angle vision of work, vocation, ministry.

Let start with Crouch's definition of culture—it is what we *make* of the world which God has created.[4] It is not just about high art or architecture. It is whatever we make of the stuff God created, ranging from an omelet to a Mona Lisa. Culture always bears the stamp of our creativity, even if, as so often is the case, it appears we are pretty derivative or unoriginal in what we make. We have, says Crouch, this innate design and desire to make something more of what we have been given. It is part of being in the image of a God who is both Creator and Ruler, both Sustainer and Redeemer.

Crouch goes on to stress that culture is also about what we make of what there is, which is to say, what *sense* we make of what exists. The world requires some interpreting, some explanation. It would appear that we are the only creature on the planet that asks why: "Making sense of the world, interpreting its wonder and its terror, is left up to human beings alone . . . We *make sense* of the world by *making something* of the world. The human quest for meaning is played out in human making: the finger-painting, omelet-stirring, chair-crafting, snow-swishing activities of culture. Meaning and making go together—culture, you could say, is the activity of making meaning."[5]

Thus far culture sounds like an exercise in hermeneutics, or interpreting things that already exist, like a movie critic, for example. But

Crouch goes on to insist that culture in fact shapes and reshapes the mere material world that exists. Humans do not merely observe or interpret the world, they construct it, they make it, in various senses of that term. "Culture, not just nature, has become the world that we must make something of."[6]

Crouch quite naturally asks us to consider the sort of work that goes into road-building and how it changes things, and not merely the landscape. I have been watching this process for some weeks now. As I drive to work in Wilmore, Kentucky, a whole new four-lane highway is being constructed, and in the process various bits of this or that horse farm is being torn up, vivisected, displaced. Pretty soon one of my favorite horse farms will no longer be beside Harrodsburg Road because that road will now go well behind the farm. This will make travel to Wilmore quicker and easier and less windy, and so my trip into work will be different, my purview different, my outlook different. The making that we do, whether we call it work or not, is culture-making, as it remakes our world, both the world out there usually called nature, and the world within my mind. Work changes the world, and imposes a new culture on what previously existed. *Culture-creating is inevitable for human beings, the only question is whether Christians will meaningfully and self-consciously engage in such activities as part of their work and realize that in so doing they are creating a new world.*

Crouch points out how the car and the highway system made impossible what had previously been taken for granted, namely traveling considerable distances on horseback. You can't do that now on a normal highway—it's prohibited, and anyway, there are not enough inns and horse barns along the way to support such a mode of travel over any considerable distance. Furthermore, if you tried it, it would endanger the horse, and the fumes would probably overcome man and beast in due course. This is why even the Amish hitch rides in cars and on trains when they want to go any real distance. The world has been changed by culture-making human work. It is thus no surprise that Crouch concludes: "Without culture, literally nothing would be possible for human beings. To say that culture creates the horizons of possibility is to speak literal, not just figurative or metaphorical, truth."[7] 'Culture' in this sense is very broadly defined, and not to be associated just or even primarily with the high arts. I have to say, however, that my mother the pianist would entirely resist calling the building of an interstate highway "culture-making."

What this means, in plain and simple terms is that work, our work, Christian work, creates a world, and without hard work even the fulfilling of the Great Commission would be just a nice idea. Grace is conveyed to other human beings through work. Grace and works were not meant to be seen as sparing partners in an eternal theological boxing match. They were meant to be seen as partners in a row boat both pulling in the same direction. Likewise, Christianity should not be set over against culture, it should ever and always be set in motion to create culture and worlds.

One of the real problems with Christians is that they can be too insular, living in their own little bubble, and this trend has only accelerated with the enormous rise to prominence of home-schooling, or solely Christian schooling in this country. But if all you ever do is sing in the choir or preach to the choir, how is that culture-making and world-changing in anything like a Christian sense when we are called to make disciples of all nations?

Consider again what Andy Crouch says: "Culture requires a public: a group of people who have been sufficiently affected by a cultural good that their horizons of possibility and impossibility have in fact been altered, and their own cultural creativity has been spurred, by that good's existence. This group of people does not necessarily have to be large. But without such a group the artifact remains exclusively personal and private."[8] In America we tend to think that things that are as deeply personal as religious beliefs ought to be private matters, but this will never do for an evangelistic religion. We have to become both Gospel sharers, but also culture-makers, and the latter involves work. Indeed one's work, if one is not a preacher, teacher or priest, may largely consist of culture-making in the most basic of all senses, senses that would not be perceived by most as involving sacred tasks. Christianity, to be truly Christian, *has to go public, or become a shared public good, not merely a private self-help program for the already convinced.*

One of the most convincing points Andy Crouch makes is that family is perhaps the most elemental and crucial culture-making institution in a society. What goes on in a home need not stay in a home, but in the milieu of a home and in the context of a family all sorts of positive cultural constructions happen. Cooking, for example, is a form of work that is not only culture-making but Kingdom-making if you invite people over for dinner, or have some of your Christian meetings in homes, or even if you just engage in friendship evangelism in such a context. "Family [including Christian family] is culture at its smallest—and most powerful."[9] If you don't believe this, just watch the classic movie "My Big Fat Greek Wedding."

It is, of course, true that any talk about changing a whole culture or changing a whole world is in most cases over-ambitious. When John Wesley, who had quite the work rate, said "the world is my parish," interestingly enough, some people believed him, and not primarily because he had already been to Georgia and back. But when we talk about making our work something that is culture-making in a way that is glorifying to God and edifying to others, we have to talk about economies of scale. Here is how Crouch puts the matter: "Finding our place in the world as culture makers requires us to pay attention to culture's many dimensions. We will make something of the world in a particular ethnic tradition, in particular spheres, at particular scales. There is no such thing as "the Culture," and any attempt to talk about "the Culture," especially in terms of "transforming the Culture," is misled and misleading. Real culture making, not to mention cultural transformation, begins with a decision about which cultural world—or, better, worlds—we will attempt to make something of."[10]

One of the most important insights to be gained from the whole study of culture is the dawning recognition that those who chase the will-o'-the-wisp that is called new/fresh/trendy will be forever changing and not having much enduring impact. Crouch rightly warns "there is an inverse relationship between a cultural layer's *speed of change* and its *longevity of impact*. The faster a given layer of culture changes, the less long-term effect it has on the horizons of possibility and impossibility."[11] Those who follow the fads will find that growth may happen in a church or in a business with hard work, but whether they are accomplishing something of lasting value is another question, a question a Christian must always ask about their work.

Is my work of some lasting value? Did it make a difference? Was it worth doing in the first place, or was it in vain? Did this work have some meaning, some purpose, and if so what was it? Of course answering such questions is not always easy, as the impact and/or quality of some piece of work may not be seen for years to come.

When the tenement house collapsed in Miami, Florida, without any apparent provocation or cause, the investigation led to the conclusion that twenty years earlier, though the building looked alright on the outside, it was built with inferior materials, in a poor fashion and, most importantly, was not built with an eye on safety and ongoing durability. It could not have passed a stress test, had one been administered. Disposable culture in a disposable society with all too rapid change can be criticized for having little long-term value. Crouch is willing to be emphatic about this—"Nothing that matters, no matter how sudden, does not have a long history and take part in a long future."[12]

Change and Culture

What is perhaps most eye-opening, and indeed depressing about our work is that it is possible to change things for the worse quickly, whereas making things of value or changing things for the better almost always takes considerable time. For example, think of 9/11 and the World Trade Towers, how rapidly they fell into dust. But how long did it take either to construct them in the first place or clean up after the devastation? Or consider a great work of art like Michelangelo's David, which took months to carve, but could be destroyed in the blink of an eye if someone took a hammer to the statue. It is not just works of art that are easily destroyed, almost anything of worth is, including human lives. Take time to read the lament of the vendors, sycophants, and clients of Rome in Revelation 18 with the refrain "it all happened in a hour."

What must be stressed is that our American culture is addicted to "the latest," and assumes that the "latest is the greatest, the newest is the truest." This is why in our culture it is called "news." But alas, the latest is quickly yesterday's story. Says Crouch: "So hope in a future revolution, or revival, to solve the problems of our contemporary culture is usually misplaced. And such a hope makes us especially vulnerable to fashion, mistaking shifts in the wind for changes in the climate. Fads sweep across the cultural landscape and believers invest outsized portions of energy and commitment in furthering the fad, mistaking it for real change."[13] How different this is from the Good News. When Jesus came proclaiming

Good News, what he in fact did was not announce a total "novum" but rather announced the fulfillment of the old Jubilee vision of Isaiah and others before him (see, for example, Luke 4 and parallels).

Perhaps then more emphasis should be put on the work of culture-making by Christians, and less on the hope that a revival will change one's milieu. Crouch quite rightly takes on those who think that the way to change the world is simply to change the worldview of the world, on the theory perhaps that "as a man thinks, so he is."

The problem with this is that thinking, even new thinking, is not the same as new doing, is not the same as going to work and changing things. The thoughts must be embodied in deeds, and this takes hard work. If you merely change the thoughts going on inside the horse's head you by no means have changed the direction the horse is heading—you have to turn the head itself! The problem with so much Christian worldview talk is not merely that we suffer the paralysis of analysis, we hardly get beyond analysis, for the problem is not just wrong thoughts, it's also wrong behaviors. Culture is not just about thinking, it's about doing and so it is about our work. Crouch reminds:

> Embodiment may not flow as naturally from thinking as many books on worldview imply. The cartoonist Sidney Harris's most famous drawing shows two scientists standing in front of a blackboard covered with a series of equations. In the middle of the equations is written, "Then a miracle occurs." One scientist says to the other, "I think you need to be more explicit here in step two." When we say, "The Christian vision can transform our world," something similar is happening. Is it really true that simply perceiving the radical comprehensiveness of the Christian worldview would "transform the world"? Or is there a middle step that is being skipped over all too lightly? . . . The danger of reducing culture to worldview is that we may miss the most distinctive thing about culture, which is that *cultural goods have a life of their own*. They reshape the world in unpredictable ways . . . The language of worldview tends to imply, to paraphrase the Catholic writer Richard Rohr, that we can think ourselves into new ways of behaving. But that is not the way culture works. Culture helps us behave ourselves into new ways of thinking.[14]

What Crouch is trying to make us see is that the only way to change the cultural landscape is to make more of it, of a variety you endorse. It is never enough simply to change people's ideas about the culture, their worldviews, though that's a start.

Consider the example of the Amish. They are pacifists especially famous for their dislike of handguns of any sort. If you go and visit them in east Ohio or western Pennsylvania where they are particularly thick on the ground, as I have done as I lived alongside them for eleven years in Ohio, you will discover that they don't just sit around and discuss how bad it is to have handguns around where children and others can be accidentally harmed, which discussion would be followed by various nodding heads. No, they've actually *banned* handguns in their communities, a rule they enforce rigorously.

Go be part of an Amish community and you will be in a culture and ethos and environment that *is* handgun free. Unless a "Yankee" or total stranger shows up in their community toting a handgun, no one is going to get shot with such a thing, no strawberry stand is going to be robbed with such a thing, no Amish hardware store is going to be terrorized with such a thing. And anyone who made such an idle threat in an Amish hardware store who *didn't* have a gun but *believed* in them, might well be taken and confined to the interior of a composting toilet for a while until they regained their senses. *Ideas and worldviews alone don't change the world, behavior and hard work does. Cultural change happens when a new way of doing things displaces the old way of doing things.*

Crouch reminds us that merely condemning or critiquing culture seldom changes things much, *unless someone has something better or more compelling to put in its place.* Sometimes what Christians do is simply copy culture and think that will change the world. Consider the evolution of the Christian rock music industry.

Christian rock musicians are hardly ever out there leading the cultural trends, in fact, mostly they are following them, only changing the lyrics. I remember the day when you would go into a Christian bookstore where there were Christian albums and cassettes and there would be signs over the bins saying things like "X sounds like Led Zeppelin," or "Y sounds like Crosby, Stills and Nash." Alas, it was almost always the case that X and Y were less filling and didn't taste as great either as the secular originals. Imitation may be the most sincere form of flattery but it's still imitation, rather than adequate creation. Christian musicians needed to learn to gain their own voices, make their own music with a high degree of creativity and skill and excellence.

One of the more recent trends in Christian music is Christian hip-hop and rap, or Christian Indie music, on the philosophy of "if you can't beat them, join them." The styles, the tunes, the clothes of the culture are very much adopted from the secular mainstream. When I was in the music business, we were thrilled when a Christian artist like Amy Grant would crossover into the mainstream. We thought maybe finally the mainstream could be transformed by the Christian message this way. Alas, it didn't happen. In fact, Christians imitating mainstream music were more likely to be the one's converted to a very different gospel. Consider, for example, the recent mega-group the Kings of Leon who came out of a Pentecostal background—like men fleeing a burning building.

One of the tasks Christians must take seriously in the twenty-first century is culture-making, dedicating their work and energies to creating culture that will be winsome and habit forming to those not already a part of it. And as Crouch warns, creativity, not knock-off imitation, is in the long run the only viable way to change a culture. Christians must work hard to produce the best art, the best movies, the best neighborhoods, the best restaurants, the best athletics possible, not merely by copying, but by coming up with something fresh, new, interesting, life-changing.

And lest we despair, we have a track record of having done it before. For example, consider the coffee culture. You may think Starbucks invented the coffee culture, but actually coffee was first brewed in Ethiopian monasteries then was exported north and west. The very word cappuccino is named after the Capuchin monks whose habits are the same color as this brew. Coffee is a Christian beverage in origins, but you'd never know it today.

Creating a Culture

Crouch is not suggesting that we start *de novo*. Culture is of course cumulative, it keeps building on and recycling from the stuff that existed before. "When it comes to cultural creativity, innocence is not a virtue. The more each of us knows about our cultural domain, the more likely we are to create something new and worthwhile."[15]

Thus Crouch says that real culture-making begins with the cultivation of the good things a culture already has and does. One doesn't need to completely reinvent the wheel to create good new culture. One needs to become fluent in the good aspects of the cultural tradition one is already a part of and nurture them. One also needs to sift the wheat from the chaff, and affirm the wheat.

Having spent a good deal of my life making music or listening to it, I can tell you that making music well requires an enormous amount of practice and discipline. Creativity that makes a lasting impact, work that makes a difference, is seldom a matter of sheer spontaneity or mere native talent. If Christians truly want to make an appealing and winsome culture that may actually attract people to Christ it will require hard work, discipline, and practice, practice, practice. "So underneath almost every act of culture making we find countless small acts of culture keeping. That is why the good screenwriter has first watched a thousand movies; why the surgeon who pioneers a new technique has first performed a thousand routine surgeries; and why the investor who provides funds to the next startup has first studied a thousand balance sheets. Cultural creativity requires cultural maturity."[16] Are there options for Christians other than cultural capitulation, accommodation, or some modified form of rejection of culture? Crouch thinks there is are, and he reminds that even Christians who practice home-schooling and generally avoid the more obviously objectionable forms of modern culture, are nonetheless cultural beings. Indeed, even the Amish don't entirely avoid mainstream culture. I have a wonderful picture from when I lived in Ashland, Ohio, of an Amish buggy stopped at the take-out window at McDonalds.

Indeed, many Christians with separatist tendencies do still drive cars, watch TV, go to movies (not the X-rated ones), attend sporting events, and the like. This is not real rejection of a dominant or secular culture. That would look like a person who withdraws and lives in a hut in the Amazon rainforest for the rest of his life with no technological tools or toys to amuse him or keep him informed.

Nor can the church simply withdraw from the dominant culture, especially if it wants to continue to bear witness to that culture. Crouch reminds us that:

> Fundamentalist Christians, like modernist ones, indulged in an attractive but specious distinction between the church and the

culture. Their unspoken assumption was that "the culture" was something distinguishable from their own daily life and enterprises, something that could be withdrawn from, rejected and condemned. In this respect they were just as modern as everyone around them, in accepting too uncritically an easy distinction between the "sacred" and the "secular." This distinction, which served liberals by carving out a sphere of public life that did not have to entangle itself with religion and religious controversies, served fundamentalists by assuring them that it was possible to eschew "secular" pursuits altogether.[17]

This may be the only thing fundamentalists and liberals may agree on about culture. There is a place and a time to condemn culture (think Nazi or apartheid culture), to critique culture (think art that promotes anti-Christian values), to copy culture (think of some of the good contemporary Christian music has done, which largely follows and copies the larger musical trends), and to consume culture (participating in the good aspects of our culture). All of these things can be part of our work and works as Christians building a better future. What Crouch is calling us to is creating culture, which is not simply identical with any of these aforementioned activities. In fact, he offers a clarion call for us to be what God called Adam and Eve to be in the first place—creators and also cultivators of all that is good, true, beautiful in the world, wherever one finds it.

Creatio ex Nihilo?

Most of the creativity Crouch is talking about is not *ex nihilo* or *de novo*, but a sort of making of things out of pre-existing materials. No one would mistake a beautiful saltpeter-glazed water pitcher for a mere lump of clay, but that is where it came from. The middle term was the potter who fashioned that wet lump of clay into something it had no capacity to be left on its own. It takes intelligence, skill and, yes, imagination to create culture well, though all too often today we just stress the imaginative aspect when we use the word "creativity." I often wonder what would happen if people approached their normal work with intelligence, skill, and creativity? Of course some do, and sometimes remarkable tasks are accomplished and remarkable things are made.

When I was in Singapore I was given a non-battery flashlight. No, it did not have a solar cell. No it did not have an electrical plug. It was in fact rather like one of those hand-flexers you use to strengthen your hands. From time to time you just squeezed it, using mechanical energy to power the light bulb in it—no muss and no fuss. It was a flashlight that did not need a constant infusion of artificially produced or chemical energy. It created no waste, such as batteries do.

God in fact expects creativity out of us, not least because we are created in God's image. Andy Crouch points to the example in Genesis 2 of how God brings the animals to Adam and asks Adam to name them. Of course, God could have named them and given Adam the zoological dictionary, but he didn't. He wants his human creatures to participate in the creative act. This was part of Adam's initial work.[18]

> In order for humankind to flourish in their role as cultivators and creators, God will have to voluntarily withdraw, in certain ways, from his own creation. He makes space for the man to name the animals; he makes room for the man and the woman to know one another and explore the garden. He even gives them freedom, tragically but necessarily, to misuse their creative and cultivating capacities.... God's first and best gift to humanity is culture, the realm in which human beings themselves will be the cultivators and creators, ultimately contributing to the cosmic purposes of the Cultivator and Creator of the natural world.[19]

I remember the days before air conditioning. I remember sleeping on the wooden floor in front of the open front door on a hot, humid summer night in Wilmington, North Carolina. You hoped for a breath of a breeze in the morning, but this particular morning not only was there none, you could have cut out a piece of humidity from the air on the front porch and eaten it! When air conditioning came along to beat the heat, all manner of Southerners like myself said huzzah! The world can be a wilderness for humans unless we cultivate it, unless we create things to help us cope with it, unless we turn a tangled mess into a garden. This is what Crouch is calling us to, and he is saying that it is the primeval task God gave to us in the first place. We must make something out of our world, not merely admire it. While Nature may abhor a vacuum, I do not abhor a vacuum cleaner, as ordering, cleaning, beautifying, creating is part of the human task.

In one of his more interesting insights, Crouch points out that while God meant Adam to be a gardener and ruler, the Snake tempted him to be a consumer rather than a creator and cultivator. "We can only sigh with disappointment as Adam and Eve swallow, so to speak, the idea that a fruit could bring "wisdom," even as we recognize how adroitly contemporary advertisers persuade us of equally unlikely results if we will just consume their cosmetics, cars or cigarettes."[20]

As it turns out, what being in the image of God means is not only that we have the capacity for personal relationship with God in a way that other creatures do not, we also, like God, have the capacity to be mini-creators, makers of culture, cultivators of gardens, and equally creators of chaos (read the tower of Babel story in Genesis 11).

Perhaps the most helpful insight of all offered by Crouch is the following:

> Jesus had a profoundly cultural phrase for his mission: *the kingdom of God*. It is hard to recapture the concept of *kingdom* in an age where monarchs are often no more than ornamental fixtures in their societies, if they exist at all. But for Jews of that time and place, the idea of a kingdom would have meant much more. In announcing that the kingdom of God was near, in telling parables of the kingdom, Jesus was not just delivering "good news," as if his only concern was to impart some new information. His good news foretold a comprehensive restructuring of social life comparable to that experienced by a people when one monarch was succeeded by another. The kingdom of God would touch every sphere and every scale of culture. It would reshape marriage and mealtimes, resistance to the Roman occupiers and prayer in the temple, the social standing of prostitutes and the piety of Pharisees, the meaning of cleanliness and the interpretation of illness, integrity in business and honesty in prayer.[21]

Kingdom as Creating Culture

As it turns out, if we truly want to understand work from a Kingdom perspective, then we must look at it in the way that Jesus viewed the matter. If the Kingdom of God is coming to town this is ever so much more than saying a new ruler or sheriff is coming to town, to better reinforce pre-existing laws and rules. No, this King is coming to town to clean house (i.e., the Temple), and to set up and cultivate a new way of structuring social life, and thus create a new culture—a culture of conversion, new creation, and all that implies. The interesting thing is—the chief work, at least at the outset, was the remaking of humankind. The cultural artifact Jesus was most interesting in remolding and retooling, and reforming was human beings themselves. He did not chiefly come to be a carpenter, or to build a new Temple, or to construct a new political system or party, or to introduce a new line of clothing or art, or food. He came to breathe new life into human beings. No wonder Paul was to call him the new Adam, only this Adam was life-giving spirit. But after one becomes a new creature, what then? What does culture look like after that transformation?

Consider the Last Supper, the Garden of Gethsemane, the Cross. The work that Christ chiefly came to do, was not a doing, but a suffering. Unlike Adam in that first garden Jesus did not come to consume but to be consumed, did not come to do his own will, but the will of God, did not come to eat of a tree that would bring knowledge and death, but rather came to be impaled on a tree, the fruit of which would be death, but then life.[22]

> Of all the creators and cultivators who have ever lived, Jesus was the most capable of shaping culture through his own talents and power—and yet the most culture-shaping event of his life is the result of his choice to abandon his talents and power. The resurrection shows us the pattern for culture-making in the image of God. Not power, but trust. Not independence, but dependence. The second Adam's influence on culture comes through his greatest act of dependence; the fulfillment of Israel's calling to demonstrate faith in the face of the great powers that threatened its existence comes in the willing submission of Jesus to a Roman cross, broken by but also breaking forever its power . . . In the kingdom of God a new kind of life and a new kind of culture becomes possible—not by abandoning the old but by transforming it. Even the cross, the worst that culture can do, is transformed into a sign of the kingdom of God—the realm of forgiveness, mercy, love and indestructible life.[23]

One of the things Christians often seem oblivious to is that they are bearing witness, and making culture whether they realize it or not. Every people group has a presence, an ethos, a way of making something of the world and Christians are no different. They see themselves as a family of faith, and like any family they have their struggles and differences. *Christians will be more often judged by the way they live in the world and what they make of the world than by their overt witness. They will be judged by, among other things, their work ethic—do they work hard, do they come to work on time, do they accept hardship without complaining, do they have honesty and integrity?*

The world, the fellow workers, the foreman is watching. And Christ will be honored or not by how we perform and what we do with the world while watching eyes are upon us. If all we ever do is complain about things, including about our culture's problems whilst at work, people will notice that as well. We might as well wear a T-shirt reading "Buzz kill for Jesus" if that's what we make of and do with the world.

I suspect that one reason Christians don't see themselves as makers of culture, even when they are at work, is that Christianity is supposed to be a universal religion, a one-size-fits-all religion, a body of believers of every tribe and tongue and people and nation. A cultural religion with specific cultural practices would be Judaism or Hinduism. Christians seem to think real Christianity is transcultural just because it is multi-ethnic. This is not so. The various different forms of Christianity all have their own ethos, their own way of making culture and making sense of the world, and creating an environment within their larger culture where things Christian can happen and prevail, including of course worship. And worship is supremely an expression of culture-making. African-American worship often looks very different from middle class suburban praise worship. What we need to understand is that whether we are at our job or we are at worship in our church, we are at work constructing a culture, and helping to advance the cause of the Kingdom or not.

Indigenization—Can You Dig It?

A key word for a Christian to understand is indigenization. Christianity has the ability to be indigenized in many different cultural expressions and still be Christian. Crouch puts it this way: "As the scholar Lamin Sanneh has pointed out, this translatability sharply differentiates Christianity from Islam, which requires the Qur'an to be read in its original language. The gospel, even though it is deeply embedded in Jewish cultural history, is available in the "mother tongue" of every human being. There is no culture beyond its reach—because the very specific cultural story of Israel was never anything other than a rescue mission for all the cultures of the world, initiated by the world's Creator."[24]

It is precisely 'translatability' and 'indigenization' that makes it possible for a Christian to assume most any good job worth doing, and work most anywhere. There is a freedom in being a Christian that other religious groups do not have, precisely because Christianity *works* differently, it constructs culture differently, and it is able to adopt and adapt the best of many cultures and still be true to the essence of its character and credo.

Suppose we did Christianity again the early church way, by which I mean we took seriously that we are family and we took care of one another? What would happen in a culture of rising unemployment if the church took care of, shared the burden with its widows, its orphans, its unemployed? What if a community of Christians not only did this, but was welcoming to strangers, was prepared to go the extra mile to help them as well? Suppose once again church became a sanctuary and a safe haven, not just a place where we as God's sheep meet, greet, bleat, eat, excrete, and retreat?

Before and during the Middle Ages, Christians provided the doctoring and nursing to strangers during epidemics when the pagan priests and medics had fled the major cities. Christians provided the food, clothing, and shelter for the poor. They did not pass these responsibilities off on the government. They were proactive and created their own worlds of work and service. They stuck together, and lived and died together during the plagues, the famines, the natural disasters such as earthquakes. They had no governmental assistance, and waited for no insurance companies to bail them out or to rebuild. They simply rolled up their sleeves and did it.

> The church had no magic or medicine to cure the plague, but it turns out that survival even of a terrible disease has a lot to do with one's access to the most basic elements of life. Simply by providing food, water and friendship to their neighbors, Christians enabled many to remain strong enough that their own immune systems could mount an effective defense. [Rodney]Stark engages in some rather macabre algebra to calculate the "differential mortality" of Christians and their neighbors compared to pagans who were not fortunate enough to have the same kind of care—and concludes that "conscientious nursing *without any medications* could cut

the mortality rate by two-thirds or even more." The result was that after consecutive epidemics had swept through a city, a very disproportionate number of those remaining would either have been Christians or pagans who had been nursed through their sickness by Christian neighbors. And with their family and friends decimated by the plague, it is no wonder that many of these neighbors, seeking new friends and family, would naturally convert to Christian faith. The church would grow not just because it proclaimed hope in the face of horror but because of the cultural effects of a new approach to the sick and dying, a willingness to care for the sick even at risk of death.[25]

In our current economic crisis the church has once more the chance to make and change culture, to build a world, and to bear better witness to the Christ who said "inasmuch as you have done it unto the least of these, you have done it unto me."

The New Jerusalem as Cultural Artifact

What if what Revelation 20–22 is telling us is that in the Kingdom humans and their culture will be purified and rescued? What if we are being told that not just nature and human nature gets an upgrade, but also human culture? Crouch says the fact that the story ends with a city, the ultimate cultural artifact, points in this direction. And notice it is a city that is built by taking the things of nature, and transforming them into cultural artifacts—gems become jewels in the kingdom, and the bounty and best of human products are brought into the city to celebrate the return of the King.

I suspect Crouch is right that the world to come will not be as drastically different from our own world as we might expect—it's just that there will no longer be the shadow of sin, sickness and sorrow, disease, decay, and death. And I would suggest there will be plenty to do as well—for instance, picking the fruit from all those trees along the central river which will require no more bug spray or artificial anything. We're going all natural in the Kingdom, all glorious, and all the best of humanity and its culture. Notice how nature flourishes in the middle of the new Jerusalem, nature is incorporated into the eternal city. We will not have to choose between urban and rural, here and there, now and then. It will all be present at once and available to all.

In his discussion of Revelation's ending, Crouch finally collects his thoughts on human work and its importance, and potential to last and make a difference. Listen to what he says:

> We should ask the same question about our own cultural creativity and cultivating. Are we creating and cultivating things that have a chance of furnishing the new Jerusalem? Will the cultural goods we devote our lives to—the food we cook and consume, the music we purchase and practice, the movies we watch and make, the enterprises we earn our paychecks from and invest our wealth in—be identified as the glory and honor of our cultural tradition? Or will they be remembered as mediocrities at best, dead-ends at worst? This is not the same as asking whether we are making "Christian" culture. "Christian" cultural artifacts will surely go through the same winnowing and judgment as "non-Christian" artifacts. Nor is this entirely a matter of who is responsible for the cultural artifacts and where their faith is placed, especially since every cultural good is a collective effort. Clearly some of the cultural goods found in the new Jerusalem will have been created and cultivated by people who may well not accept the Lamb's invitation to substitute his righteousness for their sin. Yet the best of their work may survive. Can that be said of the goods that we are devoting our lives to?
>
> This is, it seems to me, a standard for cultural responsibility that is both more demanding and more liberating than the ways Christians often gauge our work's significance. We tend to have altogether too short a time frame for the worth of our work. We ask if this book will be noticed, this store will have a profitable quarter, this contract will be accepted. Some of these are useful intermediate steps for assessing whether our cultural work is of lasting value, but our short-term evaluations can be misleading if our work is not also held up to the long horizon of God's redemptive purpose. On the other hand, knowing that the new Jerusalem will be furnished with the best of every culture frees us from having to give a "religious" or evangelistic explanation for everything we do. We are free to simply make the best we can of the world, in concert with our forebears and our neighbors. If the ships of Tarshish and the camels of Midian can find a place in the new Jerusalem, our work, no matter how "secular," can too.[26]

In the World, but Not of the World or Other-Worldly?

The issue of Christians and their work, and culture-making can in one sense be boiled down to the issue of how Christians are to live in the world, without simply becoming 'of' the world. How is this nice little walk along a high wire, without falling off on either side, achieved?

One way Christians have done it in America, surprisingly enough, is to simply baptize the American culture and call it good, and embrace it as their own—with liberty and justice and hot apple pie for some. This has led to odd distortions of the Gospel, such as the prosperity Gospel or the health and wealth Gospel. The church it seems has been more changed by, than done much changing of culture, no matter how hard we work at it.

This is one reason I love to take my students on cross-cultural trips to the lands of the Bible and deliberately take them to places where they will contract cultural vertigo—say, for instance, standing in the magnificent temple in Luxor staring at hieroglyphics whilst overhearing the Muslim call to prayer from the nearby mosque, and watching with one eye a group of Japanese tourists clicking photos on the right and a group of Germans listening intently on the left. When cultural vertigo is suddenly contracted, most Americans look for comfort food, which is why our guide pointed my students to the other side of the road saying, "and there is the American Cultural Embassy." What we were looking at, and some students were beginning to drool at, was McDonalds. No wonder we Christians haven't much changed our culture—we love it too much just like it is, warts, wrinkles, and all. But what a sad commentary on America that one of the few universal cultural objects we have managed to export to the world is the Big Mac. Sigh.

To upgrade things in a Christian way and become culture-makers in a positive sense, we need to ask the right questions. Crouch suggests these to start with: "What is God doing in culture? What is his vision for the horizons of the possible and the impossible? Who are the poor who are having good news preached to them? Who are the powerful who are called to spend their power alongside the relatively powerless? Where is the impossible becoming possible?"[27]

The 3 ... the 12 ... the 120: On Changing Culture

It is an old cliché that all politics is local, and in fact this is not quite true. But it is more true to say that all work is local, and most work actually accomplishes something when it is done in tandem with other people, sometimes only a few other people, sometimes a lot. Andy Crouch reminds us that most anything worth doing starts small, including if the work we are engaging in is culture-making. Talking about the influence a circle of 3, then 12, then 120 can have, he puts it this way:

> The essential insight of 3 : 12 : 120 is that every cultural innovation, no matter how far-reaching its consequences, is based on personal relationships and personal commitment. Culture-making is hard. It simply doesn't happen without the deep investment of absolutely and relatively small groups of people. In culture-making, size matters—in reverse. Only a small group can sustain the attention, energy, and perseverance to create something that genuinely moves the horizons of possibility—because to create that good requires an ability to suspend, at least for a time, the very horizons within which everyone else is operating. Such "suspension of impossibility" is tiring and taxing. The only thing strong enough to sustain it is a community of people. To create a new cultural good, a small group is essential.[28]

What is most striking about this point is that it describes the way Jesus set about to change the world—with an inner circle of three disciples (Peter, James, and John), and a slightly larger circle of 12, and then after Easter a group of 120 (Acts 1:15) when the church was about to be birthed. Now Crouch did not arrive at these three numbers on the basis of analysis of the Bible, but rather on the basis of his sociological analysis of how cultural change and culture-making actually transpires in the vast majority of cases. It starts small and branches out, like the ripples in a pond from a small stone thrown in it. The good news about this is that all work that really matters and makes a difference starts small, and locally. Consider the example of Mother Teresa in Calcutta. And she did not advertise. Even so, eventually the world beat a path to her door.

Perhaps you will remember the movie "Six Degrees of Separation" based on the theory that we are only six persons away from being in touch with all six billion people on the planet. There is considerable truth to this, and what it proves is that networking and work on the Net can have influence right across the globe in ever-widening circles. This, of course, is one of the reasons I do my blog, which involves my soliciting no advertising dollars at all, but simply going directly to the world that can plug in to the Internet. The Internet is of course the greatest culture changer and re-arranger in our lifetimes. It has been the ruination of my much-beloved music shops, and it may be the ruination of major labels and the production of albums on CDs eventually, since increasingly people just download particular songs they like.

Christian work, calling, vocation, ministry which is oblivious to cultural change and is clueless about being a culture-maker may not be labor in vain, but it is certainly labor that is not maximizing what can be accomplished for the Lord. This is one of the things which makes Crouch's eye-opening book so crucial. He provides us with a window on how the world works, and doesn't work, when it comes to culture-making and cultural change. Crouch is right to stress however, lest we miss the point that it is not just all about networking, it is ultimately about creating community, the body of Christ. The goal of all ministry and mission is to increase the size of the body of Christ so more people will be in right relationship with God and fulfilling their destiny to love God and neighbor wholeheartedly.

I completely agree with Crouch when he says that the sacred vs. any work that is good and godly, any work worth doing can be done to the glory of God and for the help of humankind. And while we are at it, any such work is full-time ministry.

> The religious or secular nature of our cultural creativity is simply the wrong question. The right question is whether, when we undertake the work we believe to be our vocation, we experience the joy and humility that come only when God multiplies our work so that it bears thirty, sixty and a hundredfold beyond what we could expect from our feeble inputs. *Vocation*—calling—becomes another word for a continual process of discernment, examining the fruits of our work to see whether they are producing that kind of fruit, and doing all we can to scatter the next round of seed in the most fruitful places.[29]

This whole discussion brings to mind a quote from my friend Tom Wright who says:

If we are to be kingdom-announcers, modeling the new way of being human, we are also to be cross-bearers. This is a strange and dark theme that is also our birthright as followers of Jesus. Shaping our world is never for a Christian a matter of going out arrogantly thinking we can just get on with the job, reorganizing the world according to some model we have in mind. It is a matter of sharing and bearing the pain and puzzlement of the world so that the crucified love of God in Christ may be brought to bear healingly upon the world at exactly that point ... Because, as he himself said, following him involves taking up the cross, we should expect, as the New Testament tells us repeatedly, that to build on his foundation will be to find the cross etched into the pattern of our life and work over and over again.[30]

In the End Is Our Beginning, In the Doing Is Our Being

The psalmist has some good and sobering words to offer as we end this essay on work and culture-making. He tells us that unless the Lord builds our house, our labor is in vain, or in the words of Ps 90:17 we are told that we ought to pray that the Lord will establish the works of our hands, make them of lasting value. The true test of the value of something is not merely whether it stands the test of time but rather if it stands the testing of the Lord, a test which all of our works will one day undergo (see 1 Cor 3:13–15). Work worth doing in the world, must be work about which the Word says—"well done good and faithful servant, inherit the kingdom."[31] God has placed it in our hands to help shape a better future, one that can receive such an approbation. After all, at the end of the day, doing and being are intertwined even if we often misunderstand their relationship. I once had a colleague who had a coffee cup with the following profound insights painted on the side: 1) Line One: To Be is to Do—Plato; 2) Line Two (just below One) To Do is to Be—Aristotle; 3) Line Three (below the first two) Do Be Do Be Do—Frank Sinatra. Let us hope that Christian America's contribution to culture-making will be a bit more substantive than Sinatra's words.

The question is: Will we be creators of cultured pearls, a human endeavor that involves properly interacting with nature, creating pearls of great price that can be placed in the gates of the New Jerusalem, or instead will we continue just to be diggers and divers for pearls and wearers of those we find?

It is my hope that there are some pearls of wisdom to be found in the reflections in this essay so that we may find ourselves, not like W.B. Yeats' rough beast lumbering its way toward Bethlehem and thence to Jerusalem, but rather like those who heard and heeded the words of the poet who said, "but those who wait on the Lord will renew their strength. They will mount up like eagles with wings of great length. They will run and not be weary, they will walk and not faint, bringing hope to the hopeless, and power to God's saints." Amen.

Endnotes

1. See Crouch, *Culture Making*. A special thanks to Andy Crouch who gave me his blessing to use some more extended quotes from his fine book on culture-making to more adequately reflect and interact with his helpful discussion on work.
2. This summary courtesy of the Wikipedia article on H. Richard Niebuhr, http://enwikipedia.org/wiki/Richard_Niebuhr.
3. This is one of the blurbs that appears on the Amazon page for this book, http://www.amazon.com.
4. Crouch, *Culture Making*, 23.
5. Ibid.
6. Ibid., 27.
7. Ibid., 35.
8. Ibid., 38.
9. Ibid., 45.
10. Ibid., 48.
11. Ibid., 56.
12. Ibid., 57.
13. Ibid., 58.
14. Ibid., 62–64.
15. Ibid., 73.
16. Ibid., 76.
17. Ibid., 85.
18. Ibid., 108.
19. Ibid., 109.
20. Ibid., 113.
21. Ibid., 138.
22. Ibid., 141.
23. Ibid., 144–45.
24. Ibid., 155.
25. Ibid., 156
26. Ibid., 170.

27. Ibid., 214.
28. Ibid., 242.
29. Ibid., 256.
30. Wright, *The Challenge of Jesus*, 188-89.
31. A special thanks for all the good stimulus for this discussion that is in Andy Crouch's book. This chapter is, of course, heavily indebted to that discussion.

Afterword: With God on Our Side

JOHN G. LACEY

The great American Jewish-Christian poet Bob Dylan sings:

> Oh my name it is nothin'
> My age it means less
> The country I come from
> Is called the Midwest
> I's taught and brought up there
> The laws to abide
> And the land that I live in
> Has God on its side.[1]

As we arrive at the conclusion of this book, perhaps you and I share a similar conviction with Dylan that, "God is on our side." Although it may seem a preposterous idea, we often operate out of this paradigm both theologically and ethically, affecting everything and everyone around us. I hope and pray that these twelve chapters have challenged you, as they have me, to think and live in new ways.

    Jaroslav Pelikan in his wonderful work, *Whose Bible Is It?* recognizes the divisive power of the mutual ignorance of language in regard to the children of Abraham: Judaism, Christianity, and Islam who, as people of the Book, all claim "God is on our side." Pelikan notes a time in the Middle Ages where, "at least for an occasional moment, Jews, Christians and Muslims, by the power of the Book and in the heritage of Abraham, the father whom they shared, managed to transcend their separations without losing their identities."[2] I believe these twelve authors, from differing faith-traditions, have accomplished just that, bringing dialogue to the issue of *The Bible and the American Future*. They have modeled for us how we, too, can transcend our separations without losing our identities!

Because Judaism, Christianity, and Islam all cohabitate this one-World house, they each share the basic needs to which these pages speak so eloquently:

- Security and the biblical response of *Shalom*
- Economy and the biblical response of *Jubilee*
- Ecology and the biblical response of *Sabbath*.

As a pastor-teacher in the local church, I have found ground-breaking perspectives presented in this book that are fresh and user-friendly from old familiar passages of the Bible. The authors have presented a plethora of diverse biblical alternatives; a new word from God's Word for our world, as opposed to just ideologies and preconceived agendas. I hope you will join me in preaching, teaching, and living the practical, authentic theology contained herein with individuals in your scope of influence.

An amazing thing about this book is that you, the reader, get to choose the burning platform you jump from in response to its perspectives. Your words and deeds in social justice can make a difference, create a culture, and shape a future as you partner with the quilt-making God of history and redemption.

Perhaps your own personal call-to-action may be drawn from the prophet Isaiah's overwhelming experience with the sovereign majesty of the thrice-holy God who asks, "Whom shall I send, and who will go for us?" May we echo Isaiah's earnest reply, "Here am I; send me" (Isa 6:8).

Endnotes

1. Dylan, "With God on Our Side."
2. Pelikan, *Whose Bible Is It?* 139.

Bibliography

Abrams, Ray H. *Preachers Present Arms: The Role of the American Churches and Clergy in World Wars I and II, with Some Observations on the War in Vietnam.* Rev. ed. Scottsdale: Herald, 1969.

Ahlstrom, Sidney E. *A Religious History of the American People.* New Haven: Yale University Press, 1972.

Ainger, Arthur C. "God is Working His Purpose Out." In *Worship and Rejoice*, 198. Carol Stream: Hope Publishing, 2001. (Composed 1894.)

Albanese, Catherine L. *Sons of the Fathers. The Civil Religion of the American Revolution.* Philadelphia: Temple University Press, 1976.

Allen, Leslie C. *Jeremiah.* Old Testament Library. Louisville: Westminster John Knox Press, 2008.

Allitt, Patrick, editor. *Major Problems in American Religious History: Documents and Essays.* Boston: Houghton Mifflin, 2000.

Amar, Akhil Reed. *America's Constitution: A Biography.* New York: Random House, 2005.

"America's Agricultural Land is at Risk." American Farmland Trust. 31 Aug. 2006. N.p. Online: http://www.farmland.org/programs/protection/default.asp.htm.

Bailyn, Bernard. *The Ideological Origins of the American Revolution.* Cambridge: Harvard University Press, 1967.

Banning, Lance. *The Sacred Fire of Liberty: James Madison and the Founding of the Federal Republic.* Ithaca, NY: Cornell University Press, 1995.

Barr, James, "The Bible as a Political Document." *Bulletin of the John Rylands Library* 62 (1980) 268–89.

———. *The Concept of Biblical Theology: An Old Testament Perspective.* Minneapolis: Fortress, 2003.

Barrett, C. K. *The New Testament Background: Writings from Ancient Greece and the Roman Empire That Illuminate Christian Origins.* Rev. ed. New York: HarperCollins, 1989.

Barringer, Felicity. "Endangered Species Act Faces Broad New Challenges." *The New York Times*, June 26, 2005.

Barton, John. *Understanding Old Testament Ethics: Approaches and Explorations.* Louisville: Westminster John Knox Press, 2003.

Bibliography

Baumgartner, Frederic J. *Longing for the End: A History of Millennialism in Western Civilization.* New York: St. Martin's Press, 1999.

Beckman, Gary. *Hittite Diplomatic Texts.* 2nd ed. Society of Biblical Literature Writings from the Ancient World Series 7. Atlanta: Scholars, 1995.

Bellah, Robert N. *The Broken Covenant: American Civil Religion in Time of Trial.* San Francisco: Harper & Row, 1976.

Benfey, Christopher. "The Storm over Robert Frost." *New York Review of Books* 9 (Dec 4, 2008) 48–50.

Birch, Bruce C. *Let Justice Roll Down: The Old Testament, Ethics, and Christian Life.* Louisville: Westminster John Knox Press, 1991.

Block, Daniel I. "All Creatures Great and Small: Recovering a Deuteronomic Theology of Animals." In *The Old Testament in the Life of God's People: Essays in Honor of Elmer A. Martens,* edited by J. Isaak, 283–305. Winona Lake, IN: Eisenbrauns, 2009.

Bock, Darrell L. *Acts.* Baker Exegetical Commentary on the New Testament. Grand Rapids: Baker, 2007.

———. *Luke 9:51—24:53.* Baker Exegetical Commentary on the New Testament. Grand Rapids: Baker, 1996.

Boer, Roland. *Novel Histories: The Fiction of Biblical Criticism.* Playing the Texts 2. Sheffield: Sheffield Academic, 1997.

Borowski, Oded. *Agriculture in Iron Age Israel.* Boston: American Schools of Oriental Research, 2002.

———. *Daily Life in Biblical Times.* Atlanta: Society of Biblical Literature, 2003.

Bottorff, William K., and Arthur L. Ford, editors. *The Works of Joel Barlow.* Gainsville: Scholars' Facsimiles & Reprints, 1970.

Boyer, Paul S. "The Growth of Fundamentalist Apocalyptic in the United States." Pp. 149–51 in *The Encyclopedia of Apocalypticism,* vol. 3: *Apocalypticism in the Modern Period and the Contemporary Age,* edited by Stephen J. Stein., 149–51. New York: Continuum, 1998.

———. *When Time Shall Be No More. Prophecy Belief in Modern American Culture.* Cambridge: Harvard University Press, 1992.

Bozak, Barbara. *Life "Anew": A Literary Theological Study of Jer 30–31.* Analecta Biblica 122. Rome: Pontifical Biblical Institute Press, 1991.

Bremer, Francis J. *John Winthrop: America's Forgotten Founding Father.* Oxford: Oxford University Press, 2003.

Brison, Susan J. *Aftermath: Violence and the Remaking of a Self.* Princeton: Princeton University Press, 2002.

Broshi, Magen. "The Role of the Temple in the Herodian Economy." *Journal of Jewish Studies* 38 (1987) 31–37.

Brueggemann, Walter. *A Commentary on Jeremiah: Exile and Homecoming.* Grand Rapids: Eerdmans, 1998.

———. *Divine Presence and Violence: Contextualizing the Book of Joshua.* Eugene, OR: Cascade Books, 2009.

———. *Finally Comes the Poet: Daring Speech for Proclamation.* Minneapolis: Fortress, 1989.

———. "Prophetic Ministry: A Sustainable Alternative Community." In *Like Fire in the Bones: Listening for the Prophetic Word in Jeremiah,* edited by Patrick D. Miller, 142–67. Minneapolis: Fortress, 2006.

———. *Solomon: Israel's Ironic Icon of Human Achievement.* Columbia: University of South Carolina Press, 2005.

———. *Theology of the Old Testament: Testimony, Dispute, Advocacy.* Minneapolis: Fortress, 2005.

Brueggemann, Walter, and George Stroup, editors. *Many Voices, One God: Being Faithful in a Pluralistic World.* Louisville: Westminster John Knox Press, 1998.

Buggeln, John D. "Van Dyke, Henry." In *American National Biography*, 22:208-9. New York: Oxford University Press, 1999.

Bush, George W. "National Day of Prayer and Remembrance for the Victims of the Terrorist Attacks on September 11, 2001." Spoken at Washington, (D.C.) National Cathedral service on Sept. 14, 2001.

Butler, Jon, Grant Wacker, and Randall Balmer. *Religion in American Life: A Short History.* Oxford: Oxford University Press, 2003.

Carey, Benedict. "Brain Researchers Open Door to Editing Memory." *The New York Times*, April 5, 2009. Online: http://www.nytimes.com/2009/04/06/health/research/06brain.html?emc=etal.

Carroll, Robert P. "Whorusalamin: A Tale of Three Cities as Three Sisters." In *On Reading Prophetic Texts: Gender Specific and Related Studies in Memory of Fokkelien van Dijk-Hemmes*, edited by Bob Becking and Meindert Dijkstra, 67–82. Biblical Interpretation Series 18. Leiden: Brill, 1996.

Carroll Rodas, M. Daniel. "La Cita de Isaías 58:6 en Lucas 4:18: Una Neuva Propuesta," *Kairós* 11 (1992) 61–78.

Chaney, Marvin L. "Bitter Bounty: The Dynamics of Political Economy Critiqued by the Eight-Century Prophets." In *The Bible and Liberation: Political and Social Hermeneutics*, edited by Norman K. Gottwald and Richard A. Horsley, 365–75. Maryknoll, NY: Orbis, 1993.

———. "Whose Sour Grapes? The Addressees of Isaiah 5:1–7 in the Light of Political Economy." *Semeia* 87 (1999) 105–122.

Christensen, Duane L. *Deuteronomy 21:10—34:12.* Word Biblical Commentary 6B. Nashville: Nelson, 2002.

Clark, Jonathan C. D. *The Language of Liberty, 1600–1832: Political Discourse and Social Dynamics in the Anglo-American World.* Cambridge: Cambridge University Press, 1994.

Clines, David J. A. *Interested Parties: The Ideology of Writers and Readers of the Hebrew Bible.* Journal for the Study of the Old Testament Supplements 205. Sheffield: Sheffield Academic, 1995.

Cohen, Charles H. "Winthrop, John." In *American National Biography*, 23:660–65. New York: Oxford University Press, 1999.

Cole, Steven W. "The Destruction of Orchards in Assyrian Warfare." In *Assyria 1995: Proceedings of the 10th Anniversary Symposium of the Neo-Assyrian Text Corpus Project Helsinki, September 7–11, 1995*, edited by Simo Parpola and Robert M. Whiting, 29–40. Helsinki: Neo-Assyrian Text Corpus Project, 1997.

Collins, John J. "Models of Utopia in the Biblical Tradition." In *A Wise and Discerning Mind: Essays in Honor of Burke O. Long*, edited by Saul M. Olyan and Robert C. Culley, 51–67. Brown Judaic Studies. Providence: Brown University Press, 2000.

Bibliography

Collins, John J. "Sibylline Oracles: A New Translation and Introduction." In *The Old Testament Pseudepigrapha*, edited by James H. Charlesworth, 1:317–472. Garden City, NY: Doubleday, 1983.

Collins, John J. *The Scepter and the Star: The Messiahs of the Dead Sea Scrolls and Other Ancient Literature*. Anchor Bible Reference Library. New York: Doubleday, 1995.

Cross, Frank M. *Canaanite Myth and Hebrew Epic: Essays in the History of the Religion of Israel*. Cambridge: Harvard University Press, 1973.

Crossan, John Dominic. *The Birth of Christianity: Discovering What Happened in the Years Immediately after the Execution of Jesus*. San Francisco: HarperSanFrancisco, 1998.

———. *God and Empire: Jesus against Rome, Then and Now*. San Francisco: HarperSanFrancisco, 2007.

———. "Jesus and the Challenge of Collaborative Eschatology." In *The Historical Jesus: Five Views*, edited by James Beilby and Paul Eddy, 103–30. Downers Grove, IL: InterVarsity Press, 2009.

Crouch, Andy. *Culture Making: Recovering Our Creative Calling*. Downers Grove, IL: InterVarsity Press, 2008.

Dahl, G., and A. Hjort. *Having Herds: Pastoral Herd Growth and Household Economy*. Stockholm: Dept. of Social Anthropology, University of Stockholm, 1976.

Darr, Kathryn Pfisterer. "Troubling Texts." *Journal for the Study of the Old Testament* 55 (1992) 97–117.

Davis, Ellen. *Scripture, Culture, and Agriculture: An Agrarian Reading of the Bible*. Cambridge: Cambridge University Press, 2009.

Davis, Lance E., and Robert A. Huttenback. *Mammon and the Pursuit of Empire: The Economics of British Imperialism*. Abridged Edition. Interdisciplinary Perspectives on Modern History. New York: Cambridge University Press, 1988.

Deissmann, Adolf. *Light from the Ancient East: The New Testament Illustrated by Recently Discovered Texts of the Graeco-Roman World*. Rev. ed. Translated by Lionel R. M. Strachan. 1927. Reprint, Eugene, OR: Wipf & Stock, 2004.

Dempsey, Carol J. "The 'Whore' of Ezekiel 16: The Impact and Ramifications of Gender-Specific Metaphors in Light of Biblical Law and Divine Judgment." In *Gender and Law in the Hebrew Bible and the Ancient Near East*, edited by Victor H. Matthews, Bernard M. Levinson, Tikva Frymer-Kensky, 57–68. Journal for the Study of the Old Testament Supplements 262. Sheffield: Sheffield Academic Press, 1998.

Diamond, A. R. Pete, and Kathleen M. O'Connor. "Unfaithful Passions: Coding Women Coding Men in Jeremiah 2:1—3:25 (4:2)." In *Troubling Jeremiah*, edited by A. R. Pete Diamond, 387–402. Journal for the Study of the Old Testament Supplements 260. Sheffield: Sheffield Academic, 1999.

Domeris, William Robert. *Touching the Heart of God: The Social Construction of Poverty among Biblical Peasants*. New York: T. & T. Clark, 2007.

Domke, David. *God Willing? Political Fundamentalism in the White House, the "War on Terror," and the Echoing Press*. Ann Arbor: University of Michigan Press, 2004.

Dorrien, Gary. *The Making of American Liberal Theology: Imagining Progressive Religion—1805–1900*. Louisville: Westminster John Knox, 2002.

Dowling, William G. "Dwight, Timothy." In *American National Biography*, 7:192–94. New York: Oxford University Press, 1999.

Doyle, Michael W. *Empires*. Cornell Studies in Comparative History. Ithaca: Cornell University Press, 1986.

Dunn, Elizabeth E. "Backus, Isaac." In *American National Biography*, 1:836–38. New York: Oxford University Press, 1999.

Dylan, Bob. "With God on Our Side." 1963. Renewed by Special Rider Music, 1991.

Edwards, Jonathan. *History of the Work of Redemption*. Reprint, New Haven: Yale University Press, 1989.

Epsztein [or Epzstein] Léon. *Social Justice in the Ancient Near East and the People of the Bible*. Translated by John Bowden. London: SCM, 1986.

Exum, J. Cheryl. "The Ethics of Biblical Violence Against Women." In *The Bible in Ethics: The Second Sheffield Colloquium*, edited by John W. Rogerson, Margaret Davies, and M. Daniel Carroll Rodas, 248–71. Journal for the Study of the Old Testament Supplements 207. Sheffield: Sheffield Academic, 1995.

Eyre, Christopher. "The Agricultural Cycle, Farming and Water Management in the Ancient Near East." In *Civilizations of the Ancient Near East*, edited by Jack M. Sasson, 1:175–89. New York: Scribners, 1995.

Fager, Jeffrey A. *Land Tenure and the Biblical Jubilee: Uncovering Hebrew Ethics through the Sociology of Knowledge*. Journal for the Study of the Old Testament Supplements 155. Sheffield: JSOT Press, 1993.

Fechner, Roger Jerome. "The Moral Philosophy of John Witherspoon and the Scottish-American Enlightenment." Ph.D. dissertation, University of Iowa, 1974.

Ferguson, Everett. *Backgrounds of Early Christianity*. 3rd ed. Grand Rapids: Eerdmans, 2003.

Ferguson, Niall. *Colossus: The Price of America's Empire*. New York: Penguin, 2004.

Fishbane, Michael. "Sin and Judgment in the Prophecies of Ezekiel." *Interpretation* 38 (1984) 131–50.

Fishbane, Michael. *Sacred Attunement: A Jewish Theology*. Chicago: University of Chicago Press, 2008.

Forti, Tova. "Bee's Honey—From Realia to Metaphor in Biblical Wisdom Literature." *Vetus Testamentum* 56 (2006) 327–41.

Fredriksen, Paula. *Jesus of Nazareth, King of the Jews: A Jewish Life and the Emergence of Christianity*. New York: Knopf, 1999.

Fredriksen, Paula. "Judaism: The Circumcision of Gentiles, and Apocalyptic Hope: Another Look at Galatians 1 and 2." *Journal of Theological Studies* 42 (1991) 532–64.

Fretheim, Terence E. *About the Bible: Short Answers to Big Questions*. Rev. ed. Minneapolis: Augsburg, 2009.

———. *Jeremiah*. Macon, GA: Smith & Helwys, 2002.

———. "The Prophets and Social Justice: A Conservative Agenda." *Word & World* 28 (2008) 159–68.

———. "Salvation in the Bible vs. Salvation in the Church." *Word & World* 13 (1993) 363–72.

———. "Theological Reflections on the Wrath of God in the Old Testament." *Horizons in Biblical Theology* 24 (2002) 1–26.

Gadd, C. J. *The Assyrian Sculptures*. The British Museum. London: Harrison, 1934.

Gaustad, Edwin S., and Mark A. Noll, editors. *A Documentary History of Religion in America*. 2 vols. 3rd Edition. Grand Rapids: Eerdmans, 2003.

Gaustad, Edwin S. *Roger Williams*. Oxford: Oxford University Press, 2005.

Bibliography

Georgianna, Sharon Linzey. *The Moral Majority and Fundamentalism: Plausibility and Dissonance*. Studies in Religion and Society 23.. Lewiston, NY: Mellen, 1989.

Gitin, Seymour, J. Edward Wright, and J. P. Dessel, editors. *Confronting the Past: Archaeological and Historical Essays on Ancient Israel in Honor of William G. Dever*. Winona Lake, IN: Eisenbrauns, 2006.

Glick, Daniel. "Putting the 'Public' Back in Public Lands: An Open Letter to the Next President." *National Wildlife* 46 (Oct–Nov 2008) 24–30.

Goodman, Martin. "The First Jewish Revolt: Social Conflict and the Problem of Debt." *Journal of Jewish Studies* 33 (1982) 422–34.

Gordon, Pamela, and Harold C. Washington. "Rape as Military Metaphor in the Hebrew Bible." In *Feminist Companion to the Latter Prophets*, edited by Athalya Brenner, 308–25. Sheffield: Sheffield Academic, 1995.

Gossai, Hemchand. *Justice, Righteousness, and the Social Critique of the Eighth-Century Prophets*. 1993. Reprinted, Eugene, OR: Wipf & Stock, 2008.

Gottlieb, R. S. *A Greener Faith: Religious Environmentalism and Our Planet's Future*. Oxford: Oxford University Press, 2006.

Green, Garrett. *Imagining God: Theology and the Religious Imagination*. San Francisco: Harper & Row, 1989.

Guelich, Robert. *The Sermon on the Mount*. Waco, TX: Word, 1982.

Gunn, David M. "Colonialism and the Vagaries of Scripture: Te Kooti in Canaan (A Story of Bible and Dispossession in Aotearoa/New Zealand." In *God in the Fray: A Tribute to Walter Brueggemann*, edited by Tod Linafelt and Timothy K. Beal, 127–42. Minneapolis: Fortress Press, 1998.

Haag, Herbert. "חמס ḥamas." In *Theological Dictionary of the Old Testament*, edited by Johannes Botterweck and Helmer Ringgren, 4:478–87. Translated by Geoffrey W. Bromiley. Grand Rapids: Eerdmans, 1980.

Hall, Timothy L. *Separating Church and State: Roger Williams and Religious Liberty*. Urbana: University of Illinois Press, 1998.

Hamilton, Marci A. "The Reverend John Witherspoon and the Constitutional Convention." In *Law and Religion: A Critical Anthology*, edited by Stephen M. Feldman, 54–66. New York: New York University Press, 2000.

Harland, Peter J. "Bs': Bribe, Extortion or Profit?" *Vetus Testamentum* 50 (2000) 310–22.

———. "What Kind of 'Violence' in Ezekiel 22?" *Expository Times* 108 (Jan 1997) 111–14.

Harrelson, Walter. *The Ten Commandments and Human Rights*. Overtures to Biblical Theology. Philadelphia: Fortress, 1980.

———. *The Ten Commandments for Today*. Louisville: Westminster John Knox, 2006.

Hasel, Michael. *Military Practice and Polemic: Israel's Laws of Warfare in Near Eastern Perspective*. Berrien Springs, MI: Andrews University Press, 2005.

Herman, Judith L. *Trauma and Recovery*. New York: Basic Books, 1992.

Heschel, Abraham. *The Prophets*. New York: Harper & Row, 1962.

Hess, Rick. "The Book of Joshua as a Land Grant." *Biblica* 83 (2002) 493–506.

Hesse, Brian. "Animal Husbandry and Human Diet in the Ancient Near East." In *Civilizations of the Ancient Near East*, edited by Jack M. Sasson, 1:203–22. New York: Scribners, 1995.

Hicks, Roy H. *Another Look at the Rapture*. Tulsa, OK: Harrison House, 1982.

Hill, Samuel S., and Dennis E. Owen. *The New Religious Political Right in America.* Nashville: Abingdon, 1982.

Hillers, D. R. *Micah: A Commentary on the Book of the Prophet Micah.* Hermeneia. Philadelphia: Fortress, 1984.

Holladay, John S., Jr. "Hezekiah's Tribute, Long-Distance Trade, and the Wealth of Nations ca. 1000–600 BC: A New Perspective ('Poor Little [Agrarian] Judah' at the End of the 8th Century BC: Dropping the First Shoe)." In *Confronting the Past: Archaeological and Historical Essays on Ancient Israel in Honor of William G. Dever*, edited by Seymour Gitin, J. Edward Wright and J. P. Dessel, 309–31. Winona Lake, IN: Eisenbrauns, 2006.

Holladay, William L. *Jeremiah 2: A Commentary on the Book of the Prophet Jeremiah Chapters 26–52.* Hermeneia. Philadelphia: Fortress, 1989.

Holman, Jan. "Micah." In *The International Bible Commentary: A Catholic and Ecumenical Commentary for the Twenty-First Century*, edited by William R. Farmer, 1153–63. Collegeville, MN: Liturgical, 1998.

Hopkins, David C. "Life on the Land: The Subsistence Struggles of Early Israel." *Biblical Archaeologist* 50 (1987) 178–191.

Horsley, Richard A. *Covenant Economics: A Biblical Vision of Justice for All.* Louisville: Westminster John Knox, 2009.

———. *Galilee: History, Politics, People.* Valley Forge, PA: Trinity, 1995.

———. *Hearing the Whole Story: The Politics of Plot in Mark's Gospel.* Louisville: Westminster John Knox Press, 2001.

———. *Jesus and Empire: The Kingdom of God and the New World Disorder.* Minneapolis: Fortress, 2003.

———. *Jesus and the Spiral of Violence: Popular Jewish Resistance in Roman Palestine.* San Francisco: Harper & Row, 1987.

———. *The Liberation of Christmas: The Infancy Narratives in Social Context.* 1989. Reprint, Eugene, OR: Wipf and Stock, 2006.

———. *Scribes, Visionaries, and the Politics of Second Temple Judea.* Louisville: Westminster John Knox Press, 2007.

Horsley, Richard A. with Jonathan A. Draper. *Whoever Hears You Hears Me: Prophets, Performance and Tradition in Q.* Harrisville: Trinity Press International, 1999.

Houston, Walter J. *Contending for Justice: Ideologies and Theologies of Social Justice in the Old Testament.* London: T. & T. Clark, 2006.

Hudson, Winthrop S., editor. *Nationalism and Religion in America: Concepts of American Identity and Mission.* New York: Harper & Row, 1970.

Hull, Jeff. "The Final Frontier." *Audubon* 107.5 (2005) 46–48.

Isaak, Jon, editor. *The Old Testament in the Life of God's People: Essays in Honor of Elmer A. Martens.* Winona Lake, IN: Eisenbrauns, 2009.

Jacobsen, Thorkild, and Robert M. Adams. "Salt and Silt in Ancient Mesopotamian Agriculture: Progressive Changes in Soil Salinity and Sedimentation Contributed to the Breakup of Past Civilizations." *Science* 128 (1958) 1251–58.

Janzen, Waldemar. *Old Testament Ethics: A Paradigmatic Approach.* Louisville: Westminster John Knox, 1994.

Jeffrey, Grant R. *Armageddon: Appointment with Destiny.* New York: Bantam, 1990.

Jeffrey, Grant R. *Messiah: War in the Middle East and the Road to Armageddon.* Rev. ed. New York: Bantam, 1992.

Bibliography

Jewett, Robert. *Mission and Menace: Four Centuries of Religious Zeal in America*. Minneapolis: Fortress, 2008.

Johnson, Chalmers. *The Sorrows of Empire: Militarism, Secrecy, and the End of the Republic*. New York: Holt, 2004.

Johnson, Luke T. *The Literary Function of Possessions in Luke-Acts*. SBL Dissertations. Missoula, MT: Scholars, 1977.

Jorstad, Erling. *The New Christian Right 1981-88: Prospects for the Post-Reagan Decade*. Studies in American Religion 25. Lewiston, NY: Mellen, 1987.

Kagan, Robert. *Dangerous Nation: America's Foreign Policy from Its Earliest Days to the Dawn of the Twentieth Century*. New York: Knopf, 2006.

Kalmanofsky, Amy Beth. "The Rhetoric of Horror in the Book of Jeremiah." Ph.D. dissertation, University of Michigan, 2005.

Kessler, Martin. "Jeremiah 26-45 Reconsidered." *Journal of Near Eastern Studies* 27 (1968) 81–88.

Kessler, Rainer. *Micha: Übersetzt und ausgelegt*. Herders Theologischer Kommentar zum Alten Testament. Freiburg: Herder, 1999.

King, Philip J., and Lawrence E. Stager. *Life in Biblical Israel*. Library of Ancient Israel. Louisville: Westminster John Knox, 2001.

Knowles, Michael. *Jeremiah in Matthew's Gospel: The Rejected Prophet Motif in Matthaean Redaction*. Journal for the Study of the New Testament Supplements 68. Sheffield: JSOT Press, 1993.

Koch, Adrienne. *Jefferson and Madison: The Great Collaboration*. New York: Knopf, 1950.

Kuhn, Thomas S. *The Structure of Scientific Revolutions*. Chicago: University of Chicago Press, 1965.

Ladizinski, G. "Origin and Domestication of the South West Asian Grain Legumes." In *Foraging and Farming*, edited by D. R. Harris and G. C. Hillman, 374–389. London: Unwin Hyman, 1989.

LaHaye, Tim F. *No Fear of the Storm*. Sisters, OR: Multnomah, 1992.

———. *The Beginning of the End*. Wheaton, IL: Tyndale, 1991.

Lambert, Frank. *The Founding Fathers and the Place of Religion in America*. Princeton: Princeton University Press, 2003.

Laniak, Timothy. *Shepherds after My Own Heart: Pastoral Traditions and Leadership in the Bible*. New Studies in Biblical Theology 20. Leicester, UK: Apollos, 2006.

Lapsley, Jacqueline. *Can These Bones Live? The Problem of the Moral Self in the Book of Ezekiel*. Beihefte zur Zeitschrift für die alttestamentliche Wissenschaft 301. Berlin: de Gruyter, 2000.

Leibiger, Stuart. *Founding Friendship: George Washington, James Madison and the Creation of the American Republic*. Charlottesville: University Press of Virginia, 1999.

Liebman, Robert C. and Robert Wuthnow, editors. *The New Christian Right: Mobilization and Legitimation*. Hawthorne, NY: Aldine, 1983.

Lieven, Anatole. *America Right or Wrong: An Anatomy of American Nationalism*. New York: Oxford University Press, 2004.

Lindsey, Hal. *Planet Earth-2000 A.D. Will Mankind Survive?* Palos Verde, CA: Western Front, 1994.

———. *The Rapture: Truth or Consequences*. New York: Bantam, 1983.

———. *The Terminal Generation*. Old Tappen, NJ: Revell, 1976.

Lowery, Richard H. *Sabbath and Jubilee*. Understanding Biblical Themes. St. Louis: Chalice, 2000.

Lundbom, Jack R. *Jeremiah 1–20*. Anchor Bible 21A. New York: Doubleday, 1999.

Luther, Martin. "Commentary on St. Paul's Epistle to the Galatians," 1535. Cited in Darrin M. McMahon, *Happiness: A History*. New York: Grove, 2006.

Maier, Aren M., Oren Ackermann, and Hendrik J. Bruins. "The Ecological Consequences of a Siege: A Marginal Note on Deuteronomy 20:19-20." In *Confronting the Past: Archaeological and Historical Essays on Ancient Israel in Honor of William G. Dever*, edited by Seymour Gitin, J. Edward Wright and J. P. Dessel, 239–43. Winona Lake, IN: Eisenbrauns, 2006.

Maier, Charles S. *Among Empires: American Ascendancy and Its Predecessors* Cambridge: Harvard University Press, 2006.

Malchow, Bruce. *Social Justice in the Hebrew Bible: What is New and What is Old*. Collegeville, MN: Liturgical, 1996.

Marin, Louis. *Utopics: Spatial Play*. Contemporary Studies in Philosophy and the Human Sciences. Atlantic Highlands, NJ: Humanities Press, 1984.

Mazar, Amihai and Nava Panitz-Cohen. "Honey and Bee-Keeping in the Bible and the Ancient Near East." *Near Easterm Archaeology* 70 (2007) 202–19.

McBride, S. Dean. "Polity of the Covenant People: The Book of Deuteronomy." In *A Song of Power and the Power of Song: Essays on the Book of Deuteronomy*, edited by Duane L. Christensen, 62–77. Winona Lake, IN: Eisenbrauns, 1993.

McCartney, Paul T. *Power and Progress: American National Identity, the War of 1898, and the Rise of American Imperialism*. Baton Rouge: Louisiana State University Press, 2006.

McConville, J. G. *Deuteronomy*. Apollos Old Testament Commentary. Leicester, UK: Apollos, 2002.

McCoy, Drew R. *The Last of the Fathers: James Madison and the Republican Legacy*. Cambridge: Cambridge University Press, 1989.

McKivigan, John R. *The War Against Proslavery Religion: Abolitionism and the Northern Churches 1830–1865*. Ithaca, NY: Cornell University Press, 1984.

McLoughlin, William G. *Isaac Backus and the American Pietistic Tradition*. New York: Little Brown, 1967.

McTaggart, William J. and William K. Bottorff, editors. *The Major Poems of Timothy Dwight (1752–1817): With a Dissertation on the History, Eloquence, and Poetry of the Bible*. Gainsville: Scholar's Facsimiles & Reprints, 1969.

Meyers, Carol. "The Family in Early Israel." In *Families in Ancient Israel*, edited by Leo G. Perdue, Joseph Blenkinsopp, John J. Collins and Carol L. Meyers, 1–47. Family, Religion, and Culture. Louisville: Westminster John Knox, 1997.

Migliore, Daniel L. *The Power of God and the Gods of Power*. Louisville: Westminster John Knox, 2008.

Milgrom, Jacob. *Leviticus: A Book of Ritual and Ethics*. Continental Commentary. Minneapolis: Fortress, 2004.

Miller, Patrick D. *The Religion of Ancient Israel*. Library of Ancient Israel. Louisville: Westminster John Knox, 2000.

Miller, Perry. "The Contribution of the Protestant Churches to Religious Liberty in Colonial America." In *Essays in American Colonial History*, edited by Paul Goodman, 152–83. New York: Holt, Rinehart & Winston, 1967.

Bibliography

Minor Latin Poets Volume 1. Translated by J. Wright Duff and Arnold M. Duff. Loeb Classical Library 284. Cambridge: Harvard University Press, 1935.

Moo, Douglas J. "Nature in the New Creation: New Testament Eschatology and the Environment." *Journal of the Evangelical Theological Society* 49 (2006) 449–88.

Moore, LeRoy. "Religious Liberty: Roger Williams and the Revolutionary Era." *Church History* 34 (1965) 57–76.

Moore, R. Laurence. "Roger Williams und die revolutionäre Ära." In *Zur Geschichte der Toleranz und Religionsfreiheit*, edited by Heinrich Lutz, 276–307. Darmstadt: Wissenschaftliche Buchgesellschaft, 1977.

Moorhead, James H. *American Apocalypse: Yankee Protestants and the Civil War 1860–69*. New Haven: Yale University Press, 1978.

Morris, Richard B. *Basic Documents in American History*. Rev. ed. Princeton: Van Nostrand, 1965.

Moynihan, Daniel Patrick. *On the Law of Nations*. Cambridge: Harvard University Press, 1990.

Muir, Patricia. "Consequences for Organic Matter in Soils." Online: http://oregonstate.edu/~muirp/orgmater.htm.

Murphy, Cullen. *Are We Rome? The Fall of an Empire and the Fate of America*. New York: Houghton Mifflin, 2007.

Nelson, Richard. *Deuteronomy*. Old Testament Library. Louisville: Westminster John Knox, 2002.

Newsom, Carol A. *The Self as Symbolic Space: Constructing Identity and Community at Qumran*. Studies on the Texts of the Desert of Judah 52. Leiden: Brill, 2004.

Nichols, James Hastings. *Democracy and the Churches*. New York: Greenwood, 1969.

Noll, Mark A. "The Bible in American Culture." In *Encyclopedia of the American Religious Experience: Studies of Traditions and Movements*, edited by Charles H. Lippy and Peter W. Williams, 2:1075–87. New York: Scribner, 1988.

O'Leary, Stephen D. *Arguing the Apocalypse: A Theory of Millennial Rhetoric*. New York: Oxford University Press, 1994.

Obama, Barack. "A New Beginning." Spoken in Cairo, Egypt, on June 4, 2009.

Odell, Margaret S. *Ezekiel*. Smith & Helwys Bible Commentary. Macon, GA: Smith & Helwys, 2005.

Olyan, Saul. *Disability in the Hebrew Bible: Interpreting Mental and Physical Differences*. Cambridge: Cambridge University Press, 2008.

Parenti, Michael. *Against Empire*. San Francisco: City Lights Books, 1995.

Paul, Shalom M., and William Dever. *Biblical Archaeology*. New York: Quadrangle & New York Times, 1974.

Pelikan, Jaroslav. *Whose Bible Is It? A History of the Scriptures through the Ages*. New York: Viking, 2005.

Perry, Ralph Barton. *Puritanism and Democracy*. New York: Vanguard, 1944.

Peters, F. E. *The Children of Abraham: Judaism, Christianity, Islam*. Princeton: Princeton University Press, 2006.

Philbrick, Nathaniel. *Mayflower*. New York: Viking, 2006.

Phillips, Kevin. *Bad Money: Reckless Finance, Failed Politics, and the Global Crisis of American Capitalism*. New York: Viking Adult, 2008.

Pilgrim, W. E. *Good News to the Poor: Wealth and Poverty in Luke-Acts*. Minneapolis: Augsburg, 1981.

Pleins, J. David. *The Social Visions of the Hebrew Bible: A Theological Introduction*. Louisville: Westminster John Knox, 2001.

Pollan, Michael. "An Open Letter to the Next Farmer in Chief." *New York Times*, October 12, 2008. Online: http://www.nytimes.com/2008/10/12/magazine/12policy-t.htm.

Powell, Marvin A. "Salt, Seed, and Yields in Sumerian Agriculture: A Critique of the Theory of Progressive Salinization." *Zeitschrift für die Assyriologie* 75 (1985) 7–38.

Rad, Gerhard von. *Old Testament Theology*, vol. 1: *Theology of Israel's Historical Traditions*. Translated by D. M. G. Stalker. New York: Harper & Row, 1962.

———. *Old Testament Theology*, vol. 2: *Theology of Israel's Prophetic Traditions*. Translated by D. M. G. Stalker. New York: Harper & Row, 1965.

Rakove, Jack N. *James Madison and the Creation of the American Republic*. New York: HarperCollins, 1990.

Reece, Erik. "Moving Mountains: The Battle for Justice Comes to the Coal Fields of Appalachia." *Orion Magazine* 25.1 (2006) 54–67. Online: http://www.grist.org/news/maindish/2006/02/16/reece.htm.

Richter, Sandra L. *The Deuteronomistic History and the Name Theology: lešakkēn šemô šām in the Bible and the Ancient Near East*. Beihefte zur Zeitschrift für die alttestamentliche Wissenschaft 318. Berlin: de Gruyter, 2002.

Richter, Sandra. "Environmental Law in Deuteronomy: One Lens on a Biblical Theology of Creation Care." *Bulletin of Biblical Research* (2009) forthcoming.

Richter, Sandra L. *The Epic of Eden: A Christian Entry into the Old Testament*. Downers Grove, IL: InterVarsity Academic, 2008.

Richter, Sandra L. "The Place of the Name in Deuteronomy." *Vetus Testamentum* 57 (2007) 342–45.

Roberts, J. J. M. "Amos 6.1–7." In *Understanding the Word: Essays in Honor of Bernhard W. Anderson*, edited by James T. Butler, Edgar W. Conrad, and Ben C. Ollenburger, 155–66. Journal for the Study of the Old Testament Supplements 37. Sheffield: JSOT Press, 1985.

———. "The Context, Text, and Logic of Isaiah 7.7–9." In *Inspired Speech: Prophecy in the Ancient Near East in Honour of Herbert B. Huffmon*, edited by John Kaltner and Louis Stulman, 161–70. Journal for the Study of the Old Testament Supplements 378. London: T. & T. Clark, 2004.

———. "The End of War in the Zion Tradition: The Imperialistic Background of an Old Testament Vision of World Wide Peace." In *Character Ethics and the Old Testament: Moral Dimensions of Scripture*, edited by M. Daniel Carroll Rodas and Jacqueline E. Lapsley, 119–28. Louisville: Westminster John Knox Press, 2007. Reprinted from *Horizons in Biblical Theology* 26 (2004) 2–23.

———. "The Enthronement of Yhwh and David: The Abiding Theological Significance of the Kingship Language of the Psalms." *Catholic Biblical Quarterly* 64 (2002) 675–86.

———. "Isaiah 2 and the Prophet's Message to the North." *Jewish Quarterly Review* 75 (1985) 290–308.

———. "Isaiah 33: An Isaianic Elaboration of the Zion Tradition." In *The Word of the Lord Shall Go Forth: Essays in Honor of David Noel Freedman in Celebration of His 60th Birthday*, edited by Carol L. Meyers and M. O'Connor, 15–25. Winona Lake, IN: Eisenbrauns, 1983.

———. "Isaiah and His Children." In *Biblical and Related Studies Presented to Samuel Iwry*, edited by Ann Kort and Scott Morschauser, 193–203. Winona Lake, IN: Eisenbrauns, 1985.

———. "Isaiah's Egyptian and Nubian Oracles." In *Israel's Prophets and Israel's Past: Essays on the Relationship of Prophetic Texts and Israelite History in Honor of John H. Hayes*, edited by Brad E. Kelle and Megan Bishop Moore, 201–9. Library of Hebrew Bible/Old Testament Studies 446. London: T. & T. Clark, 2006.

———. "A Note on Isaiah 28:12." *Harvard Theological Review* 74 (1981) 49–51.

———. "Security and Justice in Isaiah." *The Stone-Campbell Journal* 13.1 (2009) forthcoming.

———. "Solomon's Jerusalem and the Zion Tradition." In *Jerusalem in Bible and Archaeology: The First Temple Period*, edited by Andrew G. Vaughn and Ann E. Killebrew, 163–70. Society of Biblical Literature Symposium Series 18. Atlanta: Society of Biblical Literature, 2003.

Roebuck, David G. "Fundamentalism and Pentecostalism: The Changing Face of Evangelicalism in America." In *Faith in America: Changes, Challenges, New Directions. Organized Religion Today*, edited by Charles H. Lippy, 1:85–106. Westport, CT: Praeger, 2006.

Rogerson, John. *Theory and Practice in Old Testament Ethics*. London: T. & T. Clark, 2004.

Roosevelt, Theodore. *The Foes of Our Own Household*. New York: Scribner, 1926.

Rosen, Baruch. "Subsistence Economy in Iron Age I." In *From Nomadism to Monarchy: Archaeological and Historical Aspects of Early Israel*, edited by Israel Finkelstein and Nadav Na'aman, 177–78, 339–51. Washington, DC: Biblical Archaeology Society, 1994.

Ruether, Rosemary R. *Gaia and God: An Ecofeminist Theology of Earth Healing*. New York: HarperOne, 1994.

Sabin, Scott. "Environmental Emigration: The World on our Doorstep." *Creation Care* 37 (Fall 2008) 37–38.

Sasson, Jack. "Should Cheeseburgers Be Kosher? A Different Interpretation of Five Hebrew Words." *Bible Review* 19.6 (2003) 40–43, 50–51.

Scary, Elaine. *The Body in Pain*. New York: Oxford University Press, 1985.

Schloss, Dietmar. "Joel Barlow's *The Vision of Columbus* (1787) and the Discovery of the Ethnic." In *Colonial Encounters: Essays in Early American History and Culture*, edited by Hans-Jürgen Grabbe, 139–55. Heidelberg: Universitätsverlag Winter, 2003.

Schloss, Dietmar. "The Nation as Spectacle: The Grand Federal Procession in Philadelphia, 1788." In *Celebrating Ethnicity and Nation: American Festive Culture from the Revolution to the Early Twentieth Century*, edited by Geneviève Fabre, Jürgen Heideking, and Kai Dreisbach, 44–62. New York: Berghahn, 2001.

Schwartz, Regina M. *The Curse of Cain: The Violent Legacy of Monotheism*. Chicago: University of Chicago Press, 1997.

Schweitzer, Steven James. "Reading Utopia in Chronicles." Ph.D. dissertation, University of Notre Dame, 2005.

Scully, Matthew. *Dominion: The Power of Man, the Suffering of Animals, and the Call to Mercy*. New York: St. Martin's Griffin, 2002.

Sebald, W. G. *On the Natural History of Destruction*. New York: Random House, 2003.

Shattuck, Gardiner H. *A Shield and a Hiding Place: The Religious Life of the Civil War Armies*. Macon, GA: Mercer University Press, 1987.
Sieger Derr, Thomas, with James A. Nash and Richard John Neuhaus. *Environmental Ethics and Christian Humanism*. Nashville: Abingdon, 1996.
Slouka, Mark."Dehumanized: When Math and Science Rule the School." *Harper's Magazine* (Sept 2009) 32–40.
Smith-Christopher, Daniel L. *A Biblical Theology of Exile*. Overtures to Biblical Theology. Minneapolis: Fortress, 2002.
Smoak, Jeremy. "Building Houses and Planting Vineyards: The Early Inner-Biblical Discourse on an Ancient Israelite Wartime Curse." *Journal of Biblical Literature* 127 (2008) 19–35.
Snowball, David. *Continuity and Change in the Rhetoric of the Moral Majority*. New York: Praeger, 1991.
Stager, Lawrence E. "Shemer's Estate." *Bulletin of the American Schools of Oriental Research* 277/278 (1990) 93–107.
Stephanson, Anders. *Manifest Destiny: American Expansion and the Empire of Right*. New York: Hill & Wang, 1995.
Stulman, Louis. *Jeremiah*. Abingdon Old Testament Commentaries. Nashville: Abingdon, 2005.
Stulman, Louis, and Kim, Hyun Chul Paul. *You Are My People: An Introduction to Prophetic Literature*. Nashville: Abingdon, forthcoming.
Tal, Kalí. *Worlds of Hurt: Reading Literatures of Trauma*. Cambridge: Cambridge University Press, 1996.
Tangley, Laura. "Saving the Forest for the Trees." *National Wildlife Federation* (Dec 2008–Jan 2009) 24–30.
Theissen, Gerd. *The Social Setting of Pauline Christianity: Essays on Corinth*. Edited and translated by John H. Schütz. Philadelphia: Fortress, 1982.
Tigay, Jeffrey. *Deuteronomy*. Jewish Publication Society Torah Commentary. Philadelphia: Jewish Publication Society, 1996.
Tone, John Lawrence. *War and Genocide in Cuba, 1895–1898*. Chapel Hill: University of North Carolina Press, 2006.
Trible, Phyllis. *Texts of Terror: Literary-Feminist Reading of Biblical Narratives*. Overtures to Biblical Theology. Philadelphia: Fortress, 1984.
Tuveson, Ernest Lee. *Redeemer Nation. The Idea of America's Millennial Role*. Chicago: University of Chicago Press, 1980.
Underwood, Paul A. *The Kariye Djami*. 3 vols. Bollingen Series LXX. New York: Bollingen Foundation and Pantheon, 1966.
Van Dyke, Henry. *Fighting for Peace*. New York: Scribner, 1917.
Van Houtan, Kyle S. "Extinction and its Causes." *Creation Care* 37 (Fall 2008) 15.
Vaux, Kenneth. *America in God's World: Theology, Ethics, and the Crises of Bases Abroad, Bad Money and Black Gold*. Eugene, OR: Wipf & Stock, 2009.
Walzer, Michael. *Exodus and Revolution*. New York: Basic Books, 1985.
———. *The Revolution of the Saints: A Study in the Origins of Radical Politics*. Cambridge: Harvard University Press, 1965.
———. *Thick and Thin: Moral Argument at Home and Abroad*. Notre Dame: University of Notre Dame Press, 1994.

Bibliography

Watterson, Henry. "Editorial." *Louisville Courier-Journal* (April 20, 1898). Reprinted as: "The Right of Our Might." In *The Annals of America*, 12:194. Chicago: Encyclopaedia Brittanica, 1976.

Weems, Renita J. *Battered Love: Marriage, Sex, and Violence in the Hebrew Prophets*. Overtures to Biblical Theology. Minneapolis: Fortress, 1995.

Weinfeld, Moshe. "בְּרִית *berîth*." In *Theological Dictionary of the Old Testament*, edited by Johannes Botterweck and Helmer Ringgren, 2:253–79. Translated by Geoffrey W. Bromiley. Grand Rapids: Eerdmans, 1975.

———. *Social Justice in Ancient Israel and in the Ancient Near East*. Publications of the Perry Foundation for Biblical Research in the Hebrew University of Jerusalem. Minneapolis: Fortress Press, 1995.

Wennberg, Robert N. *God, Humans and Animals: An Invitation to Enlarge our Moral Universe*. Grand Rapids: Eerdmans, 2003.

White, James Boyd. *When Words Lose Their Meaning: Constitutions and Reconstitutions of Language, Character, and Community*. Chicago: University of Chicago Press, 1984.

Wilcox, Clyde. *God's Warriors: The Christian Right in Twentieth-Century America*. Baltimore: Johns Hopkins University Press, 1992.

Wills, Garry. *A Necessary Evil: A History of American Distrust of Government*. New York: Simon & Schuster, 1999.

———. *Under God: Religion and American Politics*. New York: Simon & Schuster, 1990.

Wilson, E. O. *The Creation: An Appeal to Save Life on Earth*. New York: Norton, 2006.

Wilson, Robert R. *Prophecy and Society in Ancient Israel*. Philadelphia: Fortress, 1980.

Wilson, Woodrow. "War Message." In *The Annals of America*, 14:77–82. Chicago: Encyclopaedia Brittanica, 1976.

Wink, Walter. *The Powers That Be: Theology for a New Millennium*. New York: Doubleday, 1999.

Wood, James. "God in the Quad: A Don Defends the Supreme Being from the New Atheists." *New Yorker* 85.26 (August 31, 2009) 75–79.

Wright, C. J. H. *Walking in the Ways of the Lord: The Ethical Authority of the Old Testament*. Leicester, UK: Apollos, 1995.

Wright, Jacob. Review in *Journal of Biblical Literature* 125 (2006) 577.

———. "Warfare and Wanton Destruction: A Reexamination of Deuteronomy 20:19–20 in Relation to Ancient Siegecraft." *Journal of Biblical Literature* 127 (2008) 423–58.

Wright, N. T. *The Challenge of Jesus: Rediscovering Who Jesus Was and Is*. Downers Grove, IL: InterVarsity Press, 1999.

Yoffee, Norman. "The Collapse of Ancient Mesopotamian States and Civilization." In *The Collapse of Ancient States and Civilizations*, edited by Norman Yoffee and George L. Cowgill, 44–68. Tucson: University of Arizona Press, 1991.

Ziff, Larzar. *Puritanism in America: New Culture in a New World*. New York: Viking, 1973.

Zimmerli, Walther. "Knowledge of God according to the Book of Ezekiel." In *I am Yahweh*, 29–98. Translated by Douglas W. Stott with an introduction by Walter Brueggemann. Atlanta: John Knox, 1982.

Index of Ancient Documents

Hebrew Bible

Genesis

	135, 210, 211
1–3	46
1:1—2:4a	210
1	108, 231
1:1	209
1:3–13	210
1:3	63
1:9	211
1:11	211
1:13	211
1:14–31	210
1:24	211
1:26	109, 211
1:29–30	211
1:31	211
2	109, 254
2:1	211
2:2–3	211
2:7	63
2:15	109, 123
9:10–11	117
11	255
15:12–16	99
17:6–8	99
22:2	31
22:12	31
28:15	99
46:3–4	99

Exodus

	98, 188, 194
2:23	98
2:24–25	98
2:24	98
3:14	46
6:6	98
15:1–18	2
15:2	99
15:18	2
15:21	2
19:1–6	158
19:8	2
20	2
20:2	4
20:8	125n
21:2	213
22:1	174
22:21–27	107n
22:25–27	167
22:25	187, 197
22:26–27	198
22:27	101
22:28	124
23:10–12	113

Index of Ancient Documents

Exodus (continued)

23:10–11	212
23:12	212
24:3	3
24:7	3

Leviticus

	113, 130, 188, 194
5:16	174
17	121
19:2	210
19:9–10	107n, 112, 113
19:18	107n
19:34	107n
23:22	112, 213
25:2b–7	212
25:4–7	113–14
25:8–17	166
25:9–10	187
25:11–13	213
25:13–17	125n
25:17	115
25:23	115, 187, 214
26:34–35	115
25:35–37	187
26:43	115

Numbers

5:7	174

Deuteronomy

	x, 12–19, 108–23, 125n, 188, 194, 217
1:8	110
4:40	110, 115
5:12–14	212
5:12	125n
5:14–15	119
5:15	212
5:33	100
6:3	110
6:5	81
6:10–15	13
7:8	99
8:7–18	13–14
8:7–10	112
8:19–20	14
10:17–19	98, 107n
11:9	110
12:10–12	111
12:15	121
12:22	121
14:5	121
14:21	120, 128n
14:22–23	110
14:28–29	124n, 173
15:1–3	173
15:1–2	187, 213
15:7–12	173
15:7–11	99–100, 167
15:7–8	187
15:7	16
15:12–18	213
15:12–15	187
15:13–15	15
15:15	15
15:19–20	111
15:22	121
16:18–20	107n
16:11–12	15
16:12	15
17:16–17	17
18:3–5	111
20:6	115
20:19–20	118
20:19	115, 116
22:1–2	173
22:6–7	118
23:19	173
24	112
24:7–15	173

Index of Ancient Documents

24:17–18	15
24:17	15
24:19–22	16, 100, 107n
24:19–21	173
24:19	112
24:20–22	113
24:20	112–13
24:22	15
25:4	119
25:13–16	107n
25:13–14	173
26	111
26:1–11	186
26:1–9	111–12
26:9	110
26:12–15	124n
26:15	110
26:16–19	3
27:3	110
28	12, 110, 214
28:1–2	214
28:7	214
28:15	214
28:25	214–15
28:68	12–13
29–34	110
29:28	110
30:9	122
30:19	110
31:20	110

Joshua

	4, 6
4:22–23	4
13–24	125n

Judges

2:18	98

Ruth

	70n

1 Samuel

8:5	6
8:14	112
8:20	6
22:20–23	6

2 Samuel

2:8ff.	90n
5:2	138
7:7	138
8:17	6
11–12	6
12:7	143

1 Kings

1:7	7
1:8	7
2:13–25	7
2:26	7
2:28–35	7
3:1	6
4:22–23	8
4:25	116
4:32	8
5:11[25]	112
6:20–22	8
7:8	6
7:48–50	8
8	9
8:13	9
8:15–16	9
8:56–57	9
9:15–19	8
9:24	6
10:22–25	8–9
10:26	8

Index of Ancient Documents

1 Kings (*continued*)

11	10
11:1	6
11:3	9
11:9–11	11
18:30–32	189–90
19:19–21	189

2 Kings

15:37–38	90n
16:5–9	90n
21:1–2	216
21:3–16	216
21:17–18	216, 217
22	12
22:11	13
23:29–30	215
25	160n

1 Chronicles

27:28	112

2 Chronicles

33:1–2	216
33:3–10	216
33:11–13	216
33:14–17	216
33:18–20	216–17
35:20–24	215–16

Ezra

	188

Nehemiah

	188

Job

	117, 217, 218
1:8	217
1:10	217
1:11	217
2:7	217
2:11—31:40	217
32:1—37:24	217
38:1—42:6	218
39:5–6	117
39:26–27	117
42:7	218

Psalms

	166
8	38
14:6	167
22:24	167
25:16	167
34:6	167
40:17	167
69:29	167
72	82
90:17	264
101	82
104	117
104:10–11	117

Proverbs

	179
10:4	179
13:7	179
14:4	124n
14:31	179
17:5	179
22:2	179

Ecclesiastes

12:13	81

Isaiah

	72–91, 131, 166
1:10–17	84
1:11–15	106
1:16–17	97
1:21–28	78
1:21–23	84
1:26	63
2	48, 76
2:1–4	79
2:2–4	87, 222
2:3–4	56
2:4	36, 210
3:13–15	84, 188
3:14–15	100, 167, 173
3:16—4:1	85
3:17	160n
3:18–24	100
5:7–8	173
5:8	84, 188, 214
6:8	268
7:1–9	90n
7:2	74
7:9	76
8:5–8	78
8:11–15	74, 79
8:12–15	79
8:23—9:6	79
9:3	83
9:6	82
10:1–3	173
10:1–2	84
10:2	167
10:5–15	78
10:16–19	76
10:20–23	76
10:27b–32	74, 90n
10:33–34	76
11:1–10	79
11:1–5	82–83
11:4	83
11:6–9	220
11:6	34, 70n
11:9	70n
11:10	87
14:24–27	78
14:28–32	77
17	76
17:4	76
17:12–14	76
18	77
19	77
19:1–15	77
19:18–25	77
19:20–22	77
20	77
25:6–8	222
28	78
28:1–6	77
28:12	85
28:21	78
29:1–8	78
30:12–17	85
30:17	78
30:27–33	78
31:1–3	78
31:4–5	78
31:8–9	78
32:1–8	79
32:1–2	82, 83
32:6–7	173
32:9–14	85
33	90n
33:1–24	79
40	39
40:1	93
44:28	138
55:8	32
58	166
58:1–9	106
58:3	173
58:6–7	173
58:6	166
58:10	173
61	166
61:1–2	165

Index of Ancient Documents

Jeremiah

	17–18, 146–61
1:1–3	148
1:1	17
2:1—4:2	148, 156
3:15	138
3:22–25	161n
3:22	157
4:23–26	148
4:5—6:30	150
5:26–28	173
6:11–12	150
6:15–17	148
6:20	106
6:22–23	150
7:5–6	173
7:26	195
10:17–22	150
10:21	138
11:1–18	148
11:7	17
12:10	138
13:1–11	148
13:20–27	150–51
13:20	150
13:22	150
13:25–26	150
13:26	150
17:16	138
18:1–11	148
19:1–15	148
22:3–5	92, 94
22:15–16	19
26–29	160n
30–33	160n
30–31	160n, 161n
30:5–7	154
30:12–17	154
30:17	153
30:18–20	153
30:18	153
30:19	155
30:20	156
30:27	153
31:1–14	153
31:1	161n
31:3b	157
31:6	157
31:8	154
31:10–14	156
31:11	152
31:12–14	156
31:13–14	153
31:15–34	156–57
31:15	161n
31:16–17	157
31:18–19	157
31:20	157
31:21–26	157
31:22	157
31:23	153
31:25	152
31:27–28	157
31:29–30	157
31:31–34	157–58
31:31–32	158
31:31	152
31:34	158
31:35–37	152
32:21–23	17
39	160n
52	160n

Ezekiel

	131–43
1	145n
2:1–7	145n
6:9	145n
7:11	136
7:23	136
8	134
8:12	134
8:17	136
11	140

11:19–20	140
12:19	136
12:22	144n
16	135–36, 145n
16:39–40	160n
16:49	137
16:52	145n
16:53–54	135
16:54	145n
16:60–61	135
16:61–63	145n
16:61	145n
16:62–63	136
16:63	145n
17:22–24	145n
18	134–35
18:1–32	145n
18:2	134
18:12–18	173
20	145n
20:11	144n
20:43	145n
22	136–38
22:3	136
22:6	136
22:7	136
22:9	136
22:10	136
22:11	136
22:12–13	137
22:12	136, 139, 145n
22:13	139
22:25	136
22:26	136, 137
22:27	136, 137, 139
22:29	136
23	145n
23:27	145n
23:35	145n
28:16	136
29:16	145n
32:24	145n
32:25	145n
32:30	145n
33	138
33:1–11	145n
33:15	173
33:30	138
33:31	138, 139
33:31b	138
34	131, 138
34:1–8	138
34:1–4	103
34:3	138
34:11–24	145n
36–48	139
36	140
36:22	144n
36:26–27	140
36:31–32	145n
36:31	145n
37	131
37:24	140
38	131
39	131
39:26	145n
40–48	131
43:10–11	145n
44:13	145n
45:9	136

Daniel

	50
3	3
10–12	207n

Hosea

	11–12, 18, 85, 156
1–3	156
2:13	11, 12
4:6	12
6:6	106
8:14	12
12:12	112

Index of Ancient Documents

Hosea (continued)

13:6–8	12
13:6	12

Joel

3:10	210

Amos

1:13	160n
2:6–8	173
5:11–12	173
5:21–24	105
5:22	105
5:23	105
6:1–7	90n
6:5	90n
6:8	90n
8:4–6	173
8:5	31
9:7	20n

Jonah

	70n

Micah

2:1–2	84, 173, 188
2:6	96
3:1–3	92–93, 173
4	48
4:1–5	87
4:1–4	221–22
4:1–3	56, 70
4:2–6	79
4:3	210
4:8	87
4:11–13	87
5:5–6	87
5:15	221, 222

6:6–8	106
6:10–11	173
6:12	104
7:10	221
7:16–17	221

Haggai

	188

Zechariah

	188
7:9–10	173
8:20–23	222

Malachi

3:5	173

Apocrypha and Pseudepigrapha

1 Enoch

94–104	207n

Psalms of Solomon

2	207n

Sirach

29:8	180n

Testament of Job

9:7–8	180n

Tobit

4:6–7	180n
4:16	180n
12:8	180n
14:10–11	180n

New Testament

Matthew

	145n, 168, 189, 191, 192, 195, 197, 207n
2:1–18	192
4:1–11	95
5–7	198
5:3	165
5:14	48
5:21–22	65
5:45	232
6:20	165
6:24	165
11:4–5	180n
11:5	165
11:28	234
12:1–14	85
13:22	165
13:39	219
13:49	219
19:21–24	165
19:21	180n
20:1–16	104
23:23	85
23:37	195
24–25	88
24:3	219
28:20	219

Mark

	168, 189, 191, 194, 196, 207n, 232
1:16–20	189
3:13–19	189
4:18	165
4:35—8:26	190
6:6–24	190
7:1–13	190, 195
7:18–19	82
10:2–45	190, 197
10:17–31	190, 197
10:21	165, 180n
10:25	165, 190, 197
10:31	219
11–12	190
11:25–27	195
12:1–12	195
12:13–17	193
12:28–31	198
12:38–44	196
12:41–44	165, 180n
12:41–42	180n
13	88
14	191
14:12–25	191
14:22–25	196
14:43–72	191
15:1–32	191
15:6–9	232
15:7	232
16:1–8	191

Luke

	164–75
1	169
1:16–17	165
1:50	164
1:51–53	164
1:52–53	172
1:52	166
1:54	164

Index of Ancient Documents

Luke (continued)

2:1–20	192
3:14	164
3:22	166
4	167, 249
4:16–19	180n
4:18–19	165
4:18	165–67
4:24–27	166
6	167, 199
6:20–49	198
6:20	165, 166, 167, 180n
6:22	166
6:24–26	166
6:24	165
6:26	166–67
6:27–34	199
7:22–23	180n
7:22	165, 167, 171
8:1–3	167–68
8:14	168
9:3	165
10:2–16	190
10:4	165
12:4–5	80
12:13–21	168–69
12:16	165
12:20	7
12:21	165
12:33	165, 169–70
12:34	175
12:48	43
13:34–35	195
14:12–14	170–71
14:12	165
14:13–14	180n
14:13	165
14:21	165, 171, 180n
14:28	165
16	178
16:1–9	197
16:1	165
16:9	178
16:13	165, 171, 198
16:14	165
16:19–31	171–73, 180n
16:19–22	165
16:27	165
16:30	165
18:18–30	173–74
18:22–25	165
18:22	46
19:1–10	174–75, 180n
19:2	165
19:8	165
19:15	165
19:23	165
21:1–3	175
21:2–3	180n
21:3	175
21:13	165
22:5	165
22:35–36	165
23:40	81

John

	232
3:16	233
10	131
17	39
18:36	232

Acts

	60, 175–77
1:15	262
2	176
2:44–45	163, 175–76
4:32–37	163
4:34–37	175–76
5:4	176
6	163
6:1–5	176
8:9–25	176–77
13:16	81

13:26	81
16:21	224
17:7	224
17:26	41
24:17	177

Romans

	37
1–3	62
1:14–17	38
2:6–11	88
2:24	144n
8	38, 46, 109
8:20–21	109
10:5	144n
12:2	123
13:11–12	224

1 Corinthians

	145n, 224
1:26–29	162
3:13–15	264
7:26–31	224
15:20–28	224
15:20	227
15:24–25	227
15:24	227
15:28	227
15:44–45	57
15:51–52	226

2 Corinthians

3:18	224
5:14	24

Galatians

2	235n
3:12	144n
3:28	80
4:4	39

Ephesians

5:5	170

Colossians

2:16–23	82

1 Thessalonians

1:6–8	225
2:19	227
3:1–7	224
4:15–17	224–25
4:15	226, 227
4:17	224, 226
5:23	227

2 Thessalonians

1:5–10	88

1 Timothy

4:1–5	82
5:21	85
6	178
6:6–8	178
6:9–10	178
6:17–19	85, 179

James

2:1–7	85

1 Peter

	79–81
1:16	210

Index of Ancient Documents

1 Peter (*continued*)

2:13—3:7	80
2:17	81
3:14–16	79
4:1—5:11	88

2 Peter

3:4	144n
3:9	27

1 John

1:8	82
1:10	82
4:18	81
4:20	4

Revelation

	48–67, 88, 209–10, 227–31, 260
1:1	227
2:16	227
3:11	227
6	38
13	230
13:3	230
13:12	230
13:14	230
13:18	230
14:7	81
14:8	230
14:20	209
16:19	230
17:5	230
17:8	230
17:9–11	230
17:9	230
18	248
18:2	230
18:10	230
18:21	230
19	230
19:17–18	228
19:17	230
19:18	230
19:21	230
20–22	259
20	48, 50, 65
20:8	131
21:3–4	209
22:1–2	131
22:7	227
22:12	227
22:20	227
22:21	209

Dead Sea Scrolls

1QS (Community Rule)

1:11–12	176
5:1–3	176
6:2–3	176

CD (Damascus Document)

9:1–15	176

Jewish Literature

Babylonian Talmud, *Beṣah*

32b	172

Josephus, *Antiquities*

11.326	225
18.20	176

Josephus, *War*

	207

Mishnah, *Abot*

5:13	180n

Philo, *Good Person*

12 §86	176

Qur'an

5.32	24
12.108	23
17.1	23
17.60	23
49.13	23

www.ingramcontent.com/pod-product-compliance
Lightning Source LLC
Chambersburg PA
CBHW032052220426
43664CB00008B/966